WANG MENG

a life

WANG MENG
a life

Memoir of China's Former Minister of Culture and Renowned Author

Zhu Hong and Liu Haiming
Translators

MerwinAsia
Portland, Maine

59 West St., Unit 3W,
Portland, ME 04102 USA

www.merwinasia.com

Distributed by the University of Hawai'i Press

Library of Congress Control Number: 2018947233

978-1-937385-60-6 (Paperback)
978-1-937385-72-9 (Cloth)

Printed in the United States of America

The paper used in this publication meets the minimum requirements of the American National Standard for Information Services—Permanence of Paper for Printed Library Materials, ANSI/NISO Z39/48-1992

CONTENTS

Introduction

Wang Meng is among the best-known Chinese writers of our time. He became a *cause celèbre* in 1957 for his hugely popular 1956 short story "A Young Newcomer at the Organization Department." The story was critical of "bureaucratism" among Party cadres, which had been singled out as a great problem by a recent Party congress. But then the wind shifted and the "hundred kinds of flowers," his story being one, that were supposed to "flourish" were recast as "poisonous weeds" by the same Party leadership, even though Mao Zedong seems to have initially supported him. He was exiled to Xinjiang Province in China's far west for the next thirteen years. Undaunted he learned the local Uighur language and anonymously translated some local stories. Eventually he was allowed to return to Beijing and to resume writing under his own name. He became a symbol of the more open climate of the first years after the Cultural Revolution, and was recruited to rise from being a Party cadre in the Communist Youth League to join the Party Central Committee and eventually to become China's Minister of Cultural Affairs (1986–1989). The end of his tenure in 1989 was no coincidence. He had refused to publicly support the persecution of the students and professional intellectuals who had demonstrated for political reforms. His removal from office saved his reputation, and was not unwelcome to him. As he wrote, he had hoped for a while to be relieved of his post to get back to writing.

Wang Meng's personal history might have led others to a disillusioned, cynical, or aggressive rejection of China's one-party rule and the fallout from its unpredictable twists and turns. However, the reader will be disappointed if he or she expects a probing self-reflection and critique of the tyranny exerted by the communist state over the life of its citizens. Wang Meng's autobiography does not offer a Chinese counterpart to the treatment of Stalin's rule in Arthur Koestler's *Darkness at Noon* or Alexandr Solzhenitsyn's *Archipel Gulag,* or to Vaclav Havel's writings on Czechoslovakia under Communism. Like many in his generation Wang Meng is a writer who remains committed to the Communist ideals of his youth. He remains loyal to the Communist Party and shares its basic agenda, but the suffering he endured and witnessed has also given him a critical perspective on the flaws in the realization of these ideals. This is not to say that the story Wang tells about his life lacks self-criticism or honesty. His writing is engaging and intimate.

Following Wang Meng's narrative gives the reader a first-hand experience of the tumultuous trajectory through which China passed during a single lifetime. Born in Beijing in 1934, Wang Meng was just fifteen when the Communist army marched into the city after it had been ruled during the war by Japan and during the ensuing civil war by the Kuomintang, The Nationalist Party. By then, however, Wang was already a student activist and enthusiastic new member of the Communist Party. The following first years of the People's Republic were enshrined in his memory as China's golden age and helped fortify Wang Meng's youthful idealism into a lifelong commitment to the Party and its cause. He recalls that this was a time full of hope and great prospects. The atmosphere was infectious. A mood of song and dance also permeates his novel in this period, which came with the enthusiastic title *Long Live Youth!* It was a time of romance, a time of idealism. Wang Meng was working as a Party cadre in the Youth League. The world seemed to belong to them and they were the masters of new China. His memories of these early years are punctuated by falling in love for the first time, dancing through the night on Tiananmen Square after National Day Celebration on October 1, singing and enjoying merging with the sights and sounds of that time. Bubbling with youth, energy, and idealism he and his peers eagerly absorbed the cultural offerings of the Soviet Union with their diverse palette of music, poetry, song, and fiction. These offerings from the big "brother country" next door, about which Wang Meng had only read, showed the grand prospects of socialism and helped him develop a world outlook that enabled him to endure through the most trying circumstances.

His decision to become a writer instead of continuing a career as a Party cadre was a very personal one, driven by a passion for writing that never left him. The idea of becoming a writer first dawned on him when he read a Chinese translation of the Soviet author Sergei Antonov's story "My first job." Years later, relating his feelings thirty years before in 1954, Wang Meng claimed that his real reason was that "life is too short, and life is too beautiful. I do not write for personal advancement. I honestly believe that our age is unusual. We have witnessed the passing of the old and even taken part in the struggle for the new. We had seen life in all its aspects and personally tasted its many flavors. Time and life, they are here today and gone tomorrow. If one does not write and leave a record, there will be a blank. A blank—for you, for others, for the world, for history—one will be staring at blankness if one does not write . . ." Two years later, his "The Young Newcomer" would make him an overnight celebrity in the literary as well as political arena, heading for his downfall a year later. The "Young Newcomer" had been inspired by another Soviet work, Galina Nikolayeva's novella with the unwieldy title *The Chief Agronomist and the Director of the Machine Tractor Station,* which had just been made mandatory reading for educated Chinese Youth League cadres. The "The Young Newcomer" does what Youth League cadres were supposed to do—"learn from Nastya," the young woman agronomist who shakes up the old ways of the machine tractor station. The young man in Wang's story, who has a copy of Nikolayeva's novella in his pocket, is a Party member newly assigned to the Party's Organization Department in the capital, but contrary to his enthusiastic expectation, this office is suffering from a bureaucratic work style. With youthful idealism and enthusiasm, he challenges the Department's leadership and criticizes their work ethic. In a challenge to prevailing ethics, he falls in love with an unhappily married young woman in the organization. Although pure hearted, her spirit appears to have been crushed by the leadership's disregard for her personal concerns. Sharing their love for Soviet and Russian literature and music, the two sit on the floor in her room under a poster entitled "Moscow Spring" and listen to Tchaikovsky's "Capriccio Italien." At the end of the story, Wang Meng's young man has not brought about any change in the Department, but bravely continues the fight.

The "The Young Newcomer" was published during a time when Mao had proposed to "Let a Hundred Flowers Bloom and a Hundred Schools of Thought Contend" to publicly articulate the criticism needed to restore the dynamism to a Party drowning in bureaucratism and becoming ever more distant from the "masses." After the publication of "The Young Newcomer," all the important national publishers were courting Wang Meng to publish new works with them, but after "The Young Newcomer" had been branded as a "poisonous weed," no publisher would take anything from him. Soon after that, Wang Meng with his young family—he was married in 1957 before all the turmoil—Wang was sent to work in the countryside. Hoping that he might be allowed to write again, he and his family moved to Xinjiang in 1962. But this hope was in vain. The local party leaders in far-off Xinjiang did not have the power to make such a decision. Except for one short story he published soon after "The Young Newcomer" in early 1957, Wang Meng was not able to publish another work of his own until after the Chinese Cultural Revolution in the 1960s.

Given this history, the mostly unchanged tone of the autobiography seems surprising, even taking into account that the author is a staunch believer in socialism. Through the meticulous details of his narrative and the sincerity of his reflections, however, the human dimension emerges. The suffering and the resilience of the individual shines through. The anchor for his survival, he writes, was his loving wife. Without the happiness in his life he owed to her, it would have been difficult to survive the many years of unending turmoil.

After his dream of being allowed to write again was dashed by the long hand of the central Party apparatus, he took the unusual steps for a Han Chinese to learn Uighur and make friends with the local people. Yet, he was restless. All his thoughts were on being able to write and publish again, but the answer to his requests was an unmitigated "bu neng yong" (cannot be reinstated). Finally he realized that the meaning of this phrase was a political life sentence without judgment or appeal. He would have to wait almost thirty years before another change beyond his control opened the door for him to write and publish again.

He was rehabilitated after the end of the Cultural Revolution and allowed to return to Beijing with his family. He was welcome back with warmth and trust by old friends and by party leaders, most of whom had just been restored to their jobs and apartments after years in the political desert.

Suddenly he was overwhelmed by requests for manuscripts from different journals and publishers. Still unsure at first of the political climate for literature, Wang published what he considered works suited to the party line as best he understood it. Soon after, however, the new paramount Party leader Deng Xiaoping gave hope to writers by remarking that politics should no longer interfere in literature as it had during the previous decades (Deng also said, as Wang Meng reminds us, literature should help promote the cause of the Party's four modernization policy and help educate the people). Wang Meng's literary creativity now burst forth. What had been kept submerged for more than twenty years now flowered into a series of experimental short stories. During the late 1970s and early 80s, these included "A Bolshevik Salute," "Butterfly," "Eyes of the Night." "Reverie by the Sea," "Kite Streamers," "The Loyal Heart," and "The Sound of Spring." Characterized as Chinese examples of the literary technique of "stream of consciousness," they caused quite a stir. As one critic put it, these stories represented a new way of writing (other than socialist realism), which might be called "subjective authenticity." In other words, the stories no longer reflected an "objective" socialist point of view on issues and problems, and they were not out to serve a social/political purpose. They were written from a subjective point of view motivated by what Wang Meng described as "an aching feeling that the author himself could not quite define; a resignation perhaps, with surface calm and inner torment, a smile hiding sorrow, and a hope for life returning to its normal course. These are memories recollected, echoes from the distant past, hope peppered with hesitation." It is worth noting here that although Wang Meng still harps back to Soviet and Eastern European literature and culture, which helped form his youthful idealism, he does not mention engagement with other foreign authors, not even Kafka, Borges or Gabriel Garcia Márquez, whose works were translated and published for the first time during the late seventies and early eighties.

Riding out big and small political waves during the 1980s, Wang Meng remained steadfast in his devotion to literature. His suggestion to the Party and to readers not to overestimate the social role and impact of literature, was rebuked from both left and right. As he put it, those on the left accused him of trying to do away with the Party's control over the direction of literature, while those on the right thought of him a defeatist, "negating and trivializing their serious struggle." In his own defense, Wang Meng offered this self-reflection when it was rumored that he was chosen to be a member of the Central Committee of the CCP: "I . . . was but a writer inclined to be free and unrestrained. I derived pleasure in words taking wing, in impassioned and nuanced expressions, in weaving intricate plots, in heartwarming laughter, in flights of fancy, irony, and satire. All this would have hardly qualified me for membership in the esteemed Committee dedicated to serious political strife."

Wang Meng did become and remained a member of the Central Committee of the CCP from 1982 to 1991. From 1986 to 1989, he also was the editor-in-chief of PRC's flagship literary journal *People's Literature*. Being completely disinterested in politics, he said that he was not a very active member of the Central Committee. By editing *People's Literature,* however, he was able to foster an atmosphere of openness, encourage young authors, and publish their works.

Looking back to his own literary development, he attributed his sense of humor and the use of satire in his writing as the fruits of his life among the Uighurs in Xinjiang. "They taught me to laugh, . . . their dark humor was infectious." His sojourn in Xinjiang certainly marked the darkest period of his life without any hope of publishing or taking an active role in society. Reflecting on this period, however, Wang was grateful for the friendship shown him by ordinary people. This allowed him to foster a memory without recrimination or bitterness. His description of leaving Xinjiang conveys the general tone of the memoir. "More than forty people came to see us off at Urumqi Railway Station, and everyone was in tears. Ruifang (Wang's wife) simply couldn't stop crying. We would be forever indebted to Xinjiang, for it was the people of Xinjiang who took us in and offered us refuge. Their manners and outlook shaped me, and their Uighur humor set me straight."

Perhaps the most moving and most probing parts of this autobiography are the pages about his parents and the deep-seated peasant mentality they conveyed to him even though he spent most of his life in in the city. His parents had a very unhappy and tumultuous marriage. Although both of them were at the time studying in Beijing, their marriage was arranged by their parents. Wang Meng' father was a graduate of Peking University, and he continued his studies in the field of education at Tokyo University. He knew Japanese and German. However, some of Wang Meng's earliest memories was being transported from Beijing to the village from which his parents originally came, and then back from this village to the city as a refugee once the war with Japan had begun. With all his education, Wang's father was not able to hold onto the high paying job he enjoyed once he returned from studying abroad. Life in the household became a nightmare with the parents fighting all the time and the father first unable and later also unwilling to shoulder his responsibilities. Yet, he loved his children. Wang Meng grew up with his mother, his aunt, and his maternal grandmother running the household. Their job was to corner his father for money when he returned home. The situation tormented young Wang Meng. From his autobiography, it is clear that he loved his father but at the same time understood the weakness of the man. This in a way represents a profile of a generation which emerged from the Chinese countryside to receive the most advanced education the era was able to offer, yet was unable to become practical modern men and women and to apply their knowledge to change their relationship to each other and to the world around them. Perhaps, this early childhood experience made Wang Meng in later life extremely kind and forbearing of those who might be weak under pressure.

The autobiography begins with Wang Meng choosing his identity as that of a person from the countryside. He does this with a clear agenda: to know a man you must know where he comes from. The choice of the countryside as his origin, although he was born and lived most of his childhood in Beijing, was deliberate. His roots are in the countryside. It is not a romantic concept but full of contradiction, it is dear to him and at the same time painful to him. From here he hails and from here he must face the contradictions of sympathy and pain. In choosing this identity, Wang Meng points a path both for us to understand him and for him to navigate his life.

This is not the autobiography of a hero. Wang Meng comes across as an upright and decent man without pretense. What we learn to appreciate is his attempt at understanding—understanding individuals, understanding the times, and understanding the socialist ideals that formed his earlier youth and continue to support his moral universe today.

Zhu Hong and Liu Haiming offer a translation that is excellent in its accuracy and readability while conveying a sense of the original tone of the author. However, readers should be aware that Wang Meng's original came in three thick volumes and that this is an abridged translation of the work. Many episodes and detailed descriptions have been cut. Given Wang Meng's particular relationship to the Chinese Communist Party, this autobiography is intimately linked to the history of PRC. While the translation is effective in transmitting the spirit of the time through Wang Meng's narration, regrettably, the reader is not given basic background information concerning the particular historical events mentioned in the text. Nonetheless, Wang Meng's life itself carries much of the historical background information as well as offering a heartfelt and heartrending story of survival and triumph of a major literary figure in modern China.

Catherine V. Yeh
Boston University

WANG MENG

a life

Chapter 1

My Native Place

I was born in Peking (changed to Beijing in 1949), in a dorm of Peking University. The dorm was a traditional-style courtyard house tucked away on a street known as Shatan Street. At the time of my birth, my father, Wang Jindi, was a student at Peking University, and my mother was also attending school in Peking. But I have always taken pains to identify myself as a native of Longtang Village, Luguan Township, Nanpi County, Canzhou Prefecture of Hebei Province of North China. I would announce myself as a "native son of Longtang" in the countrified local accent. I also claim that the local "Hebei bangzi" opera, known for its long-drawn-out tragic notes, was my favorite among all forms of opera. I do not disavow my roots, I face them squarely and hold on to them, they are dear to me, but also a pain; they are burdensome but also solemn. They are my starting point, my background, the basis of many of my choices as well as an index of my values. I must add that they are also my original sin, a secret nagging pain. They are the object of my empathy as well as of my rejection: my fellow villagers, my forefathers, especially my parents.

I had been taken back to my native village by my parents a year or two after my birth. The event still lingers in my mind; actually it is the fabric of my earliest memories, the beginning of my existence. I was always perplexed by the question: where was the "I" called Wang Meng before this first memory and first consciousness of existence? I remember being rudely awakened from a nap one summer afternoon by two cats; their brownish eyes lightly streaked with red. Now I cannot remember whether we had really kept those two cats in our family home.

I once had a dream: I was playing under the pear trees in the back garden of our family home; I lost my footing and fell into a big hole. I was in shock and actually sniffed the fragrance of pears in the air.

I also have vague memories of the death of my grandmother; it must have been the same summer. I remember people moving about in the common room, the atmosphere tense. Word was out that my grandmother had died. When I think back, it seems that I was woken up during the wee hours of the morning—I have memories of people flitting about like shadows.

I know nothing about my grandmother; my mother Dong Min had nothing good to say about her, referring to her as the "old hag." My father spoke of her with great respect; he was born after his father's death, and only knew his mother. Years later, I learned that my grandfather was called Wang Zhangfeng, that he had taken part in the reformist Gongche Petition,[1] and had campaigned for the abolition of foot binding of women. He should be classed among the reformers grouped around Kang Youwei[2] and Liang Qichao[3] during the late nineteenth century.

Another memory surfaces: the term "running for refuge." Running from what? It must be running from the Japanese attack after the July 7 Incident of 1937.[4] Was it running away from Peking, or running to Peking? I have no idea, though I guess that the latter was more likely. These are the meager memories from my early years before I turned three. I remember my mother holding me as we made off in a horse drawn carriage. I remember stopping at an inn and hearing the horses chewing hay. It was late at night, I was fast asleep and awakened by the sound of hay being cut and catching the smell of dried hay and fresh grass. The

1. Gongche Petition, Joint Petition of Imperial Examination Candidates to the Emperor, led by Kang Youwei in 1895, to oppose the signing of the Treaty of Shimonoseki and to institute reforms, marking the beginning of the Reform Movement of 1898.
2. Kang Youwei, 1858–1927, scholar and reformer of the late Qing dynasty.
3. Liang Qichao, 1873–1929, scholar and one of the leaders of the 100 Days Reform Movement in 1898.
4. When the Japanese army attacked at Marco Polo Bridge on the outskirts of Peking, and eventually occupied north China.

figure of one big horse dominates my memory of that flight.

I am sure that I spoke the local dialect throughout the years of my childhood until I started school, when I learned Mandarin. I was born in old Peking, but because of the years in my home village, I did not speak the Peking dialect as the street kids did, I spoke the official Mandarin slightly tinged with the pronunciation of my local dialect. Up until my early teens, I still spoke the local dialect at home with my parents, though my younger sister and brother could not speak it at all. All the above is meant to proclaim loud and clear the fact of my lowly beginnings! How tortuous the path before me! We were so countrified, so poor, so backward, so uncultivated, so far removed from civilization. If I do not face up to this, I would be denying reality.

Many years later, when I went back to my village, I heard for the first time that our home was formerly situated in a Muslim autonomous county and that we had only moved to Nanpi County for a change of *fengshui*,[5] when there had been too many deaths in the family. So my forefathers lived in close quarters with Muslims. That must have left an imprint on my genes.

In 1984, I visited my native village for the first time since becoming an adult. What I saw was a dead white film of alkaline covering the fields. As for the people, even the local cadres who received me were a dismal sight, their clothes in tatters, their homes crumbling. I checked the county gazeteer, and saw that the inhabitants were merely listed as Zhao the Hunchback, or Li the Rock. The situation was best summarized in a folk ballad:

Goat shit turds
Rubbing against my feet,
I am the little brother,
You are the elder.
Got a bottle of wine
Let's drink together.
When drunk
Beat the wife.

5. A form of geomancy to determine the location and positioning of a house or a tomb or the arrangement of furniture, all of which is believed to affect the family fortune.

What if she dies?
Got money,
Marry another.
No money,
Hit your drum and sing a rice-sprout song.

To this day, I am still struck by the bleakness of this ballad. This is my native place, this is rural north China. This is life for most of us, we the descendants of the race of the Middle Kingdom.

Father would often say that there was no toilet paper when he was a child—even the pieces of rock or clumps of clay had been exhausted, so people rubbed their bottoms against the end of a collapsed wall, until the corner of the wall was rubbed down to a shiny stump.

That visit in 1984 had put me on the spot. A young fellow looked me up in Beijing, showing me the verdict on his brother for stealing a cow. He assumed that I had the power to free his brother and expected me to find work for him as well. I managed to get him work on a construction site in the county, but that was not what he wanted. He then came up with a new request: his forbears had been forced into slave labor in Japan and he wanted reparation money. I was not able to help. Back in my native place, faced with the locals, I was helpless. I could only talk as if I were trying to talk myself out of their problems.

Twenty years later, during the Spring Festival of 2005, I joined up with other relatives in Beijing and we visited my native village of Longtang. The change was spectacular. Rows of ditches had been dug in the fields to dispel the alkaline. Huge tents stood here and there, for raising hothouse fruits and vegetables. All my fellow villagers were properly clothed, some with leather jackets. The village was dotted with newly built houses. Local enterprises flourished, the Nanpi County Electric Bulb Manufactory, the Automobile Parts Manufactory, the Cotton Knitting Factory, the Pickle Factory and more. The Nanpi County Hospital boasted a newly installed CT machine imported from Germany, just as good as the one in Beijing Hospital. The villagers' only complaint was the quality of their drinking water, but all in all, it was another world compared with what it had been twenty years before. I was very happy at the changes. The younger generation in our group still complained under their breath about the muddy roads, the sticks of furniture in the homes. But I was happy.

The neighboring county of Wuqiao, also under the jurisdiction of Cangzhou Prefecture, was known far and wide for its martial arts. To this day, the International Acrobatics Troupe of Hebei Province is named after Wuqiao. When I was Minister of Culture, I had approved the founding of the Wuqiao Acrobatic Training School. In a word, my native place is endowed with a martial arts tradition, which is a fine thing. On the other hand, it had also been a base for the Boxer Rebellion[6] during the late Qing dynasty. Its strength in martial arts and acrobatics could also become an obsession and feed into a group mentality about the superiority of the Chinese race, to which all other barbarians could not compare. The core issue was a lack of culture and scientific information, and the refusal to face up to reality.

Also under the jurisdiction of Cangzhou Prefecture was Huanghua County, best known for the construction of its seaport. There was a vast expanse of swamp covered with reeds, reaching beyond the horizon. In the old days it had been infested with bandits. At the outbreak of the War of Resistance against Japan, the Communist Party's Eighth Route Army had tried to recruit them. The bandits challenged the communist soldiers to a competition: strip and get into the swamp to see which group could best withstand the attack of mosquitoes which swarmed the swamp. The communist soldiers won, and the bandits joined the communists. This is more legend than history.

Cangzhou has been ridiculed for boasting of only "one street, one building, one policeman, one monkey." The one street referred to Shuqian Street, where the police were quartered, and where my maternal grandmother's home had once stood. The one building, known in the old days as the "Western-style building," referred to the Catholic Church; the earliest Western medicine clinic was located in the same building. During the days of the Japanese occupation, there had been talk of setting up a zoo; only one monkey had been acquired, and that was the long and short of the Canzhou Zoo.

6. Armed struggle waged by northern peasants and handicraftsmen in 1900, under the rallying cry of "support the Qing and oppose the foreigners," targeted Western missionaries and Chinese Christians.

Cangzhou was also known for its cast-iron lion. The saying goes: "Cangzhou's cast-iron lion, Jingzhou's tower, and Dongguang's cast-iron Buddha." Cangzhou's lion was cast very vividly, head high and legs splayed. For the previous several hundred years, it had never rusted. Later a shelter was built to keep out the sun and the rain, and strangely, the cast-iron lion started to rust and nothing could save it.

One's native place is a matter of fate. I do not understand why I am a native of Nanpi County, Cangzhou Prefecture; the question cannot be answered in terms of logic. It is a divine plan, a decision already made. All my sorrow, my humiliation, is contained in the term "native place." All intensely identify with it. Native place is the alpha and omega of my existence, the primary motivating force, the mechanism of all future growth and changes. That is how I began, and so did we all. The older I am, the more I wish to relive my origins in my native place, my beginnings, and the earliest definitions of who and what I am, my secret DNA. I hope to discover something, and decode something.

Another reason that I consciously emphasize my native place and my origins is because I vaguely feel that as private life and family life are being urbanized and society is being modernized and globalized, and as we are speeding along with passing time, I fear that my native place and my own beginnings will be washed away. I fear that my native place, my origins, not having anything to define itself with, will be overlooked, and spurned, and forgotten. I fear that the pains of my childhood—the pitiful, unformed, and naïve experiences and regrets of my childhood—will be wiped away, and from that point on, it will be impossible to interpret myself based on my origins, impossible to reminisce, that there will be a wall and big blank spaces which will block my interaction with others or with my readers.

Chapter 2

My Father and My Mother

My father, Wang Jindi, courtesy names Shaofeng and Yuesheng, graduated from the Philosophy Department of Peking University. His roommates there had been the poet-critics He Qifang[1] and Li Changzhi.[2] My name was given to me by He Qifang. At the time that I was born, He Qifang was reading *Lady of the Camilias* by Alexander Dumas fils. The name of the hero Armande had been alternately transliterated into Chinese as *amang* or *ameng*, and Mr He Qifang conferred on me the name Wang Ameng. The problem was that in naming their children, people in the south often used the diminutive prefix *a* followed by the word for *puppy* or *tabby*. To put a distance between this practice and the naming of his son, my father decided to drop the diminutive *a* and keep the *meng*, and thus I became Wang Meng. Mr Li Changzhi, entrusted with the naming of my sister, conferred on her the name Wang Sa, *sa* being derived from the famous painting Mona Lisa.

After graduating from Peking University, my father spent three years in Japan, studying education at the Imperial College in Tokyo.

On graduation, my father returned to China and was appointed principal of the Municipal Advanced Commercial Institute. It was the highest position that he ever reached and it didn't last long. But while it

1. He Qifang, 1912–1977, poet and literary critic, later director of the Institute of Literature, Chinese Academy of Social Sciences (CASS).
2. Li Changzhi, 1910–1978 poet and literary critic, labeled *rightist* during the anti-rightist campaign of the 1950s.

did last, my father really lived it up. At the time, the position of principal of a professional institute was rated much higher than what such a title would warrant nowadays. We rented a traditional style house in a hutong behind Beihai Park. The house was laid out with inner and outer courtyards, and we installed modern conveniences.

I remember that a friend of my father's, the German sinologist Wolfgang Franke,[3] had been a guest at our house. My father hired a housekeeper, a rickshaw boy and a cook. We also co-owned a rowboat with Mr. Franke. When we went boating in Beihai Park, we did not line up to rent a rowboat, but headed to a quay for our own boat. I remember sitting on Uncle Wolfgang's shoulder as a boy to go holidaying in the park. Shaded shelters had been set up on the lake to capture the cool breeze. The elusive fragrance of lotus wafted on the breeze while lotus leaf porridge and buns were served. Those were the days.

Father, tall with regular features, carried himself well, though he never managed to acquire a perfect Mandarin accent. He was a follower of the New Culture, admired Europe and America, and loved consorting with Westerners. He enjoyed conversation, but could not stick to a point, always rambling on about this, that, and the other. As for the care of us his children, Father was fixated on the problem of body posture and bathing. He would rattle away as if the future of the nation depended on it. Even late in life, one of Father's pleasures was to take his sons and grandsons to the public bath for a three-generation collective ablution. Another of Father's fixations was athletics. It would always make him happy to hear that I had been running, or swimming, or mountain climbing. Although Father tended to go to extremes, we children did grow up conscious that good posture, personal cleanliness, and sports were markers of modern civilization. Another of Father's obsessions was table manners. He made us go through the ABCs of table manners, especially when it came to Western food. He showed us how to order, how to use a knife and fork, how to lay down a knife and fork to signal that we were done or that we were not yet done. Father literally revered table manners. As for those people who ate while squatting or lolling on their chairs or bent over a

3. Wolfgang Franke, 1912–2007, Sinologist and scholar on the history of the Ming and Qing dynasties; studied and taught in China from 1937 through 1950 and returned to Germany to teach at Hamburg University.

book, he absolutely detested them as public enemies. Father was also an upholder of good social manners. Faced with the gaucheness of some of our local people, men and women alike, Father would literally squirm as if he were in physical agony.

Mother rarely ate out. Even when she did, she would never stop saying with every mouthful of food "Oh how expensive, how sinfully expensive . . ." Not so Father. As far as he was concerned, he would enjoy himself to the last mouthful even if he was down to his last penny. Better, of course, if someone else was treating. I once flung a piece of sarcasm at Father, saying, "It seems that a good dinner could change your whole attitude toward life, from extreme despair to outright optimism." Father actually agreed, claiming to be quoting Marx, as he retorted, "Certainly, it is the Smile of Matter!" God knows where he got that "quote."

I remember one bad experience when dining out with Father. It was in a restaurant in Xidan, in the western part of the city, and there was a lady guest. After dinner, Father took us for a long walk. It was getting dark, and all I wanted to do after dinner was go home. But Father ignored me as he chatted with the lady. I heard him say, "Look at us, a man and a woman holding a child between them, don't we look like a family?" "Nonsense," the lady retorted. Father then said something else and again was told off. Exclamations of "Nonsense!" "Nonsense!" followed one after another. I did not understand what was going on, all I knew was that for the moment, Father had completely forgotten about me.

The next day I reported to Mother every last detail of the dinner, and the result can be imagined, though by now I have forgotten how it ended. Several decades later, when Father had been dead for more than ten years, I accidentally came across this very same lady friend of my father's. It was on one of my trips in the south that I heard of her as being a professor of Chinese and author of some articles on Chinese literature. When we did meet, I could not see any trace of her past attractions. It was as Mother had said, Time wipes out everything. There had been a rumor floating around, that back then Father and Wolfgang Franke had both been interested in the lady. Later, by a freak accident, I came across an old letter written by this same lady to Franke wherein she mentioned Father in very unflattering terms. It is the way of the world, I suppose. Father had fared indifferently in life, and could not expect a lot of respect. Anyway, I had a good conversation with the lady at that chance meeting, and later on even helped get a book she wrote published.

Coming back to the fortunes of our family, when Father's term as principal of the Commercial Institute was up, he was not reappointed. It was to be expected, as he was not good at dealing with practical matters. He would set a glorious goal, so detached from reality that it made people question his sanity. He knew his own mind, knew what he liked, what he aspired to, but he had no clue as to how to get there, much less did he consider his own abilities and the practical measures needed to achieve his goal. He had disdain for petty concerns, which for him included money. He was definitely unsuited for the job of principle of an academic institution. I would say he was unsuited for a job as section supervisor, or a group leader, and equally unqualified as a head of household. Mother definitely agreed with the last, though she conceded that he did love his children. All he cared for and excelled at was manners and etiquette. He was liberal in sprinkling his sentences with "thank you" and "pardon" and "just a moment" and "see you again" and the like, but he would not repay your loan. He admired Marx and Hegel and Fuerbach and Rousseau, but did not know how and where to buy a shirt for himself. His head was always in the clouds: he harangued colleagues on theories of running the country and saving the nation, he advocated Western civilization, he called for Englightenment. About his fall from grace at the Commercial Institute, Father summed it up thus, "I was the early riser, but only caught the last bus!" Is this the working of Fate, or the consequence of character?

The consequence of Father's non-reappointment, however, was swift and obvious. The traditional courtyard-style house had to be given up. We moved to modest quarters. From then on we moved from house to house on a downward sliding scale and ended up in the slums. To make a living, Father burned the midnight oil translating philosophical papers from German into garbled Chinese for the pitiful royalties of the *Sino-German Academic Review*. His half-baked German was obviously self-taught, as was his smattering of English, Japanese, and Russian.

My mother, born Dong Yulan, was formally renamed Dong Min when she started to work as a teacher after Liberation and qualified for a pension. Father told me that when the marriage proposal was put before him, he had put forward two demands—first to get a look at the girl with his own eyes, and second, that she must get an education. The viewing was conducted at the Cangzhou Second Girls′ School. After the viewing, Father agreed to the proposal. At the time, my mother′s father, my maternal grandfather, was a doctor at the school clinic. The matchmaker was a literary figure of an earlier generation named Wang Jixiang.

Later, when I was in primary school, Wang Jixiang once paid us a visit. Mother spoke up and blamed him for his matchmaking, which she claimed had ruined her life. Mother had a quick and ready tongue and was never afraid to speak up. She was sometimes guilty of malapropisms, though, like saying "What a lucky draw!" when she meant to compliment people for their achievements.

Mother must have enjoyed some happy times, I suppose. I remember that in the early years when I was not yet in school, she would regularly attend a temple fair in the west part of town to learn to sing Beijing opera arias. There was also a time when Mother and her sister Dong Zhilan had been briefly hired as library staff at the Peking No. 1 Girls′ School. There they had met two other young women and the four of them spent time together singing popular songs from the movies. Their songs had been my first introduction to popular music. Mother also loved local Hebei opera—its harsh tones might have allowed her to release her own feelings. Mother also loved reading. She had read all the best-known writers of the time—the short stories and novels of Bing Xin,[4] Ba Jin,[5] and Zhang Henshui,[6] the poems of Xu Zhimo[7] and others—and she was familiar with the new thinking of the May Fourth Movement.[8] The more

4. Bing Xin, 1900–1999, through a writing life of seventy years, left a rich legacy of poetry, short stories, familiar essays, and writings for children.
5. Ba Jin, 1904–2005, was dubbed "a child of the May Fourth Movement." His vast volume of work, especially the *Torrents* trilogy, reflected the restlessness and rebellious mood of the young generation of his time.
6. Zhang Henshui, 1895–1967, one of the earliest novelists to publish in installments in the daily press. Altogether Zhang published one hundred novels and is known as the father of modern popular fiction.
7. Xu Zhimo, 1897–1931, was a romantic poet. He spent time in England and was a representative of the Crescent School of poetry of the 1920s.
8. A political and cultural movement of the early 1920s, agitating against the feudal tradition, advocating science, democracy and a new, modern culture.

she read and learned of the new culture, however, the more she deplored her own fate.

Mother did not drink milk, did not use cream on her face, did not drink tea, did not smoke or drink or eat out, considering all the above as sinfully wasteful. She seemed the exact antithesis of Father in every way. Overall, Mother's life was tense, one source of tension being a lack of economic security, the other a sense of being cheated. Father claimed to have provided large sums of money to the family, but he never realized that a family needed a steady income to keep going. He would act on impulse and give lavish dinners that halved his salary at one go. He would also fall recklessly into debt, or buy on credit without any savings to fall back on. It was painful to watch him unconscionably dispose of the poor little errand boys sent to collect his debts.

As long as he had money in his pocket, Father acted the gentleman, eating out at Western restaurants, consorting with social celebrities, throwing lavish dinners, opening his pockets for good causes. He would have nothing to do with mundane affairs and totally despised money for its own sake. He said that as long as his potential was released, he did not see why money should be a problem. He declared that he was meant to be rich, meant to be master, that being a rich master, he would be generous and kind and well mannered. Father enjoyed spending money but never concerned himself about how to make money or how to pay his debts, much less did he think of cutting expenses and saving against a rainy day. It was Father's fate to be up against wife, children, and relatives, who were often hungry. By putting it thus, I am not trying to be dramatic. I distinctly remember evenings at home when my mother, my aunt, and my maternal grandma would look at each other, not knowing how to get through supper. We would be out of flour, out of rice, and out of cash. Pushed into a corner, one of them would fish out an old wrist watch, or a felt hat, or a padded jacket from somewhere, go to the pawnshop and come back with two pounds of coarse flour, and thus we would get over the problem of supper for the time being.

Understandably, Mother was not happy with the situation, not to mention the fact that she could not get along with the kind of man that Father was. She did not trust him. She gradually found out about his affairs. Whatever the case, at least it was clear that Father wanted to spend time with more beautiful and more modern young women. The situation worsened when my aunt and my grandma joined our household. The three women would often gang up to devise strategies to deal with Father. I was too young to understand the situation—all I knew was that the two sides did their best to fight each other, rubbing salt where it hurt most and finding satisfaction therefrom.

Sometime after he lost his job at the Commercial Institute, Father took up teaching, first at Peking University and then at Peking Normal University, but those jobs, too, soon disappeared. Father then left Peking for Qjngdao (in Shangdong Province) to take up the post of principal at the local Lizhuang Teacher's School. The irony was that once Father was down on his luck, he would be on his best behavior, sweet-talking Mother, bending over backward to pacify her. The three women would lap it all up, talking a blue streak about "the repentant son is worth his weight in gold" and so on, predicting that Father would mature and improve with age. But once his situation improved, Father would change back to his old self, and hostilities resumed with renewed venom.

It was in 1944 around the Spring Festival that Father sent a letter and presents to us children, probably brought by someone traveling from Qingdao to Peking. His letter to the family reiterated his message on the importance of regular bathing—once a day minimum, preferably twice. His gifts were absolutely stunning. There was a set of Snow White and the Seven Dwarfs, carved out of wood, each figure on its own stand. Additionally there was a contraption, which when struck with a hammer, would release a shot and bring down one of the seven dwarfs. I and my sister were spellbound and could not stop playing the game. Father also brought back a book designed in Japan, a book wherein the pages were cut into three sections, the top sections painted with heads in various headgear, the middle sections with pictures of the upper body in various kinds of clothing, and the bottom sections with pictures of the lower body in various designs of clothing and shoes to match. We could turn the pages of the three parts to form various combinations of figures in different outfits. In truth I found the whole contraption a bit freaky. Mother gnashed her teeth in fury at this display of frivolity when the family had run out of daily necessities. She regarded the toys as a personal taunt, a statement of rejection of the family. "A foreign monkey," she muttered, by which she meant that Father was inscrutable and unpredictable. Later she went further to denounce him as a "public enemy." In response, Father lumped Mother and Aunt and Grandma together as an unholy trinity of ignorance and cunning.

As a child, I was often taken by Mother on a round of visits to friends and relatives to mount a campaign against Father. To this day, I remember that one of the people we called on was Yu Tianxiu, professor of Chinese at Peking Normal University. The conversation would turn on Father's irresponsibility, leaving Mother to bring up the children on her own. This accusation would be followed by appeals for monetary assistance. My presence—I, being well behaved, quick-witted and obviously undernourished—would add weight to her appeal.

Thinking back on it now, it is unbelievable that a family of six or seven people could have survived all those years without a regular income. Mother was fixated on our physical survival and holding the family together. Father had more than once raised the question of divorce, but the minute Mother mentioned alimony, he would back down. Meanwhile the family grew from two children to three and then to four. In that unhappy home in Nanweir Hutong, I remember peeking at Father's diary from his days in Japan, and reading that he had been with a prostitute. Another entry complained of Mother's letters as "no affection, no inquiries, just demands for money, what can I do? . . ." The words shocked me. I made a resolution then and there not to be someone like Father when I grew up. I made a resolution never to be mean to women. I had mastered the knack of learning by negative example.

Looking back, I remember that Father had owned two things that I loved. One was an album of the eight famous sights of Peking; it made me conscious of the beauties of the city, and I have saved it to this day. Another was a tea container carved out of a coconut shell and decorated with scenes of Mt. Fuji It was cracked with age and is not around anymore. Father loved reading; he sometimes spent long hours reading as he sipped tea. Under Mother's influence, I would ask him why he didn't drink water, as tea was so expensive. I also felt that too much reading was boring. Father also loved walking and riding and was an avid swimmer. In his old age he would spend three hours every day swimming. Sometimes he would take me to swim as early as mid-May. Father had no ear for music and could not sing a note, but I did learn something about Chinese folk music and Chinese opera from some of his phonograph records.

Father loved making friends, and enjoyed conversation. He always greeted new acquaintances warmly, so much so that my sister and I felt that it was like fawning. He was very hurt when we raised this with him. Later, in the 1950s, Father liked to quote Khrushchev who, according to him, had said that "It is a crime to be cold to people." Father loved coffee, but when asked how to make coffee, he was completely lost. Obviously he had only taken coffee served in restaurants. Father also loved talking about philosophy: Socrates, Plato, Hegel, Fuerbach . . . Late in life, Father had been dubbed Wang-erbach by his friends. Once, when I asked him about philosophy, he replied that according to Russell, philosophy was like looking for a black cat in a dark room, looking for a cat that did not exist. According to a friend of mine, Father was not a good teacher, tending to ramble on in all directions without a sustained train of thought.

Father was severe on his home village, accusing it of ignorance, backwardness, cruelty, young men masturbating and smoking opium, young women taking pleasure in eavesdropping and probing into other people's private affairs. Later, Father also deplored the sadistic cruelty of the Land Reform (of the 1950s). Father worshiped Science. While the family had run out of rice and flour, he went and bought a thermostat to check the heat and humidity of the room. After Liberation, I once gave him a bottle of cod liver oil. He was so happy with it that he swallowed it in great gulps and was not bothered even when it gave him diarrhea. Once, Father, professing to love the arts, signed up my younger sister at a Beijing opera training school. I am not sure whether it was love of the arts or the tuition-free program that had attracted him. Luckily, Sister was not accepted.

Despite his advanced views, Father had never been on an airplane, and had never gone abroad again after returning from Japan. He never had any savings in the bank, and till the day he died he had never owned a proper wristwatch. At one time I had looked back at Father's life with pity and disdain. I consider him to have accomplished nothing his whole life. But later, many years after his death, my half-brother and I met over his grave, and my half-brother had said that Father's greatest achievement was that he had left Longtang Village behind him. Father had said that the local landowners' greatest wish was for their sons to start smoking opium at an early age so that they would never leave their native village and would not be affected by the new revolutionary trends outside the village. I was struck by the truth of his remark. To leave Longtang Village was a big deal. If he had never left, what would Wang Meng's life be like? Chance, heaven and earth, space and platforms, who can afford to ignore them? Thank you, dear Father. Your own pursuits did not amount to much, but you provided the minimum conditions. Taking cheap shots at you is a sin, punishable by life and by history.

Chapter 3

Home and Family

All in all, there were four elders in my family, Father, Mother, Grandma and Aunt, and they all loved me. I grew up enveloped in love. I remember one occasion when Father took me to see a dentist. As we were waiting to get on the bus, he left abruptly muttering about something he had left behind, and joined me soon after. He had a felt hat on his head when he left but had returned hatless. When I asked him about his hat, he ignored the question. I remember that the dentist not only fixed my teeth, but also flossed them. Later, I pointed to the entrance which Father had dived into on that particular day, and Mother ordered me to shut up. It was only later when I could read that I realized it was a pawnshop. Whenever Father brought back food, or took us children to eat out, he would hover over us, saying that he felt like a happy mother hen which had caught a lot of worms for her chicks.

Dispite Father's occasional show of affection, from early childhood we children were imbued with the idea that Mother was good and Father was bad, thanks to Mother's insinuations. We were often resentful of Father. When he was around, he mostly lectured us on how to speak correctly, how to express thanks, how to greet people, how to maintain a good posture while sitting or standing, how to walk properly and avoid turning out our toes, in a word, a list of do's and dont's on social behavior. We children felt humiliated and resentful—you didn't provide us with food and clothing, you didn't help with our homework, you were never around when we needed you, and when you did show up, all you did was lecture us. What a nuisance! Mother, on the other hand, served us children hand and foot. I remember once we were having noodles for dinner. Mother had used too much salt, and I refused to eat it. Mother added vinegar to neutralize the saltiness and only made it worse. I burst out crying and Mother acted terribly contrite, apologizing repeatedly. To this day, I feel ashamed of my behavior. Sometimes when I was hungry, Mother would make flour paste, add black sugar, and that would be a treat for me. Other times she would cut up corn bread into little cubes, throw in a dash of sesame oil, soy sauce and a pinch of chopped spring onions, and that would be another treat.

Grandma would take me to temple fairs. At a fair, she would buy a concoction for removing warts, probably some sulphurous mixture, and apply it to my face. After the burning pain, my warts would disappear leaving a couple of dents, and a few days later new warts would resurface on another part of my face. We had mostly lived in the western part of the city, and the temple fairs at the White Pagoda Temple and the Huguosi Temple were sources of delight during my childhood years. I loved the singsong hawkings of the roadside peddlers selling cotton cloth, or artificial flowers, or candied haw, or fried-flour drinks, or energy pills . . . I also loved the acrobats and the weird singing of roadside "opera actors." Moreover, the beautiful Tibetan-style White Pagoda was worth seeing. However, my visits to temple fairs once caused a near-disaster. Standing on my bed, I had tried to imitate the acrobatic performers and with one spring dashed my head on a clay pot on the floor, hurting myself badly.

Grandma had tried to help with my first schoolwork—tracing calligraphy. Chinese characters were printed in red on rice paper, and I the student was expected to trace the strokes in black ink. At the time, there was no ready-made writing ink. For a start, we students had to grind our own block of ink on a grindstone to make ink before we could apply the brush to trace the strokes. After some messy grinding, I dipped my brush in the ink and applied it to paper. However, the brush seemed to have a will of its own and would not follow the movement of my hand. I burst out crying. Grandma personally took charge and tried to do my work for me. Grandma had never been to school though she could recite from the ancient *Thousand Character Reader.*[1] And thus between the two of us, black ink was splattered everywhere—on our hands, our faces, all over the paper, everywhere but on the strokes of the calligraphic characters where they were meant to be. Furthermore, due to my excessive use of force, the tip of the brush fell off the holder, and we had to go out and buy glue to reattach it. That of course drove me to distraction. I do not remember how this episode ended.

Of the three women in the household, Aunt seemed the most literary. She was tolerably good at calligraphy, and loved reading. Whenever she had a little money, she would rush to the lending library. Like Mother, Aunt was familiar with the works of all the popular novelists of the time—the romances of Zhang Henshui, Geng Xiaodi and Liu Yunruo,[2] and the martial art novels of Zheng Zhengyin and others. Her conversation was sprinkled with platitudes from the popular romances, such as "Feuds should be played down, not played up," or "Enemies tend to run into each other," or she would describe resentments as "hatred as deep as the ocean," and so on, although sometimes Aunt misquoted some of the snappy sayings.

Aunt often offered to help with my writing assignments. Once, the topic of my essay assignment was "Wind." After describing flying stones and clouds of dust, Aunt tagged on an exclamation: "Oh wind, blow! Blow away the darkness of the world!" I did not know what was meant by the darkness of the world, or what it had to do with wind, but I added the sentence all the same. The tagged-on exclamation was actually highlighted by the teacher. Obviously Aunt's exhortation had met with his approval.

Aunt smoked and drank. She smoked the cheapest kind of cigarettes which cost a few cents per pack, and she drank the cheap white wine sold by the ounce. She would say: "I have no husband, no son, no daughter, no house, no land, no money. All I have is a puff of smoke and a mouthful of drink." Aunt would often mumble to herself with animated expressions on her face. In the morning, Aunt did her makeup as if going

---

1. Ancient primer for children in rhymed sentences of four characters each, written in the sixteenth century by Zhou Xinsi.
2. Liu Yunruo, 1903–1950, prolific novelist from Tianjin, known for his novels of social exposure.

through a ritual, talking to herself non-stop, sometimes even cursing and spitting as she did her hair. Right up to age fifty-nine, when Aunt joined us in Xinjiang, her hair was jet-black.

I often felt lucky that I was born into this family, just as I sometimes felt unlucky. As far as I was concerned, the best thing about our family was that we children were not beaten. At No. 18 Shoubi Hutong, our next-door neighbor, by the name of Bai, had a houseful of children. The sounds coming from that house of children being punished were blood curdling. Sometimes the screams were heard even before the beating started— like the sounds from a slaughterhouse. It was whispered that the children were made to kneel and were beaten by wooden planks or straps. The next morning these children would emerge from the house with bruises, especially the eldest, a girl. Worst, still, was the humiliation. It was whispered that they were beaten for bad grades, or for playing hooky. It was a reminder to me of the importance of study. From this example, I sometimes ask myself: is it fair to say that the New Culture of the May Fourth Movement had left our family untouched? At least, we children were not beaten.

I sometimes ask myself, to tell or not to tell? As a writer writing about my elders, don't I have the right to touch it up a little? To pass over a little of what is too negative or too humiliating? Isn't it my moral duty, isn't it the least I should do? But my memoir is facing my ancestors, facing my parents and my elders, facing the age and the times—loaded with moral obligations right and left—facing history itself, facing the future, facing heaven and earth, the mountains and rivers, facing hundreds of thousands of readers present and future. However much I reveal, however hard I try, it can never be the whole truth. I will always feel that I have let down my readers. Such being the case, how dare I keep back something, or distort something to my advantage? I must say what I have to say.

In one of the prose poems I wrote in my early youth, I had written, "In this peculiar family of mine, there is too much discord, too much togetherness . . ." The problem was not limited to the discord between my parents. When Father was not around—which was often—what Father had dubbed the unholy trinity of Mother, Aunt, and Grandma would be torn asunder in fierce combat. I cannot remember the substance of those quarrels, but one theme running through it all was money. The less money one possessed, the more reason to suspect the other two of trying to take advantage. There was a pervasive air of tension and suspicion of one's nearest and dearest—a state of mind which Father had dubbed "Innate Evil." Though I could not tell what they were fighting over, the situation and the language used are stuck in my memory. They would jump up and down as they cursed one or the other according to the occasion: "run over by a car the minute you step out," "a sore on your tongue," "your brains dried up," "your body cut up into bits and pieces," "your body pierced by a thousand arrows," "dead and nowhere to lay down your carcass," "harlot supporting a fancy man," "already in your death throes". . . The above were just some of the abuses Grandma, Mother, and Aunt flung at each other. There was another form of abuse, the "vow and curse" variety, where one vowed that if one did what one was accused of, then one was willing to take the consequences of the curse. On the other hand, if one was innocent of what one was accused of, then the vengeance, whatever it was, would be turned against the accuser. Those fights would end in the three women each doing their own cooking. They really personified the saying that "hell is the other."

Sometimes, the three women would repent and make up. Once the three of them made a visit to our home village, but getting off the train on the way back, Grandma was missing. The two sisters were very upset and went everywhere looking for "our mom." Then Grandma appeared, and the three fell into each other's arms and had a good cry, vowing never to fight again. And of course the fights resumed. Hostilities had even extended beyond the boundaries of our home. There was a suspicion that our neighbors had been bad-mouthing us, so the three women launched a verbal onslaught across the dividing wall right into the neighbor's yard. The little daughter of the neighboring family was my classmate. Later, she joined the Party on the eve of Liberation and married a leading cadre, actually a scholarly man. Unfortunately she was labeled a *rightist* in the 1950s and committed suicide during the Cultural Revolution. I had used her story for the characterization of Haiyun in my novella *Butterfly*. I must add that the influence of the venomous verbal wars among the three women eventually extended to my two sisters, poisoning their young minds. This aspect of the family feud had inspired the description of the girl Ni Ping in my novel *The Transformer*. The most fortunate person, despite the feuding, was none other than me. All three elders, Grandma, Mother and Aunt, no matter how much they fought each other, all loved me. And that instilled in me a sense of superiority as well as a sort of disdain and pity toward these feuding women. I was above the fray. A spoiled little boy stuck in a backward, barbarous corner of the world—that was the young Wang Meng.

Grandma and Mother and Aunt even took their fights into court. Grandma had adopted a son from another branch of the family, but later Grandma and Mother and Aunt had all disapproved of the young man and had formally annulled the adoption. I remember hearing them savor the satisfaction of seeing Grandma dressed in silk and giving evidence in court—that was in the old days. Later, after Liberation, Grandma and Mother and Aunt had all gone to the local police in one or another of their many quarrels. They knew how to hit where it hurt most: Mother had reported that Grandma was a "landowner," and Aunt had exposed Mother's son, meaning me, as a "rightist."

As for Father, he was in the habit of using the term "a cesspool of evil and iniquity." Father believed that in old China every town, every street, every family, every corner was what he referred to as "a cesspool of evil and iniquity." Father believed that the cesspool was present right inside the family and that it could only be cleared away by a revolutionary storm, though he could not work out the problem of people's livelihood in the aftermath of the storm. It was beyond his mental horizon, and Father did not bother his head about it. Father condemned the feudal tradition under which his marriage had been a torment to him; the irony was that his second marriage based on free choice was an equal if not a more lethal torment. He went through the same fights and curses and repeated attempts at another divorce.

All his life, Father had been at odds with himself, caught in the gap between life and livelihood, good breeding and practical ability, personal conditions and the general environment, temperament and character. In a word, his upbringing and his capacity were at sixes and sevens, and he was his own worst enemy. During his last years when Father was blind and lame, the partner of his second marriage was paralyzed and confined to a wheelchair. Even so she had wheeled herself to all the little stores in their neighborhood, warning storekeepers not to sell good cigarettes to Father even if he had cash on him.

Father was a victim of the barbarity of his native place, and he himself had also hurt others barbarously. Then he became a victim of his own obsession with the sweep of Western enlightenment. And finally, he became victim to the pettiness of the petty Peking-er, and hurt others just as well. In a word, Father had never been happy, and had never made others happy.

In old age, Mother often bemoaned her own fate. She would say, "Look at Bing Xin! Look at Sun Qingling.[3] Look at what they made of their lives, and look at me! Would that I had never known anything about them! Now that I do know something, what good does it do me! Nothing! All my life, I was never happy. I have nothing to console myself with. Why am I doomed to such a life!" I did not understand why Mother should compare herself to Bing Xin and Sun Qingling. But then I asked myself, who am I to decide whom Mother compared herself to? Later, when I considered myself a revolutionary figure, I had even criticized my parents. Alas, the "cesspool of evil" is not to be drained in one bold sweep. The root of evil, the tentacles of evil are passed down generation to generation. All I can offer my Father and Mother are my tears. May your tortured souls find peace in the other world!

3. Sun Qingling, 1893–1981, widow of Sun Yat-Sen and vice-president of the People's Republic of China since 1949.

Chapter 4

My Education

I attended the Fragrant Mountain Kindergarten, which used to be the site of the Temple of the God of Earth, close to where we lived in the western part of town. Later on, the institution was taken over by the No. 3 Girls School and then converted to the No. 166 Middle School. During the surge of reform and opening-up in the eighties, the site reverted to the Temple of the God of Earth, hopefully to draw in some tourist income.

All I remember of life in kindergarten was that I could not dance, I could never get the movements right. I believe it was part of the result of a defective education and lack of proper nutrition. For grade school I attended the primary school attached to the Peking Teacher's Academy, at the time considered a very good institution, not open to "riffraff." For instance the son of a worker at a coal station in our neighborhood, Little Five, could not get into my school try as he did, and we kids taunted him over it.

When I entered school, I was one month short of six years old. I was thin and small for my age and had no clue as to what school life meant for a little boy. But I scored top grades for the first two semesters and was ranked No. 3 in class by grade average. My family, concerned that I might be bullied by the bigger kids, reminded me to always go to the teacher if I had a complaint. I ended up the champion complainer in the class, and a pain in the neck for the teacher. Once he was so annoyed at yet another complaint of mine that he ignored the substance of the complaint and ordered me to get up on my chair and remain standing for the duration of the class. Standing on my chair as a spectacle made me very uncomfortable. After a while I asked if I could get off the chair. The question seemed to further aggravate the teacher, who gave me a loud scolding then and there. It was a lesson that I will always remember. The "boss" likes people who help him solve problems, not those who bring problems to him.

It was in my second year that I flowered as a good student. My writing assignments were often praised by the teacher, Miss Hua Xialing, and I always complied with the rules. Once, a girl student had reported a boy for some offense. It ended with the boys and the girls of the class pitted against each other in a big shouting match. I was the only boy who did not take part against the girls, and one girl held me in a tight embrace, claiming me as one of their own. I did not know whether it should be considered an honor or a disgrace. Thinking back, it is a sweet memory.

Though a good student, I also had some memorable punishments. Once, both I and a girl student had forgotten to bring our writing utensils for the writing class. According to the rules, the teacher ordered both of us to go stand outside the classroom for the duration of the class. The girl got up and declared that Wang Meng was always a good student, and she begged the teacher to let her stand for the both of us. I immediately shouted: "I agree!" For this the teacher taught me a lesson that I will never forget! It was behavior that I am ashamed of to this day. On another occasion during a test, I checked the textbook on the sly. Teacher Hua saw me cheating, but waited till later to teach me another unforgettable lesson. I will never forget my teacher Hua Xialing.

Once, teacher Hua did me a special favor by taking me to the opening ceremony of a municipal sporting event held at the stadium near the ancient Xiannongtan Temple· a memorable experience that I used in my novel *Long Live Youth.* After the closing ceremony, however, I lost Teacher Hua in the pushing and shoving of the crowd. I mistakenly took a tram going in the opposite direction of our house and ended up in the eastern part of the city, far away from home. However, I did not panic; I hopped on a rickshaw and gave him the exact address and arrived home into the arms of Mother, who was worried sick and now praised me for my quick wits. Under normal circumstances, it was out of the question for me to hire a rickshaw on my own.

Starting from second grade, I was indisputably the best student in class. In the third grade, we once had a writing assignment on the topic "If . . ." I started my essay with the words: "If I were a tiger I would devour all the rich!" This may be considered the first budding of my leftist leanings, simply due to the poverty at home.

In the third grade, I took part in a speech contest for the first time. The topic was "How to Be a Good Student." Aunt helped me with the draft, which emphasized good health, good behavior and good grades, just the usual requirements, which were also the standard for students after Liberation. I stepped up to the podium, and goodness, I was faced with a mass of black-haired heads and black eyes staring up at me. I decided that win or lose, this is the moment. I took a deep breath and rattled through my speech. Probably it was a good start: all my life I was always able to deal with speaking in public.

It was also during the third grade that our grade teacher, Miss Shen, left and was replaced by Miss Dong, newly graduated from Peking Normal University. Many girls cried at Miss Shen's departure, but not me. I did not feel that a change of teacher was worth a cry. Perhaps it was the first inkling of rationality, or even coldness, in my emotional make-up. The new grade teacher Miss Dong took me home. She showed me photographs of herself in cap and gown, and also told me the good news that I was chosen by the school to take part in a competition for a scholarship provided by the Municipal Bureau of Education. For this, I had to copy out all my homework from the previous semester as part of the application. It was hard work, and I did not get the scholarship after all. But it was a good lesson for me: you gain some and you lose some. And anyway, I was already enjoying the rewards for being a good student—free tuition, approval from my teachers, and appreciation from my family.

But I also have lapses. Once, as class was about to start, a classmate caught a bird and did not know what to do with it. I took the bird and shoved it into my desk. Then class started and we had to open our desks to take out our writing utensils. The minute the top of my desk popped up, the bird flew out and the whole class burst out laughing. The teacher was furious and ordered me to remain standing throughout the class hour. The story has become the most popular in my repertoire—my children and grandchildren never tire of hearing it.

I was never meant to be an artist. I always got low grades for art. The only "A" that I ever got for an art assignment had been my sister's work from the previous year, with her name painted over and replaced with mine. Cheating. I stuck to reading and memorization. I memorized sections from *The Great Learning*[1] and from classical poetry. I also memorized passages from Bing Xin and Ba Jin, and later I included passages from *Wild Grass* by Lu Xun.[2]

I loved holidays. Every summer, I had to go through the preparation for finals: the debilitating heat, the lack of sleep, the exhaustion. I would be near collapse. Once final exams were over, the first thing I did on the first day of the summer holidays was to take a good nap. If a summer shower had just passed through, I would go to Beihai Park or thereabouts to listen to the cicadas and the drip drip of water from the eaves and the chirping of birds, and take out my favorite book of the moment. I was in seventh heaven. I like to be able to plan my own schedule. I love holidays, not for play but for the freedom to read. At the beginning of every summer, I would make out a long reading list of uplifting books and a study plan. Although my plans did not work out to the last detail, yet after every summer holiday, I would feel that I had achieved some growth, intellectually as well as physically.

To this day, I love going through the days gainfully according to my own plan.

---

1. An ancient text of personal improvement, author unknown, listed as one of the four Confucian classics.
2. Lu Xun, 1881–1936, a major literary figure on the Left in national politics, left a vast body of writing, mostly essays, short stories, literary criticism, and translations.

Chapter 5

A Turning Point—Progressive Contacts

Japan surrendered in August of 1945, when I was in the fifth grade. We were deliriously happy. After school, we would go to the office of our grade teacher, Miss Zheng Yi, to talk about national affairs. Teacher Zheng said that Chiang Kai-shek had launched the "New Life Movement"[1] and there had been hope for China, but that the Japanese aggression had upset the tide of affairs. I was filled with righteous anger and patriotic fervor, ready to die for my country any time, any where. By the way, Miss Zheng Yi was honored as a Model Teacher after Liberation, but did not escape the *rightist* label in 1957.

It was also in the summer of 1945 that I made the decision to skip sixth grade and apply directly to junior high school. I once came across a cartoon by the famous cartoonist Feng Zikai[2] showing four kids bound together by one leg each: the fast walker could not move ahead while the slow one was painfully dragged along. I was inspired by that picture. That fast walker was me, I decided. There was nothing that I did not know in the textbook that my sister, one grade above me, was using; actually I had been helping her with her homework all along! I could not apply to a public school, since I could not produce the required certificate of completion for grade school. So I applied and was accepted at a private

1. Launched in 1934, the movement declared "a battle on the spiritual side," trying to introduce personal hygiene and social manners among the masses, and relying on women's role to effect social change.
2. Feng Zikai, 1898–1975, painter, cartoonist, art educator, and art critic.

school, the Ping Min Middle School, now renamed the No. 41 Middle School. Having skipped a year, I was still at the top of the class.

By then Father had returned from Qingdao and for the moment there was peace at home. One evening, he brought home a friend, Comrade Li Xin. At the time, Li was working for Ye Jianying,[3] the Communist Party representative to the Executive Headquarters at Peiping.[4]

Uncle Li Xin was an instant inspiration. I was quarreling with my sister as he walked in, and he quietly taught me "criticism and self-criticism," which opened a new vista for me in personal behavior. Next, Uncle Li Xin found out that I was chosen to give a speech representing my school at the Peking Middle School Students Speech Contest sponsored by the Guomindang Political Department of the No.1 Battle Zone. The requirement was that the speech must be on a political / topical subject. Father waved it away, but Uncle Li insisted that I should seize the opportunity. He further suggested that I should talk on the "Three Principles of the People"[5] laid down by Sun Yat-sen,[6] and the "Four Freedoms"[7] spelled out by President Roosevelt—the gist of the speech being that we were neither implementing the Three Principles of the People nor enjoying any of the Four Freedoms. There was no doubt at all that in the junior section, my speech was the best. I still remember the thrill as I said, "Look at the children combing the trash heaps for scraps. Can we say that the Three Principles of the People have been implemented?" The moderator in his summing-up gave my speech an honorable mention, saying that my voice resonated like a cast iron bell. But I was only awarded third prize. Obviously the sponsors sniffed something incendiary in my speech. For me, it was a first lesson in the

---

3. Ye Jianying, 1897–1986, top military leader of the CCP, instrumental in bringing down the "Gang of Four," thus ending the Cultural Revolution and setting China on a new course.
4. Set up in January 1946, it was composed of representatives from the Communist Party and the Guomindang to correlate relationships and administer ceasefire negotiations, with assistance from the U.S. Army military personnel.
5. Nationalism, democracy, and the people's livelihood.
6. Sun Yat-sen, 1866–1925, founder of the Guomindang Party and President of China's first Republic.
7. Four fundamental freedoms: freedom of speech, of worship, and from want and fear.

political tactics of the Communist underground. I should mention, by the way, that the speaker for senior high was Yang Hushan, later a professional diplomat and at one time ambassador to Libiya.

After Liberation, Comrade Li Xin turned to academics and became an authority on Party history.[8] As the first Communist Party member that I had ever met, I was completely bowled over by his eloquence, his self-confidence, his steadfastness, his creativity, the thoroughness and clarity of his thinking. To me, it was like a divine revelation. Moreover, the force of theory was being reenforced by living reality. With open arms, I had welcomed the National Army, and I had welcomed the American army. But after the excitement was over, people were just as poor as before. Not to mention the abuses of the Guomindang takeover, the instant metamorphosis of collaborators into "underground resisters," and American jeeps running over people with impunity. When I saw fat heads emerging from high class restaurants and sniffed the aroma of rich foods wafting from within, I felt myself boiling with righteous anger and confirmed in my belief that what people wanted was communism, representing equality and justice.

The books that I read also confirmed my belief—the novel *Destruction* by Ba Jin, the play *Sunrise* by Cao Yu,[9] the novels *Decadence* and *Midnight* by Mao Dun,[10] and many other works of literature. They combined to highlight the idea that the society was rotten, that China was in crisis, and that what China needed was a thorough change, to be achieved through a baptism of fire and blood.

There was a tradition of baseball in our school, and a student from senior high was on the team as third baseman. He Ping was a lively fellow and used to get a lot of cheers, even when he missed a catch. One day, I happened to be close to the baseball field, waiting for class to begin and he strolled over to chat. By then I had made a name for myself through that public speech. He Ping asked me what I was reading lately. I mentioned

8. Director, Institute of Modern History, CASS (Chinese Academy of Social Science).
9. Cao Yu, 1910–1997, playwright of modern China, representative works: *Thunderstorm*, *Sunrise*, and others.
10. Mao Dun, 1898–1981, novelist, representative works: *Midnight*, the *Decadence* trilogy and others.

several books, and after a pause, I suddenly spurted out "Leftist." His face lit up. By a stroke of luck, He Ping was an underground Communist Party member! From then on, he became my guide on the road to revolution. At the time, to make such a "leftist" announcement as I did was risky. I could have gotten myself into trouble. But events unfolded as they did—it was part of the Scheme of Things, I suppose.

Father joined Comrade Li Xin, and together they headed for Yan'an.[11] Father was going to seek out his previous mentor, the historian Fan Wenlan,[12] at the time head of Northern University.[13]

Compared to my father's friend the historian Li Xin, He Ping was young and ardent and idealistic and full of energy. He devoted himself to showing me and another student—Qing Xueru—the way to revolution. He opened his home to us with his shelves of books; it was a veritable "Party School" for us two youngsters. We burrowed through the writings of Ai Siqi,[14] whose *Philosophy for the Masses* provided answers to everything under the sun, and we studied the works of Hua Gang,[15] whose *Outline History of Human Society* inducted me into the five forms of production and the immutable laws of social development. To me they were all infallible truths that brooked no contradiction. Having read these books, I felt myself armed with truth and invested with justice. And then there was the *Social Science Series* brought out by the New Knowledge Bookstore. Last but not least, there was Mao Zedong's *The New Democracy,* which made me realize how clear-cut and simple were the basic principles of revolution. The memoir *Back from Yan'an* by the liberal-minded educator Huang Yanpei[16] filled me with hope and confidence in the revolution. And then there were novels from the Soviet Union and other socialist

11. The Communist base in the rural northwest.
12. Fan Wenlan, 1893–1969, scholar and one-time professor of Chinese history at Peking University.
13. Set up in 1945 in the communist occupied border area adjoining the provinces of Shanxi, Hebei, Shandong, and Henan.
14. Ai Siqi, 1910–1966, Marxist philosopher, faculty member at the Central Party School.
15. Hua Gang, 1903–1972, Marxist historian, professor at Shangdong University. labeled a *rightist* and died by suicide.
16. Huang Yanpei, 1878–1965, renowned social activist and progressive-minded educator.

countries such as Katayev's *A Son of the Working People,* Vasilevskaya's *Rainbow,* and more. *How My Steel Was Tempered* by Ostrovsky was virtually the bible for all revolutionary youth. The much quoted "for man, life comes only once, but . . ." would ring in my ears and make my heart throb. The characters Zhukhlai and Paul Kochagin were my idols. Another book which influenced me was co-authored by a group of British Fabians, *Travels in the Soviet Union.* The writers praised the achievements of the USSR, but they also criticized the restrictions on freedom of speech, and I had been puzzled when I read that. In 1987, I visited Great Britain in an official capacity and had a conversation with Mr. Fisher, minister of culture of the Labour Party shadow cabinet. I talked to him about my reading of the Fabians in my youth. By the way, this goes to prove that nothing one reads is ever wasted—it will come around in its own good time. Apart from novels, at a progressive bookstore that He Ping had taken me to I found a newspaper, the "Three-day Report," published by Time Publishers, which operated as a Soviet-owned business. It was two pages, folded at the center, and it carried regular reports about life in Yan'an. It was a breath of fresh air for one living in old Peking. I went to the bookstore several times on my own, and one day it was closed down, presumably by the authorities. I was saddened by the sight of the shuttered little place.

A year or so after we met, He Ping graduated from high school and got a job, and the target of his underground work shifted from students to the young working population. Since then comrade Li Guang took over as our contact with the Party. Li Guang was a professional revolutionary and a member of the High School Committee under the North China Bureau Urban Work Committee of the Chinese Communist Party (CCP) underground network. According to the practice of underground activities at the time, I and the other student, Qin Xueru, not being Party members, were identified as "progressive contacts." Li Guang, under the pseudonym Liu Feng, was our guide and mentor in the person-to-person secret network.

Liu Feng was a fine figure of a man, handsome, with a resounding voice like that of an actor. He was everything that one expected an underground revolutionary figure to be. However, unlike my former contact He Ping, who was lively and talkative, Liu Feng personified a revolutionary outlook which was rather grim. Serious and reserved, steady in his faith, he always got right to the point when he spoke, inspiring confidence in those around him.

Being part of the student underground network opened up a new world for me. One of the forms it took was singing. I loved singing. "Strong in Unity," a classic of the student movement, was my favorite. Another favorite of mine, "We Can Take a Fall," was sung in the aftermath of the breakup of a student demonstration. My first Party contact He Ping had taught me "Katiusha," a Russian revolutionary/romantic song from WW II. Later, Liu Feng taught me to sing "How Vast Our Motherland," a Soviet song unrivaled for patriotic pride and fervor. Another song with the words "Life is like a muddy stream/Machines bite into our flesh . . ." had been a favorite of Lenin's, it was said. Moreover, folk songs, love songs, and songs from our own national minorities were adopted and widely sung and actually became the signature songs of the progressive student movement. In 1948 the Communist underground organized a huge get-together of students from Peking and Tientsin, and many folk songs were sung on that occasion. Years later, a poet from Taiwan told me that as a young man on a school outing, he and his friends had tried to sing one song after another, but were always warned that what they were singing was a "communist" song.

It gradually dawned on me that the student movement was steadily maturing. Many demonstrations were being held against the ruling Guomindang. Moreover the movement was also expanding at the periphery to include recreational activities as well as study programs and financial aid to deserving students with good grades. A wide base was formed through those various activities, from which the communist underground, the progressive students, and the vast student body were tightly linked together in a struggle for a better future, and the ruling Guomindang could do nothing about it. At Liu Feng's suggestion I myself had once joined a short winter program run by the School of Technology of Peking University. A college student gave us lessons in trigonometry. That was all there was to it, trigonometry, but at the same time the seeds of revolution were sowed.

How did revolution come about? To me, revolution came about through make-up lessons in trigonometry, through singing and dancing;

through reading; through dissatisfaction with the world, through social, family and personal conflicts, through dreams of a new society. Take the incessant fighting between my parents, for instance. I believed that only revolution could resolve their mutual resentment. I also remember an argument that I had with my mentor Liu Feng. Once he happened to ask what I was reading and I told him I was reading *Rickshaw Boy* by Lao She[17] and Liu had dispproved. I claimed that no matter what Lao She's personal political convictions were at the time, the novel itself demonstrated that the society was going to pieces and was beyond saving. I further pointed out that not only Lao She's writing, but even the elegant prose and pastoral writings of Bing Xin, were all pointing to the revolution in one way or another. But I sometimes wondered why it was that Lu Xun had never explicitly mentioned the revolution or the Communist Party? Why was it that the communist writer Ding Ling[18] had never called for revolution in her novels, and why was the description of revolution in the Soviet novels *Cement* and *Iron Flow* so chaotic, so brutal?

As a "progressive" youth, I did not limit myself to reading novels and singing songs. With myself and my partner Qin Xueru as the main contributors, I had started a handwritten journal called *The Mini-Weekly*. We soon put out the first number, with an editorial and articles exposing social inequality, rounding off the whole thing with calls to overturn the old order. We made multiple copies with carbon paper and distributed them to our classmates. Two days later, the school principal, who was on the Guomindang Municipal Committee, called me into his office and gave me a lecture, thus putting an end to my editorial ambitions.

During this period as a "progressive contact," I was neither a member of the Communist Party nor a member of any of the various youth organizations attached to the Party. Later, on January 1 of 1949, the Party made the decision to form the New Democratic Youth League [YL], an amalgam of the various existing youth organizations. At the time, Liu

17. Lao She, 1899–1966, best known for depicting the lives of the poor of old Peking; representative works include the novel *Rickshaw Boy* and the play *Tea House*. Lao She committed suicide during the Cultural Revolution.
18. Ding Ling's (1904–1986), short stories "Miss Sophia's Diary," "When I Was in Xia Village" and other works broke new ground in the depiction of women in a male-dominated society. Labeled a *rightist*.

Feng had suggested that I join up, but I refused. I was mainly interested in singing and reading and was not ready to join an organization. To me, formal membership implied some sort of leadership role, and I was not ready.

But I reveled in the secret consciousness of being "progressive," feeling myself above the common herd, with my stock of theories, and terms, and topics to mull over while I went about my everyday activities undetected. I was living in an aura of romance while also enjoying a sense of superiority. People would pale at the mention of Communism, but I knew better. I knew facts from lies, I held the truth in my grasp, I saw a future which no one could envisage, I was full of confidence and strode on boldly toward that future. Nobody knew this side of my life, including my family. Actually my sister had already joined a communist youth organization, but I only found out after Liberation.

After several months, Liu Feng still had not shown up. I went from door to door in his hutong, but could not find him. Cut off from my "contact," I was saddened, frightened. Without my connection, I was nothing. Purely on my own merits, I was a teenager, weighing less than 100 jin,[19] barely 1.6 meters tall, capable of accomplishing nothing. Only by being connected to a great organization does one have a sense of strength and power. Now I felt helpless. I saw Liu Feng in my dreams, but only woke up to find him not there.

I graduated with a diploma from junior high in 1948, the only diploma I ever earned. Our school paper put out a special edition for our graduation and wanted to include one of my essays. With the fiasco of my own editorial ambitions in mind, I submitted "The Heart of Spring," a show-off of verbal facility with no substance at all. Many years later the writer Liu Shaotang[20] saw my piece in a collection that someone had put together and noted that the essay had already shown the first signs of so-called "stream-of-consciousness."

With regard to choice of senior high school, we could apply to as many as we liked provided we paid the application fees. And that was exactly what many of my classmates did, to be on the safe side. I applied

---

19. Unit of weight, equivalent to half a kilogram.
20. Liu Shaotang, 1936–1997, child prodigy who was published at age thirteen, Liu made his name by writing about his native rural north China. Labeled a *rightist*.

to two senior high schools, No 4, and Hebei Provincial Senior High School. I was accepted by both. After talking with Qin Xueru, fellow "progressive contact," we both decided to give up the prestigious No. 4 High School and sign up for Hebei Provincial, the main reason for our choice being that Hebei Provincial Senior High boasted a revolutionary tradition. It had taken the lead in high school student activities during the December Ninth movement.[21] Rong Gaotang,[22] one of the leaders of the student movement at the time and later a national leader, had been a student at Hebei Senior High. Moreover, a year earlier, on April 17, 1947, a political incident at Hebei Senior High had caught the public eye and made its way into the papers—a folksy song and dance show had been broken up by Guomindang spies, and seventeen students were arrested.

One month after I had started school at Hebei Senior High, Liu Feng showed up! It turned out that he was actually the hand that had directed the underground movement in our school, and at that moment he was implicated in the setback that the student movement had suffered in the aforesaid April 17 Incident.

Without much ado, Liu Feng offered to induct Qin Xueru and myself into the Communist Party! He made us read a copy of the Chinese Communist Party Constitution and was ready to act right away. To this day I have no idea how he learned that I and Qin Xueru were in Hebei Senior High. Given the aftermath of the April 17 fiasco, I suppose Liu Feng was glad to see the two of us. We had arrived in the nick of time to fill the void. We were of course glad to see Liu Feng again after we thought we had lost him. But still the invitation to join the Party took us by surprise. I had always thought of Communist Party members as towering figures one looked up to, high-minded, fearless, holding high the torch of revolution, leading the masses forward. I, on the other hand, was weak and ignorant. I was actually somewhat disappointed by this turn of affairs—if someone as insignificant as I could join the Party, doesn't that deflate the Party's image? On the other hand, I felt the thrill

---

21. A demonstration staged on December 9, 1935, by Beijing students, for resisting Japanese aggression, which turned into a nationwide movement.
22. Rong Gaotang, 1912–, leader in the student movement, later commissioner for Sports and Athletics under the Central Government.

of the call to arms. There was no turning back, no time for regret. There was only one way, and that was forward, and only forward!

A few days later, on October 10, 1948, Qin Xueru and I met with Liu Feng at a location behind Beihai Park. We both announced that we had thought things through, and that we were ready to join the Party and dedicate our lives to the cause of communism, and so on and so forth. Upon which, Liu Feng inducted us into the Party as probationary members. Qin's probationary period was one year, while mine was to be prolonged until I turned eighteen. Liu also warned us that due to the tense political situation, we should act with caution and not expose ourselves unnecessarily and that we should limit our efforts to spreading leftist influence and expanding the peripheral youth organizations. He mentioned that he had to do self-criticism for the fiasco of the April 17 student action of the previous year.

On the way back I never stopped singing, tears streaming down my face. I sang a song written by Xian Xinghai:[23] "The road we have opened / the trees we have planted/the high rises we have built / heroes are fearless / with iron fists / let us build a new world!" The song perfectly reflected my mood. It was my personal oath of loyalty to the Party.

Back in school, we organized a walkout to demand that the school fire the English teacher for regularly showing up late for class. But Liu Feng advised caution, so we limited ourselves to spreading the word through casual conversation, reading groups, study sessions, cram classes, spring outings, movies, get-togethers, Christian fellowships (many of which were infiltrated by Communists), and other such activities to spread the idea that the situation was hopeless and that Liberation was inevitable. As the hour of Liberation approached, I had also inducted a few students into one of the youth organizations. Liu Feng introduced another comrade, Xu Baolun, whom we asked to join us, thus forming a three-member cell, with the newcomer Xu Baolun as secretary. Later on, two more comrades joined and we became a five-member Party cell. Except for the fact that we had secret codes for communication, our mode of operation was nothing like what is presented in the movies.

On the eve of Liberation, we were assigned the task of preserving the city from destruction. According to past experience, there would

23. Xian Xinghai, 1905–1945, celebrated leftist musician and songwriter.

be social unrest and rampant crime on the eve of Liberation. Our cell was assigned the job of ensuring the safety of the area from Tiananmen to the Drum Tower. We inspected the area and prepared sleeve bands, flags and posters, and we organized students to be on the spot when the hour arrived. It was actually quite dangerous. If we were discovered, the consequences could have been disastrous.

On the eve of Liberation, our job was to distribute leaflets issued by the military command and the Fourth Field Army. We were each given stacks of leaflets, and we started distributing them, first to our friends and family, then to teachers and acquaintances. We were directed to target the higher intellectuals—scholars and men of letters—who were considered influential in the society. Later on, we gave out the leaflets indiscriminately, sticking them through door cracks, and I even saw someone pasting up a poster right on the public bulletin board! We also ran into our art teacher distributing leaflets and realized that he was a comrade! For us victory was within grasp and darkness was swept away. For the first time, I knew through personal engagement what is meant by the collapse of an old regime and the victory of a new one.

Chapter 6

A Revolutionary Spring and a Stint at the Youth League Academy

It was a cold, cold winter, the last days of 1948 and the beginning of 1949. Due to the ongong civil war, most of the students of Hebei Senior High could not go home for the winter holidays and stayed in their dorms. The school authorities, making a virtue of necessity, kept the dorms open and called it "winter camp." The Guomindang provincial governor even made a visit as a gesture of support. I also stayed in school over the winter holidays, anticipating the coming Communist victory. The dorm was so cold that I sometimes put a table upside down over my blanket, as if it could hold down some warmth. Actually some students would get up in the middle of the night and hack furniture to pieces to make a fire. As for food, I could hardly swallow the lumps of turnip and scraggy cabbages boiled in salt water without a drop of oil. When I had some pocket money, I would walk into town to a store where I could buy a cup of milk—it was what I could afford, one cup of milk. There was lots of social unrest: rumors, runaway inflation, student protests . . .

Meanwhile, the civil war up north had led to the Communist takeover of the northeastern provinces, and now the major cities of Peking and Tientsin were under tight siege. The Communist Party [CP] victory was just a matter of time. In school, students from affluent families were very despondent. As for me, I was openly reading leftist writings during evening study time. One fellow sneered, "Oho, little Wang Meng, you're quite something, heh?" But I didn't give a damn. We stepped up our underground activities. A boiler man in our school happened to be a comrade, so we used the boiler room as our base. Although not officially announced, our cell of five members merged with the larger CP cells of second and third year students. We prepared posters and wrote out slogans on strips of paper, actively preparing for the arrival of our troops. We would parade through the streets, singing the songs and dancing the folk dances of the Yan'an red area. I would stand up and make impromptu speeches, telling everybody that we were soon to be liberated and so on. Sometimes my speeches were wildly applauded, sometimes ignored, and on some occasions I was booed. Those were heady days.

Eventually, Peking was liberated peacefully through peace talks with General Fu Zuoyi.[1]

I was a witness to the ceremonial march of the People's Liberation Army [PLA] into the city in early January, I saw Chairman Mao Zedong and I saw the tanks, heavy artillery, armored cars, and infantry of the PLA as they entered the city of Peking. The oppressed masses had finally become the masters.

The general meeting of underground Communist Party members in Peking was held in the No. 4 Auditorium of Peking University. The hall resounded to the strains of the Internationale; the hammer and sickle banner, unfamiliar to me, was draped over the platform. The leaders of the underground—Peng Zhen,[2] Nie Rongzhen,[3] Lin Biao,[4] Ye Jianying and Li Baohua, son of the martyred Li Dazhao,[5] took turns mounting the platform to give speeches. The meeting started at two in the afternoon and lasted till midnight. Halfway through the meeting, the organizers went out and brought back tons of food, pancakes, stuffed buns, bread, cooked meat . . . they must have bought out all the food stalls in the area. I was in seventh heaven. Who was I? What had I done to deserve being part of all this? There is nothing in the world as exhilarating as being

1. Fu Zuoyi, 1895–1974, general in the old national army, remembered for his critical decision to cede Peking to the besieging communist army, to save the ancient capital from destruction.
2. Peng Zhen, 1902–1997, mayor of Peking.
3. Nie Rongzhen, 1899–1992, military leader, one of the ten Marshals in the People's Liberation Army.
4. Lin Biao, 1902–1971, military leader, Minister of Defense.
5. Li Dazhao, 1889–1927, professor at Peking University, one of the founders of the Communist Party, later executed by the warlord Zhang Zuolin.

part of a successful revolution.

Later, at another meeting held in the auditorium of the National Art Institute, Zhou Enlai gave a speech on the significance of the Second Plenary Session of the Seventh CCP Committee. He pointed out that we had only taken the first step in a ten thousand-*li* march, that we must guard against sugar-coated bullets fired at us by the enemy, and so on and so forth. Zhou Enlai had a flair which swept us off our feet.

Finally there was a meeting of underground CP students, called by the Student Committee of the North China Bureau of the Urban Work Department. The leaders were called up one by one to meet us face to face for the first time—the members for the College Students Committee, the members of the Middle School Students Committee, and so on. I was deliriously happy to see these leaders in the flesh for the first time. The secretary for the Middle School Students Committee was Yang Bojian, later Party Secretary for the city of Beijing, one time ambassador to Sweden, and finally president of the Institute of Diplomatic Affairs. The deputy secretary of the High School Students Committee was a young woman named Du Ping, who later became an official at the Middle School Department of the Ministry of Education. There was another young woman in a leather jacket, quite unusual at the time, and she made me think of the early Russian revolutionary heroine Sophia. These young leaders carried themselves with such a dashing air, I had no doubt that all the best and brightest in the society had flocked to the Communist Party. I was also excited by the new terms: Party, committee member, secretary, party cell, implement, masses, active element, role model, core, work style, ideology . . . I lapped them up like heavenly manna. Thus I threw myself into the revolution. The world was ours! Peking was ours! I already knew of the coming change of its name from Peking to Beijing!

It was more than half a century later, in 2005, that I asked myself—why is it I had not foreseen that the revolution had come to me too easily, and that an easy victory bore within itself the seed of danger? In fact, very soon I had to pay the price for my self-satisfaction and self-congratulation. But of that, more later.

In late August of 1949, I was assigned to the Central Youth League Academy. It was the second year since the founding of the Academy, and I was assigned to Class 15. My classmates, mostly from Beijing, were scions of prestigious families with revolutionary pedigrees, or from families within the United Front, while still others had significant revolutionary credentials under their belts. The Central Youth League Academy was situated in the suburbs—symbolic of Mao Zedong's dictum about the country besieging the city, we students decided facetiously.

I was lucky to have sat in on the lectures of many famous people through the summer and during my stint at the Academy. The most memorable lecture was given by Mao Zedong's secretary, Tian Jiaying,[6] whose topic was Mao Zedong Thought. Tian's talk began in the afternoon and lasted till late at night. The talk was conducted in the open. We were all busy taking notes, but by evening we had to stop now and then to deal with the fireflies flitting about. Halfway through the lecture, I handed in a note reminding the speaker to keep track of time. When the note was read out loud, some among the audience expressed shock that someone had the nerve. Tian continued talking anyway. Even to this day, I remember Tian saying that Mao Zedong Thought was like the sea, from which everyone could draw sustenance, and yet its waters will never be exhausted, and that Mao Zedong Thought was like a piano on which people could play an infinite variety of tunes, depending on the skill of the person playing. According to Tian, on the topic of the so-called "intelligentsia," Mao had dismissed that lot as "lost in petty squabbles feuding over nothing," and that they needed to be "politicized" and "organized." That was something that had never been revealed in public. In the 1980s, when I was in the United States for the first time, I saw a piano over which hung a scroll saying that life is like a piano—its quality depends on how you play—and my thoughts went back to Comrade Tian Jiaying and his tragic fate.

In the eight months of my life at the Central Youth League Academy, our study of theory was also applied to the practical examination of our own ideology, to root out sinister influences inherited from family background, or acquired through reading the wrong books, or being just plain wrongheaded. We would do our breast-beating for letting down the people, letting down the Party, and so on. Somehow, the more thickly you lay it on, the more proof that you have benefited from your study. And thus I completed my stint at the Central Youth League Academy.

6. Tian Jiaying, 1922–1966, committed suicide.

Chapter 7

Down to Earth, Facing Reality

In May of 1950, I graduated from the Youth League Central Academy and reported back to the Beijing Youth League Committee. From there I was dispatched to the Third District of the Beijing Youth League Committee, first in charge of middle school affairs, later moving to organizational work. The Third District was renamed the Dongsi District and soon merged with the Dangdan District to form the enlarged Dongcheng District, covering the eastern part of the city.

There is a well-known collection of reportage titled *Daily Life in the District* by the Soviet writer Ovechkin. I had never written a book like that, but I have lived the life described in the book. For instance, we at the District Youth League Committee were often called upon by the District Communist Party Committee to help out in one or other of the ongoing campaigns of those times. One of the earliest was the campaign to wipe out the quasi-religious sects, noticeably the *Yiguandao.* The vacuum in religious discourse in our society had actually left a space for such superstitious sects to take advantage of the ignorant. We conducted the campaign vigorously, firm in the belief that we were combating superstition in the interest of science and progress, and the sects didn't have a leg to stand on. We then turned our attention to the Catholic Church to implement the "Three-Self" program, trying to help make the church independent of outside support or influence. We mobilized ordinary church members to expose the foreign preachers and their associates; we outlawed the Legion of Mary and other such organizations. The papers exposed the atrocities at an orphanage annexed to the Xishiku Cathedral in the western part of the city. Filled with righteous anger, I rounded up the children of a Catholic orphanage in my own district and tried to make them stand up and expose their imperialist overseers. I gave a rousing speech, but the children remained stone-faced, unmoved. As I was about to leave, the children rose up as one and started to recite a prayer in a loud voice, obviously as an act of defiance. At the time I believed firmly that they were poor, helpless, isolated and brainwashed, and that I as a revolutionary had an obligation to rescue them. I had used part of this experience in my novel *Long Live Youth.*

Working at the Communist Party District Committee was an eye-opener for me, getting to know a group of cadres different from what I had been used to when operating among my peers with a student background. The cadres at the Party District Committee were mostly from the so-called "old" area, that is, the rural Yan'an base. They were more direct in speech, more homely in lifestyle. They all boarded in the office building, and were on familiar terms with each other. Moreover, they brought over some of the practices of the "old" area, such as addressing each other familiarly as "Old"—Old this or Old that. On one occasion, the secretary rang me up—"Is this Old Wang?" It sounded so strange, since I was barely seventeen at the time, but I felt warmed by her greeting.

Among the veterans from the "old" area, some were quiet, but what they said mattered. Others were grumpy, but when you come down to it, you must admit that they spelled out what others had wanted to say but wouldn't. Some of them were quarrelsome, but they were not mean. There were meetings which seemed a waste of time, but they had to be held because the leadership had ordered it, or because the different parties needed to meet and coordinate their efforts. Some cadres talk openly of rank and office and payment. And this was not limited to old cadres either. Even former student leaders who had confronted the police and their hoses were now talking about salaries! Salaries! I had even seen an application on behalf of an old comrade who had died to have his rank raised by one notch so that he could be eligible for a spot in the Babaoshan Revolutionary Martyrs Cemetery!

I was shocked and repelled. During those early days after Liberation, we were truly pure in mind! At the time, I often thought of Mayakovsky's famous lines: "Oh Commune / all I have / is yours / except / my toothbrush!"

Indeed, at the time, our lifestyle had retained many traces of wartime communism. We ate from the "big pot"—only a handful of leaders above a certain rank had specially prepared meals. Our daily meal consisted mostly of sorghum porridge and vegetables. Meat appeared only during national and other holidays. When out on business we used office bikes. New bikes of a better build were reserved for leaders only, and even that made the rank and file resentful.

In 1954, we as cadres under the District Party Committee were finally paid salaries. We were actually the last batch. Cadres under the government had long been paid salaries, and at a much higher rate than we were.

Here, I must add a few last lines about my parents. Ever since I became a "progressive contact," not to mention when I had joined the Party, I had an answer for every problem under the sun, and the answer was that people's unhappiness had its roots in the corrupt social system, and that a victorious revolution would wipe out people's unhappiness and unravel all their knotty problems, including those of my parents. I had thought that with Liberation, my parents' relationship would also enter a new stage.

The fact was, right after Liberation in 1949, Father, dressed in a gray cadre's uniform, returned from a spell in Yan'an, having been there in the capacity of research fellow in Department Four of Northern University. My mother, on her side, had been a delegate to the local District People's Congress. Thus, I was led to think that all their problems were solved. But when I discovered that Father had spent those years in the Yanan liberated area without even joining the Party, and that he had not done anything to speak of at Northern University, and that on his return he had got a teaching job in the Philosophy department of Catholic University but that the response to his lectures had been cool. I was very disappointed. As for Mother, she had given up the job at the All-China Federation of Women, obviously she could not stand the hard work.

The minute I graduated from the Youth League Academy, Father approached me about the divorce problem. He did not raise the problem with my mother, he put it before me. It was all about his sufferings, his potential stifled because of an unhappy family life, his talents unreleased, his sensitivity overlooked. I was so helpless, and angry that barely out of my teens I had to be responsible for the problem of my elders. My mother demanded a monthly alimony of 50 yuan. I advised Father to accept, though his monthly salary was only 70 yuan. My plan was that I would give my mother 50 yuan every month, and then try to get the money out of my father. Anyway, the first step was to get the divorce settled, give Father his freedom, and let Mother retain her dignity.

Now that the divorce was agreed on, Father was all teary—taking pictures with the family, even taking a separate one with Mother as a keepsake—to the extent that we children thought he had changed his mind. The financial arrangement did not go as smoothly as planned. At some point, I had to borrow money to make ends meet.

After the divorce, Father remarried in haste and repented soon after. He would often come to my office to complain: marriage a fiasco, not appreciated at work, did not get along with colleagues, not respected by leadership, not enough money, not enough nutrition, neighbors rude, my younger brother and sister refusing to see him, his articles not accepted for publication, no social life . . . Father would go on and on, sprinkling his litany of complaints with quotations from Lu Xun et al. I cannot bear the memory. The lesson I learned was that a man must bear his own burden, not pass it on to the younger generation. A man must grit his teeth and bear his burden on his own shoulders.

One thing I do not understand about my father: he complained about everybody and everything, but remained steadfast in his belief in Marxism and communism. He would read Lenin's *Notes on Reading Hegel,* and get delirious with excitement. He would read Mao Zedong's *On Practice* and *On Contradictions* and be full of praise. He was totally sincere—he had no need to pretend.

During the campaign to criticize Hu Shih[1] Father wrote an article and mailed it to the *People's Daily*. I had pooh-poohed the idea that *People's Daily*

1. Hu Shih, 1891–1962, historian, philosopher, literary critic, Hu was the target of a criticism campaign in 1954, though he was not personally on the mainland.

would publish anything of *his*. But *People's Daily* sent him the galleys for corrections, actually preparing to publish. Father was in seventh heaven—finally he could prove himself, finally he would show them . . . not to mention taking us to Western restaurants on his writer's fees. He made all the corrections that the editor, Wang Ruoshui,[2] had requested, and sent back the galleys, every day expecting to see his article in print. One night Father rushed into my office with a letter from Wang in his hands—his article had been rejected after all! Father was a wreck. The description of Fan Jin[3] was nothing compared to Father's condition that night. To his dying day, Father lamented the stifling of his potential—his potential—a will-o'-the- wisp to be mourned over in song and fable, no substance, nothing to hold on to.

I helped Mother get a job as a teacher in an elementary school and she did hold down her job. At one point she thought she was going to join the Party, but it all came to nothing, perhaps on account of my *rightist* status. My juggling with the alimony was finally uncovered and Mother settled for thirty-five yuan a month.

---

2. Wang Ruoshui, 1925–2005, scholar of philosophy, at one time general editor of *People's Daily*.
3. Character in the novel *The Scholars*, Fan was obsessed with passing the imperial examinations.

Chapter 8

Nineteen, and in Love

June 1950, the outbreak of the Korean War. We sang songs in praise of Kim Il Song, in praise of Sino-Korean friendship. I pored over the papers in those days to study the comparative strengths of the socialist and the capitalist camps—the comparative figures for the production of iron, coal, electricity, etc. I watched Korean documentaries and was convinced that the United States was the enemy of all the people of the world.

At the time, the main content of thought reform for the educated elite was to straighten out their attitude toward the United States—to get rid of their pro-America tenencies, overcome their fear of U.S. power, and drop their awe of everything American. Luckily for me, I had not been favorably disposed toward the United States since the Dongdan Square incident in Beijing of December 1947, when an American G.I. sexually assaulted the college student Shen Cong. Since then I had always considered the United States an enemy. I once came across an article which gave the figures for American military aid to Chiang Kai-shek during the civil war—on average one bullet per person, which means enough to kill off every man, woman, and child of the population of China.

With the evolving situation at the front, many students sent letters written in their own blood, offering to go to the front. We at the rear sent food and letters and held street performances in support of the war. We attended speeches given by members of goodwill delegations returning from the Korean front and we sat through speeches by writers such as Yang Shuo who had been to the front and written about the war. One of our jobs at the District Youth League Committee was to recommend candidates for enrollment at the Military Academy, that is to say, to send the best and brightest of our youth to the PLA. And thus we spent the tumultuous years of 1950–51.

The years 1952–53 were also years of particular significance. In 1952, the country launched the "Three-*Anti's*" "and "Five-*Anti's*" campaigns. The former was *anti*-waste, *anti*-graft and *anti*-bureaucratism. The latter was *anti*-bribery, *anti*-tax evasion, *anti*-cutting corners in labor and supply, *anti*-theft of public property, and *anti*-theft of classified information regarding the economy. The culprits were alluded to as "tigers." A newly appointed principal of Hebei Senior High was uncovered as a "major tiger" and arrested right off the stage following the mass rally to denounce him. A few months later he was quietly released. A colleague from the Bejing Youth League, on assignment in the south, was suspected of one or another of the *anti's*, and hauled back in handcuffs. There was another case of a nice young man from the Beijing Youth League being ferreted out for this or that of the *anti's*. He was soon cleared and released, but not soon enough to find himself divorced and his wife remarried.

Each and every work unit had to meet its own quota for the amount of stolen yuan to be uncovered. The three *anti's* and five *anti's* were really eye-openers for me, one so impulsive, so primitive, so simplistic, one reflecting a naïve disregard for evidence and legality. But I was bowled over by the enthusiasm and the atmosphere of determined combativeness unleashed by the campaigns. The general public, earlier disgusted by the pervasive corruption under the Guomindang regime, now threw themselves wholeheartedly into the two campaigns, and I was caught up in the spirit, notwithstanding some of its excesses.

The Youth League District Committee where I worked was situated at No. 39, Lane 11, Dongsi. It was confiscated enemy property, and consisted of a traditional-style house with three courtyards. The rooms on the south of the first courtyard housed the Youth League and the Women's Federation. The District Communist Party headquarters occupied the central courtyard. The organization branch was housed in rooms on the western side, while the propaganda branch was housed on the eastern side. The Party Secretary had his office in the main room, overlooking a flowerbed set in the center of the courtyard. The last row of rooms was the singles' dorm and had a back door leading to Lane 12.

At the time, the main office was used exclusively for directing the three-*anti*'s and five-*anti*'s campaigns. It was the winter holidays and several high school students—CP members—were drafted to help at the office, among them Cui Ruifang from the No. 2 Girls Middle School. I stepped into the office one night and was very moved by the sight of the young people at work. I wanted to write a stage play—an office, winter, a fire roaring away in a big stove, a clock striking midnight, the latest news coming in, the leaders planning and directing, the dregs of the old society being cleaned up, young people dreaming of a crystal bright new world. There was friendship and love among the comrades. There were also enemies trying to subvert the revolution by hook or by crook, and there were young people who had fallen by the wayside, taken in by the wiles of the enemy or their own weaknesses. There was curiosity and there was innocence, there were dreams and hopes for a beautiful new world.

When I thought of Ruifang, the world seemed to whirl around me. When I realized that she and I were working in the same place, I felt warmth suffusing my whole being. I looked for appropriate ways to express my feelings. I would start a conversation with her, or lend her books, or take walks with her. I wrote her moving letters.

I recommended a flimsy booklet to her—*A Diary of Youth*. Ruifang later told me she was furious that I had handed her a juvenile reader while she noticed that I myself was reading *Anna Karennina*.

I was eighteen at the time, and Ruifang was nineteen. Although only eighteen I was a "leading cadre"—though not a big shot—and already knew my own mind. Being pursued was upsetting for Ruifang—she had refused me a couple of times, and we had resumed seeing each other a couple of times. To me everything was so beautiful, even being refused in a friendly way.

In late September 1952, we had stopped seeing each other when out of the blue Ruifang called me, asking if I was interested in watching a midnight rehearsal of the program for the coming National Day celebration. We not only watched the rehearsal, but later we went to the best movie theater in town in Dongdan and watched a new Soviet movie.

The three *anti's* and the five *anti's* petered out to a peaceful ending, while the Korean war had reached a stalemate, with peace talks in the works. The papers now were all out for peaceful construction and the Five-Year Plan and calls for students to study hard to rebuild the country. I remembered what Chairman Mao had said in his "People's Democratic Dictatorship," pointing out that what we knew was about to be put aside, that we were being compelled to deal with what we didn't know, and thus we needed to study, and so on. I was inspired with a consciousness of history. "World," "peace," "life," "happiness," "years," "days" and other such touching words began to fill the public sphere. The newly revived magazine *Translations* published a Soviet short story, "Her First Job," which described newly graduated young architect Nina and her struggle on her first job, conveying a sense of hardship and happiness and what is meant by dealing with life, and peaceful construction, and the new affinity between people and the city.

We were living through a totally unrestrained period when being in love was so thrilling; it never occurred to us that dating was inappropriate for students. That is why I later alluded to this period as "The Season of Love"—the period from 1949 to 1957. Working for the Youth League District Committee, I was always rubbing shoulders with student Youth League cadres from the various girls' middle schools. I certainly do not claim to be Jia Baoyu, but I do share his view that girls are pure and boys tend to be dirty-minded. The idea was spelled out strikingly in the great classical novel *Dream of the Red Chamber*. I am sure that most boys would agree in a general way. Those young female Youth League cadres from the various middle schools were so good-looking, so earnest, so smart, such good speakers—beating the boys in every conceivable way. Without young people's participation, there would be no revolution; without young women there absolutely would be no revolution. When you try to envisage the Russian revolution, isn't Sophia the first image that comes to mind—I'm referring to the nihilist heroine whose lover attacked the Czarist governor at a signal from her.

Actually, Ruifang and I had already met two years earlier, in the summer of 1950, when she had attended a meeting at the Youth League District Committee to discuss the supervision of student activities over the summer holidays. Her smile and her good will were so charming. At the time, she was president of the Student Union of the Beijing Second Girls' Middle School. I learned that she had been a member of the underground Democratic Youth League as early as 1947 and had joined the Communist Party in the summer of 1949.

Young people of different eras have their own way of being in love. Zhang Sheng and Cui Yingying (characters in *Romance of the Western Bower*) had first run into each other by accident and then held clandestine trysts. Jia Baoyu and Lin Daiyu (*in Dream of the Red Chamber*) made gifts of handkerchiefs with inscriptions and analyzed each other's hearts. Right now young people express themselves in popular songs such as " How I Miss You," or "If This is Love, So be It," or "My Heart is Too Soft," or "Tonight, Tonight" and stuff like that. During my time, however, all I knew was Sophia, or Katiusha, or wedding rites under the scaffold, or last partings. Or it was the poetry of Surkov in which a beautiful girl would tell her love-stricken admirer to win a Model Worker medal before aspiring to her hand.

As for me, whenever I thought of Ruifang, I could not help calling to mind her revolutionary credentials since early youth, her heavy burden of work while still a student . . . the goals she set for herself. I could not but admire her dedication as she burned the midnight oil working on the numbers, trying to keep up with the steady progress of the ongoing three-*antis* and the five-*antis* campaigns. Her presence literally lighted up the sprawling courtyard building of the District Youth League Committee.

To me, love was wind, love was song. As soon as I realized that I was in love with Ruifang, I felt swept up by wind, I was flung into space by a tornado, towns and countryside passed beneath me, stars and firmaments, mountains and rivers whizzed around me. I started singing. I sang "Over the whole wide world I roamed/I could not find love/But in my homeland Russia/love is beckoning to me . . ." I sang in Russian to release my feelings. What else could I do! Our own folksy love songs—"not all horses are equally tall, among men my love is the best of all . . ."—are so simplistic, sometimes even laughable; they do not express what I was feeling.

I kept track of what was going on around Ruifang . . . that her review of a Soviet film, which she wrote for a class assignment, was warmly praised by her teacher, that she had been in an accident and slightly wounded by a soldier on horseback. On the night of May First celebrations, I roamed through the crowd in Tiananmen Square looking for her, and actually found her, and we partied on the Square all night.

First love bring memories of Beihai Park and its pagodas, winding open pavilions, waterfalls, weeping willows, lotus leaves, and drifting boats. Love made our hearts throb at thoughts of the city, of life, of youth. Beihai Park was where we often saw each other, and where we had encountered rain and thunder and windy weather. Our office was quite close to the rear gate of Beihai, so our Youth League activities were often held there. One evening, as I was about to stand up and speak to a Youth League audience, the sunset blazed in dazzling splendor, and I suggested that we start our meeting by admiring the sunset for one silent minute. The audience was stunned. However, it was not in Beihai but in Zhongshan Park that we had our first date. My heart was singing all the time. From the Park, we went to see a movie and I was in seventh heaven. As we came out of the cinema, however, Ruifang announced that we should stop seeing each other. In a split second, my world collapsed.

From then on, Ruifang's mood went through many ups and downs; she was a middle school student, after all, how could she know her own mind? Sometimes she was warm; at other times she said that I did not understand her, she wanted to bury the past, she wished me a great future and so on. So we stopped seeing each other. We did get together briefly the next year, during the May Day celebrations in Tiananmen Square. I remember a song sung by the Art Troupe of the navy's political department—"Onward Marches the People's Navy," sung to the accompaniment of a brass band. Since then, for me that song is inextricably linked to youth and love. As for Ruifang, she actually phoned to blame me for avoiding her! What could I say, except to hum a song or read a novel, or down a beer? What can I say to that! It is true, first love is like wine, one glass after another. When one is reveling in first love, life is exhilarating.

When the Youth League summer camp of 1952 was over, Ruifang joined a study camp held for student cadres at Hongshan Pass, on the outskirts of Beijing. I made my way there to see her. Ruifang saw me off as I left, walking down the country road to the accompaniment of a loudspeaker from a worksite nearby. She later told me that something clutched at her heart as she gazed at my retreating figure. By then I might say that our relationship had found a sure footing. Back in the city, I wrote a letter to the camp leadership. I mentioned that as I walked down the road, I felt the embrace of fall. When the letter was passed around, everyone at the camp, including Ruifang, had liked my phrase "the embrace of fall."

The next year, 1953, I turned nineteen. The nineteen-year old Wang Meng was steeped in emotions and poetic feelings and runaway streams of thought. It was in this year that Ruifang and I started dating seriously, and it is also during this year that I started to write seriously.

I often thought to myself: if I could have a wish, I would certainly not wish for wealth or position or glory or anything strange and unattainable. I would ask to be nineteen again.

Can I claim to have had a *first* love? The girl that I fell in love with was Ruifang. My bride was Ruifang. And the person with whom I am about to celebrate a golden wedding anniversary is Ruifang. But I still consider the days at the District Youth League in the early fifties as my first love. First love is beautiful, but first love often does not last.

As for the progress of our relationship, I would say that our reunion during the summer of 1956—that was true love. It was like being hit by lightning, it was a transcendental experience, a part of the mystery of life, its profundity surpassing that of my existence, an inalienable part of my existence to be treasured—all frivolity, all confusion, all ignorance to be forever banished. I was at a performance of *Swan Lake* in Moscow in 2004. I watched as the prince was misled by the Black Swan, and just as he was beginning to forget Odetta, a frame opened up in the background showing the White Swan as she flashed by. My eyes welled up in tears as the past flashed by in my mind. These trials, these turning points, these pitfalls do exist in life. We can easily fall into them never to be extricated. I have witnessed more than one such instance: leaving one's true love, marrying in haste, spending a lifetime trying to change one's fate. We are sometimes our own worst enemies.

As for myself, looking back I see that I have often been mistaken, have fallen into traps, have got myself into terrible fixes through my own gullibility. But I am basically decent, I have never hurt people intentionally, have never been underhanded, and I have come out of it all in one piece. In a life and death matter such as love and marriage, I have never been cast in a bitter sea. Ruifang and I have stuck to our first choice and we have kept it that way. This has preserved me from known and unknown dangers. Not everyone is thus blessed.

Chapter 9

A Budding Writer

I love work and I enjoy holidays. At the District Youth League Committee, I spent most of my holidays reading or watching movies or attending stage performances. The fact was that as a youth worker, I got free tickets. I saw a lot of the shows staged by the Youth Drama Troupe. I enjoyed modern operas such as *The White-Haired Girl,* which give free rein to revolutionary passion. Other examples of local opera, such as *The Underage Husband,* although a bit simplistic, had very sweet arias that conveyed ordinary people's yearning for happiness. I also enjoyed classical operas such as *Lady of the Camelias* sung by professionals returned from the West, Zhang Quan,[1] for example. When Violetta sang "Let us leave this sinful world for a faraway place . . ." I had wanted to say "let us destroy the sinful old world, and build a shiny new world . . ." For me, the art of Puccini and Verdi, too, could also point the way to revolution.

I also listened to classical music on the radio: Beethoven, Tchaikovsky, Mozart . . . What a fabulous world of music. From music, I learned that man could be so loving, so civilized, so full of charm and imagination . . . As for reality, it is as one Chekhov character says: "How barbarous is life . . . !"

Apart from the enjoyment of art, I spent even more time reading. I loved Ehrenburg's *The Fall of Paris, The Storm, The Waves.* I was aware that Ehrenburg could be slapdash at times. Nevertheless, consider his

1. Zhang Quan, 1919–1992, one of China's earliest sopranos returned from training abroad. Labeled a *rightist.*

panoramic sweep in *The Fall of Paris,* consider his masterful strokes, his colorful memories, his keen insight. Under the circumstances, he had stretched the limits—merging history, geography, war, diplomacy, politics—and turning the countries of the Soviet Union, France, and Germany into one complete entity.

I read Tolstoy's *Anna Karennina,* enjoying the telling details which highlighted for me the magic of life, of love, of the mystery of the emotions. Turgenev I could read in a more relaxed mood, while Dostoevsky stunned me—his writing is like a rolling wave driving on mercilessly, hitting you where it hurts most. His writing destroys all your hopes, all your heart's desires, driving you to madness. How tormented the writer must have been!

I spent all the nights of late fall and early winter of 1952 reading Balzac. The precision of his descriptions bowled me over. I felt as if I was transplanted right to the spot. There are so many great moments in a man's life, but they can only be remembered when immortalized in literature. Literature is greater and more lasting than life itself.

I read and re-read Lu Xun. "Regret" is like a prose poem. "Solitary" and "In a Wine-shop" read as if they were written with the writer's own blood. I love best the stories and essays collected in *Wild Grass., Nights in Autumn, Kites,* and *Good Stories.* There is also *Snow*—"desolate snow, the soul of rain . . ." Reading Lu Xun, I was caught up in the spirit of sorrow and anger at the people who live in total insensibility, hurting others without even knowing what they were doing . . . I was lost in a deep depression.

I fell in love with Chekhov, his melancholy, his insights, his sighs . . . his eyes always filled with tears. I was mesmerized. I loved Ru Long's translation, smooth and elegant, every word pregnant with meaning.

During the middle fifties of the last century, a Soviet director staged *Uncle Vanya* with the China Youth Troupe. I got hold of Jiao Juyin's translation from the English of *The Seagull, Three Sisters, Uncle Vanya, The Cherry Orchard!* I felt transported! How did Chekhov manage to turn everything into drama: everyday life, a view, a mood, disappointments, broken dreams . . . The dialogue in his plays sounds poetic . Everything that I had been looking for was right there. I memorized the lines. Uncle

Vanya says: "the rain is over . . ." Sonya says "we will get our rest . . ." At the end of *Cherry Orchard,* an unusual sound is heard from off stage, the sound of an axe falling on cherry trees. An age is dead and gone, a social class is dead and gone, a generation of people is wiped out. Tanya is still dreaming of a new life, but there is no clue as to what it would be like . . . To me, all the above was Revelation: I was soaked through, I was reborn, I was baptized, my soul was uplifted, I was trembling, I was released, I was terrified. I had stood in a long line to buy a ticket. I wrote to the Central Broadcasting Station, begging them to broadcast the performance live. They promised to do so, but they never did and offered no explanation.

I firmly believe that literature lifts people out of themselves, that it makes all men heroic and all women desirable. Literature makes all life beautiful and all struggle meaningful. It makes all thoughts profound and all emotions moving and all language charming. It gives life to heaven and earth, the moon and the stars, all birds and animals, all flora and fauna, all the five elements. Literature and Revolution, they are alike in seeking self-sacrifice, in seeking perfection, in seeking the sacred and the everlasting. What a dazzling thing is literature.

But coming back to our own writing, I do not understand why is it that in stories about agricultural cooperation, the characters think of nothing except agricultural cooperation; that in stories about wiping out illiteracy, the characters think of nothing except wiping out illiteracy; that in stories about raising pigs, the characters think of nothing except raising pigs, even feeding pigs with human milk. Why are the characters in our writing so dry and fixated on one thing at a time?

It is my good fortune as well as my misfortune that I was deadly serious about art and literature. For me, art and literature involved all my emotions, all the ardor of my young life. For me, art and literature was everything good and artistic and talented and emotional and eternal; it was my standard of value, the embodiment of my ideal, the ultimate meaning of life, the object of my lifelong pursuit, my quasi-religion. I like young people, sincere people, emotional people, because they share my love of art and literature. I cannot get along with a certain kind of people and I cannot stand a certain kind of language, because they spoil my pleasure, and deaden my feelings for art and literature.

Likewise in my work, I enjoyed certain assignments because they fired my artistic imagination; I was bored by the kinds of work that shut off the imagination and deadened any spontaneity. Literature sharpened my love of life and my dedication to the cause, and it brought me closer to like-minded friends. Literature also heightened my disdain for the mundane routine of daily life, so lacking in romantic creativity and risk-taking. In the race between life and literature, I let literature get the upper hand—a clear sign of the immaturity and shallowness of raw youth. Between my one-track-mind fixation on literature and the shallowness of raw youth, disaster was sure to strike!

I must own up to the fact that by now I saw the other side of my daily work, the drudgery, the endless planning and summing-up and reporting, the long-winded speeches and lengthy meetings and repeated platitudes. I decided to quit and sit for the national exams for college. I wanted to study architecture, I wanted to offer up my youthful energy to the building site, I suppose it was the influence of Antonov's novel *My First Job*. No surprise, my application to quit was turned down by the leadership.

The fact was, by now I have become the backbone of the Committee, actually the deputy-secretary of the now expanded Youth League Committee for the Eastern District of Beijing. How could I be let go? I had refused when offered a chance to return to senior high school, and now out of the blue I want to apply for college! It didn't make sense!

However, to be frank, I was convinced that with more learning under my belt and more skills at my command I was destined for higher things; I did not want to be lost among the common herd, saying things by rote, a creature of habit. I wanted to be creative, I felt like a long distance runner waiting for the signal to start—I was not going to muddle my way through life. Suddenly, a thought flashed across my mind: suppose Wang Meng wrote a novel? A full-length *novel*? A *full-length* novel!

Now that I think of it, it is true that I had always loved writing; from as early as the second grade I had stood out in my class for my compositions. Moreover, I thought to myself, I had the unique experience of a young revolutionary, with unique insight into the sensitivities of the youth of my generation. I was mature for my age, and I had a stock of memories and experience.

I had a brainstorm! I could write a unique book, describing the passing of the old and the birth of a new society, describing adolescence passing into youth, describing social and political activities phasing into economic construction, describing darkness giving way to bright light, restrictions giving way to freedom, humiliation giving way to dignity. I could write a novel describing how our eyes are opened and a world is unveiled for youth. Singing the praises of a new age, I could write a rhapsody for everlasting youth. I wanted to write about youthful ambitions, youthful sentiments, youthful dreams, youthful pursuits and discoveries . . . I wanted to write about young people, their first political decision, their first artistic experience, their first awakening of love, their first righteous anger, their first sadness and dejection, their first emotional crisis . . .

I was overwhelmed by my own decision. That I had the nerve to make such a decision was Wang Meng through and through! It is the Wang Meng who had joined the communist underground at age fourteen, had left school to be a communist cadre at age fifteen, and had the audacity to pursue the girl of his heart at age eighteen! Now why shouldn't this same Wang Meng pick up the pen and write a novel at age nineteen?

Thirty years later, the French paper *Liberation* asked me: "Why do you write?" I replied that I write because life is too short, and life is too beautiful. I do not write for personal advancement. I honestly believe that our age is unusual. We have witnessed the passing of the old and even taken part in the struggle for the new. We had seen life in all its aspects and personally tasted its many flavors. Time and life, they are here today and gone tomorrow. If one does not write and leave a record, there will be a blank. A blank—for you, for others, for the world, for history—one will be staring at blankness if one does not write . . ."

Now that I had decided to write, I was suddenly energized. All my emotions, all my memories, all my interests were summoned. At the same time, however, I felt hopelessly disabled. No matter how good I used to feel about myself or what people used to say, the minute I started writing, I felt so awkward, so dull, so lacking in confidence as to what the future might hold. I knew that I would ultimately succeed, but I also foresaw that the road was rocky. I knew that I was a cut above average, but also that I was unrecognized. I knew that writing would make my name, but I was also aware that fame comes at a price.

Now that I had made the decision to write, I realized that everything that had taken place in my life—every experience big or small, happy or sad, all the significant moments and the homely details—all would be meaningful. The high note of my life was vibrating. Through my pen, this great age would leave its mark, the flowering of youth would leave its mark, the passions of New China's first generation of youth would leave its mark. To accomplish this, I would have to give up many of the pleasures of everyday life. My love of life had led me to this commitment, but once committed, I would be detached from everyday life, detached from the working community, even detached from the leadership. No matter how broadminded, no leader would be happy if members of his team were all mooning over art and literature. One of our revolutionary elders, a man widely liked and respected, once remarked in private: "With so many young people obsessed with writing, our country will be ruined!" I understood him completely. Later I myself often said: "Let's not crowd into the straight and narrow path of creative writing."

By now I was the deputy-secretary of the Youth League Committee of the Eastern District of Beijing, installed in an office of my own. My desk was covered with documents. There were instructions coming from above—from Party Central, from Youth League Central, from the Party North China Bureau, from the Beijing Party Committee, from the Beijing Youth League Committee . . . Then there were documents coming from below: reports, summings-up, plans, letters asking for instructions coming from the various Committees of the various Youth League branches . . . There were forms, writing paper, carbon paper, staplers, ink, glue, paper clips and all the paraphernalia of bureaucracy. I would take up a sheet of paper to write my novel. When the door opened, I would hide my draft under a file and deal with the intruder, hoping to end the conversation quickly.

Only now that I was starting to write did I really understand how hard it is. You must plan the characters, the relationships, the events, the weather, the venues, the background, the props, the sound effects, the trees, the flowers, the birds and insects, the sunlight and moonlight, the dawn and dusk, the seasons, the farewells and reunions, the births and deaths, the rights and wrongs—you are creating a world: you are the Creator. Your thoughts wander aimlessly here and there, you change your mind every couple of minutes, you stand at a crossroads undecided over the choice of a word. There are endless choices and endless ways of expression. Everything can potentially lead to success; anything can happen to lead you down a hole. It was terrifying. My nerves were a wreck. My peers Cong Weixi the novelist and Shao Yanxiang the poet had already made a name for themselves.

Insomnia, the bane of my life, returned to torment me. I was a mental wreck. I was in a continuous whirl of anxiety about the possible success or failure of my novel. All the ideological transgressions that I had laid on others now came back to torture me: "worrying over petty loss and gain," "vying for self-aggrandizement," "dreaming of instant fame," "disdain for solid work," "refusal to be part of a larger whole," "obsession with fame and glory," "self-centered," "trying to be better than everybody else". . . All these accusations came back to haunt me, I became emotionally fragile, on the edge of a nervous breakdown.

My writing affected my relationship with the masses and with the leadership. The consequence? In the year 1954 (or 1955?), all cadres at my level got a raise—all except me. What's more, my case had been kicked upstairs, and I got a mild reproof from a leading member of the Beijing Party Committee.

Meanwhile, my first draft kept creeping forward.

One Sunday I went to a free concert at the Sino-Soviet Friendship Association. I think it was a new symphony by Shostakovitch. As I listened, it suddenly occurred to me: this is the key to structure! This is the opening to a full-length novel! The first movement: the violin and the oboe! The second movement: the cello and the tuba! A variation, a harmony and then discord! Suddenly, a celestial note from outer space! A blast from the clouds! Percussion getting worked up! A cheerful solo from the side drum! Departing and returning, connecting and severing, responding from far off and gently fading . . . And a final assertion! Hurrah! Now I know how to write a novel!

Chapter 10

Young Newcomer on the Literary Scene

After a year of struggle with writing, suffering insomnia and nervous disorders affecting every part of my body, I finally managed to finish the first draft of my novel *Long Live Youth*.

I copied the completed draft into a large notebook. To be on the safe side, I made another copy on traditional-style writing paper with five hundred squares on each page to accommodate as many characters as possible, asking my younger sister Wang Ming and a friend to help out in the copying. When everything was completed, the winter of 1954 had set in. It was a whole year since I had first put pen to paper.

I called to mind a friend of my father's from his youth, Comrade Pan Zhiding, who had joined the revolution early on and was currently a scriptwriter for the Beijing Film Studio. I looked him up at his residence in the northern part of the city. His wife was a stage actress who had kept her youthful looks. She said to me: "Why don't you write a play and we could stage it." I was thrilled.

I heard back from Uncle Pan very soon. "You have real talent," he wrote, and told me that he had passed my manuscript on to Comrade Wu Xiaowu, head of the editorial section of the China Youth Publishing House. Wu was himself a writer, better known under the pen name of Xiao Yemu.[1] He had published a short story in *China Youth* magazine titled

---

1. Wu Xiaowu, 1918–1970, writer and literary editor. Labeled a *rightist* and died in a "May Seventh Cadre School" during the Cultural Revolution.

"Between Husband and Wife." The story described the estrangement between an educated husband and his working-class wife. For instance, while the husband gazes at the moon, his wife complains that round as it is, the moon could not fill your belly like a pancake. Ding Ling, herself targeted for her advocacy of one-book-ism[2] now led the attack on Xiao Yemu for representing a suspicious "tendency." Looking back at the critical attack now, one could say that it was comical. But at the time, the effect of the critical attack was decidedly lethal. Xiao Yemu was never the same man again. Later, whenever I see him, I noticed that he always had that hangdog look.

But back to the fate of my manuscript! I was in an agony of waiting. I tried to call, asking in a quavering voice for the decision regarding my novel. Xiao Yemu, himself now disgraced for his offensive short story, told me that my manuscript was in the hands of Comrade Liu Lingmeng, another member of the editorial staff. The problem dragged on till spring and then into the summer of the following year, 1955, I called and called and could not reach Comrade Liu Lingmeng. Then news leaked out that Comrade Liu, who was supposed to be reading my manuscript, was unfortunately compromised in the ongoing witch-hunt for the "Hu Feng clique."[3] China Youth Publishing House was actually quite close to my office. I got on my bicycle and made my way there, but was blocked outside the gate. I waited through the year. I became superstitious. If it rained in the morning, there will be good news; if a crow croaked at me, it meant that my novel had been turned down.

A year later, by the winter of 1955, I finally heard from Comrade Xiao Yemu. He made an appointment for me to meet with the deputy head of the Youth Work Committee of the Chinese Writers' Union—the veteran writer Comrade Xiao Yin[4] himself!

---

2. A catch-word phrase concocted by Ding Ling, who was trying to encourage budding young writers to concentrate on their first work—one of the offenses that she was accused of.
3. Hu Feng, 1902–1985, an influential man of letters on the left, close associate of Lu Xun. Hu upheld the autonomy of the literary imagination and claimed that "life is everywhere," for which tenets Hu was convicted of heading a counterrevolutionary clique. Hu received a 14-year sentence, which he served in full.
4. Xiao Yin, 1915–1983, a reporter during the War against Japanese Aggression and prolific writer on the Left, had held leading positions in writers' associations

Comrade Xiao Yin rated my novel highly, saying that I was gifted with a nose for the artistic, the only problem being that the work lacked a *main thread* running through the whole!

Now, finally, we had identified the root of the problem, put our finger on the vital *acupuncture point.* So far, I had only known that *structure* was the main stumbling block in writing a novel, but now the "main thread running through" has cropped up out of the blue! As he chain-smoked, Comrade Xiao Yin pointed out that so long as I could put my finger on the "main thread," the novel will be a major success. Xiao Yemu, who was present, cheered me on from the sideline, encouraging me to keep "rubbing" at my draft. Somehow, the word "rubbing" made my heart sink. Comrade Xiao Yin ended the conversation by telling me that the Chinese Writers' Union would send out a formal notice to my workplace that I had been granted a six-month leave from work to concentrate on revising the first draft of my novel!

I must add that in the yearlong interval, from late 1954, since first handing in my manuscript of *Long Live Youth,* to the final positive response in the winter of 1955, I had not been idle. I had written and published a few short pieces: a short story, "Little Beanie," in *People's Literature,* and a familiar essay, "Spring Festival," in the magazine *Works in Art and Literature.*

Now the year of waiting was over. The official letter of the Chinese Writers' Union, offering me a six-month leave of absence to concentrate on revising my draft of *Long Live Youth,* was approved by my superiors. I remember that Comrade Wang Jianiu, deputy secretary of the Beijing Youth League, had been suitably impressed—"Wow! The Chinese Writers' Union!" he had exclaimed. In those days, the professional associations and unions had meant something in people's perceptions.

In the spring of 1956, as I was enjoying my six-month leave to revise my manuscript, I was invited to the first national gathering of young writers convened jointly by the Chinese Writers' Union and the Communist Youth League Central Committee. It was designed as a meeting for "*young people writing*"—not "*young writers.*" The wording was framed so that these young people would not be carried away by self-aggrandizement.

---

and periodicals, outstanding for his work in guiding young writers on the make.

"Young writers" or "young people writing"—whatever you call it—we the invitees were in seventh heaven. At the time, I had only two short pieces under my belt—"Little Beanie" and "Spring Festival."

It was either 1955 or 1956 when Youth League Central issued a call to the youth of China to read Ovechkin's novella *The Agronomist and the Tractor Station Master* and learn from the example of the heroine Nastya. Nastya was a young newly graduated agronomist who through unrelenting struggle against bureaucracy brought about a change in the collective farm. China Youth Publishing House issued several million copies of the translation. By then I myself was no longer a "young newcomer." I had several years of work experience and was already a regular cadre. I did not believe in Nastya's golden touch. It was pure utopia. I myself had just handled a sticky problem involving an unruly Youth Leaguer by the name of Lu Dabiao. Lu was a lively fellow. He didn't defer to the leadership and was always making complaints or offering criticisms, as a result of which he got a two-year probation on his Youth League membership. When his case came to my desk, I consulted a leading comrade at the Beijing Municipal Youth League Committee who had studied in the Soviet Union. The comrade laid a finger precisely on the nature of Lu's problem. "*The opposition,*" he had said, "*people who are always in the opposition will end up being the enemy.*" That was an eye-opener for me. (Later I helped Lu restore his Youth League status and got him into a college, albeit an obscure one.)

So that was what Nastya was—the opposition.

Nastya represented a cheap and easy utopia. On the other hand, Nastya's innocence, fervor, and idealism had its attractions for me, just turned twenty-one, and a budding writer. Literature had a life of its own, it could wander off into hidden nooks and crannies, or it could soar to unknown heights. In real life there are people who are always getting into scraps, being their own worst enemy, but they are no harm to others. I am almost sympathetic to that type. Take the characters Lin Daiyu, Jia Baoyu or the saucy maid Qingwen and the opera singer Fangguan. They would be in real trouble if they were our colleagues in real life, but in the novel *Dream of the Red Chamber,* they belong, and they each have a role to play.

My revision of *Long Live Youth* progressed smoothly. I sometimes stayed at my father's place in the western suburbs of Beijing, where I was not disturbed. By then I was in complete control of the manuscript. I knew where I was and where I was heading. I knew where and when I should hark back to a previous passage, and where I should make a break and branch off in a new direction. I have discovered that writing a novel was like composing a symphony, there must be a first, a second and a third movement, there must be harmony and there must be variations. There must be continuous flow and there must be sudden twists and turns. As for the "main thread running through," it is more of a feeling than a format or a sustained flow. How wonderful it is—to feel the harmony, the rhythm, the pace of music while working over a literary manuscript! To write a novel is like composing music, what happiness! My feelings and instincts were completely merged in my design for the novel. The writing just flowed from my pen. *Long Live Youth* was a rhapsody to youth, full-blooded youth, moving ahead with crystal clarity, unsullied purity, and burning enthusiasm, just waiting to be brought to life by Wang Meng. *Long Live Youth* was like the angel of youth, flying into every home, nourishing every young heart, lighting up every young face, setting off ardor in every young breast.

I was in my best working mood. So I undertook a second project, and I worked at the two projects simultaneously, as I usually do, to avoid monotony.

In April of 1956, when I was twenty-one-and-a-half-years old, I dashed off "Young Newcomer at the Organization Department," and my life was changed forever.

Chapter 11

"Young Newcomer at the Organization Department"

"Young Newcomer at the Organization Department" may be said to be my personal version of Ovechkin's *Daily Life in the District.* In this story, I could romanticize my own daily life in the Youth League District Committee. I could question the credibility of Nastya's story. I could finally give form to what I had first conceived as a stage drama. I could make use of my own experience, my maturity, my political experience, my uniqueness, and my difference from the usual run of "literary youth." I could bring into the story all my worldliness, all my confusion, all my sentiments, my sighs and my artistic instincts. In this story, I could turn days and events into poetry; I could pour my poetic sentiments into days and events. I was confident of my own loyalty and my own courage, I was confident of my own understanding of the world and my skill in handling its many perplexities. I had confidence in myself.

I dashed off the story in May of 1956 and sent it off to *People's Literature* magazine. Within a month, I heard back from the editorial staff, saying that deputy editor-in-chief Qin Zhaoyang[1] was very impressed. There were a few rough edges, which I smoothed over very easily. I was elated. I went over the manuscript lovingly, touching it up here and there. I could recite it by heart. I was no more the raw apprentice writer of *Little Beanie.* Here was a major work, all twenty-thousand characters of it. It was actually a novella. I submitted it a second time.

---

1. Qin Zhaoyang, 1913–2002, editor and critic, labeled a *rightist.*

"Young Newcomer at the Organization Department" appeared in the September 1956 issue of *People's Literature* magazine. It appeared just after *The Little Miner,* a short story by Yang Daqun, a writer from the Northeast. I myself actually saw the number of that magazine which carried my story, not in Beijing, but in Taiyuan, capital of Shanxi Province. At the time, Ruifang was studying at the Technical College in Taiyuan and was one year short of graduation. It was September of 1956. We were together again, and I was going to pay her a surprise visit.

Later, Ruifang often recalled how she was in her dorm and heard the crisp tap of leather soles in the corridor as I approached. Ruifang's roommates found an empty room in the dorm and I stayed the night. Her roommates liked me and disliked another fellow who was trying to steal her from me. Ruifang and I went out together. We had a Western dinner, saw a local opera, and walked to the outskirts of town. We went to see the famous sights in the suburbs and almost missed the train which would take us back to town.

Ruifang saw me off at the Taiyuan train station. As we were waiting, the latest number of *People's Literature* magazine on a newsstand caught my eye. I bought a copy and flipped through the pages. I seemed to be looking at something alien, mysterious, and moving—not only to the reader, but to the writer as well. I noticed some changes in the text which did not make sense. But so what! What mattered was the fact that my work was published in *People's Literature*!

At the time, I was still immersed in the elation of getting back together with Ruifang. At the end of that summer holiday, Ruifang had looked me up before going back to college. It was my salvation. If not for this, I would never have survived all that befell me later. So many memories of the past, so many streets, so many dates, so many longings spilled from my memory! How can I help shedding tears? Thanks to life, thanks to the heavens, everything had been salvaged.

Though I had been considered a natural talent since childhood, I had been used to seeing human thoughts and emotions being treated as ideological phenomena, though I had become an old hand at criticism and self-criticism . . . yet to me literature was literature. To me—as well as to you and to future generations—novels and poetry are not material to be pounced on by ideology, not mouthpieces for or samples of ideology. But having said all this, I still could not help blurring the lines between literature and everyday work and everyday reality. I was lost in my writing, starting to think that it was not mere scribbling, that it had a message for real life. At one time I was even deluded into thinking that I should dedicate my short story to my leaders at the workplace.

Actually I should have realized that "Young Newcomer at the Organization Department" was my own joy and stirred my own emotions, my own bitterness, and my own disappointment. I should have known that it was my own individualized imagination, my own particular topic of interest. It was the very taste of life itself, like that train ride back from Taiyuan—dizziness and the fun of covering distance at a hectic pace, coupled with a nameless sense of elation and also of loss. The story was the fruit of my youthful self-confidence, innocence, love and regrets, hesitation and resolve, pride and yearning—like joining the Party, like first love. "Young Newcomer at the Organization Department" was my poem. Whatever it was, it had hit the mark on the first try. On the other hand, it was actually cast into waters of unknown depths in uncertain winds.

"My Young Newcomer at the Organization Department"! It was the script of my other language, the language of the heart. It was my love letter, written to all who love me, and whom I love. It was a message that I leave. One day I will not be around, but my note will still be lying there—the thought made me weep. It was a song that I hummed, a confession made when I had taken a drop too many; it was a vow that I made to myself when I saw green grass and mountain flowers in bloom; it was a little flower that I offered to life. It was a word of comfort that I offered to myself, to youth, and to life when things do not go the way we want. At the same time, "Young Newcomer at the Organization Department" was an offer of thanks to a great age, to the newly born great nation of New China, to the great lands and mountains and rivers, an offer of thanks to the sun and the moon and the stars, to all creation and to life itself. "Young Newcomer at the Organization Department" was my personal question mark, exclamation mark, and full stop. To be frank, it was only someone like me—self-anointed darling of creation, self-styled genius indulged by history, self-confirmed Communist Party member—only a creature so endowed could give voice to such poetry, could so open his heart, and breathe forth the words of his soul. Or more to the point, only a prodigy like me could be capable of such self-indulgent rompings with literature.

Chairman Mao had said that this writer was "talented."[2] It was Mao of course, who could spot talent at a glance. However, certain people on the other shore included the story in *Bitter Fruit,*[3] an anthology of Chinese writing, with the subtitle "The Uprising of the Intelligentsia behind the Iron Curtain." Although the anthology was ideology-oriented, the editor made a point of saying that Wang Meng's story was in a "different style."

But, considering the politically sensitive subject matter of the story, its writer was too young, just too young. It seemed that the story, like its writer, suffered from malnutrition. Its conception was not grand, its confidence was not firm, its analysis did not cover all the issues, its presentation was not forceful, and its argument was not clear-cut. What was it trying to do? In a forceful age which encouraged confrontation, relied on realpolitik, and believed that the world was on the edge of a decisive battle between two ideologies, in an age which upheld the slogan "whatever our enemy opposes we will uphold, whatever our enemy upholds, we will oppose"... in such a grandiose but roughshod age when the nation was determined to build up a proletarian state, what could the gentle murmurings of the half-baked wisdom of two young creatures accomplish—those two gentle, pure, well-meaning, and totally useless creatures? Wasn't the whole conception ridiculous? What could one say?

I once joked: Overcome bureaucratism with a novel? No way! Overcome the novel with bureaucratism would be a safer bet! Needed here were other criteria, other value systems, and other kinds of narrative. Across the span of half-a-century, the above is what the writer of "Newcomer at the Organization Department" had to say about the "different style" of his work.

As for the writing of *Long Live Youth,* I not only devoted myself to planning the characters, the episodes, the locality, the setting—I could memorize every passage, and savor the tones and rhythms as I rolled the

2. For Mao's comment, see Roderick MacFarquar, Timothy Creek, Eugene Wu eds., *The Secret Speeches of Chairman Mao,* Harvard Contemporary China series, Harvard University Press, 1989.

3. *Bitter Fruit—Uprising behind the Iron Curtain,* Harvard-Yenching Library.

words off my tongue. I wanted each word to be relaxed and suggestive and elegant and neat and bright. For instance I described how a group of "progressive minded" students stomped into the protagonist Su Ning's room and redecorated it with revolutionary books and artifacts, getting rid of her photographs of movie stars and sentimental fiction of the pre-Liberation days. I ended the paragraph by stating: "And thus, amid the laughter and banter of those young girls, the glorious New World made its presence felt in that little room." I could not help patting myself on the back for that *mot d'eclat.*

I now know my destiny, I am born to be a writer. My head was always swimming with words and ideas, making me forget where I was—a far cry from the good communist and hard worker of the old days. Any little thing in daily life could strike a chord in me: a breeze would make me realize that was how one of my characters was feeling; a light bulb slightly misshapen, exactly what I could use for the lamp in my description of a room; the crush at the bus stop gave me the inspiration for the ending of the novel; a burst of laughter would make me realize that I must fix the ending of a chapter. How would I describe the process of my writing? Sometimes it was planned, and sometimes it sprung to life on the spur of the moment. Some passages, on which I had prided myself, had to be deleted; others I felt I had to change after I saw a tree, or after I got back from jogging. The rhythms of life, the sudden outbursts, the expected and the unexpected, the weather of the day or my diet, sounds and smells, my mood or my digestion, my blood pressure or my muscles, the view of the mountain or the color of the night, the full moon or a waning moon, clear weather or gloomy—they all, all, defined the mood and make-up of my writing. Blessed is the novelist! Everything that happens to him has a value of its own, even that which is considered negative—failure, embarrassment, desperation—all could be gist for his mill.

The novel is creative writing not only because it provides newly created characters and settings, but also because the process of writing itself is spontaneous, so much so that sometimes the writer is surprised. Thus the initial surprise of creation is reserved for the writer—"How did I write that?!" And then the reader is pleasantly surprised while reading. This seems to be inflating the ego of the writer, but let's face it: if a story does not even delight the writer, how can it move the reader? There is hardly another writer who had done for New China what Wang Meng has done—describe the birth of a new nation and rhapsodize about the first generation of that nation's youth. There would be a blank if *Long Live Youth* had never been born.

But *Long Live Youth* itself had gone through many ups and downs. Started in 1953 and completed in 1956, it was stifled for a quarter of a century and never saw the light of day.[4] It was first published in 1979, and did not get much attention from the literary specialists. But up to this day, the book has been reprinted every three years, and by now four hundred thousand copies have been printed. From the birth of New China to the end of the Cultural Revolution, many fine works have been written and published, but none has survived those years and is still being read by the youth of the nation. For an "old" book, which still carried the rawness of youth, to have survived the test of time as has *Long Live Youth*—a writer could not ask for more.

---

4. Except for excerpts serialized in *Wenhuibao Daily*. See chapter 14.

Chapter 12

"Young Newcomer" under Attack

A couple of days after the appearance of "Young Newcomer at the Organization Department," a staff member of *People's Literature* magazine arrived at my door, bringing me a 476 yuan writer's fee. It was a considerable sum, almost five times my monthly salary of 87 yuan, 60 fen. And then the reaction . . .

The initial reaction came from people who identified themselves with characters in the story, some of them my colleagues and friends: "I am not like that . . ." was the typical complaint.

Then *Works in Art and Literature* magazine, co-edited by Wei Junyi[1] and Huang Qiuyun,[2] published a series of comments. The first piece was titled: "The Stream of Life Is Leaping Forward." This positive comment was followed by a harsh attack, which pointed out that the male protagonist, Lin Zhen, was no revolutionary vanguard but a petty-bourgeois hothead.

A couple of newly emerged young writers including Liu Shaotang, Cong Weixi,[3] and Liu Binyan[4] liked the story. On the other hand, my colleagues and friends at the Youth League were mostly negative in their

---

1. Wei Junyi, 1917–2002, later General Editor of People's Literature Publishing House.
2. Huang Qiuyun, 1918–, prolific writer of essays and reportage, held leading positions in literary associations and literary periodicals.
3. Cong Weixi, 1933–, novelist, labeled a *rightist*.
4. Liu Binyan, 1925–2005, investigative reporter, labeled a *rightist*.

reaction. Seeing that my story was stirring up so much interest, seeing one article after another being published and my own name repeatedly spelled out in print, I was happy. I owned up to myself in a shamefaced way that I enjoyed being the center of attention.

Meanwhile, my full-length novel *Long Live Youth* had passed through editorial scrutiny at the China Youth Publishing House and was slated for publication. We signed a contract and I was paid an advance of 500 yuan. It could be said that I went to bed one night and woke up the next morning to find myself famous.

But at the same time, the critique of "Young Newcomer at the Organization Department" was intensifying. The editor and deputy editor of *China Youth Daily,* both of them my elders and well-meaning friends, had a confidential conversation with me. They were worried. They felt that I was in big trouble: certain people, they told me, had compared my story to Wang Shiwei's[5] "Wild Lilies" They told me to be careful, that a newly assigned leader of my district had remarked of me: "Wang Meng is turning a deaf ear to exhortation"!

In February of 1957, *Wenhuibao Daily* suddenly—at least that was how I felt—published a long article by Li Xifan[6] attacking "Young Newcomer at the Organization Department," pushing the issue to the verge of the enemy category, equivalent to a death sentence. I saw the seriousness of the situation. I must deal with it. Everything else was trivial in comparison. I clung to my glorious revolutionary pedigree—Li Xifan could not be more revolutionary than I was; he had no right to critique me in the name of the revolution. I wrote a letter to the highest literary authority, Zhou Yang, explaining who I was and requesting an interview.

Zhou Yang's answer to my letter came much faster than I had expected.

---

5. Wang Shiwei, 1906–1947, leftist writer, best-known for his essay "Lilies" wherein he pointed out the darkness in the Yan'an Communist base. Wang was subsequently executed.
6. Li Xifan, 1927–, literary critic, best known for an article (co-written with Lan Ling) challenging the methodology of Yu Pingpo's study of the Chinese classic—*Dream of the Red Chamber.* Commended by Chairman Mao, the article led to a round of critical attacks on Yu in academic and literary circles. He later became head of the arts and literature department of *People's Daily*.

I was asked to meet him at the quarters of the Propaganda Department of the Central Committee of the CCP, at the previous site of Peking University. The room was elegantly furnished in the traditional style and used to be the living quarters of Cai Yuanpei, the founding president of Peking University. Years later, when I was serving at the Ministry of Culture, I had used it briefly as an office. Later, it was converted to a reception room for visitors from abroad.

I showed up for the appointment and Zhou Yang got to the point right away. He told me that Chairman Mao had read the story and would not write it off as totally worthless and did not agree with Li Xifan's attack. What's more, Zhou Yang told me, Chairman Mao particularly did not agree with Li's statement that there was no bureaucratism in Beijing. This was constructive criticism, and it warmed my heart.

Zhou Yang also told me that he himself and some of the Party elders and veteran writers had read the story and, talking among themselves, had wondered if people's brains were bound to ossify with age, as if only the young could oppose bureaucratism? I hastened to assure him that it was not my point at all, that I had never dreamed of upholding youth at the expense of Party leaders and veteran revolutionaries! I explained that I had never planned the character of Lin Zhen as a positive hero—all that I had wanted to show was the ambiguity in the fate of a character like Lin.

I had expressed myself appropriately and modestly, and I could see that Zhou Yang was pleased.

Looking back at that Beijing Convention for budding young writers that I had attended, I could see in hindsight that certain young writers were indeed somewhat arrogant and had offended some of their elders. While on the subject, Zhou Yang frowned and said that there was a young writer who had said that Soviet literature was inferior to the literature of the prerevolutionary era, and that the literature after Chairman Mao's *Talk at the Yenan Forum on Art and Literature*[7] stood no comparison to the literature before the talks, and Zhou Yang asked what I thought. I instantly realized the seriousness of the question laid before me, and I knew that the young

7. The forum, held on May 23, 1942, which started with art and literature issues, and eventually led to the Yan'an Rectification Movement.

writer he alluded to was no other than Liu Shaotang. I answered Zhou Yang by saying that on such a major issue, one needs more data based on solid research before making a generalization. Zhou seemed pleased with my cautious answer and repeated it to himself. He then expressed concern about my well-being in general, asking particularly after my health, noting that I was too thin and recommended that I get an X-ray to check if I had tuberculosis.

Then the situation took a turn for the worse: I heard a recording of a talk by Chairman Mao at a meeting of Party Central on propaganda work. Mao said: *There is someone called Wang Meng who wrote a novel* [meaning "Young Newcomer"], *and some people are going to encircle him and destroy him.* Mao then added that *in so saying, he was of course exaggerating.* Then he stated: *I do not know this Wang Meng, he is no relative of mine, but I cannot agree with all the criticism heaped on him. For instance, his critics say that there is no bureaucratism in Bejing. Now take note,* Mao continued, *that Wang Ming*[8] *is from Party Central and claims to be a hundred percent Marxist, even ninety-nine percent does not satisfy him. How can anyone claim that there is no bureaucratism in Beijing? Personally I support a drive against bureaucratism. Wang Meng is a literary talent, he has a future* . . . Chairman Mao went on to say: . . . *the novel is unsatisfactory in certain aspects;* he pointed out that the positive hero was not done well. *Failings should be criticized,* he conceded, *but support first, then criticize, do not demolish with one swing of the club* . . . As he was speaking, Mao fumbled for a cigarette and not finding one muttered, *Out of rations.* It is said that Lu Dingyi[9] rushed to hand a cigarette to Mao, who changed the topic as he lit-up.

Thus I came out of the fix in one piece, completely unscathed. I was basking in the warmth of spring. At the same time, I kept reminding myself, *Don't let it go to your head, keep your head down.* A reporter from *Beijing Daily* interviewed me. I stated that all criticism and comments were useful, that even hostile comments could serve as antidotes. But I was against the approach of treating works of literature as mouthpieces of political opposition. Finally, I stressed that I needed to improve my writing, so on and so forth.

The Beijing Writers' Union held a symposium on "Young Newcomer."

---

8. One time Chairman of the CCP, who was outsted.
9. Lu Dingyi, 1906–1996, veteran CCP member, at one time head of the CCP Propaganda Department.

At the gathering, I got to know other writers such as Lin Jinlan,[10] Deng Youmei,[11] Ge Cuilin,[12] and others. The young writers present praised my work most generously, expressed their support, and refuted the club-swinging attacks launched at me. As for the older writers, including academics from the universities, they seemed relaxed. They laughed and joked about everything under the sun, except the story supposedly under discussion.

Now, looking back with the wisdom of hindsight, I realize that apart from the periodic class struggles which made literature a dangerous minefield, the internal bickerings and jealousies and backstabbing among writers themselves also contributed to the destructive literary upheavals of the era.

10. Lin Jinlan, 1923–2009, writer of short stories labeled a *rightist*.
11. Deng Youmei, 1931–, writer of novels and short stories, labeled a *rightist*.
12. Ge Cuilin, 1930–, writer of children's stories.

Chapter 13

Blooming and Contending

Ruifang and I married on January 28, 1957. She was one semester short of graduation and had to return to college. My royalties from "Young Newcomer" were enough to set us up for simple housekeeping: a glass bookcase, a writing desk, sofa chairs, and what not. I was steeped in happiness and wanted nothing more than to be with Ruifang.

Prevous to this, in the fall of 1956, I had been transferred to the position of Deputy-Secretary of the Youth League Committee at the Beijing 738 Electric Cord Plant. I had planned to write a novel about the life of college students after the completion of *Long Live Youth,* my novel about a bunch of high school students. But Comrade Wang Zhaohua, head of the Beijing Youth League, said "Why limit your writing to petty-bourgeois subjects?" Thus my transfer to a manufacting plant.

The plant was situated in the "electronic zone" in the industrial east end of Beijing, electronic products being one of the major items under the First Five-Year Plan of 1956.

Meanwhile, Lin Mohan[1] had written an article on "Young Newcomer" that was slated to be published in *People's Daily,* and he showed me the galleys. In so doing, Lin was following Chairman Mao's suggestion that critics should give authors an opportunity for rebuttal. Actually, the passages and the ending of the story that Lin Mohan had issue with were not mine—they were the editorial changes and insertions of the

1. Lin Mohan, 1913–2008, reporter and editor during the war years, later held leading positions in literary associations and served as deputy Minister of Culture.

publisher, *People's Literature* magazine. So I did some explaining to Lin Mohan in a letter.

Soon word was out about the editorial changes. Shao Quanling[2] called me up, saying that he would call a meeting to discuss the relationship between writers and editors and asked me to participate. I clearly felt his good will toward me, and his support.

In our conversation, Shao Quanling brought up the name of the editor of *People's Literature* magazine, Qin Zhaoyang, saying off-handedly that Qin was considered arrogant. From his words I gathered that the leadership at the Writers' Union was cooking up a critical move against Qin, obviously on account of his article "Realism, a Broad Vista." In that article, Qin had argued against the term "socialist realism," claiming that realism was realism by definition, the only difference being the age we live in, and that "realism in a socialist age" would be a better choice of terminology. That had not gone down well with our mainstream theorists, and one of them—Zhang Guangnian[3]—had published an article rebutting Qin's theory.

Later, at the meeting called to discuss the relationship between authors and editors, I was quite restrained about the editorial meddling in the original text of "Young Newcomer at the Organization Department." The fact that they had cut off my previous ending—Lin Zhen knocking at the Party leader's door—was no big deal. They actually did me a favor in deleting my hackneyed description of the Party boss as "eagle-eyed" and so on.

To be honest, at the time, I had no clue as to what was going on in literary circles. Decades later, I learned that the larger background to that meeting over "editorial license" was that Mao himself had been furious at the changes made to "Young Newcomer" by the editorial staff and had remarked that their behavior was "underhanded."

Actually I myself had much less resentment toward *People's Literature*

---

2. Shao Quanling, 1906–1971, literary critic and translator, Secretary of the Party Core of the Chinese Writers' Union. Party Core (*dang zu*) is above Party Committee.
3. Zhang Guangnian (writing under pseudonym Guang Weiran), 1913–, writer on the Left, dramatist and poet, best known for writing the libretto for the *Yellow River Cantata*. Played leading roles in the Chinese Writers' Union and Federation of Literature and Art Circles.

magazine—which, after all, had published my story—than against *Wenhuibao Daily,* which had broken their promise to serialize *Long Live Youth.* In my talk, I did make some veiled criticisms of the editors of the latter, but they were a good-humored lot and did not seem to mind at all. Mei Duo kept smiling his fatuous smile. What can you do? Following the meeting, Mei Duo and Pu Jiexiu, chief of the *Wenhuibao* Beijing office, showed up at my door. They insisted on serializing part of *Long Live Youth,* and wouldn't take no for an answer? If not for their selected serialization—*Long Live Youth* would never have seen the light of day until a quarter of a century later.

What with this, that and the other, the "Young Newcomer at the Organization Department" became an asset instead of a liability. That same year, I was elected a "Model Youth of Socialist Construction" for the city of Beijing. Later, at the National Congress of the Youth League, my name appeared as a candidate for the National Committee of the Youth League, but I did not get enough votes to be elected—it seemed that there was still some negative reaction to me among the rank and file.

Here I must add that at the time I was going through something of a mental crisis. I had never managed to blend into life at the 738 Electric Cord Plant—the long bus rides to and from work with people squeezed together like sardines, the housing units built originally for families now used as dorms, the long lines at the cavernous dining halls, the deafening roar of machines, the pervasive smell of gasoline. Everything conveyed a sense of novelty, but I never felt at home in that environment.

Every day after work, as I looked at the setting sun, I was overcome by a feeling of emptiness and desolation, and I felt that my life and my feelings were being impoverished. Back home it was also lonely, as Ruifang was still in college, her last term. I do not know if I was suffering from some kind of melancholia, or was it loneliness following my honeymoon? Was it petty-bourgeois anxiety about being detached from the laboring masses? Or was it the ominously low pressure preceding the onslaught of the *anti-rightist* campaign that messed up my *jing* / *lo* vessels and my general internal order?

As I was undergoing all the above, the Blooming and Contending of 1956—known abroad as the Hundred Flowers Campaign—was launched.

Then diverted.

Then ended.

During the Blooming and Contending, I was invited to all kinds of meetings related to art and literature, to speak up and offer my opinion. I took care not to let off steam. At a meeting called by the Propaganda Department of the Beijing Communist Party Committee, I whispered to Deng Youmei to watch his tongue, as the leaders did not take kindly to this "blooming and contending" business. At the time, my thoughts often went back to Alexei Tolstoy's trilogy *The Tortuous Pilgrimage*. The film adaption opened with a summer scene on a Crimean beach. The caption went something like: *It is the last summer, people are still enjoying themselves and they are slowly rotting; then the wind blew everything away, the fire burned everything, and the world was turned upside down . . .*

I was invited to the enlarged meeting called by the Party Core of the Chinese Writers' Union. The targets were Ding Ling and her husband Chen Qixia. To get Ding Ling, they must first take down Chen Qixia, and to take down Chen Qixia, they got the writer Liu Qi to appear as a victim and expose Chen Qixia, her one-time lover! How unscrupulous! To what end?

As for myself, on the one hand, I was flattered that I was invited to such a high-level gathering, but on the other hand, I sensed that a storm was brewing and a test lay ahead. Since Liberation, I had thrown myself into all the campaigns against feudalism, against local tyrants, against quasi-religious sects, against the three-*anti*'s and the five-*anti*'s, and not the least into the reform of private enterprise and other causes.

With the launching of the attack against Hu Feng, however, I began to harbor doubts, I felt that I could not keep up anymore with the pace of the campaigns, hoping that they would come to an end.

As for the current campaign, it was all the more stunning—how did the Blooming and Contending turn into this *anti-rightist* campaign? I felt uncomfortable; I kept reminding myself to be careful, to keep up with the evolving situation, to be in lock step with the leadership, to watch my tongue, and make sure that I myself was not involved.

At this same enlarged meeting called by the Party Core of the Writer's Union, I had stood up to make a public criticism of Ding Ling and Feng

Xuefeng,[4] who was also a target, tagging on a resolution to try harder to raise my own consciousness.

4. Feng Xuefeng, 1903–1976, senior CCP writer who had been on the Long March, Feng was one of the leading figures in the leftist literary camp, closely allied to Lu Xun. After Liberation in 1949, Feng held leading positions in literary associations and literary publications, but was labeled a *rightist* in 1957, and targeted during the Cultural Revolution, to be re-instated post mortem.

Chapter 14

Living Through the Fifties

One day during the height of Blooming and Contending when I was still at the 738 Plant, I got a notice that a car would be coming to take me to the Beijing Party Committee to read a document. I waited a couple of hours and a second notice arrived informing me that the appointment had been canceled.

Later, I realized that the "non-event" had been a turning point in my life.

The fact was that on May 15, 1957, Chairman Mao had written an article titled "The Situation Is Undergoing a Change," in which he called for a rebuttal of the *rightists* and a critique of the revisionists! The article was first circulated among leading cadres to prepare the way for the diversion of the ongoing Party Rectification [Blooming and Contending] into a movement to beat back the attacks of the *rightists.*

According to what I heard later, there had been an arrangement to circulate Mao's article among certain notable figures both inside and outside the Party, so that they would be prepared for, and be protected against, what was coming. I will never know what had transpired within that critical period when I was first notified by the Beijing Party Committee that I would be fetched to read a document, and then two hours later when told that the appointment had been called off.

Why the decision to take me off the "to be protected" list, I will never know. But one thing I do know is that the Beijing Party Committee had nothing to do with that fatal decision. The head of the Propaganda

Department of the Beijing Party Committee, Comrade Zhang Dazhong (previously head of the Beijing Youth League) told me personally that the Beijing Party Committee had nothing to do with my case. He further told me that Comrade Yang Shu, in charge of Culture and Education for the Beijing Party Committee, had tried to take over my case, but had been obstructed by the *relevant authority*. Obviously, since Wang Meng was a cadre at the Youth League Committee, his case should be handled by the relevant Party organization of the Youth League. Thus the argument ran, and the implication was very clear . . .

Why not look around and train my sights on China as a whole—China of the 1950s! The land reform, the suppression of counterrevolutionaries, controlling inflation, the liberation of Hainan Island, entering Tibet, the war to "Resist the U.S. and Aid Korea," Sino-Soviet friendship, the death of Stalin, the first People's Congress, the drawing up of the Constitution, thought reform, the overhaul of higher education, the critique of the film "Wuxun," the critique of Hu Shih, the critique of Yu Pingbo,[1] the Five Principles of Peaceful Co-existence, the Five-Year Plan, the socialist reform projects, the drive to overtake Great Britain in fifteen years . . . So many ambitious plans, so many undertakings, so many new rules and regulations, so many experiments, so many successes, so much to look forward to!

My youth had been lived on a high note, what the Soviets called "from victory to victory," and what we in China refer to as the Party's "overwhelming bounty, which lights up everything it touches!" I myself was constantly in an ecstasy of admiration, confidence, pride . . .

As for me, Chairman Mao had spoken positively regarding "Young Newcomer at the Organization Department," and I was deeply grateful. But I had never considered his doing so as a personal favor to me.

At the time, Mao had also pooh-poohed the article jointly penned by Chen Yi, Chen Qitong, and Ma Hanbin, which had openly opposed the call for Blooming and Contending, and which had even been reprinted

1. Yu Pingbo, 1900–1990. With a solid grounding in the classics, Yu had started out as a romantic poet writing under the influence of the May Fourth Movement. He later turned to research and became an authority on *The Dream of the Red Chamber*. He was criticized in 1953. With Mao's support, the criticism ballooned into a critical campaign in literary and academic circles.

in the Soviet *Literary Gazette.* On the other hand, a Yugoslavian paper had reprinted "The Herald of Film," by Zhong Dianfei,[2] an illustration of the saying—"to each his own."

Meanwhile, Chairman Mao stood firm against both "leftist extremisn" and the *rightists,* representing the correct line.

Following quickly on the heels of Blooming and Contending, the *anti-rightist* movement was launched.

I was not elated. I was on the defense, I was not righteously incensed against the *rightists* now being exposed daily in the papers, as I should have been.

I was scared. *Will I be in trouble?* I asked myself. I didn't know. A popular saying suddenly occurred to me: "Even if I have no accomplishments, at least I have done hard work." (Later on, a line was added: "Even if I have not done hard work, I am exhausted.") I smiled uneasily at the thought *Something was not right. Definitely not right.*

---

2. Zhong Dianfei, 1919–1987, specialist in film studies, labeled a *rightist.*

Chapter 15

How I Get the Rightist Label

November 1957. While working as deputy-secretary of the Youth League at the 738 Plant, I was ordered back to the Beijing Youth League Committee to participate in the ongoing *anti-rightist* campaign against the "bloomers and contenders" of the "Hundred Flowers" period. Comrade Zhang Jinlin, who was running the Committee, said to me outright that my ideology "must be straightened out."

My first reaction was: *The Party is all-seeing, I do indeed have "ideology problems." If not, why is it that I who always rallied to the call of the Party now feel listless in the current* anti-rightist *campaign?* Not only listless, I was actually out of step! How I wanted to think things through and shake off this lethargy!

At the time, the *anti-rightist* campaign was raging on all fronts, so much so that I was completely dazed by the fast changing scene. Once I attended a meeting convened by the Youth League Central Committee to criticize the young writer Liu Shaotang, now labeled a *rightist.* As I sat down, someone gave me a pat on the back, I looked back and it was none other than Liu Shaotang himself! I was scared out of my wits.

At that same meeting, a writer acquaintance of mine, D, stood up and gave a glaring speech, criticizing Liu Shaotang, laying bare his own problems, and sending a warning to fellow writer Cong Weixi. The audience applauded loud and long until stopped by a signal from the chairman, veteran writer G. He announced: "Word had just come in that D has been labeled a *rightist* by his own work unit!" We were flabbergasted. Even more unsettling, news got out that Chairman G himself would soon be labeled.

I had been ill at ease since the outset of the campaign. Now back at the Beijing Youth League Committee, I had expected to feel more at home. Most of the staff at the Youth League had been students in the Communist Party underground; they were young and educated; having gone through the ordeal of life and death, they were all staunch comrades with analytical minds. Their drawback was that they were out of touch with reality and tended to be over zealous. It had been so during the three-*antis* and the five-*antis* campaigns of the early 1950s, and now they were pursuing the *anti-rightist* campaign with equal zeal. Besides, such was the momentum of the movement that it could not be stopped even if one wanted it to be halted.

When I turned myself in to Beijing Youth League headquarters, the *rightist* "quota"[1] handed down to our unit had already been filled. But the Youth League leadership still sought to maximize the spoils of victory. Big-character posters denouncing people of this or that political offense screamed from the walls. The hunt for *rightists* rolled on, with no sign of letting up.

L was one of my colleagues at the Youth League (I refrain from naming names out of consideration for surviving families). He was well dressed, sported a mustache, and carried himself with a certain air although he was not college-educated. I once met L on the street. He looked me up and down and shook his head, "Wang Meng," he remonstrated, "have you come to this . . . ?" I knew he meant my scruffy appearance. Previous to this, I had been seen as putting on the airs of a celebrity who could get away with anything, but it simply was not true. The plain truth was that I was never fashion conscious, and did not have the means to be particular about what I wore.

Inexplicably to me, out of the blue, L was struck down as a *rightist*. After my return to the Beijing Youth League headquarters, I once came across him by accident in the reference room located in the basement of our building. When he lifted his head, I saw with horror that his eyes were glazed over like those of a blind man, and his whole face seemed

1. Meaning percentage of the staff to be labeled *rightists*, generally 5 percent, though some work units exceeded their quota.

wrapped in gray, like the face of the dead. He must have been confined to the reference room to write his confession. At the sight of him, I turned and ran away in fright.

One after another, comrades were ferreted out and struck down as *rightists,* or even arrested outright as criminals. How could things have come to such a pass, turning the former Beijing Youth League Committee workplace into a detention center for class enemies?

At the time, nailing down a *rightist* was as easy as swatting a fly. Comrade W was one of the movers and shakers in this respect. He was short, with a pair of little round grasses perched on his nose, and he was full of analytical energy. Recently divorced, Comrade W held many private talks with me, the point of which was to help straighten out my ideology, such that I could be taken back into the bosom of the people. To effect this change, according to him, one must dig and dig. One must dig out one's innermost ideological transgressions. His logic ran thus: if it is established that you have problem A, how is it possible that your problem is limited to A? You are bound to have problem B, and from B to C, D, E, ... all the way to Z and beyond.

W toasts you over a slow fire: you had reservations regarding work in the District, right? Then what do you think of work at the Municipality? What about work at Party Central?—the State Council?—the international Communist movement? You had owned that you were confused over the Stalin issue, right? What about your views of the Western capitalist countries? What about their anti-communist propaganda? Obviously his logic was untenable. But in the heat of the anti-*rightist* movement, what worked was not logic but overwhelming pressure.

My attitude toward W and his group was one of complete cooperation. I conceded that I had problems that needed straightening out, and acknowledged that they were trying to help me. I never doubted the Party's much vaunted policy to "criticize severely and close the case leniently." Comrade W and company treated me kindly. Throughout the most intense periods of criticism, they would sit with me over lunch and with their own chopsticks pick up tasty titbits to place in my bowl. Regarding my ideological problems, they kept urging me to dig deep and deeper still. I conceded that I indeed had many flaws: I was weak, overly sensitive, in a word, I was not sufficiently working class. But I also knew that I had no choice: the only way out was to raise both hands and surrender. Ideological transgressions could not be measured quantitively, it was up to them to analyze whichever way they wanted to.

One of W's famous quotes was "It's all a matter of the bum and the nose." He elaborated: "Coming across a certain opinion, or a piece of writing, use your nose, give it a sniff, and you should be able to tell right from wrong." As regards the bum, the question was, "On which side are you sitting, what is your reaction to things as they unfold? It is all a matter of where you place your bum. Once your bum is on the right spot (sitting on the side of the working class), you are bound to see the error of your ways."

Another of W's tactics was to combat "revolutionary" AQ-ism.[2]

W exhorted me not to be like AQ, but to bravely own up to all my flaws and ideological transgressions. The more you owned up, W argued, the better you would rectify your ideology, and the brighter your future will be. In a word, according to W , confession is tantamount to a great personal victory.

I was bowled over by his analytical genius, and equally aware of his pleasure in manipulating me; the man was really enjoying himself. Perhaps if we changed places, I could be equally persuasive.

And thus W and his co-workers, six altogether, worked at straightening out my ideology. They were dripping with self-confidence and self-satisfaction and a sense of mission, competing with each other in insight, depth, ardor, and force of argument, sweeping away all doubts and uncertainties in the destructive path of their critical eloquence. Perhaps they were resentful and even envious of this little nobody who had sprung out of nowhere and was on the verge of turning into somebody?

After the slow roast, I was put on the back burner. I was left to wait. The final verdict on my case came six months later, in May of 1958. I got the *rightist* label.

Years later, it was leaked out that Zhou Yang, the cultural czar (at one time head of the Propaganda Department of the Communist

2. AhQ-ism: Ah Q, the main character in Lu Xun's novella *The True Story of Ah Q*, is a comic / tragic character who interprets his defeats as moral victories; later the name was converted into a term for such attitudes in general.

Party Central Committee), had dealt the final blow. At the time, the deputy party secretary of the Beijing Communist Party Committee, Yang Shu, had strenuously argued against giving me the *rightist* label. But W, representative from the Beijng Communist Youth League and my personal handler, had insisted. To break the deadlock, W turned over to Zhou Yang the whole ideological mess that I had confessed to under their prodding. For instance, by the end of their "straightening out," I had owned that Hyde Park was not a bad idea after all. At that Zhou Yang put his foot down—"Give him the label!"

Three days after the confirmation of my label, I went and had a photograph taken. With a jacket thrown over my shoulders, I looked relaxed, cool. I had never looked so good in a photograph before. There had been only one sleepless night when I was seized with anxiety, getting up frequently in the middle of the night.

As for W, it seemed that he was on a roller coaster and could not stop. After getting me labeled, he nailed one of his own assistants as the next target. But by then the Beijing Youth League Committee had so far exceeded their quota (for labeling *rightists*) that the wretch escaped with expulsion from the Party without getting the label.

Later, W had twice tried to kill himself with overdoses of sleeping pills. He claimed that they were accidents, but he eventually died at the beginning of the Cultural Revolution. His wife, already divorced from him by then, was very attractive. It was rumored that he was suffering from the secret agony that he could not perform.

When the ten-year Cultural Revolution was over, the Beijing Youth League Committee held memorial meetings for all the comrades who had died as victims of the Cultural Revolution, more about which later. I attended the memorial for W. I was commemorating him, and bidding farewell to an age that is gone for good.

During the period as I waited for the decision on my case, I read a lot. I was terribly attracted to Dickens' A *Tale of Two Cities*. His opening paragraph "It was the best of times, it was the worst of times . . ." struck a chord in me. I realized that life is uncertain, that there is a very thin line between good fortune and disaster. But I also believed that the good would always prevail, and that it was essential to stick it out and never lose confidence. *A Tale of Two Cities* supported me throughout those days as I waited for my verdict, though my own predicament had no relation to events described in the novel. Besides, we also believed that in the great unprecedented cause of building a spanking new China, it was perfectly legitimate to sacrifice petty little scribblers like me on the altar of the revolution.

I wrote to Ruifang, who was still in college in Taiyuan, describing in detail all my ideological transgressions and the validity of the criticism heaped on me. Surprisingly, she was not at all impressed, although she too had read Dickens. At her college, she had firmly resisted all criticisms heaped on her in a pernicious effort to cap her with the "five airs" label (a lesser evil than *rightist*), namely, "official airs," "arrogant airs," "fussy airs," "cavalier airs," and "plaintive airs." Rather than accept the labels, Ruifang chose to break with the leadership and left college outright.

Now it is clear as day that if I had not lost myself in those fanciful self-reproaches and piled guilt on myself, if I had not racked my brain to cook up all these ideological transgressions, if I had not owned up to everything that I was accused of, there would have been nothing to hang me with. In the last analysis, the overall situation at the time did affect many people's fate. But as far as Wang Meng was concerned, the last stone to damn Wang Meng was thrown by none other than the man himself. Wang Meng had capped the *rightist* label on Wang Meng.

Chapter 16

Life as a Rightist in Sanyu Village

I had never really understood the saying "a new life after being pushed to death's door" until I experienced it myself.

My father, for one, had been scared out of his wits over the situation that I found myself in. He himself had gone to the Yan'an liberated area as early as 1946, but due to his own lackadaisical attitude, he had come back uncommitted to the cause. Furthermore, during the anti-Hu Feng campaign in 1955 he had been exposed as a former member of the "national congress" under the Japanese occupation during the period when he was serving as president of Qingdao Teacher's College. At the time he had been racked by fear, expecting a death sentence at the hands of the people, and now he totally supported the sentence laid on me, encouraging me to turn my mind to manual labor, even quoting the Soviet scientist Pavlov who, according to him, preferred using his hands to using his brains.

When I had imagined myself a rising young star, I did harbor certain "unhealthy" sentiments; my fellow writers often detected in me "shadows of a gentle melancholy." But after my downfall in 1958, all that I had left were healthy sentiments. It struck me that during healthy, i.e., normal, times, you and I can safely indulge in some "unhealthy" sentiments, but during unhealthy times, you cannot afford to be anything but perfectly "healthy."

In late 1957, as I waited for my sentence to be handed down, I was assigned to work at the building site of the Youth Center. Bricks, each weighing 18 *jin*, were torn down from the ancient city walls and being used for building the Youth Center. We had to move them to the building site relying purely on muscle power. My record was moving twelve such bricks with my partner in one trip. I also gritted my teeth and carried huge pails of water, or cement, or sand, balanced on the two ends of a shoulder pole. Later, I learned to "change shoulders," shifting the pole from one shoulder to another, and my new skill allowed me to carry even heavier loads. At the building site, I scooped cement with a huge dipper and held it up to the mason. Gleefully I swung the dipper up and down, as if it were a toy. I regretted that politics had caught up with me at a tender age and deprived me of my childhood. And now, I was making up for my lost childhood. We didn't have to work during the heavy rains of summer. I went to see the Spanish film "Death of a Cyclist" with Ruifang, who was home for the summer holidays, We squeezed onto a bus in the pelting rain and missed the beginning of the film, but I was happy to be there. When we came out of the cinema, it was still raining hard, and that made me happy too.

I love life, I enjoy living. It is how I am, I cannot change myself.

On August 1, 1957, I left the Youth Center building site in the city and was assigned to a little village in the Mentougou suburbs west of Beijing. The village, renamed Sangyu Agricultural Production Team, was part of the Junxiang Production Brigade, under Zhaitang Commune.

With a few belongings strapped to my back, I got off the train at Yanchi station and started out on the 36 *li* trek to Sangyu Village. On the hilly path I saw workmen breaking stones and heard the sound of metal striking against stone mingled with the sound of water roaring in the distance. As I trudged on, the scene opened in front of me, cliffs lined up sternly one after another stretching into the distance; a mountain stream wound on relentlessly at my feet. There was no hint of tenderness, no room for melancholy sighs. I was awestruck by the untamed beauty of the scene.

Leaving Sangyu Village, I walked on to Zhaitang Commune, seat of the township, to deal with some administrative procedures. The rightists from Peking University were also located there. When misfortune strikes en masse, somehow it becomes more bearable—things happen, it is not just me.

Reform through labor is no cup of tea. This was hilly country, and I had to strap a carrier to my back and learn to move forward in a stooping position. I had carried a maximum of 150 *jin* of newly harvested corn on my back using an extra large carrier, my record. I was also quite handy with a shovel. But I was not nimble enough for farm work, which required skills such as weeding or leveling the soil. All in all, I was still my old happy-go-lucky self and mixed with the peasants as if I belonged. Obviously my cheerfulness and slapdash manners were offensive in some people's eyes. I had yet to acquire the hangdog look of the political outcast and had to watch myself every step of the way.

The fact is, the full meaning of my *rightist* label was only sinking in by stages. Publication of my novel *Long Live Youth,* already set in type, was summarily canceled. The participants in the "young people writing" convention in Beijng were effectively wiped out in the *anti-rightist* movement.

In the past, whether it was the Land Reform or the three-*antis* campaign, the campaign against counterrevolutionaries or even the Yan'an Rectification Movement of the earlier 1940s, there had been a pattern wherein the campaigns would invariably fizzle out, when policies would be implemented, ultra-extremist measures reined in, and cases closed with leniency, sometimes even ending with an apology to the injured party. I and many of my fellow rightists had wishfully assumed that the current *anti-rightist* campaign would follow such a pattern. I actually felt myself on the verge of tears at the very thought of such a happy outcome.

But no, contrary to the established pattern, the current *anti-rightist* campaign was followed by more and more ultra-extremist moves targeting more *rightists,* and issuing more calls for rigid combativeness. Obviously this was because the current *anti-rightist* campaign was of all campaigns the most elusive, the most abstract, the most controversial, with literally not one case specifically nailed down, but all wallowing in bubbly accusations, bogged down in wispy evidence based on deduction and rhetoric. Under such circumstances, if you so much as let one *rightist* off the hook, not to mention a handful, it is bound to lead to the dissolution of the whole campaign.

I was worried about Ruifang. We had been married barely a year when I was hustled away to the countryside. Her own situation at the time was not a bed of roses either. Given the circumstances, we wrote to each other daily, sometimes even twice on the same day. I was always full of good news; to judge by my letters, one would think I was enjoying the pastoral scenes. Ruifang and I had kept all those letters through the years, right up to the beginning of the Cultural Revolution, when we consigned them to flames.

At Sangyu we were granted a four-day break every two months. After my first holiday spent in Beijing, Ruifang decided to see me all the way to Yanchi, my last train stop. But all the cheap hard seats on the train heading for Yanchi had been taken. So we just went and bought two expensive soft seats on the sly, making sure we were not observed. It was like a surreptitious honeymoon.

I also remember the time when I was still back at the Beijing Youth League Committee when the criticism directed at me was at its height, I had sneaked off to the restaurant affiliated with the European-American Returned Scholars Association and had a Western-style meal, a luxury at the time. Actually, I was not self-indulgent, I was receptive of criticism. But I also believed that everything would turn out for the best, and that meanwhile I must take care of myself and keep up my zest for life.

My first child, Wang Shan, a son, was born on October 15, 1958. I did not see him until he was already three months old. It was during the Great Leap Forward, and we were all busy taking in the harvest and engaged in deep plowing according to orders from above, and thus our break was put off.

Once back home, I held my son and sang to him. I sang the theme song from the film *The Case of Xu Qiuying* (a case of wrongful indictment), and I sang the Northeast folk song "Dropping the Ring," and little Wang Shan babbled along after me. Soon, however, those two songs were banned. By then it had somehow evolved into a pattern: if there was something that people enjoyed, predictably it was bound to be disapproved of by the powers that be.

In the twenty plus years of my life so far, I had never been to a place like Sangyu Village. The natives claim that they were originally from neighboring Shanxi Province and spoke in a peculiar local accent with their own terminology. For instance, they referred to tiredness as being "over extended," and sickness as being "out of sorts." In the village, your door opens to face the mountain, with its terraced fields dotted with walnut and date trees and peach and pear trees in bloom. As you pick your way along the mountain path, butterflies flit among the wild flowers under your feet. The scene shifts and changes as you move on. Caves and cliffs leap out at every new turn; mountain streams and waterfalls surprise you at each new ascent, with tiny patches of fields ingeniously carved out between the rocks. Once you're at the top, the view spreads beneath your feet like a vast canvas, dotted with villages and framed by the highway where vehicles of all kinds speed by like lightning flashes. It was a wondrous spectacle. By a stroke of fortune I, Wang Meng, young and raw and vulnerable and sensitive, was fated to enjoy the beauty of this place, to work here, to be tempered here, and to grow here. This was how I truly felt about being in Sangyu, I was elated. But neither did I have any other choice.

This was 1958, and we were caught up in the Great Leap Forward, unprecedented in human history. Some of the fancy new practices of the Leap involved enriching the soil with cooking oil for corn planting while people went without; eating free at the communal kitchen; getting up at 3:00 am to harvest sweet potatoes and turnips, piling them into hastily dug underground storage caverns, only to see them rot; plowing so deep that the raw new soil caused a drop in the harvest; every man woman and child being made to write poetry; launching a literacy program that would eliminate illiteracy nationwide in three months . . .

On the ideological front, Chairman Mao published his article "Recommending a Rural Cooperative" in April of that same year, affirming the fast developing situation, hailing the rise of a new political consciousness, and predicting the collapse of the decadent old ideology. In the same article, Mao warned that representatives of the exploiting classes must be in step with the times, but that if some of them prefered to meet their maker with their old ideology set in stone, it would not make a dent in the glowing picture of the country as a whole.

Mao's article awed us with its breadth and scope. We *rightists* encouraged each other not to let our rightist ideology become set in stone. In response to Mao's famous saying that *All Reactionaries Are Paper Tigers,* one of the wiseguys among us said that we may be Reactionaries, but we certainly do not qualify as Paper Tigers—at best we were Paper

Rats. And to paraphrase Mao's new metaphor, the same individual added that our rotten ideology was not worthy of being set in stone; at best it could be compared to soggy corn porridge—which is what we were surviving on at the time. Moreover, it was also the established practice at the time to assess your own ideological standing by the standards of "upstream," "midstream," and "downstream." Instead of owning up to being "downstream" as befit our pariah status, we playfully proclaimed ourselves "lowdown" creatures. In the same vein we would refer to the *rightists* who dropped dead while working as "no more than soiling a piece of ground." As to the fateful moment when we were formally labeled, we would refer to it as finally "settling down." One would think that such joking would get us a new round of reprimands, but no, nothing happened; even the prim and proper leftist comrades were amused. Besides, one could argue that throwing mud at oneself shows a healthy sense of repentance, and therefore was commendable.

Come summer, the papers were raving about the superfluity of grain, so much so that the idea was bandied about to cultivate one third of the land for grain, one third to raise flowers, and one third to lie fallow. But come winter, we only had two meals of thin porridge per day. We filled ourselves with soupy porridge until our tummies were bursting and all our internal organs squeezed out of place, but it only served to make us pass water—we were still hungry. Our feces were merely a few wisps of corn skin which would float away with the wind, leaving the ground spotlessly clean. We were sick all the time, it was diarrhea one day, a high temperature the next, or coughing non-stop. The township boasted one doctor of Chinese medicine. He was lame and his wife, who doubled as his assistant, was a deaf-mute. Between the two of them, they managed to keep us alive.

I still treasure my time at Sangyu. I felt perfectly at home with nature, and I felt myself at one with the peasants. I was elated by the vastness of nature, and was happy to lose myself in its untamed beauty. I discovered new insights and new knowledge and experienced new feelings. I was tickled by the peasants' pronouncements on wine. To them, grape wine was "dishwater," beer was "horse piss," and only hard liquor was worthy of its name. To them the greatness of the city of Beijing lay in its manufacture of manure. They pointed out that the rich were concentrated in the east district, and thus the manure there fetched a higher price than human waste from other parts of the city. Li San, who led a group of peasants to collect manure for their communal fields, used to be a guerrilla leader in the old days of the civil war. Now he would say in all seriousness that the more dirty and smelly the work, the more reason to make a neat job of it.

I will never forget the scene of peasants giving up their precious jars of pickles (which they rely on for the winter) to the communal kitchen during the height of the people's commune movement. And the sight of a sprig of walnut stuck to every door at the onset of fall. I feel so blessed to have been a part of this extraordinary slice of life.

Chapter 17

From Sanyu to Yidanshi to Sanle—the Last Phase

During the spring of 1959, all the office staff from the Beijing Youth League and members of the Beijing Youth League Training Center, who were also in Sanyu for a stint of manual labor, were recalled to their various work units. We *rightists* were removed to a new locality—Yidanshi Valley—to continue our ideological straightening-out. Here the mountains were steeper, the patches of fields were narrower, and many remote fields were left to lie fallow.

During the Great Leap Forward of the previous year, 1958, the Beijng Party Committee, the Beijing Youth League Committee, and the *Beijing Daily* had jointly invested in Yidanshi Valley for forestation, and fruit orchards and farming for agricultural produce in order to supplement the diet of their own staff, leaving a certain Comrade Wang permanently in charge. The office staff back in Beijng was divided into six groups, which took turns coming down to work for one-or-two-month stints. We *rightists* in Group Eight, and folks with dubious pasts ("historical" counterrevolutionaries) in Group Seven were the permanent labor force in Yidanshi Valley.

In this new environment, I came across more varieties of *rightists.* Curiously, I found that a considerable number of these people had been labeled not for *rightist* deviation, but for being ultra-left! For instance, a young bureau-level officer at the Disciplinary Inspection Committee, a rising star, took it into his head to hand in his personal diary and his correspondence with his brother. The result: both he and his brother got the *rightist* label. Another example: a Youth League cadre, in charge of discipline and inspection, got the bright idea to make a rousing speech on July 1, 1958, celebrating the birthday of the Party, by which time the anti-*rightist* campaign had already petered out. The fellow eulogized the Yan'an tradition of high thinking and plain living, and deplored the current practice of some leading cadres who changed spouses like the proverbial Chen Shimei,[1] some of whom had even degenerated into *rightists!* Yeh? Being so high-minded, he got the *rightist* cap himself.

During the "Open Your Heart to the Party" phase in the aftermath of the *anti-rightist* campaign, a doddering old fellow who was hard of hearing "confessed" all and more, reviling himself as lower than a dog. The result, he was ushered into the *rightist* camp. Then there was that young lady with literary aspirations who had never published a word—she handed in her rejected manuscripts to the Party, and presto, she got the *rightist* cap in lieu of publication. Then there were two fellows who had been coarse and quarrelsome and foul-mouthed, a pain in the neck; they each got the *rightist* cap as a cure. One curious specimen was a barber, who had modestly confessed that he was not educated and not "qualified" to be a *rightist*; he had merely complained against the obligatory sale of grain at government fixed prices and got himself the unique title of being an "anti-socialist element." Thanks to his free haircuts, we folks in Group Eight were always presentable.

There were two leaders for our Group. Director Wang usually fell asleep and snored loudly at meetings, so the two leaders jointly presided over our "criticize and denounce" meetings, usually held in the dead of night. Once, the well-known cartoonist for *Beijing Daily*, Li Binsheng, was "criticized" to within an inch of his life, and fainted away. These noisy midnight denunciations in Group Eight became such a general nuisance that the other regular cadres working on short shifts intervened, and thus the midnight theatrics were brought to a stop.

To be fair, the disturbance should not be totally blamed on the two leaders: we the masses of *rightists* were so acclimated to the foul language and abuses piled on us that we caught on and used it on each other in

1. Character in Beijing opera who discarded his wife and children after he came in first at the imperial examination.

fits of sadistic frenzy, acting according to the principle "Do unto others what you do not want done unto to you!" What is more, one of the two leaders, in a literary mood, ordered me to write a stage play reflecting the reform of rightists, saying that it would be a contribution to the international communist movement! I knew it was a preposterous idea, but I still had to spend many sleepless nights going through the motions. Compared to attempts at the dramatic, our singing was more successful. There was a music teacher among us who directed us in singing popular songs with the words changed to fit our situation, such as: "Socialism is good, is good. Rightists cannot harm it even if they could . . ." The lyrics had been reworded by our fellow *rightist* Zhang Yongjing, who later became head of the Beijing Broadcasting Bureau.

Of course the main topic of our reform was to own up to our guilt. The logic ran thus: only by admitting that you had tried to oppose the Party can you prove that you have reformed yourself and do not oppose the Party anymore. Which means to say that if you refuse to play by the rules, that in itself would confirm that you are still opposing the Party. It is a perfect Catch-22 situation, wherein you had either opposed the Party in the past, or you are opposing the Party right now.

Here I need to remember Xu Baolun, my senior by a couple of years. Xu used to be the Party Secretary of the underground communist cell at the Hebei Senior High to which I had been admitted. Later on, Xu was transferred to the Research Group at the Beijing Party Committee. The move suited him, as he was always interested in theory, and he had actually published in *People's Daily*. Somehow I also remember him as not having a happy family life, and that he had a quick temper. Xu was in the forestation group when we met at Yidanshi. He told me that he had thought up a term—"Stalinism"—as a generalization for Stalin's policies and practices, and for that he was given the *rightist* cap. Xu was blessed with foresight, a cut above the others. I last met him before our two-week break and had even borrowed a couple of *yuan* from him, as I did not have enough cash for the trip back to town. When we returned from our bi-weekly break, Xu was missing. I asked around and learned that he had hanged himself in the library on the sixth floor of the Beijing Party Committee building. How could he have done that?! I suspected that apart from political pressure, his difficult family must have had something to do with it. Looking back at the many subsequent campaigns, I know for certain that the victims must have suffered a double agony—after the struggle sessions at work, he or she had to face a new round of torture at home. Going back to the death of Xu Baolun, I remembered that I still owed him a few yuan. I returned the money to his father, who had come down to wrap up his affairs. But I could not shake off the shock and the pity of his death.

The writer Cong Weixi was also among us. He had actually sought me out to discuss issues in literary composition. I felt that he was so out of touch, just looking for trouble and yet so deadly serious. Later it transpired that Cong Weixi and several others from *Beijing Daily* were put behind bars for surreptitiously reading the Party Program of the Yugoslavian Communist Party. What could I say to that?

All I could do was to take care not to worsen my own situation, especially now that we were supposed to be entering the stage of communism and expected to live in "communes," where, according to Mayakovsky,"everything I have / is yours / except / my toothbrush." I must not do anything rash, must not take any risks, I still had confidence in the revolution and the Party, had confidence in this great age and in our leader Chairman Mao. I still believed that a hand had been stretched out to protect me and that a better future was in store for me and for my country.

May I of 1961 was a regular holiday; we were forbidden to return to town, and we knew the reason why. As I was reading in my dorm, I heard the familiar tap tap of a woman's footsteps. It was Ruifang, nicely dressed and wearing the fancy semi-high heeled shoes that I had bought her for our wedding. She appeared to be in good spirits and brought a box of cookies with her. I don't know how she made her way to where I was. I was so moved. I could not utter a word and could not control my tears. "This is not the place for her"—that was my first reaction, coward that I was. I pulled her aside and warned her not to be too familiar with the other *rightists.* To this day I am ashamed of my own timidity. Luckily Ruifang's surprise visit was not brought up as a problem at our study meeting.

In the fall of 1961, obviously due to the concern of Yang Shu, I was finally divested of my *rightist* label and "returned to the ranks of the people," so to speak. Following this, in the winter of 1961, the situation was relaxed, the tension of struggle loosened up. Members of the educated elite and broad-minded cadres could hardly believe their eyes; they began to dream of a time when they would eventually be allowed to to get some work done.

In the spring of 1962, I was still working in the fields in Sanle, when a letter was delivered to me, a letter from People's Literature Publishing House, soliciting manuscripts. Besides which, a member of the editorial staff, Ms. Zhang Mulan, wife of the critic Xu Juemin,[2] had asked to meet me in person. I could tell that the letter had been instigated by Wei Junyi, at the time general editor of the People's Literature Publishing House, and wife of Yang Shu.

I must add here that throughout a life of vissicitudes, apart from the support of my wife, there was always a number of "noble women" [borrowing from Hardy's "A Group of Noble Dames"] to extend a helping. The letter from People's Literature Publishing House prodded the Beijing Youth League Committee to seriously consider our situation and where to place us: the remaining handful of ex-*rightists*. The first thing the authorities did was to move us back to Beijing and send us as a group to the countryside in Yanqing and Fanshan counties to investigate the general condition of the youth down there, including their lives, education, marital situation, recreation, and so on.

After the summer holidays, in September of 1962· I was assigned to Beijing Teacher's College (now Capital Normal University). And thus, my four years of reform through manual labor came to an end. Thinking back, it had been a lot of thunder and lightning but not much rain, what we call a snake's tail tagged to a tiger's head—it seemed to be the general drift of all things under heaven, from political campaigns to creative writing.

Take our batch of *rightists,* for example. After all the talk about reform and turning inside out, after all those thunderous denunciations and so on, what did it amount to? Doing some farm work, fiddling with vegetables and what not, holding stormy meetings with a lot of

2. Xu Juemin, 1921–2006, literary critic, Director of the Institute of Literature, CASS.

speechifying, signifying nothing . . .

As far as our country is concerned, however, it's another story. Having saddled itself with such an enormous population of unskilled agricultural workers at great expense (we *rightists* were still paid our salaries which, even reduced, were higher than that of real agricultural workers), no one had bothered to examine how such a luxury had affected the so-called intelligentsia, or bothered to research the political, social, economic, and financial consequences of this undertaking. A thoughtless, expensive mess, I would say.

Chapter 18

Life on Campus and the Beijing Writers' Congress

Back in Beijing, the relevant authorities were busy formulating the Ten Articles for Art and Literature, the Eight Articles for Literature and Art, and what not, in an effort to rein in the ultra-leftist extremism that had been rampant since the *anti-rightist* movement.

I sent a letter to Shao Quanling, secretary of the Party Core of the Chinese Writers' Union, requesting an interview, and enclosing a poem. Shao responded immediately, praising my poem written in the traditional style and telling me that he had advised *People's Literature* magazine to publish my work. He also told me that he would nominate me for membership in the Writer's Union. We chatted about this and that, but the most important thing that Shao brought up was his promotion of the "commonplace" character in fiction. He said that of course writers should be encouraged to hold up positive images of revolutionary heroes, but he argued that it was also commendable to portray ordinary, commonplace characters who undergo a change for the better. As he spoke, I recalled reading a story in *People's Literature* magazine about a country woman, "Sister Lai"—a vulgar, unscrupulous country woman who underwent a change of heart and ended up a decent person after all. Obviously, Shao was trying to do something to loosen up the tense atmosphere in art and literature.

There was a general air of relaxation. The film *Notes of the Flute* had come under attack, but Li Xiannian[1] watched it and saw no harm, and the filmmaker, Haimo, was let off the hook. At the same time, the *Literary Gazette* was conducting an open discussion of the film *Daji and Her Dad,* a sign that the ban on the film had been lifted. More amazing was the case of Liu Shaotang. I saw a short story of his published in *Beijing Literature* magazine—"Reporter for the *County Daily*"—its comic satire absolutely sidesplitting. I could not believe that Liu could produce something like that after what he had been through. Shao Yanxiang published a poem in *People's Literature* magazine, "Plowing by Night," and I could not help thinking of the time Shao had spent in the Great Northern Wilderness. To avoid raising suspicion in certain quarters, I did not get in touch with any of them.

As for my own work *Long Live Youth,* it was again taken out of storage and considered for publication by the China Youth Publishing House, though I did not dare get my hopes up. They invited Feng Mu,[2] editor of the *Literary Gazette,* to review the manuscript. Feng liked it—merely suggesting that some of the more fulsome descriptions of the influence of Soviet literature on that generation of Chinese youth be cut. Feng received me at his home. He was friendly and casual, without the airs of a leader, or the pedantry of a scholar.

Huang Qiuyun, who had escaped the *rightist* label by a hairs' breath, was also very kind to me. I used to visit at his home in Dayabao Alley and often found him sighing helplessly at the state of affairs of the literary scene. In October of that same year, he told me in confidence that there had been "a change of wind" again—he was referring to the Tenth Plenary Session of the Eighth Party Central Committee, which had hurled out the warning "Never Forget Class Struggle!"

During the sixties, Huang had shown me great kindness and concern, but try as he might, he was never able to help me get anything published.

After an initial loosening up, the ex-*rightists* who had managed to publish something or other were now silenced again. My elder sister told me in confidence: word had been handed down that the "unlabeled"

1. Li Xiannian, 1909–1992, ex-Minister of Finance in the 1960s, who became President of China in the mid-1980s.
2. Feng Mu, 1919–1995, literary critic, at one time Vice-President of the Writers' Union.

rightists were still *rightists* after all, and should be treated as such. She tried to dampen my spirits lest I forget my place and stick my neck out. As for the Eight or the Ten Articles for Art and Literature, they had disappeared without a trace, as if they had never been drafted.

Long Live Youth was again shelved. All my submissions for publication were returned.

Thus, without any document or explicit orders, people like me understood that they were expected to keep their heads down. It was in the air, and it seemed natural, like a change of season. Feng Mu, who had expressed approval of *Long Live Youth,* was now embarrassed when confronted with the question.

Despite the tense situation, I did manage to get something published after all.

Interestingly, the moment my two short stories ("Eyes" and "Rainy Night") were published, I heard from readers. One of the letters I got was from a student of philosophy at Peking University. He wrote to say that he was glad to see me in print again, and that to judge from these my latest works, I must have been down in the countryside for thought reform. That was the greatest reward that I could hope for. Writing is a curious business in China, you pay a very particular price, but your reward is extraordinary appreciation and concern.

In my case, I had been rocketed to instant fame and then put in cold storage. Another of my stories during this period was "Waiting"—a young man working in the village library, waiting for a girl to show up. For me, anything touching on the subject of love, even platonic love, will stir up my muse. Thinking back, the topic and the title were perfectly apt for my situation at the time. I must wait. Yes, I must keep on waiting.

Meanwhile my life had moved on to a college campus, the Chinese Department of the Beijing Teachers' College. The president was Yang Bozhen, at one time party secretary of the Middle School Committee of the Underground North China Bureau, and later secretary of the Beijing Youth League Committee. We were old acquaintances, and in hackneyed phraseology, he "understood" me. After all that had happened, it was impossible for me to stay within the Beijing Youth League system.

Never having been to college myself, it was sort of gratifying that I was now part of the faculty. I was an assistant to Wang Jingshan, the specialist on Lu Xun, at the time a senior lecturer. Professor Wang was cultured in manner and politically cautious. He had been a Party member, but had lost his membership during the *anti-rightist* campaign, though he had managed to avoid the label itself. Everything went well at the beginning, and I got along with the students. We went to Fragrant Mountain in the western suburbs for an outing; it took me back to my own student days. My job included tutoring on the language of Lu Xun, and I was appreciated. Some of the students would later turn out to be active figures in the literary world.

During my stint at the Teachers' College, I had been invited to the Beijing Writers' Conference, it was a friendly gesture on the part of the College and the Beijing authorities. The deputy secretary of the Beijing Party Committee, Deng Tuo,[3] gave the opening speech.

Although born with countrified looks, Deng carried himself with a scholarly air, like a member of the literati of ancient China. At the time, Deng Tuo's *Evening Talks in the Capital City* and *Notes on Three Family Village* (co-authored with Wu Han and Liao Mosha, and which was among the early targets of the Cultural Revolution) were about to be serialized in the pages of the *Beijing Daily*. Deng talked about combating revisionism and the negative influence of "modernism" among the young generation. The Conference was chaired by the chairman of the Beijing Federation of Art and Literature Circles, the veteran writer Lao She. Mao Dun gave the main speech, talking about "Life, Thinking, Craft." I suggested changing "craft" to "art." My suggestion was turned down by an older writer who referred to me as "the person whose name escapes me . . ." meaning "who do you think you are," effectively silencing me and putting me in my place.

As for the larger picture, the years 1961 and 1962 were the years of "adjustment" and "consolidation." The fact was, the situation was such that even a slight adjustment made a difference in our lives.

In 1963, the college assigned me a dorm room, bright and roomy. So far I had always lived in old houses in little alleys, with leaning walls and ill-fitting windows, places where rats scurried across the papered ceiling

3. Deng Tuo, 1912–1966, CCP veteran, poet and essayist, Deng had served as head of *People's Daily*.

at night. Now Ruifang and I were really happy with our two sunny rooms with clean walls and shiny glass windows. Finally we had a family life. Ruifang was teaching at the No.109 Middle School. They treated her very well, paying her the regular salary of a college graduate, despite her leaving school early on account of the *anti-rightist* campaign. We ate in the dining hall, but sometimes we surreptitiously did a little cooking over an electric cooker, getting a taste of real family life.

I had landed in a good place, I held a good job and I was happy. But I felt that I did not belong. I still clung to my dream of being a writer.

Chapter 19

Combating Revisionism in the Western Hills

In the fall of 1962, I received an invitation to take part in a two-week study session at one of the Eight Stops —the Lasting Peace Temple—in the Western Hills on the outskirts of Beijing; the subject of study—combating Soviet revisionism. Since the fall of 1959, apart from the fixation on the shortage of food, the straightened relationship between China and the Soviet Union had been the top concern on everybody's minds.

My own feelings were very torn. I had spent my own childhood and youth under Soviet influence. My youthful awakening, my spiritual yearnings, my political consciousness . . . had all been inspired by Soviet art and literature. Novels, films, songs, music, poetry, painting, and dance from the Soviet Union and the Republics had been food and drink to my soul. I was first aware of some uneasiness in PRC-Soviet relations shortly after the death of Stalin. But I did not let it bother me—as I saw it, a nation and a country that had produced such great literature and such great music should never be seen as an enemy, and could never be conquered. Following on this general uneasiness in the air was my own "downfall." Then as time went on the controversy between the PRC and the Soviet Union intensified, and the impact was considerable.

I knew for a fact that there was a link between this controversy and the anti-*rightist* campaign going on in China at the time. Certainly, some of the elderly *rightists* had been pro-American. A considerable number among the younger *rightists*, however, got the label on account of their pro-Soviet attitude. Whether pro-American or pro-Soviet, they were equally foolish and politically naïve. What's more, some *rightists* got the label for being *anti*-Soviet, which was an afterthought—coming at a time when these folks were just looking for trouble. As for myself, most of my "unhealthy" thoughts and moods had come from Soviet influence, my "original sin." And now, the *anti*-Soviet controversy involved the interests of our country and our nation—no laughing matter. I must sit up and deal with it seriously. After all, the Soviet Big Brother was not so great after all, as it had been touted in the early years; it had as many problems as China, if not more. In the long run, China had to grow out of its perceived deference to the Soviet Union. I personally think that, though never publicly avowed, Mao Zedong's two great tactical moves and contributions to the nation were first, to leave Hong Kong untouched in 1949, and second, to shake off our association with the socialist camp headed by the Soviet Union and go on to map out China's own path, including a relationship with the United States.

Of course I could not help being saddened by recent developments—the downfall of the former group of veteran leftist writers such as Ding Ling, Ai Qing, and Hu Feng. And now this current critique directed against the Soviet Union. Though I understood the reasons for it , I still could not help feeling sad. But this is no joking matter. I must sit up and study the documents. I must make a strong case against revisionism. I must stand firm and do what I am told and fight the good fight.

The Western Hills study session was actually very nicely planned. We read documents or conducted discussions in the morning sessions and watched Soviet revisionist movies in the afternoon, films such as *The Cranes Are Flying, A Sunny Day, Man and Beast, Lakeside,* and so on. We were also shown documentaries on the new direction in the art and literature of the Soviet Union, with captioned Western commentaries

Participants coming from the provinces were mainly leaders of the various local art and literature federations, editors of literary magazines, or heads of performing groups. There were three participants from Beijing: Professor Zhong Jingwen,[1] the artist Yin Shouzhu, and myself,

1. Zhong Jingwen, 1903–2002, scholar in social studies and folk studies, labeled a *rightist.*

all one-time *rightists.* I did not understand the thinking behind this arrangement.

The vice-president, doubling as secretary for the Party Core of the Federation of Art and Literature Circles, Comrade Liu Mingzhi, and vice presidents Tian Han[2] and Lao She paid us a visit in the Western Hills. They shared our meals and gave speeches, and it was all very jolly. Liu Mingzhi had been head of propaganda at the North China Bureau of the Communist Party underground network, and had presided over the critique of Xiao Jun.[3] Liu's face was totally devoid of expression as if he wore a mask, and I understand that his career seemed to have met with a setback after Liberation. Tian Han and Lao She, on the other hand, were bubbling with high spirits. Over dinner, the venerable Professor Zhong Jingwen said to Comrade Liu Mingzhi that he was determined to denounce Khrushshev, as it was the "bald pate" Khrushshev who had led him astray. I also hastened to add a few words of my own and expressed regret for "straying." Liu Mingzhi hastened to assure me that "You are still young . . ." and muttered that "Wang is very bright . . ." As for Tian Han, he announced that although a "bald pate" himself, he would still denounce the "bald pate" Khrushchev. His denunciation was comic but nonetheless firm, exuding a sense of confidence and belonging. The veteran writer Lao She spoke on anti-revisionism, saying that the Soviet Union is not to be relied on anymore, that the world is looking to China, to Chairman Mao, for direction. His speech was imbued with a sense of mission, a consciousness of being trusted, as well as an air of contentment.

I was bowled over by the veterans, Party members and non-members alike, talking confidently about the future of world communism. At the same time, I felt a sense of incongruity. But you have to admit that the Party is all-powerful: the minute it points in one direction, all will follow, no questions asked.

As for myself, I was all attention, lapping up every word. Ever since the anti-*rightist* campaign, I had it branded into my consciousness that

---

2. Tian Han, 1912–1968, dramatist, persecuted to death during the Cultural Revolution.
3. Xiao Jun, 1907–1988, prominent leftist writer from Northeast China, labeled a *rightist.*

nothing was more important than the Party, and that the Party was all-powerful to make or break anyone. There was no one to compare with Wang Meng in respecting and responding to the Party.

In the group critiques and denunciations of Soviet works of art and literature, I would delve deep into the writers' or artists' conception and seize on their lapses into pacifism, decadence, depression, essentialism as regards human nature, disappointment with the revolution, and so on, all conveyed through the language of artistic images. My fellow "students" would be bowled over by my analyses. As for myself, I believed that critiquing revisionism would be a good antidote against ideological lapses, and a form of ideological reform. An elder from one of the provinces gave me a pat on the back, so to speak, saying that I had talent and that I was sure to produce a masterpiece so long as I stuck to the right path.

I was grateful for his goodwill. But I was perplexed that people not in the business of writing were usually so cocksure about the right path for art and literature, so discerning as to where we writers went wrong, and so ready to offer a cure. On the other hand, how is it that we in the business of writing are so obtuse, such blockheads, such good-for-nothings, that we always stray from the right path, making trouble for the leadership? Is it comparable to what people say about the mountain, that being on the mountain you do not see the mountain, that you can only see it from a distance? Whatever it is, art and literature has a knack of misleading people in the business, making them lose all sense of north, south, east, west, not to mention the directions of "right" or "left."

Not long ago, the National Committee of the Federation of Literature and Art Circles had held an expanded meeting, and the recording of Premier Zhou Enlai's speech at the meeting was played for us during this particular study session. In the flow of his talk, Premier Zhou mentioned that Zhou Yang had translated *Anna Karenina* into Chinese (actually co-translated with Xie Sutai). Zhou Yang, who was present, hastened to mention that it was a mistake on his part. Zhou Enlai went on to say that the translation of the classics into Chinese should be accompanied by a foreword or afterword, directing the reader to treat the classics with proper understanding. Zhou Yang added that precisely because they were classics, the more reason to critique, since the classics could not avoid carrying poison within them —the more classical, the more lethal their negative influence. What a theory! Really scary! In the recording of the talk, Zhou Yang makes brief interruptions during Premier Zhou Enlai's talk, and in doing so mentions my name, saying that "Wang Meng got himself the *rightist* cap. Now the cap is removed. He is talented, we should help him."

The gist of Premier Zhou's talk was to prepare us for the upheaval of class struggle that was coming. He wanted us folks on the cultural front to be prepared, to stand the test, to be strengthened in the struggle, to grow in wisdom and class-consciousness, to overcome our weaknesses. As to the precise nature and form of the struggle, Premier Zhou was vague. He did not say anything precise. Perhaps he himself did not have a clear view of what was coming—all he knew was that something big was cooking. All he tried to convey was that he loved us and that we should be prepared. Premier Zhou Enlai was beloved in cultural circles. In the early forties when he was in Chongqing as the CCP representative during the Guomindang / Communist United Front, he had forged friendships with many leftist artists and writers.

The situation was changing by the day. *Long Live Youth* went through one checking after another. Apart from Feng Mu, who had given it the nod, a secretary of the Youth League National Committee joined in the censorship and pointed out that the novel had omitted to describe how the youth had allied themselves with workers and peasants. No one made a decision one way or another. The manuscript made its way to Shao Quanling's desk. Shao did not hide his admiration for the novel: the language, poetic sensibility, details and what not, but he demurred over giving the signal to go ahead with publication. He had scruples—there were no descriptions of educated youth aligning themselves with workers and peasants. In our country the appearance of a novel was a major event, he stated, and hinted—"how about you wait a bit . . . ? How about bring it out in some obscure corner?"

At the time, leaders at all levels knew that another storm was brewing, but no one knew when it would arrive, what form it would take, and what we people in literature and art circles should do to prepare for its landing. People talked about it as if it were a typhoon, or a tunnel to be taken, or a test to go through, or an earthquake. They were expecting the advent of a threat that they could not control, one which they could neither avoid nor escape from, and about which they had no clue and could not make any conjectures.

Chapter 20

Yearning for Life

Things would have been easy for me if it had just been a matter of survival. But I wanted to write, to publish. And there's the rub.

The writer in me was nipped in the bud when I had barely appeared on the scene. And now, the prospects of publishing *Long Live Youth* were nil. To date, I had five short stories and a couple of essays to my name, and I was now faced with a ban. The more absolute the ban, the more I wanted to publish. I was in a fever of anxiety. I was not myself at all. Getting all worked up like that could not change my circumstances, nor was it conducive to good writing. All it achieved was to make me even more restless in my teaching job.

For me, the significance of the study session in the Western Hills was not to make me aware of revisionism in the Soviet Union. For me, it was the starting point of my move to Xinjiang.

Leading figures from the various Federations of Literature and Art Circles in the provinces were in attendance at the Western Hills study session. As we chatted, they described the local scene in their own areas, all of which I found deeply attractive. I was firmly convinced that there was no future for me in a college job in Beijing. I was perfectly aware that in our country, literature was expected to concern itself with workers and peasants, especially with life in rural areas. Staying put in a college meant shutting myself off from real life, from society and from the living struggle going on around me. It meant cutting myself off from a writing career forever. And writing held such attractions for me. I yearned to dabble with language, to exercise my skill with words. I could not bear to stagnate on a college campus, I wanted to throw myself into the wider world.

I sounded out some of the leaders of literature and art circles from the provinces about the possibility of my moving to their area. Jiangxi, Gansu, and Xinjiang responded warmly. I felt most attracted to Xinjiang, it was so romantic to be in Xinjiang. By a lucky coincidence, the head of the Xinjiang Federation of Literature and Art Circles, Comrade Liu Xiaowu, was just back from a visit to the Soviet Union and stopped by at our study session on his way back to Xinjiang. The secretary-general of the Xinjiang Writers' Union, concurrently editor-in-chief of *Xinjiang Literature* magazine, Comrade Wang Gulin, was also present at the study session. The two men conferred and between them, made a decision on the spot. I was invited. So Xinjiang it would be.

Moving to Xinjiang was not just for my writing. Actually there was quite a distance to be covered between moving to Xinjiang and writing about Xinjiang, not to mention the political handicap that I would be working under. The move was dictated primarily by my yearning for life. I yearned for life as I yearned for writing, for me the two were inextricably tied together. I yearned for the variety of the world, for men and women, old and young. I yearned for the sun and the moon and the stars, for days sunny and days cloudy. I yearned for love and hatred, for success and failure, for joy and anger, for sadness. Just in my early twenties, how could I bear to be stagnating in a classroom? I yearned for the distant borders and an unfamiliar culture, for desolation and struggle, for Mother Earth, source of hardship and happiness. It was a big book, I was willing to pay any price to be able to open that book and read it through to the end.

I phoned Ruifang, and she agreed to move to Xinjiang; she said that she loved the songs and dances of Xinjiang! Songs and dances indeed! We really didn't know what we were doing, had no idea of the times we were living in.

Wei Junyi, my mentor at People's Publishing House, supported me in my decision, saying that in Xinjiang I could write on less controversial subject matter such as the national minorities, the natural beauties of the place, and various aspects of our great motherland. Besides, she said, I could modify my style, which has been leaning toward the fastidious. It was exactly what I had in mind too. I was not going to expend my muse on the Pagoda of the Winter Palace, or the lamps of the Western Gate of old Beijing. What I yearned for were the desert wilds, the snowcapped mountains and the frozen rivers, the Tianshan and Kunlun mountain ranges, the vast steppes, the camel herds, the aurorae borealis of the border regions. Or so I thought.

Huang Qiuyun, another veteran writer, sighed and advised me not to bring my family, so as not to cut off my exit route. But I thought otherwise. Only by taking my family with me, only by making a clean break could I remain steadfast in my resolve to make something of myself in Xinjiang. And if I failed, I would only have myself to blame.

Huang also offered to lend me money for the trip. But Wang Gulin, editor of *Xinjiang Literature* magazine and my future boss in Xinjiang, informed me that I was eligible for financial help for the move. I submitted an application and actually got 800 yuan, ten times my monthly salary! I must add that at the time, the party secretary of the Chinese Department who had to approve the stipend was no other than Mrs. Bi Ling, whose husband, Wu Xueqian, would later become Minister of Foreign Affairs. The head of personnel who handled the affair was the wife of the chairman of the All-China Workers' Union. I had actually been protected by a group of "noble dames"! This kind of support was a reminder that the human heart, whatever the circumstances, was always throbbing with kindness, and filled with decency and love. For this kind of gesture, I have never ceased to be grateful.

We were toasted everywhere. Professor Wang Jingshan of my department took us to Cuihualou Restaurant, Professor Shi Wuji, being from Hunan, took us to a Hunan restaurant. The scholar Zhong Jingwen, whose acquaintance I had made at the Western Hills study session, gave us a farewell banquet at his home. Zhong was Cantonese and on good terms with Huang Qiuyun, another Cantonese, who was also invited. The walls of Zhong's living room were hung with calligraphy scrolls. Huang read out loud the lines of a poem, which carried a whiff of emotional ambiguity. He murmured: "This is pure Zhao Huiwen, this is Zhao Huiwen to a T."

I looked up books on Xinjiang and devoured them voraciously, getting more and more excited over the coming move. I went to a Xinjiang restaurant way out of town to savor Xinjiang food, and was enraptured with the movie *Stranger from Icy Mountain,* set in Xinjiang, which featured exotic scenes set to local music.

Once the move was decided on, I made a formal application during the study session. Liu Zhiming, at the time head of the national Federation of Art and Literature Circles supported me, and the Chinese Writers' Union helped with the paper work, all which goes to prove that leaving for Xinjiang was a move in the right direction.

Ruifang and I were very excited over the move. I went to the dentist; I bought a silk-lined cotton jacket. Ruifang bought a woolen coat and woolen pants; she had her picture taken with her mother and sister.

One day in late December of 1963, having sold what we could not carry and taking our five-year-old and three-year-old sons, we started out for Umruchi, capital of Xinjiang. At the time there was no direct train, we stopped in Xi'an, stayed at a local inn near the railway station, and did a tour of the ancient city before taking the Lanzhou/Xinjiang train for Umruchi, a four-day-three-night journey.

On our way we passed by sites of ancient cities, crossed mountains and rivers, and gazed at ancient passes famed throughout our history. I committed these sights to poetry and sent them back to my colleagues at Beijing Teacher's College. They wrote back saying that I was indeed fired by lofty ambitions.

Chapter 21

Xinjiang—Flaming Red Flags

On our arrival in Urumqi, comrades at the Xinjiang Federation of Literature and Art Circles gave us a warm welcome. I was assigned to the editorial staff of *Xinjiang Literature* magazine. It was the first time that I actually worked as member of staff at a literary work unit. Our little family was first settled in the South Gate area, close to the local theaters and movie houses. Soon after arriving, I was able to start attending many performances, and that made me happy.

What first hit me among the sights and sounds of Urumqi were the various national minority songs resounding from loudspeakers at the train station and elsewhere. And then there was the unique architecture: the South Gate Bank built by Sheng Shicai[1] in his time, the People's Theater built by the Soviets in the Tashkent-style of architecture, the mosque outside the South Gate. There were huge shop signs in Uighur written from right to left. There were the meetings where speeches were translated back and forth between Uighur and Mandarin. There was the Russian cleaning lady in the building of the Xinjiang Federation of Literature and Art Circles. There were the houses, each with its own indispensable mound of coal. Then there was the temperature, dropping to 20 below, 30 below, sometimes 40 degrees below. Here reigns the god of ice and snow; here blooms the flower of fire. In winter, a fire roars away in every stove, making each home sound like a train engine. The

1. Sheng Shicai, 1895–1970, early military leader in Xinjiang.

Uighurs have a saying: "Fire is the flower of winter!" How blessed is a people with such wisdom and such a perfect form of expression. Filled with ardor I embrace the Uighur people.

Although a northerner, to me the cold in Xinjiang was still staggering. Using the public toilet or going to fetch water at the shared tap invariably involved struggling up an ice mound. Walking out in the open meant slipping and sliding over layers of snow and ice and a topping of dirty coal dust. In Urumqi, good quality coal is used for heating homes as well as for industrial purposes. A thick pall of black smoke overhangs the city. People here say that even the sparrows are black with coal dust. Bicycles leave a deep rut in the blanket of ice and snow over the street, and trap the front wheel of the bicycle following behind. My sons, Wang Shan and Wang Shi, had a good time roller-skating.

Indoors, homes are cozily heated and it feels like spring. Heating comes from a wall of beaten clay, while the cooking stove is laid with bricks. An iron-plated baking oven, a clay hot water container, a roaring fire in the stove, and inch-thick ice patterns clinging to the kitchen windows make up the average Xinjiang home scene. I now understand why Eskimos live in dwellings built of ice—the ice never melts and the dwellings are thereby kept warm. These are what I could never figure out from my primary school textbook but could easily understand once I was in Xinjiang.

At the time, the city of Urumqi had a flair of its own. Bright orange-colored high-rise buildings could stand comparison to traditional Dutch architecture for its flaming beauty. People mostly live in one-story houses topped with adobe or tin roofs. The sound of Xinjiang songs and music fill the air, giving the city a particular charm. Here people use the kilo system; to buy a *jin* of meat, you say you want 500 grams. Some articles are indispensable to the Uighur nationality: musical instruments, colorful caps, leather boots, copper drinking pots, carpets and *moherka* tobacco—I now realized that here is the source of the *moherka* tobacco mentioned in Soviet fiction and in the long poem *Vassili Tsorkin*. I still remember a line from the latter which runs:

The moherka tobacco of the soldier
is like the soldier's wife

bitter and spicy and fierce
filling his eyes with tears
something that he could not do without.

A few days after our arrival, I paid a call on Comrade Niu Qiyi, deputy head of the Secretariat of the Central Committee of the CCP of the Xinjiang Uighur Autonomous Region. Here I must bring the narrative back to Comrade Zhang Jinlin, secretary of the Beijing Youth League. The fact is, back then when Zhang heard of my decision to go to Xinjiang, he came to see me at my home. He not only came to say goodbye, but gave me a letter to take to his friend Comrade Niu Qiyi, who had been secretary of the Xinjiang Youth League, and with whom he had traveled abroad. In his letter, Zhang recommended me to Niu's attention, saying that I should report to him on arrival and he hoped that he, Niu, would look after me, and so on.

When we met, Comrade Niu suggested that I go and take a look at Turpan in south Xinjiang; the leadership at the magazine *Xinjiang Literature* was accommodating, and I was sent off on a business trip to Turpan, actually to see the sights.

Every scene, every person that I met in Turpan excited my curiousity. I saw large single-room houses built of beaten earth capped with rounded roofs, a particular structure which kept warm in winter and cool in summer. I saw open-air houses of beaten clay, used for hanging grapevines to dry. I saw stands for hanging grapevines running several hundred meters long. I saw the kariz wells dug for irrigation purposes. I visited a geological group. I called on the model worker Miss Wu Mingzhu, a specialist on the cultivation of grapes, and watched a TV program about her achievements. I send Miss Wu my deepest respects. I enjoy the sound of Uighur speech, which is like listening to a symphony. I enjoy *naan* baked with corn, as well as that baked with sorghum. I walked miles and miles to visit the site of the Tarrng waterworks project still under construction, and spent time with the farmers-turned-workers, sharing their meals and joining in their dances. And then, starting off from the work site, I followed the railway track and walked for six hours, having only to worry about prowling wolves. I walked through the night and arrived at the Peach Railway Station in the wee hours. The station had only seen two arrivals in three months, and the station-master, a native of Beijing, was glad to see me. He offered me cigarettes and a bowl of noodles in chicken soup topped with an egg. Everything that I had seen so far in Xinjiang seemed like a dream.

On my return, I published an article, "Spring in Turfan." The editor of *Xinjiang Literarure,* Comrade Wang Gulin, it goes without saying, could not approve my manuscript before he had generously applied his red pencil to it. Still, I was happy. I had been right to come to Xinjiang!

In June of 1964, I settled in at the Red Flag Commune, a commune which was expected to be a "standard bearer." The first party secretary of the Autonomous Region, Wang Enmao,[2] laid down three standards to be met by the Commune:

threefold abundance:
abundance of rice,
abundance of cotton,
abundance of livestock,
fivefold excellence:
excellent paddies,
excellent roads,
excellent forest belts,
excellent waterworks,
excellent residential centers,
and one outstanding:
referring to the members of the Commune as being outstanding people.

Xinjiang has an abundance of arable land where large-scale farming had been more or less casual, thus leaving space for a revision of the system, or [as Mao had said], "to draw beautiful pictures on a clean sheet of paper."

The Red Flag Commune was situated on dirt-poor land, where the people were simple and patient and pliable when it came to rules and orders. Shi Yutang, party secretary of the commune, was a harsh leader, running around nonstop from morning to night—checking the fields, giving orders at his office, never taking no for an answer. He was known

2. Wang Enmao, 1913–2001, veteran CCP general, the first general secretary of the Party Committee of the Xinjiang Uighur Autonomous Region.

to have ordered the local militia to tie up whoever had the temerity to challenge him. Quite a character, he was.

By Secretary Shi Yutang's orders, a commune member by the name of Abdumijit Awut was designated to be my personal assistant and teacher of Uighur. Abdumijit was staff at the local library. He sported a stylish mustache and wore a fanciful multi-colored *badam* cap. His mastery of Mandarin was limited, but matched with my native talent for guessing and deducing what he could not spell out, we got along swimmingly. The problem was that this character had a knack for disappearing—it was said that he was recently married, for the second time, and that his new wife was very attractive. Good enough excuse for the disappearing act. It only pushed me to deal directly with the native Uighurs, which was an asset for me, really.

In company with Abdumijit Awut, I visited the captain of the March 8 Brigade, Mahpurahan. This young woman, who had been sold as a child-bride in the old days, was now an outstanding member of the commune, and she had been invited to Beijing to review the parade during the October First celebrations. We also visited the secretary of another brigade, Kuwan, another notable figure. Kuwan would keep pounding on the table as he talked to us, introducing himself as Secretary Kuwan. He was big and tall and strong, his hands flailing about, his two feet planted on the ground like two boats stranded on shore, altogether like a giant in a fairy tale. The people here were so strong, so lovable. My leanings toward populism, nurtured since childhood, were now reawakened.

Being a standard bearer, the Red Flag Commune was often deluged by reporters from Urumqi. This made the place a hive of activity, with reporters writing, telephoning, and telegraphing.

Somehow, Commune Secretary Shi Yutang got wind of negative comments on his behavior made by some of the reporters. He called a meeting of all persons involved, blubbering and blustering, hectoring and lecturing. I was present and tried to lighten the atmosphere. On the spur of the moment I commented that this was a lot of fuss over a non-event, a much-ado-about nothing—words which brought down the house. Secretary Shi Yutang turned to me in fury and shouted me down, saying that I should get permission from *him* before I showed my face anywhere.

In a flash, I understood the implications of the terms "provincial," and "out yonder," and "local tyrants," and "on the spot practices". . . just as I understood the implication of the term "your own status." I did not respond to Secretary Shi, as I had already invited abuse on myself and did not want to aggravate the situation.

There is only one word which serves all purposes, and that is "endure." I had always disliked the word when I was younger but now I think it is the *fix-it-all* for any situation. Take for example what I had once witnessed in the Red Flag Commune. A peasant came to the commune to look up Secretary Shi Yutang. He had started out early and had walked dozens of *li,* arriving at Secretary Shi's office early in the morning—but Secretary Shi had already left. The man squatted down at Secretary Shi Yutang's doorstep all day from morning till midnight. I understand that the Uighurs usually bring their staple food, *naan,* with them when they travel. They would scoop up water from a canal and drink it down, sand and all. Then they would throw their dried *naan* upstream of the canal works and let it tumble down the waterfall. After three rounds, the *naan* would be nicely soaked and softened and would make a good meal. It is a lifestyle that harks back to ancient times, so innocent, so idyllic, something that modern writers would die for (sometimes not without histrionics). Yet when I questioned the man who had been waiting for Secretary Shi, he said that he had not eaten anything all day.

People sitting in an office in Beijing, even in the rural outskirts, not to mention those sitting in posh offices dealing with culture and education all their working lives, do not understand the situation in China. They are useless bookworms, heads in the clouds. This is something that I had learned from being in Xinjiang.

The cadres down here have certain pithy sayings which are worth mulling over for the likes of you and me. One saying goes, "What's the use of being *talented*? Look at the hordes doing hard labor in the Gobi Desert. They are all *talented! And so what?!*" Then there is another saying: "What's this about writers being hard to deal with? Writers? Send them to us down here. A mere section supervisor will reduce any number of them into docile little lambs . . ." And listen to this local cadre talking to a young fellow from the Xiwa Nationality: "Since you folks consume pork like the Hans, why bother setting up a separate national minority for the likes of you?" To him—as to Chairman Mao who had stated that despite our ancient hundred schools of thought there are basically only two: the proletarian and the bourgeois—likewise to this local cadre, there were only two nationalities, those who consume pork and those who don't. His is certainly a simple and forceful generalization. But isn't it scary when we think back to the price we had to pay for dealing with national affairs in simplified terms? We must face up to this barbarous reduction of everything to black and white. Further, we must understand it and even have a little sympathy. It can only be softened slowly through education and the widening of perspectives and the enforcement of the law.

Meanwhile, we must admit that despite harsh simplifications, some things do get done as we muddle along. During my stay at the Red Flag Commune at Maket, I wrote two pieces of reportage: "Flaming Red Flags" and "Mahpurahan," the latter an eulogy to the captain of the March 8 Brigade. I sent both pieces to my work unit, *Xinjiang Literature* magazine, and heard back from them in glowing terms.

Three months later, by the end of September of 1964, I set out for the return trip to Urumqi, getting a ride on the cart which was taking wheat to the capital. We set out at night, and when we got tired, we would "park" the cart on the roadside and crawl underneath for a catnap. I was thrilled by this way of traveling. Can you imagine going from the west side of Beijing to the east side in such a fashion? This trip was beyond the scope of my wildest imagination!

Like a sponge I soaked up the juicees of life in south Xinjiang. Beijing was left far behind. Once I was at an open-air film show in the Maket county center and a scene of Beijing showed up on the screen. I was struck by the thought: Beijing is so far away.

It is true, "Life is everywhere." To this day I do not know in what context Hu Feng had made this statement, and why he had been damned for it. But I say so because it is my personal conviction. Life is everywhere, an eternal source of joy and meaningfulness. I actually surprise myself: having experienced so many vicissitudes and now being thrown into such an alien environment, I was nevertheless able to mix intimately and feel at home and enjoy myself. Youth, kindness, ideals, determination, principles . . . these are the keys that can open every door to the human heart.

When I finally returned to Urmuqi, my piece of reportage "Flaming Red Flags" was already on press. But at the last minute, it was taken off. Word passed around within and outside of the Federation of Literature and Art Circles: "Wang Meng is finished. Publish his article? Don't you people have a sense of the times we are living in?"

The situation was getting more and more tense. Under fire were Shao Quanling's proposal about depicting "commonplace" characters and the proposal by Xia Yan[3] to "steer away from the beaten track." Tian Han's new play *Xie Yaohuan*, and some of Zhao Shuli's[4] stories which had purportedly described the Great Leap Forward were now perceived as something else not so benign. Some of the old targets, such as the films *Southern Scenes in a Northern Setting, Early Spring in February, Stage Sisters* and others were dragged out for a second round of condemnation. Not to mention such old targets as Ding Ling, Ai Qing, Xiao Jun et al.

Later, during the Cultural Revolution starting in 1966, this current round of criticism would be damned as a fake rectification in literature and art circles. But at the time, even the "fake" critique had been quite devastating, sending chills down one's spine.

About this time, a fierce outbreak of revolutionary fervor was unleashed throughout the land. "Mountains linked to mountains, seas merged with seas, workers of the world hand in hand . . ." made you believe that every man, woman, and child in China was ready to do or die for a new revolution. "The people's commune is good, the people's commune is surely good . . ." —it seems that the more you are out of words, the more you want to scream.

Concurrent with the rectification in art and literature and the outbreak of revolutionary extremism in the mid-sixties, another invention called the "Four Clean-ups" (also known as the "Socialist Education Movement") was going on in the countryside, justified on the premise that "two thirds of power in rural China was not in the hands of the

---

3. Xia Yan, 1900–1995, filmmaker, leading figure in literary and film circles, *The Lin Family Store* being one of his representative works. Xia had served as Vice-Minister of Culture.
4. Zhao Shuli, 1906–1970, mainly known as writer of folksy stories based on life in rural Shansi, persecuted to death during the Cultural Revolution, reinstated post-mortem.

Communist Party." Cadres and staff were being moved en masse to help conduct the "four clean-ups." In Urumqi, I was among those called up from the Xinjiang Federation of Literature and Art Circles and had taken part in some preparatory training. But a few days later, I was dropped from the project, as were many others. One artist had relatives abroad and was disqualified; one musician from a national minority group was excluded because a relative of his had defected.

I finally understood: I was not eligible to serve. It was a bigger blow than being labeled a *rightist*. In the latter case, I had been snared in a campaign. As we all know, campaigns come and campaigns go, sometimes even followed by reparations. The anti-*rightist* campaign was over and done with, and I have been "unlabeled" since 1961, yet I was still deprived of some of my rights as a citizen. It called to mind a saying which I once came across in a Soviet novel, which identified this kind of revolutionary extremism as *poisoning* people's lives. How had things come to such a pass?

All through the winter of 1964, I was completely idle. Now and then I would pick up a volume of Chinese history. I was shocked to find that our ancestors had gone through fewer times of peace than times of chaos. A period of chaos, which could endure through dozens or even hundreds of years meant the lifetime of several generations. Perhaps what I was going through was not personal; it may have been a repetition of history, the momentum of the years of chaos, a continuum of strife, a result of the struggle to maintain state power, a misguided stress on class struggle, a mistake from which we should have already learned the lesson.

I was depressed, but not despondent. I could wait. I read history. Great historical figures stride through history, having things their way, without concern for reality, without regard for people's livelihood, speaking of the people's pots and pans with utter contempt. On the other hand, it is a fact that historical figures do exercise great influence on people's lives . . .

As far as I was concerned, although life had been poisoned, I could still strive to make my life meaningful and happy. As for the past, it would not only turn into tender recollections but could provide food for thought that would not be otherwise available.

Chapter 22

"Go West, Young Man . . ."

By the end of the year 1964, I had finally heard from one of the leading figures of the Xinjiang Federation of Literature and Art Circles, Comrade Liu Xiaowu, whom I had previously met in the Western Hills. He began by saying that during my stay in Maket, I had quarreled with Shi Yutang, party secretary of the Red Flag Commune, in which case we had both been to blame. *Both*—that was actually a point in my favor. Then Comrade Liu went on to state that after consulting with Secretary Lin of the District CCCP, the leadership now wished me to go west to the countryside in Ili to be "tempered through manual labor" while at the same time doubling as deputy leader of a brigade under the commune. Thus I could continue to learn the language, delve deep into the life of the people, and ultimately take up my pen again and produce genuinely good writing. Note: not now, but *ultimately*. Comrade Liu Xiaowu added that I could bring my family if I so wished. As to the details, he said that Comrade Song Yanming of the Propaganda Department of the The Central Committee of the CCP over in Ili would take care of the move, and that since Song was at the moment in Beijing, why not wait till he returned and then the two of us could make our way to Ili together the following spring.

Idling away the last couple of months had been most dreary and I was happy over the new arrangement, especially the prospect of being in beautiful Ili. I understood that under the circumstances, it was the best that the leadership could do for me. I jumped at the chance and promptly accepted the offer. I also liked the newly concocted term "to be tempered through manual labor." The term "temper," as for steel, could be interpreted variously, thanks to the fluidity of the Chinese language.

Come April of the year 1965, I was told to get ready to depart. Leaving Urumqi for good involved many things. First, send back the elder whom we had brought over to help with housekeeping. Second, send the children back to Beijing. Third, get Ruifang transferred to Ili. Fourth, break up our household in Urumqi.

Obviously we had not moved far enough; we must keep moving, moving to the edge of the national territory. If there is no stability in the nation, where can ordinary people find peace?

There was a greater variety of minorities in the Ili area: Kazakh, Uighur, Han, Muslim, Mongolian, Usbek, Russian, Xiwa, and others. Compared to south Xinjiang, here in Ili there was more wine, more mutton, more honey and more keepers of bees and more singing. I saw more water-propelled grindmills, I saw more people planting trees, more people on rafts, more sheep and more shepherds, more fishermen and more people riding on horses instead of on donkeys. I arrived just in time to see young girls in colorful kerchiefs, hand in hand singing their way down the streets, celebrating a local festival. I felt in my bones that a new round of experiences was about to unfold for me.

Two days later, I arrived at my destination, the Red Flag (again Red Flag) Commune, located in Bayanday County, five *li* from Ghulja, chosen obviously out of concern that I would not be too distant from town.

The Uighurs of Ili come from two sources: In the distant past, the vast land of the west had been sparsely inhabited so the Qing imperial government laid out preferential policies to encourage migration, one of them being that a man could legally snatch a woman for his wife and settle there. Even to this day, in the northern parts of Ili which is mostly nomad, the wife would be seated in front of her man when the couple is riding together—the man wants to make sure that his wife does not bolt, seeing as she had been kidnapped. On the other hand, in the southern parts of Ili, the wife is always seated behind when a couple is riding together, to denote marital harmony and wifely submissiveness. The northerners of Ili were mostly nomads while the southern people were called Talanqi, a Mongolian word meaning growers of wheat.

Then there had also been a wave of immigration from south Xinjiang, since the Ili area was richer than the south. The population of Bayanday, where I was settled, was mostly made up of this last group.

After a few days getting to know the area, I was allotted to the First Team under the Second Brigade, and later was designated deputy head of said brigade. I was to board with commune member Abdrahman Nur. He was a short stocky fellow who had been dirt poor and could only afford to marry after the land reform. His wife, Haliqam, had been a widow who had one adopted daughter. Haliqam must have been very good looking when young, even now she had regular features and a good complexion. The couple lived in a small adobe house. The fact was, to avoid complications, Abdrahman had insisted on giving the bigger house to his wife's adopted daughter Setgul. The two houses, both of which Haliqam had inherited from her late husband, were connected through a yard. One could tell that this part of Ili must have been prosperous in the old days, seeing as how Haliqam's late husband, a "middle peasant," had owned such a piece of property.

There was another reason for assigning me to this household. Abdrahman had an adopted son, a Han from Gansu Province. The boy had been an orphan, but in the 1960s, when starvation was widespread and even orphanages were broken up and moved, the boy was circumcised, renamed Abdukerm, and adopted as heir of the Abdrahman household. Abdukerm was a good-looking pleasant little fellow and designated to be my interpreter.

There was a little 4 ft x 4 ft storage room in the house, furnished with a heated *kang*,[1] which in a pinch could accommodate two people, and it was my bedroom. What perplexed me about the little room was a triangular opening in the door. Soon the mystery of the Golden Triangle was unveiled: two swallows came through the opening to build their nest under the low-hanging roof. Twittering and fluttering in and out, the two little love birds managed to finish their nest by the end of the day. The neighbors were all excited. "Old Wang must be a good man," they declared, "other people have come and gone, and no birds came, but the moment Old Wang made his home here, the swallows followed . . ." Wang

1. Raised platform bed usually built of bricks or adobe, heated from within.

Meng is happy, Wang Meng is fulfilled, Wang Meng is determined to settle in the western borderlands among national minorities, determined to attain what many had never achieved (or never even tried)—to live among poor peasants, to share their food and work together side by side!

And thus I embraced a new world—the pretty town of Ghulja, the countryside in the environs of Yining County, the Uighur households on the banks of the Ili river, the adobe homesteads and the log dwellings, the walls of beaten clay . . .

Before the the Cultural Revolution broke out, I had taken part in the movement to *Learn from Dazhai*[2] and had been asked to help during the height of the *Four Clean-ups.* Moreover, this was a sensitive area near the Soviet border where masses of people had once crossed over and defected. I have never taken part in explorations on a desert, nor have I been shipwrecked at sea, nor ever came under enemy fire on the battlefield, but now I found myself in an entirely new world, and I made myself at home. I mastered one Uighur saying: "a boy's head needs be knocked about," meaning that a man must deal with things as they come, not get angry or cry like a woman. In a word, he must be a man.

The Uighurs know how to enjoy life. They usually build an extension to their house, a high platform the size of a room, covered with vines in the summer, where they spend most of the day drinking tea, chatting, and entertaining guests. They like the outdoors, calling it "swallowing fresh air." Abdrahman kept a cow, a donkey, a yearling, and a dog. His wife milked the cow twice a day. She would let the milk, about one kilo, simmer over a slow fire and skim it, using the sheet of cream for cooking or for making tea. Haliqam loved drinking tea with her friends under the canopied platform, rather like an open-air living room. There was a saying in Uighur which translates literally as "the *naan* is gone because of the tea . . ." The fact is, the Uighurs were in the habit of drinking tea while nibbling on *naan,* or, to put it another way, they were in the habit of nibbling on *naan* while drinking tea. Baking *naan* is one of women's most important tasks. They start by lighting a fire inside a huge clay container. When the fire inside subsides into fiery ashes, the women reach down

2. A model commune in Xiyang County of Shanxi Province, headed by model peasant Chen Yonggui.

and slap slabs of molded dough onto the sides of the container. The sides, having been heated up, start baking the underside of the dough while the embers at the bottom of the container bake the dough from the other side. Thus the *naan* is baked golden brown on both sides.

One memorable afternoon in May, I left "home" after lunch to work in the fields. I saw Haliqam with a group of friends drinking tea on the raised platform. After two hours, I returned for a break, and there they were, still drinking tea and chatting! Among the Uighurs, men's culinary delights are noodles or mutton or fried rice to go down with their drink; they do not consider *naan* real food. At home when dinner is ready, the men sit down to eat first; when something is left, the women finish it off. When nothing is left, no big deal, the women drink tea, nibbling *naan*. The biggest expense in the home is tea bricks, most of which are consumed by women. I tried the tea before it was mixed with cream and what not—it was so strong, like a Chinese medicinal herbal drink.

Once, I took part in road repair. Bus after bus passed us on the highway, some going from Ili to Urumqi, some going in the opposite direction. I could make out the outlines of passengers, city people, cadres, sitting in their seats as they roared by. I wondered what went on in their minds as they caught sight of me, spectacled and frail looking—an apparition? I myself had taken buses and trains in my time, and passing through rural areas had seen people working in the fields. They would look up from their work with fleeting interest and bend down again, unmoved. Now the roles were reversed.

Chapter 23

"Tempered through Manual Labor"

The leader of the Second Brigade of the Red Flag Commune, Mamut Oxur, had been a mere head of a Team under the Brigade. But he had distinguished himself in the movement to "Learn from Dazhai," got invited to Beijing and Dazhai and so on, and ended up being promoted to leader of the Brigade. He was a fine figure of a man, sporting a lively mustache, often chewing on a tobacco "snack" as he walked about on his various inspections of the fields or the canals. He was known to talk to himself, he was so absorbed in what he was doing. People admired him for his devotion to work.

I had arrived in the spring of 1965, and soon the days turned hot. But Brigade leader Mamut still walked about in his heavy winter jacket. It was said that he could not afford a new summer jacket. It was further said that his wife was a big spender and may have sold his summer clothes. It seemed as if the Uighur people took naturally to trade. They would buy a pair of boots, wear them for a month and then sell them. The Kazakhs around here often remark somewhat disparagingly on this tendency of the Uighurs to trade. There is a saying about the Uighurs that if a day goes by without making a deal, a man would sell the contents of his left pocket to his right pocket!

The People's Commune was operated on the "work-point" system. All the commune members would show up for work, and at the end of the day their work-points would be recorded. The problem was that at the end of the fiscal year, no matter how many work-points they'd accumulated, the commune members could not collect their payments in cash. For instance, if you had accumulated three thousand work-points and supposing each work-point was worth twenty *fen*, that amounts to six hundred yuan. Deduct from that sum the equivalent in cash of what you had been allotted by the commune—grain, meat, cash, etc., which amounted to two hundred yuan. So you would be entitled to four hundred yuan in cash. But the brigade has been wiped clean of cash. The money had been paid out to various people for various purposes: a work-related accident, a rescue, a work-related travel expense for cadres like Mamut, relief for destitute families, relief to the Brigade leader himself for summer clothes since his wife had wiped out his cash. The Brigade could not pay the commune members any cash for the worth of their work-points. A constant topic at brigade meetings was the leaders explaining why cash was unavailable.

The party secretary for the Brigade, Axim Yusup, was slightly older, with a wispy beard, and he worked tirelessly all day. Though illiterate, he was a sharp thinker and always spoke clearly and logically and would often deplore the thoughtlessness of the young generation who cared nothing about the revolution and the hardships of the old days. He would bare his arm and show where he had been bitten by a snake. Not able to afford treatment, he had put a tourniquet on his arm to prevent the poison from spreading, and to this day that part of his arm had remained unnaturally thin.

The bookkeeper of the Brigade, also called Abdrahman, was a handsome young man who loved reading and drawing. During the "Four Clean-ups," he had drawn a lot of cartoons on order, depicting this one as a demon, portraying that one as a bully, notwithstanding family relationships, as the targets of his art. But after hours, he would visit them in his personal capacity and pay them respects according to the generational hierarchy, drawing a clear line between public and private affairs. Over time, I noticed that this rule of behavior was quite common among the local people.

The cashier for the Brigade was a lively young man who spoke tolerable Mandarin. Once we met on the highway, biking in opposite directions. He had a bottle of wine with him and made me get off my bike and join him in the shade of the cornfield lining the highway. At his suggestion, we each screwed off the top of the bell on our bikes, turned them upside down, and used them for wine cups. We drank to friendship and the health of our families. He could have climbed higher, he confided to me, but for his wife who had dragged him down, being the daughter of a landlord. Obviously, the "Four Clean-ups" going on in the countryside had been mild down here, or our cashier would never hear the end of it. His wife, as I remember, was very appealing, looking out through a pair of big soft eyes.

Many people inimical to the Communist Party would revile village cadres. Chairman Mao himself had also conducted rectification programs against them. All of which combined to turn village cadres into "village-cads."

There was this saying about them:

> *Heroes of spring" (being newly elected),*
> *Busy bees of summer" (lots of work in the fields),*
> *Beggars of fall" (unable to pay commune members for their work-points),*
> *Criminals of winter" (targets of rectification campaigns).*

Since May of 1965, I was the designated deputy brigade leader and mixed easily with the commune members. According to orders from above, I started every morning by teaching them the newly designed alphabet for Uighur, combined with reading Chairman Mao's works. I had never realized that study for them was such an ordeal: the moment I opened my book, they all wilted, turning teary and sleepy—they would rather work at their quotas for digging cubics of earth or cut grass, than do their "study."

In my role as deputy brigade leader, I would do my part inspecting the summer and fall harvests, check on housing for leaks during heavy rains, select models for studying the works of Chairman Mao, and join in the regular farm work of Team One and Team Six under the Brigade. I also took part in the social life of the commune, visiting families, mediating quarrels, attending weddings and funerals and circumcisions and other communal occasions.

If I had any complaints, it was the mail delivery. They seemed to deliver only when they were in the mood. Ruifang and I wrote to each other regularly, on average a letter a day, but I received her letters only sporadically. They either didn't show up or would descend on me in cascades. This style of delivery completely wiped out the immediacy of the communication, which was the point of writing so regularly. One day I made my way to the post office and luckily found someone with whom I had a fleeting acquaintance. I was let into the sorting room and lo and behold, several letters from Ruifang were languishing right there among letters designated for the Second Brigade. I took them away immediately. A few days later, I tried the trick again. Unfortunately my acquaintance at the post office was not around and I came back dejectedly. Since our marriage nine years before, we had had only two and a half years of family life during the early sixties. We were always moving here and there. And now we could not even properly communicate by mail. What next?

In the summer of that same year of 1965, my main concern was for Ruifang to join me in Ili. Back in Urumqi, Comrade Liu Xiaowu, head of the Xinjiang Federation of Literature and Art Circles, had promised. Moreover, there was a formal letter from the Federation endorsing the move. Now was the time to act, Ruifang and I decided. Predictably, Ruifang's employer, the school in Urumqi where she was teaching, would not release her. To ready ourselves for the coming battle, Ruifang sent the children back to Beijing, and I traveled from Ili to Urumqi to be with her during the coming ordeal. We were ready to take action and determined to succeed, and the summer holiday was the best time to start.

As things turned out, however, this transferring of personnel—one of the most knotty businesses under the current administrative system—was solved by Ruifang in a matter of an hour.

I still remember the day she and I set out together. Dressed in a well-cut suit of gray made in Beijing, she walked firmly into the building of the municipal government, where the Bureau of Education was housed. I waited in the Western Park, directly across the street. It was a critical moment for us. The objections of her school had been overcome, but now the Urumqi municipal authority started to make a fuss, saying that orders had come down that teachers must not be released—and so on.

I waited for about an hour and then saw Ruifang come out of the building, her face radiant. She had won the argument. If you want to convince someone, the first thing is to be convinced yourself, as Ruifang used to say. We stood looking at the early signs of fall and felt great happiness at a job well done, the joy of being together, and the consciousness of hope for the future.

What Ruifang wanted was simple, to be together with me. What I wanted was equally simple, to be together with her. In this harsh age when only power speaks, how many lovers have been separated! How many families broken up! I am blessed with my own corner of the world, where husband and wife live in harmony. What more could we want? This is our good fortune in the midst of misfortune.

Now that the move was approved, we set to work immediately. We began by disposing of the furniture that we had brought over from Beijing at great trouble and expense. I piled desks and bookcases in a cart and lugged them through the streets of Umruchi, leaving pieces of them here and there with friends. Two sofa chairs and a coffee table, however, I decided to move to Ili. I got into touch with a driver, a Muslim by the name of Ma, who was driving a cargo truck carrying cement. Since cement was heavy, the storage area of the truck was barely one / third filled, and there was plenty of space for our few pieces of furniture. We stayed the night with kind friends, the couple Chen Bozhong and Lou Youqin, and got up at dawn the next day to leave with the cargo truck. And thus we started turning a new page to our new life in Xinjiang.

Moving from Beijing to Urumqi, we thought that we had removed ourselves far enough away, but obviously not—we had to move farther west. By the third day of our truck ride, we reached Kokdala, a term found equally in Uighur and in Mongolian, meaning blue wilderness. We passed Sailimu Lake, the biggest salt water lake at that altitude, reminding one of the sea that had once been there [in a mythological past]. The water was blue, like blue jade, and vied with the blue of the sky in its dazzling gaze. It took our truck one full hour to circumvent the lake before continuing on its way. Having left the lake behind, we entered the forest area. Kazakh shepherds and lumberjacks made up part of the scene. Circular-shaped log houses dotted the landscape here and there, seeming to have wandered over straight out of a fairy tale. As the truck stopped for a break, Ruifang and I seized the opportunity to take a picture with the forest background. The driver Ma snapped the shot. Moving on, we entered the Ili river valley and passed by Khorghas. We were told that we were about forty kilometers from the Soviet border!

My heart almost missed a beat! We passed by the vast holding of the Fourth Division of the Army Agricultural Plantation, and turning round reached our new home—Ghulja, capital of Ili, situated in the Ili Kazakh Autonomous Prefecture under the Xinjiang Autonomous Region.

Ruifang would teach at the No. 2 Middle School right in town, across from the cinema house, just over the Western Bridge.

Come winter, Ruifang was allotted housing in the newly built dorm for the school staff. It was a unit in a one-story building. You entered through the smaller room facing the sun, then walked into the main room, about twelve square meters, with a big window which looked into a wide alley, the No 2 Alley off Liberation Road.

Finally we had a home of our own.

I took part in the work of the commune. I liked to work on the threshing ground to winnow the wheat; I enjoyed watching the mound of winnowed wheat grow while the chaff wafted away in the wind. I also enjoyed loading and unloading both horse drawn carts and trucks. To be holding high a sack of wheat over your head and throwing it down in relief, or to walk over a wobbly plank with a sack on your shoulder—these gave me a sense of achievement.

Now and then I would work at the commune and return home to our dorm in the No. 2 Middle School, combining "tempering through manual labor" with some family time. I savored this peace away from the center of politics, while the faraway world of art and literature and learning were being thrown into turmoil and all the people involved feared for their lives.

Ruifang sometimes visited me in my village, and always brought gifts for my landlord's family. Haliqam would be very excited at her coming, scrambling up trees to gather fruit for her. And at night, Ruifang and I would share my little storeroom with the pair of swallows.

Sometimes I would bicycle home at night, passing through the deserted orchards and stretches of alkaline fields, savoring the joy of toughening it out alone on a deserted road in the dark. Once, a bag of eggs fell and smashed, smearing the road in yellow and white. Another time, I arrived too late, and the school gate was locked. I left my battered bike under that low cut window of our dorm and crawled under the school gate for ingress. Later that night, we heard two guards stop under our window, speculating about this tattered bicycle lying there untended.

We were so young at the time, so young. When one is young things happen. A youth wherein nothing happens is a blank. More worth living is a youth beset by trials. These bits and pieces, they are part of life, beyond our control, and later they turn into tender recollections.

Before setting out for Ili, Comrade Liu Xiaowu of the Xinjiang Federation of Art and Literature Circles had advised me to study the language. For many reasons—to mix with the masses, to comply with directives from above, in pursuit of the unknown, in pursuit of knowledge for its own sake, and—need I deny it—to fill a gap in my life, I now started to study Uighur. From then on, apart from manual labor and my homelife, all my energies were devoted to the study of the Uighur language.

I started with the alphabet, asking help from anyone among the locals who had been to school. I used an old textbook, which had been issued by the local government in the fifties, even before the Autonomous Region was set up. A neighborhood little girl heard me reading from the textbook and came over to help me with my pronunciation. My father in Beijing mailed me three books, Darwin's *Origin of Species,* a dictionary of Mandarin Chinese, and a copy of the latest number of the magazine *The Chinese Languages* which carried an article "Brief Introduction to the Uighur Language" written by Professor Zhu Zhining of the National Minorities Institute under the Chinese Academy of Social Sciences. I seized on the latter, and profited greatly from an article on the Uighur language. To me, every word was enlightenment—from concept, to pronunciation, to syntax, to grammar, and I even picked up some basics of linguistics. Thanks to my grounding in Russian, I had no problem at all with "case" and "past perfect" and other points of grammar. I was completely absorbed in the language, and would listen for hours to broadcasts in Uighur no matter how much or how little I understood. For every word I learned I would apply it to the life around me, and not just revert to its equivalent in Mandarin. I think I literally dreamed in Uighur. Language is a living thing: it is culture, it is people, it is life itself, it is character, it is the past and it is the present . . . I am grateful to destiny for the chance to study a language on the spot and use it on the spot . . . I feel blessed, and I am proud to have mastered it quickly and to have used it correctly and precisely for all occasions. A few months after I got started, I was able to take part in meetings in Uighur. I spoke up and pointed out the unfairness of the work-point system, saying that it did not reflect the real amount of work done by an individual member but swept everybody into the same category. My point was well taken, and I was praised as a worthy member of the commune.

Later on, the Cultural Revolution gave me a chance to re-enforce my mastery of Uighur: I memorized Mao's quotations in Uighur. I read Mao's three "compulsory pieces"—"Serve the People," "To the Memory of Norman Bethune," and "The Old Man Who Moved the Mountain"—in Uighur, I sang the songs in praise of Mao in Uighur, I shouted slogans— down with this and down with that—all in Uighur, not to mention that I shouted "Long live Chairman Mao!" in Uighur. I started to read Uighur publications: legal publications and later on those "illegal" ones seized during the Cultural Revolution. I read stories and poems and fables and folk tales. I could read not only in Uighur but also in Usbeki (close to Uighur). I had read Uighur translations of Lu Xun and translations of Gorky from Russian and translations of stories from other national minorities. Later on, during the those darkest days of the cultural desert, I came across a hand-copied Usbeki version of the Persian classic *Rubaiyat* by Omar Kayam. I was aware that it had been translated into Mandarin by Guo Moro (from the English), and now I myself also tried my hand at a few verses.

Years later in 1980, the American Sinologist Howard Goldblatt gave me a copy of the *Rubaiyat* in English, translated by the FitzGerald brothers. There is currently more than one translation into Mandarin, including into classical Chinese. I was frustrated that in going over the English translation, I could not locate my favorite verse. Finally, in the latest Mandarin translation by Professor Zhang Hongnian of Peking University, I found it—verse forty-eight!

In 1980, during my first visit to the United States, I recited verse forty-eight in Usbeki at the International Writing Center [University of Iowa], and a Turkish writer excitedly told me that he understood the words of my recital.

I have often been asked, how did you manage to master the Uighur language, and I would answer: "Easy. Sit down with an Uighur and by the time you have consumed two tons of Ilite, you will get it."

In 1999, on my return trip to Ili, the Ilite Beverage Company had asked me to leave a piece of calligraphy. I wrote: "One glass of Ilite, Two rows of tears!"

I am actually not much of a drinker. What I want to emphasize is the importance of mixing with people wholeheartedly. The crux of learning another language lies in knowing the life and heart of the other nation and to be culturally open-minded. There is a saying in Uighur: "language different, heart different," with which I do not quite agree. I would rather change it to "language understood, heart understood." To sit together over a bottle, to share the same cup, poured and passed around by a server. The one whose turn it is to drink must offer a few words, or sing a song, or tell a joke—a chance to show off his wit and eloquence. Where can you find a better language-training center? What I learned was not just vocabulary or grammar or pronunciation, what I learned was tone and situation and mood and culture and style. I am close to the heart of the Uighur people. Also, I had told my Uighur friends many stories taken from Han Chinese history and fable, broken down in a way that they could appreciate, including those from the Anecdotes of Su Dongpo[3]—a collection of clever repartee, which were much appreciated. Language links us together, and hearts touch each other. With a combination of language and heart, I have earned the friendship and trust of the Uighur people. I consider it one of the happiest and proudest achievements of my life.

Later, when asked what I had been doing in Xinjiang, I would say "Post-doc degree in Uighur linguistics." Indeed, I had done three years of *prep school,* five years of *undergrad,* three years of *masters,* three years of *doctorate,* and two years of *post-doc*—exactly what it takes.

To be honest, I should add, "There was no choice."

---

3. Su Dongpo, formal name Su Shi, 1037–1101—poet, writer, and calligrapher of the Song dynasty.

Chapter 24

On the Eve

It is hard to describe, much less *explain,* the state of society and the mood of the people on the eve of the Cultural Revolution during the middle 1960s. One must just accept the situation as it evolved. At the time, we could not foresee the future, just as looking back at all that had transpired, it is still beyond understanding.

There had been so many ultra-leftist outbreaks, putting people down, expending energy in internecine feuding, flaunting grandiose terms: "sweeping away everything in our path," "unprecedented in history," "reverberating in the clouds . . ."

The period was dominated by songs, all in praise of Mao Zedong: "sailing in the sea we rely on our great Helmsman . . . ," "commune members are sunflowers gazing upward at the Sun . . . ," "Chairman Mao is coming to our commune . . . ," "turn all the trees into pencils to write the praises of Mao Zedong . . . ," "I love my mom and my dad, but I love Chairman Mao more," and the like. One could imagine people crying as they sang, and singing as they cried. On the other side of the picture, however, was the great famine of the 1960s, when nobody knew what it would all lead to . . .

Apart from songs, there were slogans: "ants gnawing at a bone," "chicken feathers flying into the sky," "revolutionary energy plus desperation," "all for others, none for self," "the Renaissance of the East," "learn from Lei Feng . . . from Zhang Side . . . from Norman Bethune . . . from the Old Man of the Mountain . . . ," "in agriculture learn from Dazhai," "in industry learn from Daqing,"[1] "the whole nation learn from the People's Liberation Army," "fear not the imperialists, the revisionists and all other counterrevolutionary elements," and other thunderous slogans.

Apart from the songs and slogans, there was daily labor. Take harvesting, for instance. The people's commune, according to song and verse, was "good as good can be," but few people showed up for work, and the few that did show up did not work. When the commune members had dragged themselves through half a day, the group leader would call it quits. They didn't dare to be seen back in the village when the sun was still high, so they'd smoke and sit it out till sundown. So much for the people's commune! But there were huge projects too, involving hundreds of thousands of people pulled from many communes in the area, wave after wave of human muscle, lined up to dig untold numbers of cubic earth and what not, projects designed to "make the mountains bow their heads and the rivers give way," as touted in a popular slogan of the times.

Meanwhile, Chairman Mao had said, "using a novel to oppose the Party is a great discovery." It was being filtered down from the highest levels that "the Federation of Literature and Art Circles and its affiliated organizations were on the edge of deteriorating into a Sander Petofi Club[2] . . ." By then, Shanghai had already launched a mass critique of the play *Hairui Dismissed from Office.*[3]

All through some seventy years of life, I have seen many changes, but I noticed that one thing remains unchanging—life must go on and people must eat. My novel about this period, *Carnival Season,* describes, among other things, how ultra-leftist politics distorts life, while life itself has managed to dissolve politics, as pointed out very astutely by the writer Bi Shumin.[4] How to get on with their lives on a day-to-day basis was always

1. A model oilfield in the Northwest, also known for the model worker Iron Man Wang Jinxi.
2. Literary club in Hungary where men of letters gathered on the eve of the Hungarian Uprising in 1956.
3. A historical play by Wu Han, loosely based on the story of the Ming dynasty minister Hairui who had dared to remonstrate with Emperor Jiajing; perceived by leftist extremists as a veiled attack on Mao.
4. Bi Shumin, 1952– , one of the leading woman writers on the scene; initially trained as a doctor, Bi's stories often have to do with women and illness.

the top concern of the common people. One must show up for work at the commune, or one's grain ration would not be issued by the commune. One must cut grass, or one's animals would not survive the harsh winter. My landlord Abdrahman had been coming home later and later every evening. After work, he cut grass for his animals. Once home, he didn't go into the house; he went out to check on his animals. If one of them had not been properly fed, his wife Haliqam would never hear the end of it. Haliqam, meanwhile, had kept the pot boiling for upward of an hour, waiting for Abdrahman's return to start supper. Meanwhile, the couple never stopped making changes to their home, setting up a fence here, building a stove there, one day taking down the old dog house, the next day digging up the vegetable garden to grow roses. All they wanted was to improve their lives.

As for the cadres, their job was certainly no cup of tea. During those times, a meeting at the Commune Center attended by leaders at all levels—from the commune, the brigade, and the team—was an exhausting trial lasting several days. When the leaders returned each to their own communes to pass down the message, they must also begin at the beginning, and go through the rigmarole about the international situation, the struggle against imperialism and revisionism, the dazzling light of Mao Zedong Thought, the shiny examples of Chen Yonggui of Dazhai, Iron Man Wang of Daqing, Jiao Yulu[5] of Lankao County, and that starting the next day, all commune members must stay day and night in the fields for a total of a month to finish taking in the wheat, which was for the purpose of combating revisionism and supporting the world revolution, and that being in Xinjiang one must keep the world situation in mind and remember that two-thirds of the world population had not yet been liberated and that there were still people in this commune who did not show up for work, and that these people must be reminded that the path of capitalism leads to perdition, and that tomorrow an ox will be killed and its meat parceled out, one kilogram per family . . . A considerable amount of time would then be spent on reprimands and exhortations and warnings and threats to those who did not show up

5. Jiao Yulu, 1922–1964, exemplary county official who had worked tirelessly through the famine of the early sixties while suffering from liver cancer.

for this particular meeting—all this borne meekly by those who had dutifully shown up. And thus the meeting would end, with no other discernible result than the one kilogram of beef per family, which was duly parceled out the next day.

One of the bones of contention between cadres and commune members was the issue of "going down the capitalist road." The fact was, people needed some ready cash. They made rocking cradles, they tied together brooms, they made handles for agricultural instruments, they kept poultry and made milk products, all for the purpose of getting some cash, practices which were popularly known as "grabbing." Actually, Xinjiang was quite lax in this respect. There was a lot of rhetoric against "grabbing," but everybody was doing it on the sly. A safer method of conducting business, however, was the exchange of goods, with no cash involved. If you brought out your eggs or apples in exchange for cash, that would be considered "grabbing," and "grabbing" was considered "capitalism." If you brought your eggs to the store in exchange for salt or tea leaves, that would not be considered "capitalism," and you were off the hook.

The people, they have their own way of dealing with things. Take the problem of punctuality. When a meeting was called, some of the commune members might show up three hours late. To deal with the problem, the conveners would announce the meeting three hours earlier than the actual meeting time, but the late arrivals will arrive even later. As you talked a blue streak about the unattainable, they would go to sleep. When you waked them up, they would jump up to announce their resolute adherence to whatever it is you were proposing; they promised to fulfill whatever it was you had ordered; they shouted Long Live the General Line, the Great Leap Forward, and the People's Commune! And just when you were made happy by this reaction, they fell asleep again! Perhaps there is an immutable law maintaining a balance between grandiloquent words and sober reality, between theory and practice, between policies and its subversions?

At the time, the critical attack on *Hairui Dismissed from Office* and *Evening*

Chats in Yanshan[6] was going full blast. The "sixteen points" of the Cultural Revolution were about to be proclaimed. An uneasy anticipation of disaster hovered over the country. Concurrent with the above, in the early summer of 1966, the commune conducted a collective wedding. A group of newly registered couples were collected in the meeting hall of the Commune Center, red paper flowers were pinned to their chests while loudspeakers resounded to the blare of revolutionary songs. County leaders, the Party secretary of the commune, representatives of the production brigades, representatives of the parents, representatives of the newlyweds all went up on stage to sing the praises of the new-style wedding, and then exhorted each other to learn from the Old Man of the Mountain, learn from Zhang Side,[7] learn from Norman Bethune, learn from Lei Feng, learn from Mai Xiande,[8] learn from Ouyang Hai[9] and other exemplary figures and to work hard for the next three years and change the face of the commune. The leaders were pleased; they held up the advantages of the new-style wedding, and deplored the waste, the excessive eating and drinking, the virtual sale of the bride, etc., which were innate to old-style weddings.

To this day, I wonder if the leaders ever found out the truth. One night after that new-style wedding, I was dragged out of bed and taken to a re-enacted traditional wedding. We drank, we slaughtered a lamb, we sang the old songs, we danced the old-style dances, and everything was done as they were prescribed according to the old rules. The host said that they had actually spent more cash for the new-style wedding, having to buy red paper flowers, melon seeds, candies, biscuits, cigarettes, and what not. As for the traditional wedding, everything was done according to form and nothing was missing.

---

6. A collection of essays perceived to be satirical, penned by diverse hands, including members from within the Beijing Party leadership.
7. An ordinary worker whose death was commemorated by Mao Zedong in the article *Serve the People*.
8. Mai Xiande, 1945– , an exemplary communist soldier.
9. Ouyang Hai, 1940–1963, a Communist soldier who gave up his life to save others.

Chapter 25

The Sweep of the Cultural Revolution Out West

I am sometimes given to musing: how did the Cultural Revolution get under way in the commune in Bayanday? The attack against Wu Han, author of the play *Hairui Dismissed from Office,* did not cause a ripple out there. Way back in the days when I was working for the Youth League in Beijing, my boss had once gone to call on Wu, with me in his retinue. Wu Han received us and mouthed some platitudes. I then realized that despite being deputy mayor of Beijing, Wu Han was after all just a member of one of the Democratic Parties and he knew his place. I vaguely remember that he had been quite forward during the anti-*rightist* campaign. And now his own turn had come. What goes around comes around.

But the business about Deng Tuo was no laughing matter. I knew something about the make-up of the Party Committee of Beijing. If there were to be a re-shuffling at that end, it would ultimately come round to Party Secretary Peng Zhen himself!

Now the border region out there in Xinjiang was being galvanized into action. Our own production brigade had called a meeting to denounce Deng Tuo. The party secretary of the Brigade made a thunderous speech. But speaking in Uighur, he could not help using the polite form of address in the second person *plural* when figuratively confronting Deng Tuo. More serious trouble cropped up during the shouting of slogans. In Uighur, the terms "Down with," *yokalsun,* and "Long live," *yaxasun,* sounded similar. The representative of the Poor Peasants' Association—set up earlier during the "Four Clean-ups" and by now a mere formality—unfortunately confused the two terms and kept shouting *yokalsun* for Chairman Mao! The poor Party Secretary, in a panic, did his best to shout him down. Fortunately for the representative of the Poor Peasants' Association, folks down here were not interested in getting a handle on their neighbors—no one heard the *unmentionable.* If anybody did, it could only mean that he or she was thinking the unmentionable, and he or she would be appropriately dealt with!

Among the youth of the area, the Cultural Revolution provided new experiences which made them feel good about themselves. A detachment of Red Guards was formed, although later this first batch was written off as *mercenary* Red Guards. But at the time they had kicked up quite a show, putting up big-character posters with words written in yellow on red paper, ordering all beards and mustaches shaved off, all betting gadgets confiscated, all pet pigeons released, all weasels liberated, though the latter were rat exterminators. The Red Guards also confiscated a number of books. It was not clear if their activities were a proliferation of the nationwide "Smash the Four Olds" program, or just an outburst under local circumstances. Whatever it was, the Red Guards' activities had begun to infringe on the way of life of the national minorities. If not for a new turn of events which called for smashing the "Reactionary Bourgeois Line," *involving a downturn for the Red Guards themselves,* who knows to what lengths they would have gone.

Back in Beijing my mother was so frightened by the sudden outbreak of the Cultural Revolution that she came all the way to Ghulja to take refuge with us. Later, during the height of the staggering "massive national link-up" when travel was free all over the country, Ruifang took the opportunity to escort Mother back to her own home in Beijing and bring back our younger son Wang Shi. I could have gone with them, but I was timid. I traveled with them as far as Urumqi, the capital, where Ruifang and my mother changed trains for Beijing.

In Urumqi, after an absence of four years, I reported to the Xinjiang Federation of Literature and Art Circles, the work unit to which I was originally assigned when I first arrived in Xinjiang. My timing could not have been worse. The two factions within the Federation were at each other's throats. They had just gone through the "Seize Power" phase and that having ended in turmoil, they were now under military control. But that did not stop the faction fighting. Once you were there, you could not avoid the imputation of siding with either one or other of the two factions, and consequently being regarded as an enemy by both. Following which you could not help getting worked up and resentful of one or the other of the two factions, and getting into a foul mood yourself. This is how political strife poisons the mind and sets people against each other.

I finally realized that for the time being the Xinjiang Federation of Literature and Art Circles was no haven for me. With their permission, in May of 1967, I traveled to Beijing intending to bring my Aunt with me to Ghulja so that she could help take care of our younger son Wang Shi.

At the time it took the train about ninety hours to run from Urumqi to Beijing. I could not afford the sleeping car and had to make do with a hard seat. Nighttime was a trial: my whole frame felt like it was collapsing, as if all my bones had been removed, like the famous "braised boneless chicken." I could not help taking the line of least resistance—I crept under the seat and stretched myself out. The floor under the seat was littered with cigarette butts, melon seed husks, candy wrappings, dust, and trails of spittum . . . The stink was overwhelming. I would lie down for ten or fifteen minutes until I could not bear it any longer. I would then return to my seat and sit until I could no longer maintain a sitting position and repeat the crawling act. This went on for three days and three nights until I reached Beijing. On the return trip to Xinjiang, Aunt bore the long nights better than I did—she said she was used to long sleepless nights. Once off the train, there was a long distance bus. Finally a week later, Aunt and I were in Ghulja.

On arrival Aunt said that she felt dizzy. I thought it was the fatigue of the journey. A few days later, Ruifang was assigned to take her students down to the countryside to help take in the wheat, and I had my hands full with little Wang Shi. Aunt woke up one day with a splitting headache. She went to bed and again I thought it was fatigue. I left home to work in the fields in Bayanday, it being harvest time. When I returned home at night, Aunt was still sleeping! I then realized that she was not sleeping, she had lost consciousness. I called on the neighbors for help. An Uighur teacher got hold of a horse cart and helped me bring Aunt to the Friendship Hospital, now renamed the Anti-Revisionism Hospital. Aunt died four days later. A driver, Wang Pingshan, from the No. 6

Middle School, helped me take care of the funeral. From dressing the body to acquiring a coffin and choosing a burial spot, down to digging the grave and performing the last rites, everything was done properly. From then on, one member of my family has been at rest in Xinjiang soil! This made me feel even closer to Xinjiang.

I was especially moved by the people of Bayanday, all of whom attended the funeral. In compliance with their religious belief, the Uighurs attach great importance to burials. The locals affirm that Aunt was probably from this part of the earth and had wandered by mistake onto the plains of Hebei and into the city of Beijing. She had covered the miles from Beijing to lie down here in her true native resting place, they maintained. Hearing this, I was somewhat consoled but even more pained for Aunt.

This was my first experience of death, and my first experience of escorting an unfortunate soul to her last resting place.

My aunt Dong Xuewen was born in 1908 and died in 1967. She was widowed at nineteen and since then had led a poverty-stricken, lonely life. She was intelligent, loved reading, and initiated me into a love of reading. In her loneliness, Aunt took to cigarettes and drink. She told me about the advantages of smoking: when hungry, smoke and you will feel filled; when stuffed, smoke and you will feel relieved; when sleepy, smoke and you will be refreshed; when sleepless, smoke and you will feel rested. Aunt smoked the cheapest brand of cigarettes, a few cents per pack. Aunt drank the cheapest kind of wine, sold by the ounce, with peanuts to go with her libation. Later when peanuts were not affordable, she shifted to dried beancurd and salted fish. In the "Smash the Four Olds" phase of the Cultural Revolution, Aunt and my grandma had been forced to drink water which had been used for a footbath. My grandma died after this ordeal. Aunt, left alone, scrounged to keep body and soul together. Aunt was full of expectations of a happy old age living with us in Xinjiang. But that last wish had been snatched from her by Fate.

Even to this day I have tender memories of the show of national togetherness during those twisted years. The events revolving around the death of Aunt testify to this togetherness and will always remain in my memory. I am forever indebted to this land and this people.

Chapter 26

The Cultural Revolution—Scenes from a Border Town

The Xinjiang countryside had its share of the storm and stress of the Cultural Revolution. As to its spread in the border town of Ghulja, where Ruifang was teaching at the No. 2 Middle School, all that I knew was mostly through the shock of sight and sound.

As far as sight was concerned, the town was immersed in a sea of red. All buildings and walls seemed to be plastered over with Mao portraits and red paper scrolls of Mao quotations. All Mao quotations were written in Chinese and Uighur, the latter in the old Arabic script. Mao buttons of every conceivable design glittered on every chest. Red armbands clung round every youngster's arm. At one time there were four or five identical Mao portraits hanging in our living room in Ghulja. It was to make sure that whichever way we turned, we would meet the gaze of Chairman Mao. Collecting Mao buttons was the national pastime. Thanks to our relatives in Beijing, we often received by post buttons of the newest design.

Outside on the streets, the *sea of red* had the unintended effect of hiding the ugliness of the town: broken down walls, piled up garbage, untended public toilets, dirt and decay . . . now all hidden by a sea of red. Would China thus undergo a new birth and stand up as unique and invincible? These questions are beyond the understanding of you and me.

Adding to the sights were big-character posters taking up what space was left by the portraits and quotations. I cannot even begin to list the number of incorrectly written characters in those posters, and the abuses of grammar. At the same time, however, there were stunning samples of calligraphy in various classic styles among some of the big-character posters. The eye-catching "thriller" of the moment was a big-character "serial" which was sparked by abuses that a man and a woman flung at each other. Man A put up a poster, accusing man B of having slept with his [A]'s wife. Before Man B could respond, wife B rushed to the defense, asserting that Man A's wife is known for sleeping around and why pick on *her* husband? And couldn't he, Man A, tell that his wife was not a virgin. Then the mother, sister, and relatives on each side jumped into the fray, polluting the air with unmentionable words, making that particular group of posters the most read of all. Had the Cultural Revolution sunk to this?

Meanwhile, a whole line of identical eye-catching posters running down Stalin Street all the way to Liberation Road screamed for attention: "The opening of the Ghulja Bakery Is a Great Victory of Mao Zedong Thought!" Is this some kind of deconstructive joke? I should think not. The people here are not that sophisticated. Indeed, come to think of it, to enjoy a bakery while carrying on the Cultural Revolution—why shouldn't that be a victory of Mao Zedong Thought?

As to sounds, well, all I could say is that thanks to loudspeakers lining the streets, there was never a quiet moment in our little town: slogan chanting, mutual recrimination between factions, songs of praise, growls and laughter . . .

Truthfully speaking, I had been scared stiff at the beginning of the Cultural Revolution. Highlighting the "cultural" and starting with attacks against the play *Hairui Dismissed from Office* meant that this was a campaign against the educated, especially those of us in art and literature circles, and you had to take it lying down. Now thinking back, I could kick myself for rushing to burn every piece of paper with written words on it—the letters that I had exchanged with Ruifang while I was doing manual labor in the suburbs, all my correspondence with my literary friends, Huang Qiuyun, Zhang Xuan,[1] and many others.

At the time, how could I have imagined the chaos to follow? How

1. Zhang Xuan, 1934–1997, writer of novels and screenplays; among his film works, "Corner Left Unnoticed by Love" won a Golden Rooster Award for Best Screenplay in 1982; labeled a *rightist*.

could I have foreseen the downfall of those former champions in putting down the *rightists*? Their own label—the three *anti's*—*anti*-Party, *anti*-Socialism, *anti*-Mao Zedong Thought—was no better than our label of *rightist*. And now it was revealed that though some of us may have been genuine *rightists*, they, the self-styled warriors against us *rightists*, they were in fact *fake* leftists. We may have been paper tigers, while they were being uncovered as wolves in sheep's clothing. Seeing the situation in this light, I felt much relieved. I may still be in trouble but those being exposed now were in a worse fix.

And then as the movement rolled along on its own momentum beyond anyone's control, I saw decent people within the leadership taken down one by one. I just gave up trying to make sense of any of it, and was lost in a deep depression.

Our little home had experienced its own share of the drama. One night we were disturbed by a confusion of crackling noises, which sounded like mice scuttling over the papered ceilings in traditional one-story old houses. The next morning we opened the door to find a big-character poster stuck to our door: "Cui Ruifang," the accusation ran, "bourgeois lifestyle, sofa in the house, permanent waves on the head . . ." Seeing this, I now remembered that when Ruifang and one or other of the Han teachers passed the school gate, the girl Red Guards would mutter: "Wang Guangmei! Wang Guangmei!"[2] Personally I think the compliment undeserved.

And now the Red Guards were at our door!

Ruifang was totally incensed, but I told her not to get worked up, although I personally did not agree that keeping a sofa was sign of a bourgeois lifestyle. After all, in one of the portraits on my wall, Chairman Mao was sitting on a sofa! Following on the big-character poster on our door, a couple of Red Guards showed up at our home the next day, saying that they needed to take away our sofa and parade it through the streets as an example of our decadent bourgeois lifestyle, and also as one of the spoils in their drive to "Smash the Four Olds." As they were negotiating, one of the Red Guards happened to look up and was shocked to see

2. Wang Guangmei, 1921–2006, wife of Liu Shaoqi, head of the state of the PRC, 1962–66. During the Cultural Revolution Wang spent eleven years in prison and later served briefly as Director of Foreign Affairs, CASS.

Chairman Mao himself sitting on a sofa! He stood for a moment in stunned silence, muttered something unintelligible, but left with our sofa nevertheless. Two days later, the Red Guards came to the door again and returned our sofa, and we continued to sit on it notwithstanding. I must add here that our "sofa" was a makeshift contraption, with two bent iron bars on each side for armrests, a few uneasy springs in the center bordered by a bar—that was the seat, making it very hard on our legs as we bent to sit down. That this makeshift old thing should be an exhibit of the bourgeois lifestyle—the bourgeoisie of China must be a pitiful lot.

By now the Cultural Revolution has become a part of life, and life itself now proceeded to adapt the politics of the Cultural Revolution to its own ends. The "sea of red" had turned into everyday street scenes; the Mao quotations converted to songs had become popular music; the verbal warfare conducted over loudspeakers became a release for the frustrations of puberty. And then there were the uniform trench coats, the green uniforms, the army caps, the two little braids of the female hairstyle . . . In our brigade, word was formally handed down that the usual Uighur "Salaam" or the Mandarin "Have you eaten?" for everyday greetings must be replaced by "Wishing Chairman Mao ten thousand years of life," and that the answer instead of the usual "best wishes . . ." must now be changed to "ten thousand years of life, ten thousand years of life, ten thousand years of life," making it thirty thousand.

The sun, the moon, and the stars remain up on high, hot and cold weather follow each other in cycles, the five elements checked on each other, the heavenly *stem* and the earthly *branch* complemented each other. Thus on a particular day of a particular month of a particular year, these peculiar phenomena descended on this ancient land with a civilization of several thousand years behind it. New sights, new dangers, new challenges which no one could keep up with—they appeared in a flash and disappeared without a trace. Like SARS. To quote an old folk saying: "Once this village is behind us, we will never see this inn again." I am lucky to have lived through it all and come out in one piece. I count it a blessing.

Chapter 27

Another World, a Different Clime

The Red Guards in the No. 2 Middle School, where we were living, belonged to a rebel faction, and were locked in fierce combat with Red Guards from the foreign trade office right across the street. When the two sides started using firearms, we decided to get out of the way. We found rooms to let in an old courtyard house removed from the center of town. In such a little border town, even the sweep of the Cultural Revolution could not prevent people from renting out their spare rooms. You could not stop life from going on. Our little family moved into No. 5 East Xinhua Street and stayed there for two years.

Here, it was a totally different world, a world where the Cultural Revolution was no big deal. The owner was a widow, Ayim by name. Her late husband's picture hung on the wall. He had been an army officer in the old days of the nationalist revolution in Xinjiang. The old lady had a son, who had gone to school, had even been a cadre at one time, and then had been in prison. No one knew his current occupation. He would sometimes show up at his mother's, demanding money. On those occasions the old lady would be in tears while the son's voice could be heard across the yard. The old lady told me that her son was less than human.

We lived next door to the landlady, on the north side of the yard. Apart from our family there were four other renters taking up the rooms on the south and west sides of the yard. One was a railroad worker and his wife from Sichuan. They had accused our landlady of having been a landowner, a claim which the latter stoutly denied. The second tenant was an old Uighur lady living with her daughter and son. The daughter had just graduated from the physics department of Beijing University and was now waiting to be sent down to the countryside. The third renter was a very thin Khazakh lady with a sickly son who had to go horseback riding every day for his health. The horse was a bone of contention between the Khazakh renter and the landlady, who forbade horses to be stabled in her yard. The last was an old Manchu couple with a little adopted son whom they worshiped to distraction. The old mother would personally play with the little boy to protect him against the other children; she would even take part in the children's fights. I myself once had a tiff with her on behalf of our little Wang Shi, who sometimes played with her son.

After moving in, I had a great shock. There were bulbs hanging in the two rooms, but no electricity. I confronted Ayim with the problem, and she confessed that the previous tenant of these rooms had abused the right to his share of the electric bill, so she just went and cut off the electricity altogether. Now was the chance for me to impress. I put on the most cultivated upper-class tone and chose the most high-sounding elegant words in the Uighur language to convey to Ayimu that no matter what percentage of the bill I was expected to pay, from sixty percent all the way to ninety-nine point nine percent, I did not mind, but that I must have electricity. Then I made some rhetorical flourishes posing questions to no one in particular and answering them myself, all to the effect that I must have electricity. Stunned by the weight of my eloquence, the landlady rolled up her eyes in shock and had no choice but to agree. As it later turned out, Ayim was not mean about the electricity bill, after all. But we were barely settled before she tried to raise the rent. To avoid confrontation, I gave her the extra cash she demanded. Then it occurred to me I should not let her get away with this kind of meanness, so I went and talked to her daughter, who worked in a bank. The young woman had problems of her own, I was told, but she came and gave her a mother a lecture. When her daughter left, Ayim paid me back the extra money, then stomped back to her room, crying her heart out. I felt sorry and gave her back what she had just returned. She broke out in smiles when she saw the cash—I had wasted my time for nothing.

When the young graduate from Beijing University had her wedding in our courtyard, Comrade Song Yanming from the CCP Propaganda Department happened to be visiting me. The two of us went out shopping for gifts and ended up giving the newlyweds a deluxe edition, bound in red silk, of the works of Chairman Mao. We were afraid to give anything else. When would this stranglehold over our lives be ever lifted?

Living in the compound we often get gifts of noodles or cooked rice from the neighbors on festive occasions. Gifts of *naan* from the mother of the university graduate were especially frequent and generous. This old lady was constantly feuding with the landlady and understood the political art of cementing friendships to isolate the enemy.

Do not assume, however, that the Cultural Revolution had overflowed everywhere, overtaken everything, and turned the world completely upside down. Actually the petty little townspeople with their petty little lives and petty little affairs, they continue on their daily rounds totally oblivious to the world outside, like a little stream flowing in a quiet corner, carrying with it the dregs of the town and the petty concerns of its inhabitants, their joys and their sorrows. The little people, they are ignorant but not lacking in kindness; they are powerless but not lacking in resourcefulness; they are not outstanding at anything, yet interesting just in themselves.

As for me living in this little town, I had totally given up writing and forgotten all about literature. Ruifang would remind me to read and write something, but I'd tell her sincerely that I had forgotten how to write, that it is not appropriate to write, and that I had completely lost the inclination. And thus I passed the two years from October of 1967 to October of 1969 in this little isolated courtyard house in the outskirts of the little town of Ghulja.

I had left descriptions of life in this little courtyard in my novella *High Jinks*—about the landlady, about our friendship with the railway worker from Sichuan, about how we played mahjong and how we danced the "Mao Loyalty Dance," and how we would be penalized by wearing the dunce cap when we lost at mahjong. I joked that for me Fate had diverted my dunce cap to mahjong, so that I was spared the humiliation of wearing it during the Cultural Revolution.

Years later, my novel *Carnival Season* and the short story "The Captain, the Secretary, the Wild Cat and the Stump of a Broken Chopstick" described my experience of keeping cats during this idle interval in my life. The fact was, I had kept two cats. One was a well-behaved white cat with black spots, as described in *Carnival Season,* while the other cat was wild and fierce, as described in "The Captain . . ." The stories of these cats were interesting in themselves. Add to that the fact that my former landlady in Bayanday village, Haliqam, came and named the good white cat "Joint Committee" (after a mass organization which was comparatively mild in outlook) and the big standoffish tiger-striped cat she named "Red Rebel" (after the joint title of the rebel mass organizations of Ili). In fact, my novel *Carnival Season* revolved more around the good white cat than anything else; at one time, I had even considered naming the book *The Season for Raising Cats.* Tie Ning[3] saw through this in her review of the *Seasons* Series, all of one hundred thousand plus words. How happy that made me, how grateful!

The novella *High Jinks* also touched on a case of factional infighting, based on a true account of what I had witnessed. Standing in the yard one day, facing the No. 6 Middle School across the street, I saw the huge red pennant of the "Fight to the Bloody End" faction being hit by enemy fire and starting to burn, then slowly collapse to the ground in flames. A young teacher from the school had just returned from his wedding back in his native village in Hunan; he was crossing the street carrying a cotton-stuffed blanket in his arms and he was caught in the cross fire. Seven hours passed before his body was taken away. Bleeding, he had crawled more than forty meters before he collapsed. He had struggled, leaving fingernail scratches on the ground. With timely help, he would not have died. I remember a scene like that in a Soviet film about the dark days of 1941, when flags were downed and men had died. That was World War II. What is the meaning of this death in a street in Ghulja?

We all recognize the force of truth; we are all eager to seek truth and die for the truth. But have we thought about the fatal attraction of fallacy? Fallacies can appear to be more alluring, more sensational, more gripping, and very effective in rousing people to action. Between solid

3. Tie Ning, 1957–, novelist, representative works are *Rose Gate* and *Grand Ablution,* mostly based on women's lives.

plodding truth and sensational fallacies, which would you choose? The Chinese "Cultural Revolution" evoked the two false deities of Fallacy and Destruction.

At the beginning, the Cultural Revolution meant tension, risks, enmity, decisive breaks, fighting to the death . . . But after one or two years which dragged into three and then into four, people began to take big breaks, enjoying more leisure than they ever had. They were bored, that is, except for those at the top, and leaders of factions.

People found outlets for their energies. The times when only one book was read throughout the nation had come and gone. Ruifang and I went and bought cookbooks. I learned to make the famous "fried cream puffs," signature brand of the famous Muslim Dong Lai Shun Restaurant in Beijing. Ruifang learned to make pork strips in beaten egg yoke. Later I figured out how to make varieties of yogurt. Ruifang and her colleagues also enjoyed sitting together to do fancy knitting.

The favorite pastime passed down from Beijing, leader of fashion, was carpentry. People made furniture by hand and reckoned their accomplishments by the number of "legs" on each piece. Some people left on family visits, others seized the moment to have babies. Ruifang and I became the happy parents of a daughter, Yihuan. Some people dug underground vegetable storage, some built little additions to their houses, some kept cats or chickens or birds, some bought scissors and did their own haircutting, some played chess, others made salted veggies or stood in long lines for stuffed buns . . . We were left alone for several years to idle the time away. All we could do was to wait. We must go with the flow. We could only immerse ourselves in mundane things. I had taken up smoking, and I began to enjoy a drink or two. It was the only way to dispel the frustration and the boredom.

As I said, I had burned all my letters and all my papers with anything written on them, and had thrown away my pen. In 1969, I picked up my pen again, to write the baby diary for my newborn daughter Yihuan. Before she could speak, I monitored her condition mainly by observing her stool. Stool can tell a lot about a baby: nourishment, digestion, and general well being. I had read up on the subject and could diagnose a lot of baby ailments by observing their stool. Even today, my children consult me on the subject when my grandchildren have problems. The family conferred on me a title which when pronounced, sounded like "authority on history," but was actually "authority on stool."

By now the Cultural Revolution seemed to be petering out. Chairman Mao had called on the population to "Concern yourself with national affairs and carry on the Cultural Revolution right through to the end!" The problem was, after those last several years, what and where is the end? At the moment, "class background checking" was seemingly the final wrapping-up. The No. 2 Middle School, where Ruifang was teaching, seemed to take it very seriously. The leadership called a general meeting, announcing that from the next day on, everyone must bring their bedding and toiletries and remain on school premises to go through "class background checks."

The Chinese teachers were in a flurry of activity, weaning babies, turning children over to grandparents, or fetching grandparents over for babysitting. On the first day, the Uighur teachers and staff arrived smiling, with not a stitch of bedding. The leader was furious, and the Uighur teachers and staff kept smiling and saying "Tomorrow." Many tomorrows came and went, but the Uighur teachers and staff never brought their bedding or toiletries, and the checking of "class background" faded away.

In the village, however, the checking on class background was conducted by personnel from the neighboring Fourth Division of the Military Agricultural Plantation. The person in charge, Comrade S, gave me the job of translating the personal records, since they would be working in both Uighur and mandarin. I humbly accepted, of course. But when I sat down to look at the records, I got the shock of my life. All the people under investigation were already labeled "class enemies" and sentenced to be shot! Including the young student who had said in jest, "Spies in the movies are smartly dressed and dance with beautiful girls, how I wish I were a spy . . ."

The point of the investigation was supposedly to dig out "counterrevolutionary cliques." The problem was that the harder you dig, the more you find, so that at the end of the day, there were more members of "counterrevolutionary cliques" standing on the stage to be denounced than there were members of the masses in the audience to do the denouncing. All those clique members were made to bend down and were handcuffed from behind. My question: where did they get so many handcuffs? Certainly not provided by the regular police! It turned out that those handcuffs were all hastily turned out by the village ironmonger from our own commune!

Just as the hunt for "counter-revolutionary cliques" was going on at full steam, Premier Zhou Enlai's directive was handed down: the labeling of "counterrevolutionary" cliques was to be approved by the highest authority at Central, not at the local county level, not at the prefecture level, not at the provincial level.

Thus, all the "counterrevolutionary cliques" dissolved into thin air. The so-called targets have been "strengthened through ordeal," as the saying goes, and the masses have been "tempered through struggle," and things were back to what they had always been. Well, not entirely. There was a man surnamed Xu who had come from Jiangsu. It was said that he had been in trouble in 1957 and was sent down here. After being attacked and physically manhandled, he went to the highway and ran in front of a car, dying on the spot. Another person, Comrade Zhang, who was actually a friend of Song Yanming, the propaganda chief, ran to the highway and killed himself with a butcher knife. People were saying that there was another man, a specialist in Uighur linguistics who had made a great contribution by translating Uighur folk songs into Mandarin, and now he too had killed himself. Let us hope that the deaths of these innocent people will serve as a warning. Let us hope that such tragedies will never happen again.

Chapter 28

The May 7th Cadre School, and a Sequel

By the time things had quieted down in the village and the so-called counterrevolutionary cliques let off the hook, it was already the spring of 1970. During the Spring Festival break, a member of the "work team" at my unit back at the Federation of Literature and Art Circles in Urumqi suddenly showed up in Ghulja on a mission of "investigation." This meant that I was trusted enough to give information on some case that the "work team" at the Federation was working on! I was elated. But to my chagrin, apart from news that so and so at the Federation had been ousted in the latest move on "class background checking," the man knew nothing about my case and could not care less.

Since arriving in Urumqi and being sent down to be "tempered through manual labor," more than five years had gone by. What was my current status? What did my "unit," the Federation of Literature and Art Circles, propose to do with me? This man standing in front of me did not have a clue. Am I supposed to be "tempered" for the rest of my life? I was like a kite whose string snaps in mid-air. I had to do something.

In the spring of 1969, the factions at the Federation had united to form a "Joint Committee," and one of the decisions of the "Joint Committee" was to half my salary and freeze my savings account, seeing as I was not yet properly "tempered." When the order was passed on to the Commune leaders there, they asserted that the "joint committee" was not an official entity and had no power to meddle in salaries, and that Wang Meng was a good member of the commune in any case. Well-meaning as these local people were, that did not help my immediate situation. To say nothing of the fact that we had an addition to our family, our newborn little daughter.

I had always been part of a work unit; now I felt abandoned, without any unit to identify myself with. It was close to six years now, this uncertainty. What did the Federation intend to do with me? Actually as it later turned out, the answer was simple. The Federation was itself a shambles. As far as my future was concerned, they did not give a damn.

Clueless as to the state of affairs, I was a bundle of nerves and could not bear the tension anymore. Finally in the spring of 1971, I hopped on a long-distance bus, arrived in Urumqi, and made my way to my "unit," the Xinjiang Federation of Literature and Art Circles.

What met me at the Federation was a complete fiasco. There were just about a hundred or so personnel attached to the Federation and after all those years, they were still at each other's throats, claiming that the "cover-up of class struggle" at the Federation had yet to be lifted.

I found temporary housing in the singles' dorm. There I roomed with the poet Rehim· He was the most dashing figure that I had ever met among the Xinjiang educated elite—spruce in a Western suit, looking out at you through a pair of piercing blue eyes. Rehim was a hard drinker, buried in debt, and could not get along with people. At the moment, he was in the middle of a divorce, so he had no home to go to. It was said that he and his wife had divorced once before, got back together, and were now divorcing again.

During that miserable short stay at the Federation, Rehim and I commiserated and supported each other. Once, we finished off a whole bottle of liquor in one sitting. We lunched on noodles together. We chatted about this and that, especially about Ili. Without Rehim, I would have been desperately lonely.

As things turned out, I must say that my arrival in Urumqi had been most timely. One month later, orders were handed down from above:

All personnel and staff at the Xinjiang Federation of Literature and Art Circles should pack up and go down to the May 7th Cadre School[I]

I. The so-called May 7th Cadre School was named after an instruction by Mao Zedong on May 7, 1969, to send government officials, college instructors, and academics to work in labor camps in rural areas across the country during the and such work units as the Federation will eventually be dissolved!

The "Culture and Education Circles May 7th Cadre School" to which we folks at the Federation were assigned, was located in the Ulanbay area, about forty li south of Umruchi. We had stayed there for upward of two years. At "school," I shared a room with the Uighur poet Abdkerim Ho Jayef and the critic Patar Jan. I also joined the Uighur group in the daily reading of Mao's works, and that was helpful for my language study.

For me the most important benefit from my stay at the May 7th Cadre School was the fact that my *status* was finally clarified. At the time, people who were not politically tainted were called "May 7th jianqi" (May 7th soldiers). People who had not yet been cleared" were in a political hiatus; they were "shelved" for the moment and did not qualify as "jianqi."

One day there was a "jianqi only" meeting, and I was included! It meant that I had been accepted into the fold! I was a "jianqi"!

Once on this footing, I made a statement at a general meeting. I said that since I was a "jianqi" it follows that I am not being "shelved"— how can a "jianqi" be "shelved"?— the two concepts were mutually incompatible. I made this statement because a piddling little nobody at the Federation was spreading the word that I was still on the "shelf." The president of the "Cadre School" was Gong Ke, formerly a leading figure at the Ministry of Culture. He laughed at my speech, and that was the end of the matter.

I raised the issue of my "jianqi" status not for its own sake, but for my salary. If I was a "jianqi" like everybody else, by rights I should retain my full salary. Soon my back salary was paid in full, a staggering sum of two thousand-plus yuan. I wrote to Ruifang, who was in Beijing at the time, telling her the good news. Ruifang, who rarely ever indulged in political jargon, wrote back: "This is a victory for Mao Zedong Thought" and promptly bought a scarlet Russian carpet to celebrate.

The Cadre School was a military deployment, and we in the Federation group were designated Regiment No. 1. At first, I was on the night shift

---

height of the Cultural Revolution. Mao's instruction was in response to a May 7th letter from Lin Biao, who made the suggestion. Entire work units were sent down when the Cutural Revolution ran out of steam in 1970–72. With Mao's approval, public institutions were disbanded and staff sent down for manual labor as Lin Biao had suggested.

for irrigation; the work was light but the wee hours hard to bear. Then out of the blue I was selected to be deputy head of the kitchen staff. The head was Wang Yuhu, a veteran writer who had written most of the scripts for films with a Xinjiang background. I was elated by this sign of trust. The Xinjiang writer Klim Hoga, who was now a cook on my staff, talked about the "three handles": the handle of the warrior's sword, the handle of the official's chop, and the handle of the cook's chopper. All emblems of power, he stated. Poor Liu Xiaowu, formerly head of the Xinjiang Federation of Literature and Art Circles, was still on the "shelf," tending pigs. He was often late for meals and had to make do with leftovers.

At the cadre school, the only thing hard to swallow was the so-called *massive critique*—supposedly food for our re-education. One of the papers we were supposed to study was a critique of the nursery tale "Pulling the Turnip." We all know the story: one rabbit could not pull out the turnip, more rabbits came to help and the big turnip was pulled out—a fable on the strength of the collective. The *critique* stated: "The turnip was planted by poor-and-lower-middle peasants, but the story imputed it to rabbits! Now isn't this lying?"! Another *critique,* intended for our edification, was written by a newly installed bureau chief of culture. He was asked to approve a song about a "babbling brook." The man critiqued: "How can a brook babble?" and that was the end of the song. These cadres had all been dispatched from Beijing, they did not take to Xinjiang, and one by one they all flitted away.

In spite of these *critiques,* we were in a good mood.

First, we had work to keep ourselves busy, and that was a relief from the years of infighting.

Second, living in a collective can be fun.

Third, the food was much better than what we had in the countryside.

Fourth, the air in Xinjiang was fresh and clear, you would never see the moon and the stars so close and so clearly anywhere else.

We "cadre school jiangqi" sometimes held our own little celebrations on the Gobi Desert, singing and composing poetry.

Once, during the National Day holiday, I had the good fortune to be sent on a mission to fetch lumber and had a close view of the breathtaking majesty of the deep forests hidden behind the mountains.

There was a monthly holiday at the cadre school, but my home was still back in Ili. So I would stay at the Federation's old quarters in Urumqi or stay put in the cadre school as a watchman. On the latter occasions, I would abuse my privilege and make free with the kitchen larder, making stuffed buns, fried cruellers, meatballs, and other goodies while listening to snatches from one or other of the "eight model operas" on a semiconductor radio.

In the year 1972, the Lin Biao affair erupted.[2]

All the ugliness in our life vanished, and people waited happily to "graduate" from the "cadre school." Meanwhile we were abandoned to enjoying life as much as possible, busy with chess or cards, right into the wee hours.

It occurred to me that perhaps many things in the world do begin with a bang and end with a whimper.

Some wars are like that.

Some books are like that, such as the classic *Dream of the Red Chamber*. Some attempts at musical composition are like that.

The Cultural Revolution was like that.

In 1973, Comrade Saipidin Aziz, the leading figure in the Xinjiang Uighur Autonomous Region, decided that all personnel under the previous Federation of Literature and Art Circles should be taken out of "cadre school" and reorganized into a Literary Research Group under the supervision of the local Bureau of Culture, to be engaged in "research" in literary and art projects.

My first job under the Literary Research Group was to write captions for a story told in a series of illustrations. It was said that the culture czars in Beijing were thinking of putting up an exhibition of stories in illustration. So we faraway scribblers and dabblers were put to work. The contribution of Xinjiang toward this planned exhibition was to be a story told through illustrations: "Tree of Blood and Tears."

It was said that there used to be an ancient poplar tree which had stood on the grounds of what is now the Red Star Commune in Yining, and that in the old days, poor peasants used to be bound to that tree and

---

2. According to officially released information, Lin Biao fled the country with his wife, son and a couple of associates on an air force Trident aircraft, which reportedly crashed in Mongolia after running out of fuel, killing all on board.

whipped by their landlord masters. We group of three writers and artists were sent on a short business trip to the locality the better to create the illustrated series on site.

The job was a hot potato.

Now if the poor peasant was drawn as being bound and whipped, how could he fill the "heroic" role demanded by the revolutionary literary tenets of the day?

On the other hand, if you make this poor peasant turn around and fight his landlord torturer all on his own, could not that be construed as denying the role of the Party?

Or on a flight of fancy, how about we make a Communist Party member appear in the nick of time to save the peasant? Considering the early historical period of this legendary tree, would that "communist" be a genuine member of the Chinese Communist Party, or could he be from the Soviet Union? The ideological pitfalls were endless.

The artists doing the drawing, moreover, had their own priorities. Lie Yang, a veteran artist, wanted to add female characters, preferably a little concubine of the landlord carrying on an affair with the poor peasant. His partner, a younger artist, seized this business trip as an opportunity to sketch profiles of pretty country girls and had no interest in legendary old poplars.

To make these artists keep politics in mind was harder than making that proverbial camel go through the eye of a needle. I became the butt of their jokes. Once, to pass the time, Lie Yang started to tell everybody their fortunes. Pissed off by my ideological caution, he predicted that Wang Meng would one day become a "Minister" of the government! How we doubled over in laughter at that idea!

Chapter 29

Final Farewell to Ili

Back in Urumqi, life went on as usual. In spite of that very expensive "education" at the "Cadre School," we were back to where we were before.

My top priority was to get Ruifang, left behind in Ili, relocated back to Urumqi. At the moment, our younger son, Wang Shi, was with Ruifang in Ili; they were just waiting for approval to move. Our eldest son, Wang Shan, and our daughter Yihuan were with their maternal grandma in Beijing, while I was in Urumqi. Our little family, again, was scattered over three locations.

I now concentrated all my energy on getting the wheels rolling for Ruifang's transfer: I looked up the wife of Comrade Maimiao, previous Party Secretary of the Federation of Literature and Art Circles. I looked up Comrade Zhao Qunli, in charge of personnel at the Urumqi Bureau of Education. I went to Comrade Yuanru, the head of personnel of the No. 7 Middle School (where Ruifang had once taught) and through her, reached Comrade Wang Xifeng of the Urumqi Bureau of Education. Comrade Wang Xifeng gave the order for Ruifang's transfer, very straightforward, no negotiation.

All the same, I went through Wang Yuhu, the film scriptwriter, to reach Yir Hail, governor of the prefecture of Ili, so that there would be no obstacles from the government side. The minute school was closed for the summer holidays, I arranged for Ruifang and our son Wang Shi to join me in Urumqi, stating that she was not going back to Ili, transfer or no transfer. In September of 1973, Ruifang's transfer order arrived, and I made the trip alone to Ili to deal with the paperwork.

Starting from 1965 when I had first arrived, I had spent a total of eight years in Ili and I could hardly bear to leave. It was a tie of affection that had been nurtured over eight years' time. If not for the difference between country and city, if not for considerations of personal development, and if not for the so-called educated elite seeking out their own kind, I would have no reason to leave.

My first visit was to Bayanday, which I had left more than two years earlier. My landlady, Old Mother Haliqam, was suffering from trachoma and could hardly see. I had brought snacks and helped put some into her mouth. Her home had been moved to another part of the village due to some adjustment in team formation, and poor Haliqam blamed her eye trouble on the move. I cannot even begin to count the number of meals Haliqam had prepared for me. I remember Ramadan, when Muslims eat one meal after dark and one meal before daylight. The fun was that I would join their evening meal, sleep through their meal before daylight, and get up leisurely to enjoy a meal that Haliqam would prepare specially for me! Haliqam died not long after our last meeting.

May her soul rest in peace!

Finished with the paperwork for Ruifang's transfer, I was ready to leave. I spent the last few days in our former dwelling, which was by now a shambles, and struggled with mixed feelings about the imminent move. I recall what Axim-Yusuf, secretary of the Second Brigade, had said to me way back in 1971 when I had first tried to return to Urumqi: "Old Wang, you are a decent fellow. If you can't survive in Urumqi, come back here. We need you. We will fix your residential registration. We will give you a plot and build you a house with an orchard. Don't worry, we are behind you . . ."

I couldn't help looking back to the days we had spent there. Ruifang and I were interested in every aspect of the culture, eager to participate in any new experience. Sometimes people would come to our door begging for food. But when they saw us, aliens, they would turn away with an apology. We would run after them with some money, but no food, as our food would be considered unclean.

I had once endured a memorable line-up for tea bricks. During those times so many essentials were missing—people would line up for anything available even if they had no immediate need. One day, tea bricks made a rare appearance. My tea coupon was about to expire, so I rushed to stand in line. I stood doggedly in line for seven straight hours and was lucky to get hold of one of the last batch! Queuing was itself a challenge, a risk, and a pleasure. People in small towns were friendly. Standing in line we would chat. Time and again I would recognize someone who had stood in line behind me at a store, or at the bus stop—"queue mates."

One of the most interesting slices of life here in Xinjiang was the singing of the cart drivers. On this my last trip, I heard it again. As fall approaches, horse-drawn carts would start transporting coal. During those times, the few coalmines up north would be deluged with people standing in line. You arrived before dawn and got your coal by early afternoon. If you were late, you might have to wait through the night. Thus cart drivers transporting coal would start off in the middle of the night, so as to catch the early birds. They would warm themselves up with a little wine, and then drive their horse-drawn cart to the coal mine, singing all the way. Their singing could be animated or dreamy, the strains would wind on endlessly: now wild, now tender, now heroic, now plaintive. None of the greatest tenors in the world could touch me as did the singing of the cart drivers of Ili. And now I was really saying good-bye to all this.

It is my blessing to have had the chance to live among such people, in such a place—what more could I want? But I cannot free myself of worldly ambitions, cannot rise above mundane pursuits. I want to throw myself into the madding crowd, to be part of the stressful game.

I was leaving, under obligations which I would never be able to fulfill. I have let you down, good people of Ili.

On the day of departure just as the truck was about to start, a colleague of Ruifang's, Li Hong, a teacher, rushed over, bringing me a parting gift of scrambled eggs wrapped in pancake. I thought it was totally unnecessary, but he insisted and I took the package. Who would have thought that throughout that two-day trip sitting on my luggage in the truck, I could not find a single inn or eating place that was open for business! This is what it was like after eight years of Cultural Revolution!

Back in Urumqi, Ruifang was teaching at the No.14 Middle School and we lived in the school dorm. Thus we started life anew. Things were always hard for the lowly couple, but we could get by. That is life.

At the Literary Research Group, my unit at the time, I was exempt from office hours. I stayed home and did my writing while taking care of the house. I would write as I kept an eye on the stuffed buns steaming over the fire. As I wrote I filled the hot water container, or added coal to the fire, or bank the fire, whatever the situation called for I am proud of the fact that I could write despite interruptions, but sometimes I felt embarrassed. We were in the dorm of a school, after all. People did tend to wonder as they saw me always puttering around in and out of the place.

We had a little back garden of about ten square meters. My son and I had built a storage room of about four square feet. With the coming of spring, I set up a brick stove and turned the storage room into a kitchen. I would do the family cooking there as I did my writing. My biological clock would tell me when to get up and check the fire. Starting a fire, feeding the flames and banking it was one of my keenest pleasures. I don't believe in the airs that some writers put on: no noise, no interruptions and what not. Not me. I would sit writing indoors, get up for the mail, even go out to pay the electricity bill, and still be back on time to tend the fire and take up my writing where I had stopped. My experience had made me immune to adversity. After those years of being forced to join in the chorus of belittling, despising, and even denouncing the art of writing, I was just happy to have things back to normal. It is comical, and yet pathetic. I would write as I steamed baozi, and both would turn out well.

With the coming of fall, we stored turnips and cabbage. The two boys joined me in digging an underground storage room. It was a joy to have a patch of earth to call one's own. It was a blessing to be able to raise the shovel and strike deep into the earth. Inch by inch, the shovel worked over the earth, and over time, the underground vegetable storage room was ready. The boys called gleefully to their mom to come down and take a look. They even cut into one side of the dugout to form steps for her to go down and up. We also raised a wall of beaten clay and built a little storeroom aboveground.

In winter we did our cooking indoors. One of my self-invented bakery items was a mixture of corn flour, wheat flour, and mashed pumpkin sprinkled with crushed onions and a pinch of salt. I did not have equal success with bread, though, try as I might. Buying flour and grains was a trial. You might have your coupons, but flour and grains were not always available. Just as you might have coupons for tea or for meat, you rarely saw tea in the teashop or meat at the butcher's. Thus it was permissible to ask leave to buy flour and grain whenever they were available. So considerate of the leadership!

In Urumqi, unlike Beijing, there were hardly any little grocery stores dotted here and there in streets and alleys. Here the closest grocery store was six or seven hundred meters away. Besides, you never knew what would be available on any given day at any given time. When out shopping, I would bring six or seven bags and bottles, and grab whatever was on offer. Get cooking oil if you see cooking oil, get vinegar if you see vinegar. If a line is forming, get in line early and then check what it is you are queuing for. Always make sure you keep a good stock of everything in case of shortages. I pat myself on the back for executing all the above tasks conscientiously and satisfactorily. I must say, if no one else does, that I have kept the household running smoothly.

But Ruifang was under impressed. She had something to her credit, beside which all my achievements paled. She had once single-handedly, brick by brick, unloaded a ton of brick coal, and then brick by brick piled them up into a mini-Great Wall.

Life is in the details; details are ordinary, banal, but indispensable. Men of great accomplishments, geniuses, heroes, they cannot dispense with the petty details of ordinary life either. But a man's heart can be throbbing with colorful dreams and soaring ambitions. Can he be satisfied with the ordinary, the banal, the little odds and ends that make up life? Won't he secretly shed tears for letting life go by without making a splash? Will he rail against life and despise the ordinary because life had treated him unfairly? Or perhaps he will wish to turn life into a feather, a handful of dust, and let it drift with the wind? Perhaps he is resigned to seeing life, which comes only once, fade away without leaving a trace of meaning?

1976. Premier Zhou died in January. People's hearts were heavy. Certain people in high places had been disrespectful during the mourning ceremonies. Soon, the country was led through another convulsion:

"Repudiating the Rightist-Reversal Plot," aimed at Deng Xiaoping. Actually Deng had just resumed office and things were beginning to look hopeful. But now Deng was brought down again, and all our hopes were dashed. During the Spring Festival when people gathered together, public opinion had never been so united, all pointing one way. Though sadly, people still talked in terms of "loyal minister," "evil adviser," "enjoying royal favor," "royal negligence" and so on. In Chinese society, why is it so hard to move forward?

April arrived, cloudy, windy, and cold. Ruifang came running back from school one day, saying that there had been an incident in Tiananmen. On April Fifth, Festival of Ghosts, people seized the opportunity to go to the Square to commemorate the death of Zhou Enlai, obliquely demonstrating against Jiang Qing and her team, later known as the "Gang of Four." The masses were dispersed by force of arms. Ruifang and I looked at each other, silent in grief. This is what will later be known as the April 5 Incident.

Here in Urumqi, we also had to go through the motions of "study" to conform to the official version of events.

A public demonstration was held for "repudiating the rightist reversal plot," followed by a march. When the ragtag band reached South Gate, however, the first batch of spring chives went on sale and the marchers melted away . . .

At such a time, one could not help thinking of Chairman Mao Zedong. He had played such an important part in our lives. His every move affected our lives for good or for evil, for life or for death. The style of his speech so familiar to us, could make us or break us. But now he was getting old, He was losing control of his faculties. We could see that on television. It was a sad sight. It made me think that China was getting old, that we were all getting old. No one dared imagine a day when Chairman Mao would not be around. He had personally concerned himself with my story "Young Newcomer at the Organization Department," and had commented favorably on it, and it had been a positive influence on my life.

And now by 1976, I realized that Chairman Mao's passing would be a great danger, an unfathomable hole, an unknown factor, but at the same time a chance for change, a chance to untie many knots.

The cycle of life defies Greatness, defies Power, defies Ambition, defies Sadness. One day in September, we were told to listen to an important broadcast of the Central Broadcasting Station, and I knew immediately that the day had come. I dared not think on what was to follow. I was ready for anarchy and could only hope for survival.

Unlike the atmosphere during Zhou Enlai's death when people were prostrated by grief, now at Mao's death, the dominant reaction was one of gravity and unspoken fear.

That same night, Ruifang and I talked deep into the night, speculating on what was to follow.

Actually, events followed at lightning speed. I had expected change, but never dreamed that it would come so fast.

I was in grateful tears. It was a second Liberation. When the Henan opera singer Chang Xiangyu[1] set her tune to the words: "Down with the Gang of Four."[2] I could not hold back my tears of joy. Why was I so involved? Why not stand on the sidelines? I could not. My feelings were irrepressible. I know right from wrong. No matter how I tried to retreat, to accept fate, to act dumb, to spend my days keeping cats and dogs, cooking and frying, my heart still belonged to China, I am concerned about my country, concerned about the world, I looked forward eagerly to a new page in Chinese history. A new page was being turned.

---

1. Chang Xiangyu, 1923–2004, Henan folk opera singer.
2. Jiang Qing, Wang Hongwen, Zhang Chunqiao, and Yao Wenyuan.

WANG MENG

a life

Illustrations

Figure 1 – My father Wang Jindi with me (front left), my sister Wang Sa, and cousins Wang Shengsheng and Wang Rui.

Figure 2 – Photo of me in grade 2 of elementary school. Reproduction of the original photo given to teacher Mrs. Hua Xialing.

Figure 3 – Wang Meng and siblings. From left, Wang Sa, Wang Meng, Wang Ming and Wang Zhi.

Figure 4 – With He Ping and Qin Xueru (left and center).

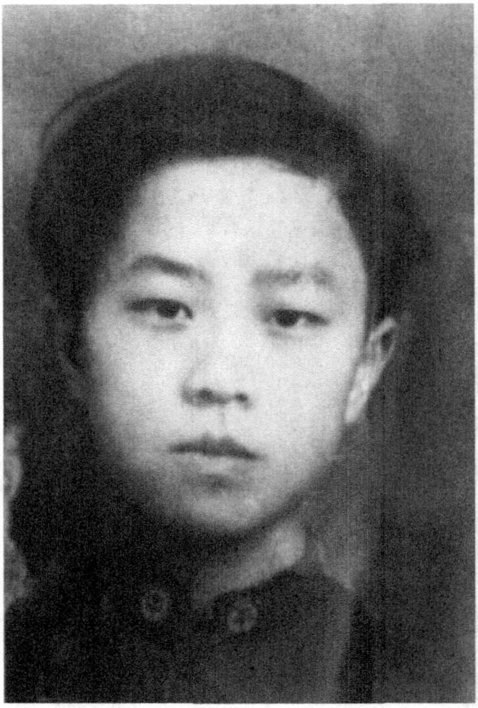

Figure 5 – This photo was taken upon my graduation from junior high school.

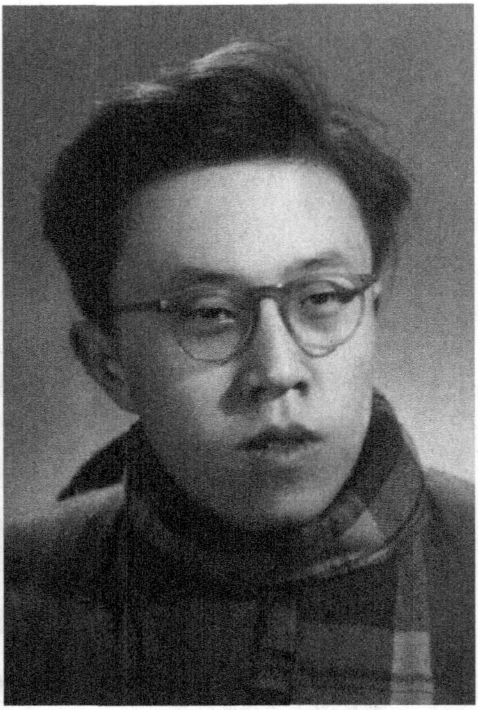

Figure 6 – Wang Meng in 1951 while working at the district committee of the Communist Youth League.

Figure 7 – Wedding photo – Wang Meng and wife Cui Ruifang on January 28, 1957.

Figure 8 – This photo was taken in 1957 after being subjected to criticism in the anti-rightist campaign.

Figure 9 – Shortly after my arrival in Ili, Xinjiang, in 1965.

Figure 10 - On the 10th anniversary of our wedding with sons Wang Shan and Wang Shi in Ili in 1967.

Figure 11 – At the home of Yisihake of Bayandai Village in Ili.

Figure 12 – This photo was taken at the town of Yining, the seat of Ili Prefecture, with me being second and poet Tieyipujiang third from right.

Figure 13 – With Aximu Yusuopu, party secretary of No. 2 Production Team of Bayandai Village.

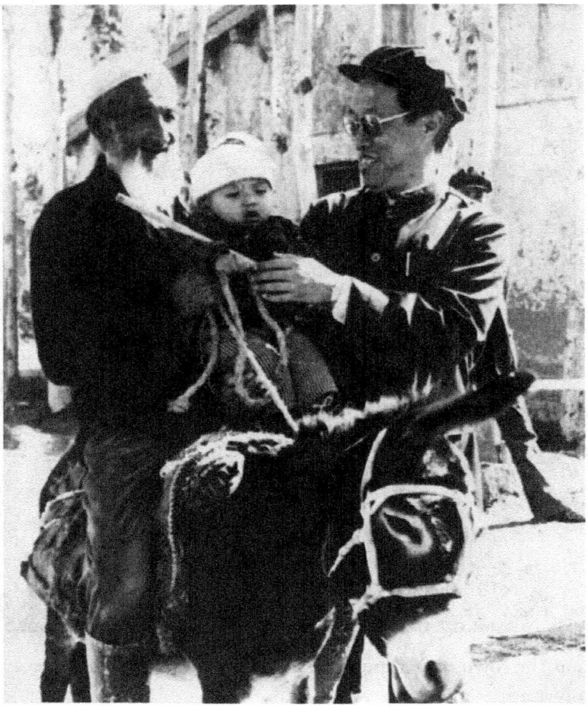

Figure 14 – Chatting with a Uighur villager.

Figure 15 – Driving horses pulling a threshing stone.

Figure 16 – With villagers at Bayandai Village in Ili.

Figure 17 – At the Herbert Hoover museum on September 7, 1980.

Figure 18 – At the farm house in Eagle Nest Village.

Figure 19 – With my wife on a rooftop terrace of the Potala Palace in Lhasa when attending the Shoton Festival in August 1986.

Figure 20 – At the home of soprano Dilber Yunus in 1988.

Figure 21 – Reunion on October 25, 1991 with my landlord Abdrahman from the Xinjiang days.

Figure 22 – During a visit to the United States on November 22, 1993.

Figure 23 – Visiting Malaysia in 1993.

Figure 24 - Visiting Japan in 1994.

Figure 25 - Visiting Alberta, Canada in April 1995.

Figure 26 – Enjoying a meal with my wife at a Greek restaurant in downtown Aachen, Germany on June 16, 1996.

Figure 27 – At Heinrich Böll's in June 1996.

Figure 28 – Visiting writer Yasushi Inoue at his home during a visit to Japan in 1997.

Figure 29 – Hosting a visit by Princess Maha Chakri Sirindhorn at my home on February 24, 2001.

Figure 30 – At the reception following my daughter Yihuan's doctoral defence at Leiden University in Holland in November 2003.

Chapter 30

Life Begins Again

The overthrow of the Gang of Four in 1976 was greeted as a second Liberation. For me, this second Liberation actually overshadowed the first. It was a critical turning point for my fate, for my very survival. That first Liberation of 1949 brought in its wake the thrill of victory, but this second Liberation was a beam of light shining through the darkness, a vista opening up when the path seemed to have reached a dead-end. Now, each day brought new hopes and unexpected pleasures.

Of course the change of direction had to be justified by a former Mao quotation, namely his 1957 talk on "The Ten Major Relationships," one of the least dogmatic of his utterances. Following which, the *People's Daily* published an editorial refuting the extremist critique of the so-called "Fixation on Productivity." The editorial pointed to the sorry condition of the economy, and ended by asking that if this was "Fixation on Productivity," should people live on empty air? Actually these pearls of common sense wisdom had long been circulating among the common people, but only whispered under their breath. Now that the political taboos had been removed, now that the Emperor's new clothes had been exposed, such a platitude when spoken out loud actually resonated like a clap of thunder! Now that we could openly state that a cloud was a cloud, such a statement actually seemed sublime, moving, dramatic, tragic, and yet so comical. To remember everything we had to go through to get to where we are today, to reach this point when we can call a cloud a cloud, and call a spade a spade! As people used to say, "To live, it means to be able to see." We see, because we are alive! But the others, they are not here anymore, they cannot see what is happening. We the timid, we the conformers, we can now rejoice in our survival, and call a spade a spade.

Little by little, life resumed its normal course. This was obvious from the start. But I must be careful. There will be relapses, setbacks, reverses. I must not stick my head out. I must keep my tail between my legs. I must go on as if nothing had happened, I kept reminding myself. But still I could not keep down my elation, so much so that well meaning friends gave me warning hints: the ways of the high and mighty are unpredictable, their intentions hard to decipher . . . My friends advised caution, caution, and still more caution. So I told myself: Enjoy yourself, but in little bites.

I first showed my hand through a short piece titled "Poetry and Math," a eulogy on the restoration of the National Examination system at the end of 1977, a momentous event which heralded the reopening of colleges and universities across the country. In the essay I quoted Mao; I quoted Hua Guofeng, Mao's designated successor; I repeated the prevalent line of attack on the Gang of Four. There was not a single word of my own, not a hint of individuality. The only thing that could be called my own was the eulogy of math as a form of poetry. I sang the praise of poetry and math as the epitome of wisdom, the cream of culture. For the record, I had said this long before the Fujian scholar Lin Xingzhai pronounced math as the highest form of poetry, much later, in the 1980s. I do not remember how I submitted this article to the *Xinjiang Daily*, but I remember the word being passed around that the leadership at the paper had been saying positive things about Wang Meng, and thus my little article appeared in the literary supplement of *Xinjiang Daily* in December 1977.

It was exactly thirteen years since May 1964 when the paper had published my article, "Spring in Turfan," shortly after my arrival in Xinjiang. Add thirteen years to the period between 1958 to 1962 when my writing had been under a complete ban, and the years from 1962 to 1964 when I had been under a "soft" ban—let me state for the record that the literary inquisition had banned me from writing and publishing for a total of seventeen years.

The article "Poetry and Math" was followed by a short story "The

Splendor of Spring," based on the true story of a young couple from inland China who had sincerely answered the call and dedicated themselves to building a new Xinjiang. It was published in *Xinjiang Literature* magazine in January of 1978.

Now the letters started coming, from the prestigious *People's Literature* magazine and other publications representing literary authority. A letter from those quarters was proof that one was being taken back into the fold. All of which just goes to show the weight of institutions and the weightlessness of writers.

Now what should I write for *People's Literature* magazine? What should I write to show that Wang Meng's pen was as nimble as ever, to show that Wang Meng was still worthy of the erstwhile praise showered on him from the highest quarter—of being "talented"? Unlike my writings of the 1950s, which had been motivated by my own feelings, inspired by life itself, I now started out from the politically "correct." I now used the material of life as a means toward the vindication of politics. In making art serve politics, the most appropriate subject matter at hand would be my experience of life in Xinjiang among the Uighurs. My short story, titled "The Captain, the Secretary, the Wild Cat and the Stump of a Broken Chopstick," joined in the prevailing chorus denouncing the Gang of Four. I sometimes think to myself, what if I had continued writing in this style, manufacturing characters and stories according to the politics of the times, as some of my peers did? I mailed the story to *People's Literature* in faraway Beijing.

The response from *People's Literature* finally arrived. As I look back to the scene on that momentous day, how pitiful it had been, how pathetic, and yet how satisfying! It was a rainy day in early summer. Ruifang was in school as usual, and I was at home making chive dumplings. I was dusted all over with flour, and the room reeked with the smell of raw chives. Suddenly Ruifang rushed in, her face flushed, sputtering unintelligibly, totally unlike her usual self. It turned out that my story had been published in *People's Literature.*

Never mind the weight of the shackles on my feet, the words which flowed from my pen had carried me through. I grabbed the newly arrived copy of *People's Literature* and pored over the printed words written by Wang Meng—reappearing after a span of half a lifetime, it seemed. My heart was warmed, saddened. I was overwhelmed by a hundred conflicting feelings.

Finally my patience was rewarded! Is this real? Is this Wang Meng appearing in print again, in *People's Literature*? I went over the printed words of my own short story, and they appeared like strangers, like old acquaintances with which I had lost touch for many years. Who wrote these words? Wang Meng! Which Wang Meng? The Wang Meng who had written "Young Newcomer at the Organization Department" at age twenty-two! Since then, twenty-three years had come and gone!

Life went on, highlighted by significant markers. In 1977, Liu Xinwu's "The Class Monitor" appeared in *People's Literature*. I was struck by Liu's exposure of the emotional devastation, the moral blindness of the Cultural Revolution, especially its brutalizing influence on a whole generation of school age youngsters. My heart missed a beat! Can you write like this and get away with it? Does it mean that nowadays you can write short stories without looking over your shoulder? My eyes misted over. And so, we wielders of the pen are finally allowed to take a stab at the destruction of learning, we are allowed to shed a few tears on our own behalf! Following on the impact of "The Class Monitor," new works appeared in succession by writers who had recently emerged from cold storage, such as former poet Shao Yanxiang, or straight out of the iron house, such as the novelist Cong Weixi.

I personally felt that I had completed my life span from 1934 to 1978 in exactly forty-four years. After all, my favorite writer, Chekhov, had only lived forty-four years but had left such a treasure house of exquisite writings. Now, at the beginning of 1978, at age forty-four, I was poised to make a new start. I looked around: is this really a new beginning? I was all fired up, ready to take the leap. At the same time, I tiptoed cautiously, prepared for any contingency. Having been tossed about on a sea of troubles for the last two decades, I now found myself safely on shore and still in one piece! How could I afford to be so naïve and trustful? How dare I let it go to my head?

On the Festival of Souls, April 1978 (now the Festival has become part of the collective memory, following on the events of April 5, 1976), I dashed off a new story "The Most Precious." Inspired by "The Class Monitor," I described how the human heart has been turned into stone, losing its sense of right and wrong, losing its sense of human values, under the demonic influence of the Cultural Revolution. I remember a film from East Germany, called *The Cold Heart*, and the theme song "Forget-Me-Not." The heart-wringing emotions stirred by that film now resurfaced, and a "cold heart" became the subject matter as well as the theme of my new story. In the heat of the Cultural Revolution, an innocent little boy unwittingly disclosed the whereabouts of a veteran cadre who was in hiding, thus leading to the old man's death at the hands of the Red Guards. Yes, in my exposure of the violence of the Cultural Revolution, I had targeted a mere boy. And so what if I did? As an old saying goes, if you cannot afford to blame the kettle, blame the teacup! Isn't it what Chinese writers have been doing all along, blaming the teacup instead of the kettle? Now what can I do except blame the boy! As to who or what made the boy do what he did, readers can figure that out for themselves. Can't they see through the tragedy of the teacup?

Whatever critics or readers say about my story, for me it was a release of pent-up emotions, of long suppressed tears. "They are like the evil witches in fairy tales, they steal people's throbbing red hearts and leave a cold stone in their place. The stone has no ideals, no principles, no sacrifice, no truth, no courage, no loyalty, no faith, no humility, no steadfastness, no warmth, no light. Written on this stone are merely cold, calculating avarice, only hypocrisy and power plays and profanity, only the dumb creature's defensive shell and the animal's aggressive horns." Is the father's admonition to the little boy in the story, or is it talking directly to Wang Meng? Has Wang Meng also undergone a change of heart? Thinking back to all the campaigns since Liberation, isn't it true that they had been couched in highfalutin language, unleashed in the name of the most glorious goals? But in practice isn't it true that these same campaigns had been set into motion by resorting to mankind's heart of darkness, stirring up their most despicable motives, leading them to lie, to betray—out of fear, out of self-interest, or simply out of spite. And have we ever stopped to think what these repeated onslaughts have contributed to the moral decay of our people as a whole?

My story "The Most Precious" was published in *Writing* magazine in late summer of that year [1978]. I later learned that the story had been translated into German by a Sinologist who was working for the *Voice of*

Deutschland radio station. He claimed that this story of a change of heart had originated in Germany. In 1964, newly arrived in Xinjiang, at a Spring Festival get-together, I picked up a cigarette and from then on discovered the pleasure of smoking— and kept it up for fourteen years. Through the years of the Cultural Revolution, in far away Xinjiang, one could not write, one could not make friends, one could not engage in chitchat, one could not even indulge in food and drink (limited by coupons for food and cooking oil, as well as by the size of your pocketbook). It was even worse after 1971 when I was reassigned to Umruchi, the capital of the Xinjiang Autonomous Region, to work at the Federation of Literature and Art Circles. I lost touch with my friends in the countryside and was stuck with the endless "class struggle" going on in the office. For six or seven years, we could not work, could not write; we could not do anything productive, except keep "unleashing class struggle" as ordered from above. Apart from "class struggle," there was a quick lunch in the dining hall—four ounces of rice plus a choice between one veggie dish and another veggie dish with a suspicion of meat. This meal would be dispatched in twenty minutes at most, and then what?

Fortunately, cigarettes came to the rescue. You open the packet, you retrieve one cigarette, you tap it on the table, you feel how loosely the tobacco is packed, you shake your head in disapproval. You take out your box of matches. You love the sight of the flame. You look at the side of the matchbox, you scrutinize the scratch on the side, and wonder at the precise point of ignition. You must not strike the little matchstick too hard on the surface, or the side will be worn off before you go through all the matches. But you must not strike too lightly either, or it will not ignite. I remember a Soviet novel which described Stalin's smoking—he never used a lighter owing to the smell of gasoline. It would spoil his enjoyment of the first whiff of tobacco. Well, well, Stalin obviously wanted the best out of everything. Now as I pulled at my lit cigarette, I tried out ways of enjoying it, holding it loosely between the lips, blowing out rings of smoke, puffing through the nose, different positions for holding the cigarette. At least this gave me a few minutes satisfaction. I sometimes used the cigarette as a test of will power: I would refuse to light up when the craving came on. Or I would snuff out a newly lit cigarette, only to go back to it twelve hours later. I'd sometimes go through half a pack in one day, but at other times I could go on for days without lighting up at all. I tried out different brands of cigarettes and tobacco, including the local *Moherka.* I used different kinds of paper to roll tobacco, though it was said that tobacco rolled in newspaper is the most poisonous due to the ink in the print.

But whatever it is, throughout my fourteen years of smoking, I had made sure that I was in control, I had never let tobacco control me. Now that life was starting all over again, now that my rights as a citizen were being basically restored, and seeing that a new historical era was dawning, why should I go on smoking? My way of quitting was unique. I had read a newspaper article which described how tobacco causes cancer. Because the term Acrylamide sounded so scientific, so authoritative, I was an immediate convert. Whenever I felt the craving, I would pick up the article, which I had cut out, and reread it, and the graphic description of how Acrylamide worked on the lungs was enough to kill any craving. Later, at a get-together with old friends in the south, one guy repeated the old saying to beware of the man who neither drinks nor smokes. Another added that the man who smokes and quits at a moment's notice was even more dangerous, capable of "plots and strategies." I related my own experience of smoking and quitting. Knowing me, they changed their minds, conceding that not all such quitters would be so dangerous after all. To be truthful, I had never inhaled when I was a smoker, always knowing deep down that I would stop at some point. This reminds me of the famous saying of the Russian sinologist Troptsev that "The Soviet Union was created not to overcome, but to be overcome." Likewise, Wang Meng had taken up smoking, not to keep it up, but ultimately to quit.

Thus, in April 1978, after fourteen years of smoking, I quit and resumed writing. Smoking, which had accompanied all the unpleasantness of those years, became a thing of the past. There is the famous saying that "there is no pain like the death of the heart." For me, throughout those painful years, nothing had given me more relief than smoking. I had enveloped myself in smoke, I had lost myself in drunken stupors, I had whittled away my time, I had shrunk into a shell. As far as writing was concerned, I confess that I was outdated (no thanks to reminders from Shanghai scribblers), I vowed to give it up altogether. I announced that I had cut the bleeding knot. I had learned, not from literary quotations, but from life itself, about the pleasures to be wrung from the "death of the heart."

Now this individual called Wang Meng is back again at his desk. What with letters and solicitations for copy, you are back. You had stopped writing just as you had started smoking. The smoking had been taken up—to be ultimately dropped; the writing stopped—to be ultimately taken up again. In spite of all your vows, in spite of all your protests, it is not up to you—you are hard wired to it, all you need to do is to turn it on, and the writing starts flowing again, as if nothing had intervened in between.

Human life is marked by age, and Wang Meng is back to writing in his forties. It is no more the writing of youth, it is the writing of middle age. Somehow, life must be lived twice. Somehow love, or revolution, or writing must be experienced twice, the first time like a poem, like a dream, like childhood, like a drifting cloud. But illusions will be dashed. The second time around it is not so pure, not so intoxicating, nor so colorful, nor so passionate. The second time you live that experience, you have become more aware, you are cautious, you have become an old hand. You sometimes reproach yourself, you remember something from the past and smile wanly to yourself . . . but then you shrug and shake it off.

Chapter 31

The Winds of Spring

In early June of 1978, I sat for three and a half days on a hard seat, minus my cigarette, heading from Urumqi to the Beijing railway station. On arrival I was picked up by a young man from the Youth Publishing House and put on another train heading for the seaside resort of Beidaihe. Traveling together with me were writers, publishers, and critics from across the country. It took our group five hours to reach Beidaihe. The modest little station at Beidaihe struck me as pleasant, standing on a fresh green lawn dotted with trees and flowers.

It was not just the scene before me that made the difference—more to the point, it was my own mood. Winter in Xinjiang is never over until after May 1. But here I am, barely a month later, basking in the sun on the beach of Beidaihe!

We were housed in the holiday resort of the Youth League Central Committee, with a stone-paved walkway leading to the beach. It was an old building tucked away in a peach grove, with stone walls and lacquered window frames. Inside, some of the rooms had cement floors, some were laid with floorboards. Unoccupied for a long time, there was a musty air hanging over the place. But it was cool, and that was good enough for us.

The ostensible reason for my paid holiday to Beidaihe was for the purpose of revising a story, "The View from This Side," which I had started in Xinjiang. I worked on the story morning and evening and spent the afternoon swimming. After lunch, we fellow guests, bare backed and in shorts, would stretch out in sagging cane chairs, slapping our tummies while talking a blue streak. The food was good. The charge was thirty yuan per month, of which we paid a small percentage while the rest was absorbed by our host, the Youth Publishing House.

We swapped stories about everything under the sun, but mostly about the Gang of Four and the atrocities of the ultra-leftist line, some of which were hard to believe. There was this story of a young fellow: as he sang the song eulogizing Mao Zedong set to the words: "The Old Three Pieces, I love to read. My heart starts throbbing when I say the words . . . ," he made a slip of the tongue and mentioned not his heart but another part of his anatomy that started throbbing. For this sacrilegious mistake he was taken out and shot. There was also the story of the donkey shelter which caught fire. The "politically alert" extremists in the village swore that the fire was started by class enemies, while ordinary folks said that the little donkey had kicked the lamp and set the shelter on fire. The Provincial Revolutionary Committee called on the population of the whole province to take part in critiquing the "donkey-kicking" theory.

One extreme leads to another: all we could do was to laugh and laugh at stories of such suffering which stretched the limit of human endurance.

As for the main purpose of this trip—writing—I never managed to get into the right mood. I was always hampered by the "three prominence theory," dogma of the Gang of Four, whereby all literary writing was supposed to uphold the perfect communist hero. My story had been based on a case of burglary of rice in the village, and the unfolding of the story was supposed to lead to class struggle, but also take in scenes of Ili as well as the charms of Uighur culture. However, cramped by a tagged-on moral, the story never did work.

My true achievement during this trip lay in swimming. We used the part of the beach set aside for the Miners' Swimming Reserve. There is a charge nowadays, but at the time it was free. My self-imposed task was two laps from the beach to the edge of the safety area. I loved swimming but my technque was bad, and I needed to control my breathing. In the past, there was always too little time for practice: barely had I got into the swing of it the season was over and I had to wait for the next summer to start over again. But now I had all the time in the world. It was June, the temperature was still low, but I swam in earnest and made great progress.

After two laps to and from the safety area, I would lie down on the sand and soak up the sun, abandoning myself to the feeling of being at one with Nature.

It was just a couple of months by the ocean in Beidaihe, but the outside world seemed to have leaped through decades. On September 1, 1978, I left Beidaihe for Beijing. My plan had been to visit family briefly and head back to Xinjiang. I missed home. But who would have known that once in Beijing, events would rush at me from all directions. Leaving Beijing was out of the question. The folks at *People's Literature*, the folks at the People's Literature Publishing House, the folks at the Youth Publishing House, my old friends, my old classmates, my old connections, all looked me up, one after another.

I made a trip to the office of *People's Literature* and met veteran members of the editorial staff as well as a new member, Xiang Qian, who had edited my short story on the "broken chopstick." It turned out to be a very fruitful visit: I was invited on the spot to join a group of writers to visit an oil field in north China. Moreover, I was designated their special reporter to attend the Tenth National Congress of the Youth League. All very welcome to me. The group visiting the oil fields included members who were later responsible for restoring the Federation of Literature and Art Circles and the Writers' Union.

We visited the oil fields, we listened to reports of the achievements of the oil workers; we visited neighboring Baiyang Lake and enjoyed the famous view of a sea of reeds stretching into the misty distance. And of course we were entertained with food and drink. In a world where everyday provisions had dropped to a bare minimum, entertainment with food and drink is not something to be scoffed at. Of course, most importantly, I, from being a non-person was now restored to the status of a writer. The scope of my life was being expanded.

Attending the Congress of the Youth League touched me even more deeply. As I set foot in the Great Hall of the People, I was overwhelmed by conflicting feelings. It was my second experience of the red carpet treatment; what struck me was not elation, but a sense of *déjà vu* and caution, and a sense of unreality. I was still in a state of disbelief, I was unsure of myself. The change had come too suddenly.

During the course of the Congress, I was included when Hu Yaobang[1] met separately with leaders of local Youth League organizations who were in attendance at the Congress. Adapting a familiar folk saying,

When fellas from the same township meet,
tearfully each other they greet . . .

Hu said:

When old and new Youth Leaguers meet,
they challenge each other to new feats.

Hu Yaobang was still the untiring cheerleader as he always was. As for me, however, I was not the youthful leader of the Youth League District Committee anymore. But I did fulfill my commitment as a special reporter for the Congress and published a piece of reportage, "The Song of Fire," commemorating Li Xining, a young man from Nanjing, who had distinguished himself in the April 5th Movement (to commemorate the death of Zhou Enlai). I also published an essay "Hail to Alloy Steel," saluting this new generation of youth as precious metal which has been tempered through fire.

I got together with the editor of People's Publishing House, Wei Junyi, in September. Used to handling major issues, she came right to the point.

First of all, she decided that my early novel *Long Live Youth,* which had never seen the light of day,[2] must be published right away. All I needed to do, she decided, was make a few alterations and write an afterword, explaining that having been written more than twenty years ago, the work was not necessarily in tune with current trends.

Second, Wei decided that now was the time for me to apply for a formal overturning of my conviction as a "*rightist,*" and to apply for a transfer back to Beijing. Wei also told me how to get in touch with Comrade Xiang Ziming at the Beijing Municipal Party Committee. Xiang had been one of the leaders of the Beijing underground; after Liberation, he worked at Party organizations in schools, and briefly had been Party

1. Hu Yaobang, 1915–1989, head of the Youth League, one time general secretary of the CCP Central Committee, forced to step down in 1987.
2. Several instalments were published in *Wenhuibao Daily*. See Chapter 15.

Secretary of Peking University, and now he was finally installed in the Beijing Municipal Party leadership. Xiang received me cordially.

I went one step further and looked up Comrades Li Guang and Shen Qian, senior leaders at the Beijing Municipal Party Organization Department. Li Guang (alias Liu Feng) had inducted me into the Communist Party, while Shen was an old acquaintance of my sister and brother-in-law. They were all part of the underground student movement in the old days before Liberation. They were very concerned about my case and readily acceded to all my requests.

I attended the memorial service commemorating Liu Ren, former Party leader of Beijing. The numbers attending far exceeded the figure allotted by the authorities, which was not surprising. The mere mention of his name would stir up feelings among members of the old Beijing underground network. Add to that the fact of Liu Ren's tragic death during the Cultural Revolution, the big turnout at the memorial service was to be expected. Later in 2006, I had a chance to visit the site of the Urban Work Division of the CCP North China Bureau, mysteriously hidden behind high walls in an out-of-the way corner of Botou, a town in Hebei Province. To members of the underground movement of North China, it is a sacred site.

I also attended a number of memorial services for former members of the Beijing Youth League Committee. Predictably there had been no memorial service for Xu Baolun,[3] and none for Comrade Li Lu[4] either. After reading my reference to him in my autobiography, Li's sister wrote to me saying that Li did not die in labor reform as I had written but that he was diagnosed with cancer after he had served his term and returned to his hometown.[5] Unremembered too was the former group leader Xue De[6] who had lived with his own demons and his petty devices. May he find peace at last!

Before starting out for Beidaihe, I had sent a letter to the poet Shao Yanxiang at the Central Broadcasting Station. At about the same time,

3. See Chapter 17.
4. Referred to as L earlier in the text, see Chapter 15.
5. Wang Meng's narrative keeps to the facts—there are no errors. See chapter 15.
6. The author's handler, previously referred to as W. See Chapter 15.

Shao had written to me, addressing his letter to the Xinjiang Federation of Literature and Art Circles. The two letters crossed, providentially linking us up. Returning to Beijing from Beidaihe, I went to look up Shao at the dormitory building of the Central Radio Broadcasting Station.

From Shao, I learned that Lin Jinlan was living somewhere on Xinfu Street, quite near my mother-in-law's place. I quickly got into touch with Lin, and attended a party at Lin's place where I met more friends from long ago—Deng Youmei, Cong Weixi, Liu Shaotang, Shao Yanxiang, Liu Zhen, and Hao Ran. Here, at Lin Jinlan's dinner party, all the talk was about good fellowship and "let's get down to the business of writing." Lin was my elder by a dozen years. Referred to as Elder Brother Lin, he was always the one who held people together, as he was doing at the dinner party that day. Even Liu Shaotang, who had been attacked by Hao Ran during the Cultural Revolution, greeted the latter in a hail-fellow-well-met manner. In fact, Hao Ran was the only one who seemed dejected and acted the injured party. Obviously he had not yet adjusted to his fall from the clouds.

The dinner party was very jolly, and we enjoyed many a good laugh at the gaffes of the ultra-leftists who had been in power during the Cultural Revolution. There was one story about Lu Ying, which had spread far and wide. Lu Ying, head of *People's Daily,* had mistakenly taken Madame Sirimavo Bandaranaike, prime minister of Sri Lanka, as the wife of the Panchen Lama and referred to her as Mrs. Panchen! Other gaffes involved someone else who had shot to the top during the Cultural Revolution: when a visiting foreigner respectfully mentioned Li Shizhen,[7] the famous doctor of Chinese medicine, this ignoramus looked around and asked: "Is Comrade Li Shizhen present?"

What can you do? We so-called literati have a larger vocabulary than other people; we know a little more history and have a few anecdotes. Those who reject knowledge are bound to expose themselves to ridicule. On the other hand, those of us who flaunt our little bit of knowledge are equally pitiful. So what if we know that Madame Bandaranaike is from Sri Lanka? What does it actually amount to?

7. Li Shizhen, 1518–1593, doctor of Chinese medicine, compiler of *Compendium of Materia Medica.*

Lu Wenfu[8] was another writer that I met up with in Beijing. In 1956, his short story "Down the Little Lane" and my story "Young Newcomer at the Organization Department" were both chosen by the Writers' Union as Representative Works of the Year. Thus Lu and I felt somehow that we were "champions" of the same year in the "imperial examination." Then we were struck down together the next year. For him, it happened this way: In 1957, several young writers in Suzhou got together and decided to start a magazine to be called "The Explorer." It was immediately damned as an anti-Party plot. Lu was implicated and demoted by three ranks. It was a heavy blow indeed. I, on the other hand, was labeled a *rightist,* but my executive rank was not lowered. A fine example of the rich variety of life in those times! Lu told me about the Jiangsu writer Zhang Xuan, who was made to collect tickets at the local cinema house during the Cultural Revolution. Now I understand why Zhang Xuan wrote the story "Memory," about a case of wrongful conviction based on the reversal of a movie tape! At the time, Zhang was trying to get transferred to Nanjing from the little town of Ma'anshan where he had been banished.

In the summer of 1978, we writers, including Lu Wenfu, who had been muzzled, found our voices again. I read his new work "Offerings" in *People's Literature* and was deeply moved. When we finally met, we felt as if we were drawn together across the distance by a common fate, and even when apart we had an unspoken understanding. As the Chinese saying goes, "to know each other, we need not meet." During those heady days, gone for good was the mutual animosities proverbially ascribed to writers. Actually the catastrophe of the Cultural Revolution had drawn writers together in unprecedented solidarity, who, sharing vicissitudes, were bonded together in life and death. Literature was so utterly fragile, yet not to be swept away overnight; writers seem so helpless, yet not to be destroyed by repeated bombardments either.

Lu's friend, the famous Suzhou writer Fang Zhi, joined us later and suggested that we pay a visit to Zhou Yang. At the time, Zhou Yang was head of the Chinese Academy of Social Sciences, and Hu Qiaomu was

---

8. Lu Wenfu, 1927–2005, Chinese writer and former honorary vice chairman of the Chinese Writers' Union.

his deputy; Chen Huangmei was director of the Institute of Chinese Literature. The Federation of Literature and Arts Circles and the Writers Union were not yet restored then; in some cases sensitive issues were involved. The time was not yet ripe for previous leaders to make a comeback, so some of them were put in storage at the Chinese Academy of Social Sciences [CASS].

Zhou Yang was in good spirits and was his same old self. I could not imagine how he had managed to come out of the Cultural Revolution in one piece. It seemed that some of our leading cadres have got the stuff to tough it out through thick and thin. Anyway, during this visit we enjoyed a lively get-together with Zhou Yang. He was concerned about my job assignment. He said that the Academy was setting up an Institute of Minority Literature Studies and that he could assign me there.

Chapter 32

Verdicts Overturned

In the fall of 1978, another major event took place: the historic Third Plenum of the Eleventh Congress of the CCP.[1] In the wake of its various reform initiatives, damning verdicts on many literary works over the past decades were overturned. I was asked to speak at a forum at the Novotel in Beijing, where literary works condemned as "poisonous weeds" in the past, including my novel "Young Newcomer at the Organization Department," were declared innocent of evil designs.

I was perplexed. What should I say? How could I revoke the verdict on my own work just by so declaring it myself? I decided my remarks should be low-key, merely pointing out that my novel harbored no antagonism toward the Party and that there was really no need for its condemnation in the first place. I do not remember what others said at that forum, but the ban on literary works of so many, inflicting so much suffering, was lifted with so little effort, like snubbing out a bothersome flame. What a contrast to the strenuous efforts invoking the forces of "two tigers and nine bullocks" when those writings were being condemned. While all this was meant to be put behind us, it was as if all that happened was merely some inadvertent mislabeling, so trivial as to be easily brushed aside. It was done in such a convenient and simplistic manner that I almost doubted if all the ratification was serious. How could history be made

1. The decision for reform-and-opening up was officially adopted by the CCP Central Committee, setting the scene for social transformation and economic growth.

and then unmade so innocuously?

Just a few months earlier, no one dared imagine that all the mass critiques and condemnation of the past two decades would unravel so quickly. Accusations that had been made out of nothing disappeared into thin air. What a turnaround!

Back in Xinjiang Ruifang heard the news on the radio about the forum and "Young Newcomer at the Organization Department" making the headlines in the *People's Daily*. She wrote excitedly that Party Central had declared to the world that the past verdict on my writings was wrong.

I was dumbfounded; only half believing all this could even be real. I returned to my humble home in Urumqi, finding it cramped, the lighting so dim and the cracked brick floors so ugly, nothing like the smooth cement floors in the homes of my friends and relatives in Beijing. How could I be so shallow—becoming anxious and discontented all of a sudden—so easily swayed by worldly temptations?

A copy of *Guangming Daily* with the epilogue to my novel *Long Live Youth,* which was written in 1953 and now printed in its literary supplement, arrived in the mail. My publisher had sent the piece to the paper without my knowledge. But what a pleasant surprise! More than twenty-five years had passed since I wrote the novel. The years spent in waiting for its publication were more than the years of my entire life when I started the novel. So absurd were the twists of fate that when it seemed to smile on me and *Long Live Youth,* the youth that had been was no more.

In January 1979, I received an invitation from the People's Publishing House to speak at a forum on fiction writing in Beijing. I flew in on a Soviet-made Illushin-62 and stayed in the Friendship Hotel. Most of the talks at the forum were about the relationship between literature, on the one hand, and society, politics and life, on the other. I made two somewhat original points. First, I expressed my hope that the Writers' Union should never find itself in the business of condemning writers and banishing them into limbo. Second, we needed a new spiritual foundation for literature, which was more important than exposé. We had once found such raisons d'etre through left-wing literary movements, in Soviet literature, and in glorifying lives and deeds of noble individuals—which pitifully had all unraveled. So the task was of some urgency.

Other than joining my neatly clad and eloquent fellow writers relishing their regained respectability at this forum, I took the opportunity to resolve a matter of personal significance: getting an official note of "correction" from the Beijing Municipal Committee of the Communist Youth League, my former employer, nullifying its wrongful political judgment made about me in 1958, and a letter to the Xinjiang regional Party committee affirming my CCP membership after a gap of more than fifteen years. As the Chinese saying goes, illness strikes like a mountain crumbling but recedes like silk being pulled from a cocoon. The political storm struck me down with lightening and thunder. I was declared politically "sick" in a solemn session akin to a funeral. Then when the reversal came, it looked so trifling as if it had all been a sick joke. No one bothered to offer an apology, wish me good luck, or even said so much as a simple "take care." No one offered anything beyond what was required.

The Beijing Municipal CCP Committee also issued a document for my transfer to Beijing, following an official mandate to correct wrongful labeling of *rightists* and "recall" those who had been exiled to remote regions. My friends in Xinjiang loathed the idea of my departure and lamented how the world had changed. I talked with the leaders of my unit about making arrangements. They offered understanding and a promise of support, but said with a sigh: what do people take Xinjiang for?—everyone talks about leaving as soon as their political stigma is removed.

While preparing to leave, I was notified by *People's Literature* that "The Most Precious" was named the best short story for 1977–78, and I was invited to attend an award ceremony in Beijing. I felt uncomfortable traveling to Beijing again so soon. I knew the travel budget of the regional office for creative writing (the regional Federation of Literature and Arts Circles was yet to be reestablished) was rather meager. Such flying back and forth was sinful. However, great significance was attached to this award event in the capital, the first ever after the Cultural Revolution, and organizers in Beijing called repeatedly urging my attendance. I had to oblige.

The event was like a reunion of shipwreck survivors: a celebration of the resurrection of literature and literary men and women, the return of exiled heroes after an absence of some twenty years. Many of my fellow writers made the prizewinners list. People wanted to have photos taken with us. I couldn't help remarking wryly to Deng Youmei how unfathomable it was that we so-called "demons and monsters" are now turned into photo-worthy exotic creatures. I told my daughter Yihuan, who was only ten, about people snapping shots of me like they do with animals in the zoo. She shouted "golden monkey!" oblivious to the irony of it all.

Writing about this twenty-seven years later, I had to marvel at how much had changed. Of those on the list of awardees, veteran writers Zhou Libo[2] and Lu Wenfu have since passed away. Zhang Jie and Jia Pingwa[3] are in their prime like the midday sun. The voice of indignant Zhang Chengzhi,[4] who had always been so aloof, is waning. Zong Pu[5] continues to create excellent stories in spite of her illness and advancing age. Some have taken and then rescinded their positions as chairmen or vice chairmen of writers' unions at various levels, while others are dedicated as always to their official perch, toeing this or that political line. Those who are still writing no longer have the same sparkle. Some of the "golden monkeys" have stopped writing altogether, while the rest, including Wang Meng, are moving into the twilight of their lives.

Back in Xinjiang, there were farewells and heartwarming parting words from my comrades. Han Wenhui, secretary general of the regional Writers' Union (who later became bureau chief at the Xinhua News Agency in Xinjiang) declared me a "man of kind thoughts." My being discreet, respectful with little ego, pretensions or arrogance had perhaps prompted him to say so. But such attributes are only natural to people down on their luck.

I kept myself busy with reading, writing, and staying abreast of all

2. Zhou Libo, 1908–1979, known for his novels on Chinese rural life and the land reform movement.
3. Jia Pingwa, 1952–, famous Chinese novelist and short story writer; winner of the 1987 Pegasus prize in literature for his *Turbulence: A Novel,* Howard Goldblatt, trans. Grove Press.
4. Zhang Chengzhi, 1948–, Chinese fiction writer, also known as the most influential Muslim writer in China.
5. Feng Zongpu, 1928–, writer and daughter of noted Chinese historian Feng Youlan, Writer of novels and short stories, *The Everlasting Stone* and *Red Beans* are among the better known.

political and cultural news (given that my fate had been so inexplicably affected by them in the past), and networking with fellow writers and relevant parties. Suddenly time became precious. I could not afford to spend much of the day drinking and playing word games with my old friends any more. Lu Xun scorned those who became arrogant once they struck it rich. I was nowhere near rich, but I had changed. I wrote about this in a short story titled "Friends and Smoke," and my drinking buddies were not impressed.

On June 12, 1979, Ruifang and I took the No. 70 train bound for Beijing. My older son Wang Shan stayed behind as he had been admitted to Xinjiang University, and my younger son Wang Shi was in a military college at Sanyuan, Sha'anxi. My daughter Yihuan had moved back to Beijing by the end of 1978 to attend primary school. More than forty people came to see us off at Urumqi Railway Station, and everyone was in tears. Ruifang simply couldn't stop crying. We would be forever indebted to Xinjiang, for it was the people of Xinjiang who took us in and offered us refuge. Their manners and outlook shaped me, and their Uighur humor set me straight. No matter what circumstances you find yourself in coming to Xinjiang, you will find it a great place, with bighearted people and much to learn. The wisdom and kindness of the folks was a woolen vest that kept out the cold and a bowl of hot tea that warmed your soul. I will cherish Xinjiang always and think of it only with the fondest memories.

We arrived in Beijing three days later, crossing a chasm of sixteen years. It was in December 1962 that I had left Beijing with my wife and young family for Xinjiang, having sold all our furniture, with a "nothing-could-be-worse" resolve, mixed feelings of adventure, recalcitrance, and striking out on our own. Now coming back to Beijing, I took up a job at the Municipal Federation of Literature and Arts Circles, while Ruifang went back to teaching physics at No. 72 High School.

My two sons were still in the Northwest. I had tried to get my older son back to a college in Beijing but to no avail. My concern for their future affected my choices. I had to excel in everything I did. I did not opt for aloofness, being a recluse, or living on the edge. One of the reasons was an obligation to my sons. I must admit I could not shirk this banal, worldly concern of mine, though it was far from noble.

We were put up in Room No. 6, a 10-square-meter room in the small guesthouse owned by the municipal Cultural Bureau. The room had a window that opened onto the common area where lodgers gathered to watch TV every evening. Opposite my room was the latrine. The sound of gushing water, the endless blare of TV, and the mixed scents of other people's soap and toothpaste wafted into my room. I had many calls from various publications requesting contributions. The stout and friendly woman at reception would bellow over the communal din every time a call came for me, "Room Number Six, Telephone!"

Here in this tiny room I wrote my novellas *A Bolshevik Salute* and *Butterfly* and the short story "The Eyes of the Night," and met with editors, reporters, and fellow writers. Those were unforgettable days. Steps away from that cramped room, with all the raucousness of a traveler's inn, was the moat quietly encircling the Forbidden City where I could see the glow of the sun on the tiles of its magnificent corner tower at dawn and dusk, the bustle and lights of Dongan Market, and the traffic flowing like a river in Donghuamen Street. Change was in the air. Literature came to the fore; significant works heralded reversals of past political verdicts and new policy initiatives. Retribution was imperative; everyone had wrongs to redress. But I was bent on doing more. I wanted to dash off one, two, or even more essays every day. I was showered with invitations, interview requests, and solicitations for stories. I became a significant being, brimming with confidence and intellectual vigor for intricate deliberations. When I wrote, words came forth as if inspired by the muses. My mirthful quips brought laughter all around, and talk of the fierce tiger no longer freaked me out. The world is everyone's as well as mine for the taking. I say to myself: you are in control. After twenty years and a metamorphosis, you again stand tall as a man!

Chapter 33

Unfamiliar Looking Eyes of the Night

I returned to Beijing after being away for sixteen years. Beijing, Beijing! Its name had been sung in many a song that gained popularity toward the end of the Cultural Revolution. I liked them even though I could not quite agree with all their feverish sentiments. In "A Paean to Beijing": "The fiery morning clouds rise over great Beijing . . ." and in a Xinjiang song simply called "Great Beijing": "We sing in your praise, great Beijing!" Hearing these rousing tunes, I was put in mind not of revolutionary imperatives, but images of its enduring landmarks—the White Pagoda, serene Shichahai Lake, the majestic gate towers and palaces of the Forbidden City, the lonely copses of trees outside the derelict Jimen gate tower, the Avenue of Perpetual Peace, and the squat Monument to Peoples' Heroes. I knew this city of my youth and its intricate web of alleyways like the back of my hand. When political fervors dissipated, Beijing could again be a beloved old town.

But when I returned in 1979, the city was changed for the worse. I was surprised to learn that a restaurant in a city park still served Western food, but when I went there with my daughter, we were asked to pay a deposit for forks and knives before we were even seated. This odd requirement, the waitresses told us, was to prevent theft of cutlery. You also had to pay a deposit when you bought a soda, even if you promised to drink it in front of the stand and return the bottle right after. When you ordered a beer in a restaurant, you paid a deposit for the crappy plastic mug. I called these pauper's mugs as they were so battered and unclean, and smelled and felt rubbery, like the stuff for insoles. Drinking beer from mugs like these, you were reminded of your rotten luck and feeble standing. Why did restaurants treat their patrons with distrust and guard against them as potential pickpockets? This made me want to cry for old Beijing.

But life in Beijing was not all sadness. From our dingy abode, my wife and I could walk westward to the broad moat skirting the Forbidden City. To the east were Beijing Department Store and Dongan Market. The name of the latter was changed to East Wind Market during the Cultural Revolution. It was pitiful that they had to change these place names according to fickle political winds. Dongan Market, the old name I preferred, was packed with shoppers and gawkers each evening and on weekends. It was heartening to see people buying and enjoying the simple comforts of life—popsicles, apricot-kernel-flavored jelly, Chinese doughnuts, dried beef, Beijing muffins, dried plums, and candies. You could also see young men with girls clutching their arms, browsing in the stores. Even such banal signs of leisure and the old days, of young people not having to hide their affection moved me to the brink of tears. Hope would be rekindled, as long as there was no more madness against life itself. All this had come at such cost—twenty-odd years taken from the lives of all in my family and that of countless others.

"The Eyes of Night," a short story I wrote then, is a reflection on the change and the promise of a new life, to which I dedicate this chapter.

It marked a shift in my writings in the late 1970s, a departure from "literature of the wounded," the prevailing genre of the time. Such literature had spurred much public debate. Its critics argued that it served no public good, calling for not writing about "scars" any more. They believed such literature would sooner or later court trouble (e.g., being deemed as anti-Party or "political whacking-off," in the words of a cultural big shot). Personally, I had never been big on "literature of the wounded," which seemed to me shallow and kitschy, even non-literature. It had served the purpose of helping to redress past wrongs and countering left extremism, meeting a public expectation that is more political than literary. But this shouldn't be cause for its condemnation.

"The Eyes of Night" came from unspecific but true feelings, feelings about art and feelings associated with my personal experiences. Its protagonist observes with solitary eye and melancholy heart the unending hustle and bustle in the city. It reflects alienation and the fear of an outsider in strange urban environs, a city of congested streets and towering buildings, of face cream ads and construction sites, and the unbreakable routine that dictates everyone's life. It conveys an aching feeling that the author himself could not quite define; a resignation perhaps, with surface calm and inner torment, a grin hiding sorrow, and hope for life returning to its normal course. There are memories recollected, echoes from the distant past, hope peppered with hesitation.

There was also Hungarian music flowing down as if from heaven:

> Just before stepping out into the hall, he hesitated and instinctively pricked up his ears. The tape recorder was now playing real music, the "Gold and Silver" waltz by the Hungarian composer Franz Lehár. In his mind he pictured a leaf swirling on the surface of a deep blue alpine lake hemmed in on three sides by tall, snow-covered peaks; beside the lake was his remote, small provincial town, a white swan in peaceful repose in the lake.[1]

Why did I mention real music all of a sudden? Why did I recall that remote provincial town? What put me in that unlikely place was not important anymore. What's important was that I had lived there for so many years at one stretch; living the best part of my life among the country folks, who comprised the majority of the nation's people, and enduring the same hardships. That life was set against a backdrop of alpine meadows, snow-capped peaks, and dark blue lakes with wild swans. Perhaps it was this backdrop that connects me emotionally with the Hungarian composer, or other European and world composers for that matter.

Seventeen years after I wrote that story, I saw a real Alpine lake with a lone wild swan in Scotland during a visit in 1996. My British friend told me there used to be a pair, but now only one was left (which also disappeared a few years later, so I was told). The scene was exactly the

---

1. From "Eyes of the Night", trans. by Donald A. Gibbs, in Perry Link, ed., *Roses and Thorns: The Second Blooming of the Hundred Flowers in Chinese Fiction*. Berkeley: University of California Press, 1984, 43-55.

same as I envisioned when I wrote "The Eyes of Night." The alpine lake in Xinjiang was my inspiration. But the remote land there had a ruggedness to its immensity and steely silence. Lehar's music added a soft touch.

There was also expediency: I did not use a Russian or West European composer's music: a deliberate effort to avoid any association with Soviet "revisionism" or the capitalist West. I had become so cautious. Yet I managed to make it seem incidental, and such seeming randomness is a constant in literature. When I was writing the story, it was indeed Lehar's "Gold and Silver" waltz that I heard on the radio. The Cultural Revolution had ended and such European music, which had not been heard for a very long time, was now being played again. I was touched.

> Streetlights, of course, are all turned on at the same time. Chen Gao knew that, but he still had the sensation that they were two beams of light shooting out of his own head.

The story begins with descriptions of subjective feelings. If I had not been away for sixteen years, if I had not become used to life at No. 2 Liberation Road in Yining or in a house on a rise at the eastern end of Unity Road in Urumqi, if my wife and I had not taken daily walks at dusk on Wangfujing Street watching the day growing old (we were yet to have a permanent home in Beijing then), I probably would not have had such a feeling about street lights in the city. The story continues:

> It takes nighttime for a big city to show off its energy and its peculiarity. At first the lights are faint and scattered, but then those attention-grabbing neon signs and revolving poles in front of barbershops come on. And you see permanents, long hair, high heels, flat soles, and the short, body-hugging dresses, and scents of cologne and face cream wafting in the air. The city, like women, is making itself pretty, and already there are people who are stirred and become agitated because of it. That's intriguing.
>
> . . . For over twenty years he was stuck in a small, remote provincial town where one-third of the street lamps never came on at all, and for the two-thirds that had light bulbs in them, a third of the nights they did not get electricity. Was it mere

> negligence or because the electricity allocation was haywire? A small matter in any case, for nearly everyone there lived the old rural way anyway, working from dawn to dusk. By six in the evening all the offices, factories, shops and restaurants were closed for the day. In the evenings, people simply stayed at home cuddling their babies, smoking, doing laundry, or chattering, saying things that are no sooner said than forgotten.
>
> There was a touch of exaggeration but no sarcasm intended in this portrayal of life in a small provincial town. It was full of sympathy and nostalgia. The way I described streetlights was far more poetic than saying city lights shining like daylight and neon signs pulsating everywhere. To me, backwaters and hardship are more conducive to poetry. They take on an enchanting quality through the prism of art. Shangri-la is only convincing in a setting of primitive living, void of skyscrapers, five-star hotels, and glitzy shopping malls. People take to simplicity, finding beauty, aesthetic appeal and moral superiority in resilience against immense hardships. But I was no the starry-eyed idealist hung up on the notion of "poetic being" glorified by Heidegger. That was more about a yearning and romantic imagining of the intelligentsia and would lose luster when translated into reality.

Xinjiang and my life in its small provincial town of Yining became my cherished past, and their contrast to life in Beijing inspired many of my stories. Those sixteen years were no easy sojourn. All the contrast and dislocation were material for literature.

> Two youths in workman garb . . . were engaged in an animated discussion: ". . . the crux of the matter is democracy, democracy, democracy . . ." Wherever he had been during the week he was in the city this time, all he heard was people talking about democracy. It was about as ubiquitous and mundane as a leg of mutton that people in his remote provincial town were fond of talking about. As food supply in the city was relatively plentiful no one was that fixated on mutton and such anymore.

There was self-mockery, but no intent to trivialize.

> The train had halted at a small whistle stop for an hour and twelve minutes because a man who had no proper identity papers but who did have a prized leg of mutton was killed under the wheels while in pursuit of a better offer for his mutton . . . He ducked under the railcar in order to dash across the tracks. Just then the brakes slipped and the train moved, killing the poor fellow instantly.
>
> Such a hair-raising detail may be incredulous to people in Beijing. Yet Chen Gao, the protagonist, finds the tale about a leg of mutton close to his heart. People would die for the prospect of profit, as birds are killed when seeking prey. How pitiful it is when man's drive for survival and getting ahead only leads him to doom. Is there an alternative? All the smooth rhetoric about democracy that Chen Gao hears in the capital renders him utterly impotent. He has learned his lessons and knows only too well that such talk forebodes peril. He remains a silent observer, trying in vain to ascertain.
>
> All the sounds, lights, and assortment of things were in these apartment buildings, which stood like dumb matchboxes. The congested spaces were strange to Chen Gao; it was hard to imagine what it would be like living here, and it even struck him as comical. The shadowy trees, as tall as the buildings themselves, cast a thin veil of mystery over the strange life he observed. In his small, remote provincial town, what he heard most at night was the sound of dogs barking, and so familiar was he with them all that he could tell from the sound of barking alone what color the dog was and who it belonged to. Beyond that, there would be the sound of heavy trucks rumbling past, their headlights piercing the darkness with such brilliance that your eyes were blinded for a time after they passed by. All the houses near the road trembled each time a truck rumbled by.

Describing buildings as matchboxes was influenced by *Dersu Uzala,* a Soviet-era film directed by the Japanese filmmaker Akira Kurosawa, though I only read its screenplay, which was made available to show the Soviet intent against China. Dersu, an aboriginal Nanai tribesman (or Hèzhé in Chinese), who prefers a life in the wilderness, refuses to move into town. My descriptions of houses trembling each time a truck rumbled by won some praises from writer Gong Liu.[2] Apparently he had lived in similar adobe houses.

> Go around or jump? Well, he wasn't that old. He backed off a few steps, and then one, two, three . . . Soft sand foiled his footing as he jumped. He fell to the bottom of the ditch. Fortunately there were no hard or sharp objects. Even so, it was ten minutes or more before he fully recovered from the pain and shock. Grinning, he brushed off the dirt and clambered out of the ditch. Once out, his foot plunged into a deep puddle. He pulled his foot up with a squish, but his shoe and sock were soaked through. His foot in the sodden shoe felt grittiness, like eating rice with sand in it. As he looked up, his eyes were drawn to a light bulb hung on a slant post by the building, with a forlorn glow of orange red in the darkness. This light bulb, at such a place and time, struck him like a tiny question mark, written on an enormous blackboard.

The small light bulb in the story was inspired imagery and a gift from the poetic muse, symbolizing "The Eyes of the Night."[3] I had the title of the story in mind before I started writing. With such an unusual title and opening, the rest of the story flowed naturally. With other stories, I could start writing without a title and only settled on one when the story was complete or partially written.

I was asked by my foreign friends, sometimes translators, if I meant "eye" or "eyes." I did not have an answer. Eye(s) of night can be interpreted as eyes of protagonist Chen Gao, which is of course plural, as he is not known to have lost an eye. It can also be that lone light bulb. Or it is the dark night itself that may have one or a multitude of eyes. I was unable to give a categorical answer to the curious international experts.

The first piece of Chinese contemporary literature published by a Soviet journal of foreign literature after bilateral relations thawed was this short story. It was also included in the anthology *Roses and Thorns: The Second Blooming of the Hundred Flowers in Chinese Fiction* published in the

2. 1927–2003, poet and army veteran; labeled a *rightist* in 1957.
3. The title in Chinese does not specify singular or plural.

United States in the early 1980s.[4] The writer Grace Paley[5] was full of praise when she flew with me from the Midwest to the East Coast in 1980. She had read it in the journal *Chinese Literature.* Mr. Zhao Jin, head of the literary supplement of *Guangming Daily,* applauded the piece as pioneering new storytelling in Chinese literature. Many years later, the novelist Zhao Mei[6] told me how she felt when reading the story in college: life and writing suddenly took on new possibilities.

I also paid a price. The plot of using back-door pull to accomplish a trivial task too closely resembles a leader in literary and arts circles in Xinjiang who had asked me to do certain favors for him. He was duly enraged. During the Fourth National Conference for Literature and Art Circles[7] in Beijing, his scolding and howling resonated in the hotel lobby and shocked the Xinjiang delegation. He thought it defamatory. I tried in vain to explain that descriptions of certain events were merely a "shell" (vehicle) of the story and completely fictitious. He became even more furious, saying I humiliated him by equating him to an empty "shell." I fell silent in the storm of his wrath. Luckily, we both managed to put this behind us afterward and were on good terms once again.

Mr. Cui Daoyi, an editor at *People's Literature,* decided to use this story when compiling an anthology for the thirtieth anniversary of the founding of the People's Republic. The collection would begin with Liu Baiyu's "The Rising Sun" and end with "The Eyes of the Night." Perfect bookends! Cui told me he felt the pain of losing all the things he had cherished when reading my story. The story was first published in the *Guangming Daily* on November 21, 1979. I remember reading it while standing with my wife at a post, near the Market, where the day's papers were pasted up. We were so thrilled that we lingered there just to see if others took note of the story.

---

4. *Roses and Thorns,* Perry Link, ed.
5. Grace Paley, 1922–2007, American short story writer, poet, teacher, and political activist.
6. Zhao Mei, 1954– , fiction writer and essayist from Tianjin, member of Chinese Writers' Union.
7. The first national conference for the Literary and Arts Circles held in Beijing where grievances over persecution during the Cultural Revolution were aired and a new leadership team was elected.

I try to bring the joy of reading to my readers. At the same time, I seek to explore the depth of human experience. It seems that all good writing, or truly satisfying writing, does not start with a high-sounding notion. More often a writer is seized by a certain mystic force, some powerful passion. Aided by a stroke of luck, he puts pen to paper and a great piece of writing, that will astound even him, is in the making. Before it takes form, he may even not have a complete vision of it. He does not argue or make a statement about it, and its real subject matter, which of course is right there, may not even be fully explained. Writing in such a vein will never be regarded as exemplary by those obsessed with the didactic function of literature.

When realism was extolled as the mainstream; when party secretaries, managers, farmers, military heroes, and exemplary factory workers were glorified as literary archetypes, people turned away and applauded quirkiness and living on the edge in writings by venerable scholar Wang Zengqi,[8] or turned to Zen and Buddhist teachings. They would seek out stories about highway robbers, celebrated courtesans, criminals on the lam, demons and monsters, fierce tigers and mad dogs; they would rather read stories that painted life in China today as not much different from that of the Ming or Qing dynasties. Who took note of such a paradox?

8. Wang Zengqi, 1920–1997, writer of stories and familiar essays; labeled a *rightist* in 1958.

Chapter 34

The Writers' Union, the Literary Scene, and Literary Friends

I returned to Beijing and became a "professional" writer on the payroll of the municipal Federation of Literature and Arts Circles. Unlike professional writers in the West who make a living by receiving royalties for their writings, "professional writers" in China at the time referred narrowly to those salaried writers who had neither to report to work every day nor to depend on earnings from their writings to make ends meet.

The municipal Federation was abuzz with all that was happening. Hao Ran, who rose to fame during the Cultural Revolution, was now down on his luck. Opinions varied. Writers such as Guan Hua,[1] Yang Mo,[2] and most of the staffers and chauffeurs in the organization thought of him favorably, because he had been loyal to his wife of his only marriage, who had little schooling, among other things. This was deemed a mark of good character. He had also been nice to humble farmers-turned-writers. Other writers, however, were not happy about his garnering fame and glory during the Cultural Revolution while others were being persecuted. They remembered a Red Guard rally where Lao She was humiliated and physically abused, which was followed by his suicide. This took place when Hao Ran headed the federation's Cultural Revolution Committee. One

1. Guan Hua, 1922–2002, army veteran, novelist and former chairman of the Beijing Municipal Writers' Union.
2. Yang Mo, 1914–1995, novelist, fought with guerrillas against the Japanese occupation during the war, chairman of Beijing Municipal Federation of Literature and Arts Circles.

writer insisted that Hao Ran once said it did not matter if someone was beaten to death. (I doubted this.) Yet other fellow writers, such as Qu Bo,[3] would become furious at the mere mention of Hao Ran's name and never wanted to be seen together with him. People always derive satisfaction in seeing high-rollers fall. Those who had been envious of his success laughed up their sleeves. Hatred for the rich and powerful is universal.

Hao Ran became very depressed and said he felt like he "had lost all his bets." The slide was crushing because he had long been a favored writer and had few setbacks. He was not accustomed to introspection and self-criticism. Writers who had been rehabilitated, including Liu Shaotang, Deng Youmei, Cong Weixi, and me, treated him with kindness. With our own suffering in the recent past, we did not wish to see yet more suffering befall other writers. For this, I was criticized for my meek-mindedness. I was not audacious enough. I was supposed to criticize what Hao Ran had written during the Cultural Revolution. The truth is we really did not care what and how others wrote. I would never make damning comments about other writers, though I wrote serious literary criticism. Only those whose creative juices had dried up would devote themselves to bigotry, trying to prove their waning worth by attacking others.

Back in Beijing, I busily attended literary gatherings. Most of these were hosted by the Literature Institute of the Chinese Academy of Social Sciences, the newly launched *October* magazine and the re-launched *Art and Literature Gazette*. I came to know many fellow writers in their prime. They included Bai Hua,[4] who was revising his screenplay in Beijing; Zhang Qie[5] from Anhui; Li Tuo[6] from Beijing; and Su Shuyang,[7] who wrote the acclaimed play *Story of Loyal Hearts*. Liu Xinwu[8] was at the height of his fame and made only occasional appearances. Discussions at these forums touched on a range of issues, including the denunciation of the so-called literary and arts fallacies during the Cultural Revolution, the purge of

---

3. Qu Bo, 1923–2002, army veteran turned novelist.
4. Bai Hua, 1930–, playwright and poet, whose screenplay *Unrequited Love* was to cause a political controversy later, labeled a *rightist* in 1958.
5. Zhang Qie, 1933–, writer and party secretary of Writers' Union.
6. Li Tuo, 1939–, story writer and playwright.
7. Su Shuyang, 1938–, story writer and playwright.
8. Liu Xinwu, 1942–, writer and former school teacher whose short story "Class Teacher" was thought to have pioneered the "Literature of the Wounded" in the post-Cultural Revolution collective soul searching.

writers and artists, the revival of realism, and the notions of human nature, compassion, and Humanism. We debated why the Japanese film *Sandakan Brothel No. 8* was banned in China, the merit or otherwise of "literature of the wounded," whether the Party's policies in the past on literature and art had been "left extremist" in nature, if there were laws of creativity that should be followed and how they could be defined.

Everybody let it all hang out at these sessions and felt contented afterward. How satisfying it was to have these occasions to say the things they had wanted to say after having to hold their peace for all those years!

These sessions were often moderated by either Feng Mu or Chen Huangmei—great supporters and friends of writers who were in their thirties and forties. I held them in great respect and felt an affinity for them. They were passionate about post-Cultural Revolution rectification and the Party's imperative on reform and opening-up. Chen Huangmei mentioned on a couple of occasions that he was often approached by people from literary and arts circles for his take on a possible future direction. They were anxious to know what the top leaders in literature and art were thinking and whether their writings would court trouble. Chen urged everyone to stop such speculation and focus on the work at hand.

On the surface, his urging seemed fitting. A writer who could weave intricate plots should surely be guided by his or her own conscience and sense of direction, rather than hunting for hints from the higher-ups. In fact, in the post-Cultural Revolution years, if you were bold enough to try and take responsibility, you could very well succeed in trailblazing work in any field of endeavor and be applauded for your efforts. Hu Yaobang, the general secretary of the Party, set a personal example in rectifying past persecution and the "anti-*rightist*" campaign. Some venerable leaders in the literary and arts circles indeed took on such a responsibility and demonstrated their courage. They took bold actions in supporting "literature of the wounded" and reform literature and reviving literary endeavors that had been stifled during the Cultural Revolution.

However, there were others who seemed to think differently. Word went around that certain literary forums and writings had raised the ire of senior CCP leaders. With the exception of Ba Jin, Xia Yan, and a few others, venerable writers mostly had reservations about the contemporary literary scene and writers in their thirties and forties. The concern that the "less-senior leaders" might not be getting the senior CCP leaders' intentions right was neither frivolous nor mere paranoia. They did not need to be reminded of what could happen if they acted against such intentions. Chen Huangmei's remarks were noble and pure, but also superficial and pedantic. Soon afterward, he was censured for allowing an internal screening of a foreign film that contained excessive nudity. Chen Huangmei and Feng Mu were themselves not having an easy time.

Sitting through the meetings in Beijing, I could sense the advent of a "New Era," heralded by Liu Xinwu. But I cared more about creating works of literature than following literary fads. I knew our luck with fair political weather was no substitute for writing. Conducive weather could be important, but literature, unlike vegetation, can come into blossom in less than ideal climes. What mattered was the act and the quality of the writing itself.

There were always smooth talkers at these sessions who appeared insightful and carried themselves with superior airs. Their exuberance and pomposity made someone like me who had just returned from the remote borderland feel subdued and out of place. They freely dropped the names of senior CCP leaders and acted as if they had just come out of a Politburo meeting, or a meeting of the top team at the CCP Organization or Propaganda Department. They were surely in the know, and I was even willing to believe that most of their comments had a factual basis. I even shared some of their sentiments about the people they liked or held in disdain. However, I was after all a bit bookish and remembered the lessons of my earlier years. I decided it was neither necessary nor appropriate, in these literary discussions, to pass judgment on senior leaders, to eagerly discuss possible leadership successions, or to judge if the current crop of political leaders were up to snuff. One of the topics that enthralled them, for example, was who should succeed Zhou Yang, the Party's propaganda chief.

I remember learning the term—"taking a stand"—during the Cultural Revolution. In fact, this meant choosing sides and getting entangled in political feuding high up. It was like placing a bet, which was something I would never do. If you made a winning bet, you might get a boost to your literary career. However, if you made the wrong bet, you could find yourself in a deep hole. I was merely five feet six, earning a paltry salary of less than ninety yuan per month at the time, with no more than three hundred thousand words in print to my name. I knew I could write well, with a knack for storytelling, not merely a passion for word craft. I needed greater precision and clarity in my narratives, but not clever calculations to take a certain political stand.

I remember my bookish friend Hao Guanzhong from my Xinjiang days. His motto was "You should never tie yourself to somebody else's chariot." How incisive. I declared in 1979 that I would respect those whom I regarded as elders and mentors, but never pledge personal allegiance. I would treat my fellow writers with decency but refrain from cronyism.

I cannot say if such an approach was virtuous, or merely clever, indicative of political maturity. I was certain however that I did not want to follow the crowd or pander to the powers-that-be. To put it bluntly, in literary circles, only those with literary pretention but no ability would be keen to take a stand and choose sides in political strife. In retrospect, I made the right choice then and thereafter by refraining from certain actions and giving up some options. I did not mix personal emotions with the work at hand, nor did I allow myself to be dragged into factional politics. History will judge my actions in a positive light.

There was also a debate on realism in literature. I voiced my concern over describing the Chinese literary scene in the late 1970s as a revival of Realism. I couldn't quite understand the notion proposed by the much-respected Mao Dun that a recurring theme in the history of Chinese literature was Realism vs. anti-Realism. Realism no doubt is a central pillar in the pantheon of literature. However, one pillar does not make a great mansion, nor one lone tree a forest. There are other literary traditions, such as Romanticism in the works of the Chinese poets Qu Yuan, Li Bai, and the French writers Victor Hugo, Prosper Mérimée; and Aestheticism in Oscar Wilde, Li Shangyin,[9] and Li He;[10] Classicism in [Shakespeare] and Tang and Song fiction, as well as Symbolism, psychoanalysis, mysticism, Impressionism, and Modernism (post-modern had yet to arrive). Surely, they cannot all be heretical or serve only as

9. Li Shangyin, 813–858 CE, late Tang dynasty poet.
10. Li He, 790–816 CE, Tang dynasty poet.

the antitheses of Realism. Wasn't Oscar Wilde's *The Happy Prince* also an exposé of society's ills, showing great sympathy for the huddled masses? Why couldn't there be a win-win situation and a collective blossoming of Realism and all the other non-Realism schools? Why must the triumph of one be the doom of all the others?

Chairman Mao's notion of "combining revolutionary Romanticism with revolutionary Realism" was a better proposition, allowing at least a creative space for writers pursuing the Romantic tradition. Of course, equating Romanticism with fairies and demons of the Chinese folk theater was naïve and simplistic. Li Tuo once summed up my thinking well, "The problem we are facing is anti-Realism and pseudo Romanticism." Our writings had too often been marred by a lack of both Realism and imagination. How could literature be devoid of fantasy, symbolism, and imagination—as discussed in an ancient text of Chinese literary criticism *The Literary Mind and the Carving of Dragons*?[11]

This discussion about Realism and anti-Realism was but a prelude to the later tempest over "Modernism."

Writers who had been rehabilitated celebrated their return to Beijing, but some came back to face extreme hardship. I visited the writer Cong Weixi, who had just been released from prison. When both he and his wife were behind bars, his mother and son shared a tiny dormitory room. When they were both freed, his wife had to live with her own mother, as their one-room home could not accommodate them all. I could hardly hold back my tears when I saw the sorry conditions they lived in.

We gathered for dinner at Liu Zhen's home to celebrate the start of her new life. Fellow writers who had suffered similar hardships were all eager to see her and her ex-husband Deng Youmei reunited, but for some reason their efforts were to no avail. One of the dishes she cooked was a whole chicken steamed in a winter melon. When this was served, the top of the pot-shaped melon was removed and the limp, cooked chicken with its drooping head still attached was hoisted from the broth. After she explained the tortuous cooking process, I quipped the dish might as well be named "*uncapped rightist.*" Liu Zhen was quite forthcoming

---

11. *Wen-xin diao-long*, sixth century treatise on literary criticism by Liu Xie (465–520 CE).

but neither was she free from hyperbole. She seemed to know a lot and gave sweeping comments on various personalities. She mimicked the stammering of an old writer who condemned her improper "class affiliations." She fumed over how bland a fellow writer's screenplay was. Her biting comments invigorated the gathering. But her own suffering during the Cultural Revolution, due to political misfortune as well as her own uncompromising personality, was more than most could bear recounting.

She did not get far in her new life. But for the moment, like everyone else she felt fortunate to have survived it all and looked forward to better days ahead. We prayed that there would be enduring peace in our lives and in the nation. A theoretician labeled such sentiment a collective yearning for stability and peace.

Her ex-husband, Deng Youmei, recounted his harrowing experience. He was forced to stand alongside plaques bearing the names of people who had been persecuted to death and endure the scoldings and beatings of Red Guards, all the while with arias of a revolutionary Peking opera blaring out in the background. (He thereafter became a staunch opponent of the restaging of these revolutionary operas.) After these mob sessions, he would be dumped into a freezing room, which was so cold that he would puke and suffer stomach cramps. Such was his journey.

In short order, those of us who were not yet members of the Writers' Union were granted membership. Not long after, we all became delegates to the Fourth National Conference of Literature and Arts Circles. Though we could claim no great literary accomplishments, we were accorded titles and status because we happened to be in the right age group, and the conditions for writers in general improved, like a swollen river raising all boats. Even those who had lingering problems with the law would soon see their troubles vaporize. If the forces that had conspired to incriminate them could be compared to that of nine oxen and two tigers, as the saying goes, their reversal now needed only three cats and two dogs. Still, no one was spared.

Looking back on this period, I could not help thinking of *October* magazine. Its editor-in-chief then was Su Yu.[12] She joined the revolution

---

12. Su Yu, 1926–, literary writer and editor.

when the CCP was an underground organization and she was a student at Yenching University. After Liberation, she stumbled along in a career rife with mishaps. Yet she kept alive the noble ideal of collective struggle for a better tomorrow. A host of other new literary journals appeared in China, including the re-launched *Harvest,* and *Dangdai Bimonthly, Flower City, Qingming,* and *Fresh Land. October* was one of the earliest. For a few years, I lived close by and often dropped in for a chat with Su Yu and her colleagues. I believed Su Yu remained an idealist all her life in spite of all the trials she had lived through.

Like Su Yu, I went to work for the Youth League in 1949 as an idealistic and dedicated young man. We engaged in criticism and self-criticism with fervor and pride. We were strict with ourselves and our fellow revolutionaries, demanding utmost devotion. Then came the years of confusion and fear. The political campaigns invariably started with pointing to undesirable tendencies in literary circles. After three decades, we came full circle. The once timid, servile writers again strutted with heads held high. The Youth League cadres and the CCP committees all seemed so remote and irrelevant, to say nothing of the labor camps. At such times, you could see the stark contrast in people's character. As for my fellow writers, I liked them all, but I could not agree with all they did. Why did they never learn?

Chapter 35

The Fourth Literature and Arts Conference

Shortly after I returned to Beijing in 1979, I heard that a national conference for writers and artists was in the works. Literary and arts circles suffered the most persecution during the Cultural Revolution. What drama would unfold at a conference of delegates from these circles, many with a legendary past?

The Fourth National Conference of Literature and Art Circles opened on October 13, 1979,[1] in the Great Hall of the People in Beijing. Venerable writers and artists arrived in wheel chairs, on crutches, or clutching each other's arms. Some, barely recovered from persecution and overcome by a tumult of emotions, spoke in mumbled speech. Venerable writers Xiao Shan[2] and Lou Shiyi,[3] after opening their remarks with "We have survived and are here to meet again . . ." could not help sobbing into their scripts on the podium. I felt even the spirits of those departed during the Cultural Revolution were hovering above that expansive stage.

Writers in their thirties and forties, on the other hand, were excited, eyes shining as they made the rounds in the conference venues. Several gave rousing speeches that brought down the house. Some of them saw their names being added to the list of candidates for the National Committee of the Federation, after such impressive speechifying.

---

1. According to an official report by the *Art and Literature Gazette*, the conference opened on October 30, 1979.
2. Xiao Shan, 1896–1983, Chinese poet and translator.
3. Lou Shiyi, 1905–2001, Chinese writer and translator.

Deng Xiaoping came to offer congratulatory remarks on behalf of the central leadership. Delegates broke into thunderous applause when they heard him say, "In the creation of literature and art, which involves complex mental labor, it is essential that writers and artists follow their own creative spirit. What subjects they should choose for their creative work and how they should deal with those subjects are questions that writers and artists themselves must examine and gradually resolve through practice. There should be no arbitrary meddling in this process." Most people remembered only six words: "There should be no arbitrary meddling." How unfathomable but marvelous that he should even say that!

My take, however, was slightly different from that of others. I was a member of the conference presidium and sat in the first row behind the podium on that massive stage. With such proximity, I could feel the powerful presence and audacity of Deng delivering his speech. His voice was that of authority and command, leaving little room for a literary man's fancies. He stressed, "This congress reflects the unprecedented unity of writers and artists throughout the country." He affirmed, "Our writers and artists, like workers in other fields, have scored considerable achievements . . . By and large our writers and artists have proved to be good." He was passing down a verdict.

I noted in particular that he said, "[Writers and artists] should remain clearheaded when confronted by the proponents of erroneous tendencies, whether from the 'Left' or from the Right, who are always attempting by one means or another to create disturbances and sabotage stability and unity, against the interests and wishes of the overwhelming majority of the people . . ." He warned against erroneous tendencies from both "left" and right, including the dangers of disturbances, which was to be borne out by later events. Overall, there was celebration, consolation, and empathy in his speech. There was also the reaffirmation of leadership and the demand for conformity. He would not tolerate letting things getting out of hand; he was firm as a rock. There was no ambiguity, nor room for compromise.

At the time, Deng Xiaoping's remarks at an earlier session on ideological issues had also been circulated. We were all reminded of the need to adhere to the "Four Basic Principles." Therefore, I was not surprised by Deng's formal remarks at the conference. It would be unthinkable for the leader of the CCP not to make such solemn statements and warn against any deviation.

I felt happy for all the previously defamed writers who, having been rehabilitated, now had a place on the presidium or were able to speak up without too much inhibition. This was an outcome that so many had paid for with precious years of their lives and even their blood. Had it not been for the great turnaround led by Deng Xiaoping, it would have been inconceivable.

I am but a literary man, who by nature is eager to make noise, to sing, and to join the fray, like frogs relishing a croaky chorus. The difference being I was aware of my frog-like urge and never foolishly thought that such reptilian tendencies could make me a dragon. I never aspired to be a spiritual leader and was adverse to such a proposition. I had my doubts about the very notion of spiritual leaders, anyway. I had to be true to myself, which, though hardly sublime and inspirational, was in fact a very high standard indeed.

A writer becoming a spiritual leader was perhaps possible in the era of Lu Xun. In fact, he achieved that status only posthumously. It was unrepeatable. No other writers before or after him attained that kind of status. Not Li Bai,[4] not Du Fu,[5] not Cao Xueqin,[6] not Homer, not Balzac, not Cervantes. Tolstoy was seen as an example of virtue and noble character in China, but not necessarily so in his native Russia. In the contemporary world, Heinrich Böll has some claims to being a guru, but he is nowhere close to being a spiritual leader. Thus I remained cool-headed amid all the hype, and my official remarks at the conference were rather low-key—I merely pointed out that the policies of the extreme left had alienated the Party against writers [in the past]. I wanted to stay away from all the hoopla. However, there was immediate fallout. Some fellow writers felt unsatisfied, not getting the anticipated kick from of my speech. They felt it too tame and uninspiring. Ever since then, I have often been subjected to such well-intentioned criticism. Some claimed that I was too much of a "leftist," that I had surrendered and sided with

4. Li Bai, 701–762, also known as Li Bo, Tang dynasty poet.
5. Du Fu, 712–770, poet of the Tang dynasty.
6. Cao Xueqin, 1715–1763 (?), Qing dynasty writer, best known for *Dream of the Red Chamber*, one of the Four Great Classical Novels of Chinese literature.

the government. Still others pointed out that I was in fact right leaning and hence treacherous.

Zhou Yang, the culture czar since Liberation, who had gone through hard times himself, apologized openly at the conference to all writers and artists, and in particular to Ding Ling and Jiang Feng,[7] whom he had condemned in the past. The venerable writer and vice chairman of the Writers' Union, Liu Baiyu, echoed this by saying that Zhou's apologies were his, too. This was met by heckling from the audience, "No, they are no substitute for yours!" In a huge auditorium seating thousands, this was stunning and embarrassing. But then what would it be like if there had been only applause and no loud objections throughout such a conference? I sometimes think it was precisely the total suppression of dissenting voices that made the occasional heckler stand out more. If someone shouted the explosive "Fuck you!" in the middle of a busy crossroad during the Cultural Revolution, wouldn't that have made him a hero?

I was impressed by Xia Yan's closing remarks. He talked about efforts against feudal tendencies, about the evergreen tree of Life, and about the Party's ideology needing improvement. He insisted that writers and artists must not cease to learn. The emphasis on learning was a perennial theme of his remarks on all such occasions, and it was music to the ears of many. Xia Yan had such seniority; he had been a CCP member since the 1920s. He was beyond reproach and was thought of by younger writers as endearing. But he could also be bothersome to others.

An odd and memorable incident [also] occurred at the conference: a few others and I were summoned by someone for a private talk. He claimed to have been asked by a senior CCP leader to *steer* us in the right direction. He was none other than Ruan Ming, who had labeled me a *rightist* even before the formal verdict was passed down by the Party committee in 1957. He was lanky and sullen with a bony face and gray eyes. He had a forced air to his arrogance and a chilling gaze. He did not look like a run-of-the-mill cadre or behind-the-scene counsel—but more like a surgeon in scrubs, with a lancet in hand, ready for the incision. He was the first to attack Zhou Yang during the Cultural Revolution,

7. Jiang Feng, 1910–1982, woodcut artist, former chairman of the China Artists Association, labeled a *rightist* in 1957.

accusing him of underhandedness in meddling with the *Notes to the Complete Works of Lu Xun*. He rose to some fame and became chairman of the revolutionary committee of the CCP Propaganda Department during the Cultural Revolution and was expelled from the Party in 1983 for his active involvement in the political tumult. He settled in the United States in 1988, became a visiting professor in Taiwan, and adviser to Taiwan "president" Chen Shuibian in 2004!

The question of literary groups not endorsed by the government was also discussed at the conference. One was led by Bei Dao[8] and included contributors to the journal *Today*. They were Gu Cheng,[9] Shu Ting,[10] Yang Lian,[11] Meng Ke,[12] Gan Tiesheng,[13] Shi Tiesheng,[14] Pan Jing,[15] and Xu Xiao.[16] These names still resonate with many today. Shu Ting's poetry and prose has been so popular that she is now a leading figure at the Xiamen Municipal Federation of Literature and Arts Circles. Shi Tiesheng, who was disabled after an accident, received popular and critical acclaim for both his writings and for the way he lived his life. Pang Jing's "An Era of Passion" won the top prize at the Shanghai Literary Awards. Yet other members of this group decided to move overseas.

In the charter of the Writer's Union adopted at the conference, a reference was made to enhancing relationships with such non-official literary groups in the interest of promoting literary creativity. It reflected a desire for unity and avoiding entrenchment in literary circles, and the promotion of stability and harmony in society. However, efforts in this regard were not entirely successful, with unresolved problems that would resurface later.

---

8. Bei Dao, 1949–, poet and the most notable representative of "the Misty Poets," a group of Chinese modernist poets.
9. Gu Cheng, 1956–1993, poet, essayist, and novelist. He committed suicide after killing his wife with a hatchet.
10. Shu Ting, 1952–, poet, leading female representative of the Misty Poets.
11. Yang Lian, 1955–, poet associated with the Misty Poets and of the "Root-Seeking School." He was born in Berne, Switzerland, and raised in Beijing.
12. Meng Ke, 1950–, poet. Settled in the United States.
13. Gan Tiesheng, 1946–, writer whose short story "Juhui" (The Reunion) was published in 1980 and caused quite a stir in literary circles.
14. Shi Tiesheng, 1951–2010, novelist best known for his novel *Life on a String*.
15. Pan Jing, 1950–, writer and literary editor.
16. Xu Xiao, 1956–, editor at *Today* and essayist.

Now, twenty-seven years later, I can recall nothing in the way of a discussion on literature and the arts proper at a conference held in their name. The support for "literature of the wounded" really meant support for post-Cultural Revolution rectification. Putting formerly banished writers into positions of leadership was part of the "rehabilitation of former cadres." This gathering of writers and artists, many of whom had been persecuted during the Cultural Revolution, was an emotional occasion for many. Those of us who had been banished for more than two decades, however, returned only with mellowness after all the trials and tribulations. A few excitable delegates took the opportunity for a bombastic airing of their long suppressed sentiments. That raised a few eyebrows. Overall, the political tone and policies announced at the conference were encouraging. There was again talk of "let a hundred flowers bloom." Deng's remarks about no more arbitrary meddling and his verdict that writers and artists had proved to be "good" certainly sent many into fits of joy.

The scale and all the ceremonial proceedings of the conference were also memorable, causing excitement and admiration in the literary and arts circles at large. Even those claiming to be indifferent and disinterested took note. What a sight to behold when several thousand delegates gathered in the Great Hall of the People, with blazing lights beaming down from the ceiling, and top leaders of the Party and the state showing up on the massive podium to thunderous applause. Many in the audience were in tears. There were rousing speeches, rallying calls, and proclamations of allegiance, which, like pre-battle chants, got everyone's adrenaline pumping. Positions and titles were conferred and claimed by the bright, virtuous and notable, who numbered in the hundreds. A new crop of chairpersons, secretaries, members of committees and high councils, and advisers, honorary chairpersons and so on came to the fore. All this was conducted in the most grandiose and ceremonious manner. Then there were also the not so ceremonial sobbing and laughing; jostling and badmouthing; scheming and anguishing.

One notable absence was Shen Rong,[17] who had published quite a few short stories. She was a secondary school teacher, but her salary

17. Shen Rong, 1936–, Chinese woman writer.

had been withheld for years because of her failure to fulfill her teaching obligations. She had spent much of her employer's time moonlighting. Liu Libang, director of the district education bureau, who was my former boss in my Youth League years, would fume with rage. But Shen Rong never repented. Without the endorsement of her employer, she could not attend the conference. She made good use of the time, sneaking into an eye hospital and gaining firsthand experience for her short story "At Middle Age" which was to bring her critical acclaim and national fame. She was eventually paid all her back salary and became a "professional writer" on the roster of the Beijing municipal Federation of Literature and Arts Circles. All this enraged Liu Libang even more. I was torn between Shen Rong, a fellow writer, and my former comrade-in-arms. For Shen Rong, not attending the conference was no disappointment, and she was amply compensated.

The conference ushered in a new era for literature and arts in China. The madness and turmoil of the Cultural Revolution was finally behind us. As a Chinese saying goes, extremity breeds its own reversal. The reversal in literary and arts circles was what this conference was about. It threw the last shovel of dirt on the Cultural Revolution. Even though some who had large followings during the Cultural Revolution lingered and attempted to eulogize the Red Guards and their campaigns, that extraordinary and insane era was gone for good.

Chapter 36

A Creative Outburst

After the Fourth National Conference for Literature and Arts, I was appointed editor-in-chief of *People's Literature* and then a member of the Secretariat of the Writers' Union. I began to feel a certain responsibility for my fellow writers, particularly when they found themselves in trouble.

One incident involved a small group of rehabilitated writers who were invited by publishers in the northeast for a tour after the conference. The over-excited comments they made there about the "Democracy Wall"[1] in Beijing drew criticism. I had declined invitations for such tours, wanting to devote more time to writing. After hearing about their trouble, I tried to think of a way to offer them some protection. Frailty, thy name is "man of letters." Such people could be indignant with righteousness one instant, but recoil at the drop of the gauntlet the next. Now that their words had got them into trouble, how could I protect them and the hard-earned, better-than-ever environment for literary expression? How could we prevent a repeat of past persecution?

Yet these writers actually yearned for attention. I ended up not being able to find a good solution. I realized I could only do what I was best at. Literature should be immune to political agitation. It belongs in the realm of the universal and historical. It cannot be too simplistic and

---

1. A section of brick wall on Xidan Street in downtown Beijing that became the focus for political dissent in late 1978. Big-character posters with news and ideas were pasted on the wall by activists.

state the obvious, like "big character posters" or public square orations. Literature of substance, multiple dimensions, and enduring qualities is a world unto its own, which cannot be easily destroyed—not by a roaring mob, not by slander. Real literature is rooted in life and the world at large, which are ultimately indestructible.

Even with all other obligations then, I insisted on being first and foremost a literary man dedicated to the craft of writing. Around that time, newspapers reprinted a quote by the senior CCP leader Chen Yun,[2] suggesting that writers who were CCP members must "be party members first and a writer second." I was asked by a Japanese writer whether this meant people had to join the Party first and then, only then, be allowed to write. I went to great lengths to explain but still could not make him quite understand.

I did join the Party first in the early years and then learned to write stories. I had no way of playing down my political background and obligations. I had admitted a personal motive also: I needed to improve my lot; I intended to demonstrate my unique attributes, experience, and versatility to get ahead and get my two sons back from Xinjiang. They were too young when we moved down there. I did not ask for their opinion, and now had an obligation as their father to give them a chance back in the city.

The period from the fall of 1979 through 1980 was quite productive. "A Barber's Tale" and "The Unforgettable and Unmemorable," both short stories, touched upon the fate of rehabilitated cadres. The opportunistic apple-polishing official in "The Unforgettable and Unmemorable" was based on a true story. She was a scheming woman that had a past on the stage. During the Cultural Revolution, she succeeded in evicting a senior cadre of the Literature and Arts Federation from his house by denouncing him as a "capitalist-roader." She herself then moved into the prized property. She was an archetype of those profiting from the turmoil of revolution. When the Cultural Revolution was over, she promptly returned to her coastal hometown, leaving her political past behind. She was never a successful actress, never remembered for her stagecraft, but she

2. Chen Yun, 1905–1995, CCP elder, chiefly known for his role in planned economic policies. He served as vice premier, Politburo member, and vice chairman of the CCP Central Committee.

thrived in political upheavals. Her worldly gains could help explain why political campaigns had attracted so many zealots. Unlike the Gang of Four or "the three bad elements" (those who damaged public properties and physically harmed others in the Cultural Revolution), they could not be convicted as criminals and put away. Even venerable cadres who had been taken advantage of found them not entirely dispensable because of their political prowess. Those in a position of power needed a few able bodies pandering to their whims.

I wrote "A Barber's Tale" following a trip to Ili in the spring of 1979 while I was still in Xinjiang and shortly before returning to Beijing for good. I stopped over in the county of Xinyuan and joined a drinking party with local officials. I got so drunk that I remembered afterward only a horrible tale or two about local cadres, but not much else. One was about a cadre being literally scared to death during the Cultural Revolution. After he and two others said something nasty about Mao's wife in private, someone tipped off the authorities. All three were rounded up as "counterrevolutionaries." The first cadre dropped dead out of sheer fear, and another went mad after repeated public repudiations. The third survived and was rehabilitated after the Cultural Revolution. Yet his arrogance and indulgence in officious "trappings" annoyed local folks. In "A Barber's Tale," Master Tang the barber was sympathetic to the survivor, now a cadre of elevated position, while trimming his unruly hair. The story won a "year's best" literary prize.

At a forum on my writings during the Horizon Art Festival in West Berlin in 1985, the German sinologist Rudolf G. Wagner read a paper on this story. He offered his analysis that the word for haircutting in Chinese is a homonym of lawmaking; the barber's surname "Tang" reflects a yearning for the golden era of the Tang dynasty. Apparently, the Chinese pedantic tradition of digging up hidden sources and meanings had followers in faraway places.

Similar to these two short stories, "Butterfly," a novella, again focused on cadres who had seen their days of glory and humiliation and then held onto their stubborn old habits. The title dawned on me during a trip I took with the Uighur poet Tieyipujiang in Xinjiang, at the end of 1979 or in early 1980. While the comfortable five-seat Beijing Jeep we rode in roared down the highway, I could not help reflecting on the poignancy of my changeable fate and the vicissitudes of life: a political outcast and then somebody riding high and in luxury from one moment to the next. Finding it unfathomable, I recalled the ancient philosopher Zhuang Zi pondering if he dreamed he was a butterfly, or a butterfly dreaming he was Zhuang Zi. Will I always know who I am?

"Butterfly" is not so much a sarcastic look at officialdom as a tale of soul-searching. The self-doubt of the protagonist is the result of being caught in uncertain, abrupt, and random changes in society. At first, he was a dedicated, selfless revolutionary, then a triumphant victor with vested interests in the post-Liberation period, then a victim of the Cultural Revolution, condemned as a counterrevolutionary, and finally a man rehabilitated to his former position, without he himself even knowing how it all happened.

Decades passed and his old flame Hai Yun, who had loved him deeply, committed suicide. Hai Yun's story is based on the true story of my hometown neighbor and former schoolmate. She had large eyes, which was unusual for girls from north China, who tend to have narrow, slanted eyes. Writer Kong Jiesheng once offered me his "finding": such a facial feature was the evolutionary outcome of living in the windy north with frequent sandstorms. Anyway, this schoolmate of mine joined a peripheral group of the CCP on the eve of Liberation. Then she met her future husband, a scholar and senior cadre of some renown. Soon, she married him when she was still in her teens. A road was specially paved to the village so the venerated cadre could arrive in his Warszawa (or Volga) sedan right at the doorstep of his in-laws. However, during the anti-*rightist* campaign, Hai Yun was persecuted and their marriage fell apart. According to her mother, a man with a crooked mouth but who was otherwise handsome then married her. It is possible that they were both labeled *rightists* and fell for each other in a labor camp. Love cannot not be banished. In the 1960s, I ran into her outside my old home after our *rightist* labels were rescinded. She said that after trying to put out a fire at the labor camp, she was suspected of starting it in the first place. She said that was "heart-rending." As the Cultural Revolution started, she could not bear all the humiliation again and hanged herself.

Hai Yun's celebrity first husband in real life—alive and well respected today—has nothing to do with the male protagonist. He is as dedicated as ever, always thinking. I offer him my cordial salute.

In "Butterfly," my focus was no longer on whether the apple-polisher should be entrusted with an important assignment, or rehabilitated cadres would alienate themselves from the people. It poses questions, rather, about human conscience, integrity, and love in times of turmoil. There is sympathy for the meek and feeble.

I must also reveal that my hometown neighbor and schoolmate—that very intelligent, beautiful and warm-hearted girl—is Sun Lisheng. The sad story of her life gave me inspiration. My sister told me what she had heard from Sun's mother after my novella was published: on the morning before the day of her suicide, Sun was seen looking up again and again, staring up at the sky, as if searching for something in the boundless blue. Then she stared at the ground, as if trying to see into the depths of the earth. Then she walked into the warehouse and never came out. Gazing up at the infinite skies and down into the impenetrable depths—I was shaken to the core.

Had I known these last details of her life, the portrayal of Hai Yun in "Butterfly" would have been better. You have to admit that life is larger than art, destiny more powerful than industry, and heaven and earth more enduring than fickle human emotions.

I also wrote "Anecdotes of Chairman Maimaiti," a short story with an entirely different subject. Its subtitle was "Uighur Black Humor." At the time, I knew little about black humor other than what the term conveyed in Chinese.

Here is the beginning of the story:

> It was May 6, 1979, according to the Gregorian calendar, a warm spring day with a light breeze blowing through the poplar limbs tender with new leaves. I chanced upon Chairman Maimaiti and his twin brother, Division Chief Saimaiti, at the Great Cross Halal Restaurant in Urumqi, after last seeing them both more than a decade before. What an impressive figure Chairman Maimaiti has grown into!
>
> *The unforgiving years etched his face with ridges and furrows,*
> *But his crown of dark hair is bouncy with life and vigor.*
> *His supple cheeks glisten like freshly buttered* naan,

And his hearty laughter brims with innocence and carefree wit.

Now look at Chief Saimaiti:

His curved spine like a taut bow trembling at each step,
His vague eyes with shadowy glimmers of the god of death Erlik,
His sigh before each utterance like a patient's moan,
Always gripped in his hand is a bottle of Nitroglycerin.

Such an opening had an obvious trace of the *Arabian Nights.* I ended the story by swiftly declaring:

> To live is to laugh. I urged we should simply stop whining and wailing and learn to appreciate all the blessings in life. As a Uighur proverb goes, "The life minus death is filled with pleasures." The word "pleasure" in Uighur implies taking a stroll, amusing oneself, being thankful, lounging about, playing or loafing. A Chinese standup comedian said famously, "Just to make you happy." Was this merely Epicurean? Yet underneath all this, there was sorrow and a letting go. As I have said before, profound joy is only possible after deep sorrow.

The joy for me in my forties was that I was entering the most prolific period of my writing. I experienced a spurt of creative energy. Stories seemed to spring forth from everywhere. They danced around me; new subject matter enchanted me; ingenious phrasing buzzed in my ears and blossomed in my heart. I turned around and ideas like specks of gold swirled in a circle. All I had to do was to pick one and put pen to paper. My world was full of stories, and all I could capture was barely a drop in the ocean. How many stories could a man write? How much luckier can I be? Such was life in those heady years of the early 1980s.

During another trip to Xinjiang, I waited for days for an air ticket back to Beijing. My old chums treated me to sweet potato noodles and fried peanuts every day. In desperation, I decided to take the train. I stopped over in Xian on my long ride home and was met by venerable local writers whom I had met before in Beijing. I was invited to a forum and was most respectful when fielding questions from these writers, all with of a proud past in wartime Yan'an. I said that the notion of "intervention in life" and "exposing the dark side of society," both being popular notions at the time, were perhaps not entirely appropriate, at least not true to our literary tradition. I would propose "intervention in the human soul" (which was first coined by the Jiangsu writer Gao Xiaosheng[3]) and "exposing conflicts," which was more specific and convincing than merely exposing the dark side. This met their approval.

I then took a two-hour ride in a boxcar to visit my younger son Wang Shi, who was a cadet at a military technology college in Sanyuan County. I had not seen him since leaving the northwest in the early summer of 1978. Boxcars were used then to haul passengers on remote rural routes. They usually had only one or two tiny square windows for ventilation, with no lighting inside and everyone resting their butts on the floor. I based my short story "The Sound of Spring" on the experience of riding on that train. It began:

> The door slid close with a loud clank and it was dark as night inside. A square spot of light, like a mellow, yellowish moon, appeared in the darkness on the opposite wall.

This paragraph led to intriguing interpretations, with one going as far as suggesting that Wang Meng meant spring had arrived with a loud clank. People often remember not what actually happened, but what they believe to have happened and what was most memorable. What was perceived would then be labeled, extrapolated, or simplified and become lodged in people's memories.

My experimental writings from this period included *A Bolshevik Salute,* "Butterfly," "Reverie by the Sea," "Kite Streamers," and "The Sound of Spring." They were branded as "stream of consciousness" and caused quite a stir. But our understanding, including mine, of "stream of consciousness" was actually rather limited. Even to this day, I haven't done any serious reading of James Joyce, William Faulkner, or Virginia Woolf—or any formal expositions on "stream of consciousness." My understanding was nothing more than what the term in Chinese connoted. To me consciousness meant psychological details, and stream, the flow of water—glistening, with surface and undercurrents, ceaseless, disappearing and reemerging, and rippled by wind and rain. Writings

3. Gao Xiaosheng, 1928–1999, Chinese novelist; labeled a *rightist.*

in such a vein could certainly be interesting and multifaceted. But they were nothing extraordinary. My essays from my high school years already showed, as fellow writer Liu Shaotang observed, such a tendency.

These writings were deemed problematic by some because I wrote about the inner world. Psychological descriptions, as in Goncharov's novel *Oblomov,* for example, were ridiculed in China. Several pages into the novel, Goncharov's protagonist is still lying in his bed debating whether to get up right away or simply stay put. Zhou Yang once quoted Goethe as saying that a social class in ascent is outward looking and becomes introspective when in decline (I have yet to locate the source of this quote).[4] Further, it would just be too arbitrary to put my writings into any category."The Eyes of the Night" was not exactly an exposé of back-door deals; "Kite Streamers" not a tale of school kids being sent down to the country for re-education; "Reverie by the Sea" not merely about the rehabilitation of purged intellectuals. What could the boxcar and the new locomotive in "The Sound of Spring" possibly imply?

This creative outburst of mine lasted seven or eight months. In *A Bolshevik Salute,* I showed much lucidity, though my narrative could at times be halting. With "The Eyes of the Night," inspirations from life, sensibilities, compelling storytelling, and underlying emotional forces (first referred to in my short story "Young Newcomer at the Organization Department") all came back. Life after the Cultural Revolution, hopes for better things, new beginnings and old memories, sad smiles and blissful dreams, all inspired me. Writer Yan Wenjing[5] told me in a letter that he was touched by my "Reverie by the Sea," that he believed it to be more poetic than poetry. This was by no means mere pleasantry. If you have read his essays, you will know that his own prose has indeed poetic elegance. By then, however, my experiment with form had made some in the literary establishment uncomfortable, thanks to their intolerance and limitations. Thus, even such a tame letter by Yan raised many an eyebrow. He was censured for affirming my latest writings. Many others, including those for whom I had great respect and admiration, shied away from

---

4. Zhou Yang might have paraphrased this direct quote from "Conversation with Goethe": "All eras in a state of decline and dissolution are subjective; on the other hand, all progressive eras have an objective tendency."
5. Yan Wenjing, 1915–2005, writer of children's literature and essayist.

making positive comments.

A family relative said with a sigh, "Wang Meng's stories caused controversy in the 1950s because of their substance. Now in the 1980s his new writings are causing a debate because of their form." Nonetheless, I continued to write. I was in my element, like a fish in a pond, an eagle soaring in the sky, a horse running free on the prairie. I saw material for my stories everywhere. Hardly was one story finished when the plan for another began to take shape. As Anton Chekhov said, any random item—a glass bottle or an old button—could be inspiration for him.

I had first tried my hand at writing short stories in the 1950s. After more than two decades of political and literary limbo, I returned to writing them again. My stories were being published in quick succession. Sometimes, as many as five titles of my stories would appear in ads for literary journals in one newspaper. My name popped up everywhere—what I wrote was in vogue. Reviewers found it hard to keep pace and were left behind seeing a trail of dust, as I raced ahead, switching from one genre or narrative style to another, so said a friend of mine. Those were the glory days, again.

"A story is but a story," as Zong Pu wrote as an epigraph to her popular novella *Stone of Three Incarnations.* But a story is also much more than a story. Such antitheses with political undertones had haunted writers in China for decades, tormenting them and at times putting their lives in peril.

Chapter 37

My First Visit to Germany

At the end of 1979, I was invited to a dinner party hosted by German Ambassador Erwin Wickert, together with writers Feng Mu, Yuan Ying,[1] and possibly Bai Hua. At this dinner in honor of the visiting Polish-born German literary critic Marcel Reich-Ranicki, the discussion turned to German Nobel laureate Heinrich Böll. The ambassador said that Böll had given the German government some headaches. Böll had been known for his harsh criticism of German society and its capitalist system. I cannot recall if it was Ranicki who wrote disparagingly, in the *Frankfurter Allgemeine Zeitung*, of Böll's language and style and that he had won the Nobel Prize for Literature more as a moralist than as a fiction writer. Ranicki grilled us with questions such as why literary writing should be subjected to control by the Party. Feng Mu and Yuan Ying offered some elusive comments, but it was hard to have any consensus on such a topic.

One thing definite was an invitation to the guests by the ambassador for a visit to Germany in the early summer of the following year, which was "happily accepted" by all.

In those days, overseas travel was deemed an immense privilege for a writer, bestowing honor even on one's long dead uncles. Writer Liu Xinwu had just returned from such a visit to Romania in late autumn of that year, and I was enthralled by his riveting observations about

1. Yuan Ying, 1924–, writer, poet, and former director of the Literary Department of the *People's Daily*.

Romanian women having their curly hair permed straight, in contrast to straight-haired women in China wanting the exact opposite, and his terrible experience of watching an aviation disaster movie midflight. I had been asked earlier by the Writers' Union to join two venerable writers—Ba Jin and Bing Xin—on a visit to Japan in the cherry blossom season of early spring the following year. With the German visit in the works, my place on the Japanese trip would be taken by someone else (writer Deng Youmei). It was all about balance and avoiding favoritism when it came to overseas travel. It turned out that Deng Youmei was a better candidate for the Japanese trip anyway: he had been forced by Japanese troops to work in Seto in Japan during World War II.

Thus in early June 1980, a Chinese writers' delegation headed by Feng Mu, with poet Ke Yan,[2] writer Ma Jia,[3] me and an interpreter, and Wang Wanqian boarded a Lufthansa DC-10 jumbo jet for our trip to Germany. Yuan Ying and his interpreter Wang Xiaoping from the *People's Daily* were on the same flight. Their itinerary mostly shadowed ours except for some media events. The only one missing was Bai Hua, who could not get approval for travel.

Our plane made a refueling stop in Tehran. Because of strained relations with the USSR, commercial flights from Beijing to Europe were routed southwest via Tehran or Karachi (later mostly Sharjah), rather than the shorter northern route through Soviet airspace. The in-flight food and beverages were a luxury. Even the pull-tab can gave me much private amusement. One fellow traveler reported swallowing the wax casing of a Babybel cheese by mistake. It took me a while to understand the label "mineral water," and I was bothered by the idea of bottling plain drinking water in lavish cans. I also had my first taste of fresh fruit juice and couldn't help but be amazed. Back home, merely having fruit from time to time was already a blessing. But to crush them into tasteful juices and then drink them—what a bourgeois concoction!

Also during the stopover on this flight (maybe it was a later flight on my second trip to Germany at either Tehran or Karachi), we were told to stay on board because of a local curfew. Wanting to get a glimpse of

2. Ke Yan, 1929–2011, writer and poet, wife of former Minister of Culture He Jingzhi.
3. Ma Jia, 1910–2004, storywriter and poet.

the airport, I tried to push close to the cabin door and bumped into a European. He immediately wheeled about with an "Excuse me!" I was embarrassed and learned later that such inadvertent body contact should always be avoided. You apologize first, no matter who is at fault. Many years later in 1993, I watched on television a Chinese judo champion recounting to an audience how she tested her foreign opponent at a reception before the final game: she deliberately bumped her opponent who then apologized to her. The Chinese champion took that as a sign of weakness and boasted to roaring applause: "I knew right then she was afraid of me." I was dismayed by the utter ignorance.

The first city we visited was Frankfurt. We saw blue-eyed, blond police officers, walkie-talkies in hand and handguns in hip holsters. We also saw glittering merchandise displayed in lavish shop windows and were stirred by blatant "sex shop" signs here and there. Exotic spirits and whiffs of perfume and cologne overwhelmed our senses and made us tipsy.

In one week, we visited Bonn, Cologne, Berlin, Hamburg, Heidelberg, and Munich. Berlin was then East Germany's capital with West Berlin being a Western enclave. West German flights were not allowed in East German airspace. Nor did it acknowledge West Berlin as being part of West Germany, but rather a territory under British, American, and French joint occupation. We flew into West Berlin on a British Airways flight, a sobering reminder of this state of affairs.

I was elated. For days I would fall asleep the instant my head hit the pillow, only to wake up a short while later and remain wide-awake. But once I got up, I would feel drowsy again. I was amazed by how clean, bright, and colorful everything was. People's clothes and faces, houses and streets, all looked neatly scrubbed. The air was clear and crisp, without the ever-present dust that we were accustomed to back home, and our shirt collars and cuffs remained clean by day's end. There were lush plants everywhere. I was told that Americans visiting Germany shortly after the war were similarly impressed by the flowers on every balcony amid the ruins and desolation of the war, and took that as a sign of German resilience. Fine dining at restaurants was not just about food but also ambience. But I was a little perturbed one morning by scurrying ants enjoying themselves on and beneath the breakfast table. The marmalade and honey was perhaps too irresistible, and people were not in the habit of getting rid of them as pests.

In Hamburg we met Anna Wang, ex-wife of the venerable Chinese diplomat Wang Bingnan and author of the memoir *Ich Kämpfte für Mao* (I Fight for Mao). She enquired in Chinese about the health of "Comrade Wang Bingnan." Our meeting was at the Hotel Atlantic over coffee and ice cream, which were dearly priced at six German marks per serving. That was a hefty sum of ten yuan in RMB. While there, I also visited the home of Professor Wolfgang Franke, an old friend of my father's, and met his wife Hu Chün-yin. I was pleased to see the framed rubbing of ancient carved calligraphy by the eccentric scholar Zhen Banqiao, a gift to him from my father. Its four Chinese characters declared, "Ignorance is bliss." I had often seen and been emboldened by this message when I was a child. I thought about my father's old house at No. 14, Nanweir Alley in Beijing. After all, your past doesn't just disappear but can be hidden somewhere unbeknown to you.

At the University of Hamburg, we were introduced to Professor Zhao of the Chinese Department—he was the brother of the well-known Peking Opera singer Zhao Rongchen—and Department Chair Professor Qiao and his wife. I was struck by their rich Mandarin pronunciation, which sounded much more gratifying than that of Beijing locals nowadays. This was the old style speech of the true "Manchu," evocative of my childhood days in Beijing.

We also met Dr. Kuan Yu-chien who had worked for China's People's Friendship Association before leaving the country during the Cultural Revolution under extraordinary circumstances. Despite all the hardships and near-death ordeals in his escape, his abiding love for and interest in his motherland was only too evident.

The prettiest town we visited was Heidelberg, which, on the picturesque River Neckar, has aged buildings and a medieval castle. We visited a poet who lived in the tower of the Old Bridge. It was interesting to note his choice of abode, though such a fortress-like home could hardly be called comfortable. The poet, according to Ambassador Wickert, was a man of great character, though not necessarily of great verse. The town of Heidelberg was spared in the Allied bombing in WW II because of its historic buildings, so I was told.

In West Berlin, the ruins of the old Kaiser Wilhelm Memorial Church, destroyed by the bombing, still stood. A new chapel and belfry were constructed right next to the ruins. This was a great idea for heritage preservation. Inside the new church was a figure of Christ with his head bent low. It was an image of profound despair and disenchantment over mankind's follies. Jesus could almost be heard saying, "People, how can I love you anymore?" I felt shaken and subdued.

It was a delightful trip overall, though short and akin to "looking at flowers on horseback." We noted how far China had lagged behind, but felt no despair as China, having come out of isolation and given up wrestling with imagined giant windmills, had begun her reform and ascendance. We were beginning to see the world for what it was and our place in it. After all, the Party had just concluded its historic Third Plenary Session of the Eleventh Congress and was embarking on a new journey.

My dialogue with German friends was helped by the copies of English translations of my short stories (published in the journal *Chinese Literature*) that I brought with me. We were also fortunate to have with us Ambassador Wickert, who had a keen interest in literature and had written a historical novel on the Taiping Rebellion in China. We were invited to his home, which he named "The Humble Administrator's Garden" after a heritage home in Suzhou in eastern China. I remember sitting in his living room looking out of the floor-to-ceiling windows over a lawn with Chinese plants and trees, while being amused by the dancing bubbles of my fizzy carbonated drink. There seemed to be so much more carbonation than the soda I was used to back in China. The refrigerator, the chilled cola drinks, the French windows, and the manicured lawn were luxuries beyond imagining for most Chinese at that time. Trees and flowers were nothing strange, no matter how much more lush there. But the large swaths of grass purely intended to please the eye were a novelty. I was struck by their rich green. The smooth luxuriance inexplicably reminded me of butter. My past experience with grass being all about hoeing weeds or pulling it up for cow feed.

The German visit was a much-needed eye-opener. To say the least, it was refreshing to see a world out there where Chinese was not the only lingua franca, where multiple political and value systems existed.

There were diverse perspectives and outlooks, in addition to a rainbow of skin and eye colors. The visit was many courses crammed into one—geography, history, anthropology, language, and architecture—about the places we visited: Berlin, Munich, Hamburg, Bremen, the Alps and the Rhine River. Valley slopes were dotted with poppies in striking colors, and village churches with ubiquitous weathervane roosters perched on their spires. I was taken on a cruise on the Rhine and remembered—as enchanting castles, churches, and dark woods swept by—a song I learned in childhood about the river spirit Lorelei:

In times of distant past,
There were tales as numerous as raindrops from the skies . . .

Such was the amazing power of literature. I was there on the Rhine, which I had never visited before, and felt like I was coming back to a place of my youth, to a song that I had learned decades ago, which were there all the while, waiting to be remembered. I recalled the tune and these first two lines plus the fourth line "The air is cool in the gloaming . . ." It is about a Siren distracting a boatman with her song, causing his boat to crash onto the rocks. I asked around for its lyrics when I returned to China. But to my dismay, no one had a clue.

It was not until 2007 that I got help from Mr. Li Zhang, Wang Anyi's husband, and got a slightly different Chinese version based on a poem by Heinrich Heine set to music by Friedrich Silcher:

A fable of old, through it streaming,
allows my mind no rest.
The air is cool in the gloaming
and gently flows the Rhine . . .

. . . Her golden jewelry is glist'ning;
She combs her golden hair.

. . . The boatman aboard his small skiff,
I think that the waves will devour
both boat and man, by and by,
and that, with her dulcet-voiced power
was done by the Lorelei.

Germany was a strange and foreign land no more, because of familiar tales and the lingering tune of *Lorelei.* The excellent Chinese translation of the song was by the noted translator and lyricist Xue Fan.

I was pleased to see and hear so much that was evocative of my youth—names and symbols associated with Germany—Beethoven and Goethe, Marx and Hegel, Bayer's aspirins and Siemens appliances. Having limited wayfaring experience is not a sin. But to reject such an experience and opportunity to learn would be unwise. We should always try in our finite lives to venture out and explore new horizons. Just as my old landlord Abdureheman had sung, "I want to leave and see the big world . . ."

After returning to Beijing, I wrote an essay, "Fleeting Impressions of West Germany," which was given a reading in German by someone at the West Berlin Arts Festival in 1985, which I attended. The interpreter, unfamiliar with the Chinese original, translated the German version back into Chinese on the spot. Amazingly, after such back and forth, it had become an entirely new piece of writing, only vaguely familiar to me. Such was literary translation then. Physically, meanwhile, I had gained much weight during the German trip, likely because of the rich servings of meat, sugary foods, and dairy products.

Then, I learned from Feng Mu of the Writers' Union that I had an invitation to the International Writing Program [IWP] at the University of Iowa. As Liu Binyan who was also invited could not go, the group included only the poet Ai Qing, his wife, and me. (Thus shortly after Germany, I was getting ready for my first trip to the States.)

Chapter 38

Four Months in the United States

From late August to December 1980, I was in the United States as a resident writer at the International Writing Program at the University of Iowa. The program was co-directed by Nieh Hualing and her poet husband Paul Engle. Apart from obligatory seminars and social gatherings, I spent most of my time there writing *A Dappled Horse,* a novella based on my horse riding trips near the Tekesi Military Ranch and Nileke summer range in Xinjiang, that I completed there. In retrospect, that remote area of northwestern Xinjiang is not that vast and empty, certainly unlike the Russian steppes depicted by Chekhov or the expansive grassland sung about in Russian ballades. That part of Xinjiang is in fact mostly alpine meadows and valleys. Not a landscape of melancholy, of boundless prairie receding into distant horizons. Rather, there are gently rolling hills in all directions, with cool mountain streams and lush vegetation, cattle and sheep grazing in the deep valleys or way up on distant precipices. Against this background was the horse of dapple gray:

> This could well be the shabbiest horse in the stable of the revolutionary committee of the commune. Just look at him: his gray coat of mixed white and chestnut hair, his bushy unkempt mane; his bruised back with its ugly scabs; sinuous veins on his barrel chest extended to his sagging haunches: all markings of a harsh existence. His worn saddle was soiled with mud and chaff and hung limply from a post. It was so tattered and brittle that it looked as if it were a patch of dry mud and

> would disappear in a puff of dust at a mere poke. "What do you expect? Everyone has his own hero and I am stuck with mine . . ." murmured Cao Qianli, who stood by his dappled gray-horse, patting its neck, scratching its chin and smoothing its hair.
>
> But the old horse stood motionless with a blank stare.

I wrote about the sorry-looking horse with numbness in his limbs and his best years behind him, dreaming still of galloping with lightening swiftness under thunderous skies. He certainly can't compare to those fabled equines of antiquity—the swift "red hare," a bay horse charging to great fame on the battlefields of the "Three Kingdoms," the black horse "Wu Zhui" ridden by the tragic general who brought down the mighty Qin Empire, the noble horses of Emperor Taizong of the Tang immortalized in a bas-relief on his tomb, the doomed "De Lu" who saved and doomed his successive masters, the white horse of monk Xuan Zhuang on his legendary pilgrimage to the West, or even Don Quixote's skinny steed, or the nervous mare Frou Frou which Vronsky, Anna Karenina's lover, rides to a terrible crash in a steeplechase.

Yet the feeble dappled horse had significance for me—it gives form to loss, confusion, and void of meaning. As the Cultural Revolution raged on elsewhere in the country, I lived in limbo, left to my own devices. My life was a numbing routine, without a sense of purpose. My being in that remote northwestern town of Ili was never by choice. Yet the chaos of the Cultural Revolution made my living there a matter of personal responsibility. My riding trip was symbolic of such aimless wandering. In my confused youth, I joined the revolution for the sense of certainty it accorded; everything was prescribed for me once I was part of the revolution. All I need do was follow instructions in work as well as in life. In that forgotten corner of mine in the feverish years of the Cultural Revolution, however, orders no longer came from the authorities. I became a negligible horse of mixed colors that few cared about.

However, when sensing danger, his survival instinct jolted him to life; it was his moment of truth.

> While Cao Qianli's nerves were yet to calm, the horse had returned to his ponderous state, his head sleepily hanging.

> Cao Qianli could not understand how the old hack could have mustered such strength to gallop from the valley bottom to the hilltop. There was not even a trail. How could he have hurled himself, as it were, up the hill? How could this pathetic and tired old hack have such alertness, dexterity, valor and energy?
>
> "Let me do it again," the horse suddenly said. "Let me run once more!" The horse frothed, clearly and with sadness in his trembling voice. "All I need is one more chance; let me run with all my strength, just once more!'
>
> "Let him, let him run!" the wind whispered.
>
> "Let him, let him fly!" the eagle echoed with his dark wings spreading wide.
>
> "He can do it, yes he can . . ." the stream murmured as if begging.
>
> "Let him run, let him take on wings and fly!" the valley echoed thunderously.

Before the end of the story, I wrote about Cao Qianli, our famished and rain-drenched hero, having gulped down several bowls of kumis and now having an alcohol emboldened vision:

> Cao Qianli mounted the horse and broke out in song. His song resonated in the valley and spurred the horse to gallop faster and faster, as if taking wing and swift as with speed like wind and lightening. [Then there was silence.] The horse surging forth became like a whale plowing through the glimmering sea, waves parting in unstoppable progression, or like a spaceship gliding in the illuminated infinity with all the stars lined up in awe of its brilliance . . . all Cao Qianli could hear now was the whooshing of the wind, the wind of the mountain, the sea, the plateau and the stratosphere . . .

Literary men are often inclined to find solace and inspiration from remote edges and desolation, the endless expanse of grasslands and desert sands, the untamed, primordial forces. They take to solitude and dejection— tears in celebratory moments and laughter in utter despair. They tend to glorify life in a world without advanced industrial production, of shipwreck, highway robberies, and wild wolves. Or at least on occasion—on many occasions—they do. Only creators of soap operas relish scenes of grand mansions, flashy cars, bombshells, big spending, endless feasts and masquerades. I cherish the experience of riding in remote mountain valleys and encountering a thunderous storm and pelting rain. My horse would amble calmly through valley meadows one moment and gallop with total abandon the next. I could be so drunk as to throw up after downing foolish amounts of fermented horse milk on an empty stomach. Standing outside the tent of a nomad Kazakh family, I laughed and wailed like a horse neighing skyward. Would I give up the opportunity for such experiences in exchange for a thousand taels of gold? No! Having lived in remote Xinjiang, Wang Meng was no longer the skinny, sensitive young man with a head full of poetic notions, a hopeless "petit bourgeois." In fact, Wang Meng could be likened to a mature, dappled horse that had seen the world for what it was and weathered rains and storms. He had not pathetically given up all hope. Nor was he tormented any more by unfulfilled ambitions. He had grown capable of accomplishing anything that he set his heart to. He could be calm or laugh as circumstances warranted; he could prevail over adversity. He was free from despair, self-pity, and remorse. I liked my vivid descriptions of the dull-spirited hack, with vascular veins on his belly, marks branded on his butt, and chaff in his mane. The portrayal of his bony frame as a "coat hanger" shaped man was inspired. However, when it comes to a noble stallion, my words often fall flat.

But why was this story about an old horse in Xinjiang written in Iowa? I stayed in Mayflower Hall four kilometers away from the main campus. I sat at my tiny side table mounted to the wall every morning after jogging along the Iowa River, across the pedestrian bridge, around the university theater and back. I tried to memorize thirty new English words every day, had buttered toast with Italian coffee and cream for breakfast, watched ABC and CBS news and listened to President Regan bashing communism at every opportunity, before my mind wandered back to the distant meadows and valleys of Xinjiang. I grew accustomed to saying "Hello!" when picking up the phone and "How do you do?" when meeting strangers. I was seeing more "foreigners" than Chinese. Most people had negative views of the Communist Party and had little knowledge of China. I could understand little of what was said on the radio or TV. In a world so foreign, much of what was going on had little to do with me. You couldn't use your Renminbi or see your leader or Party secretary who could sort things out for you when you were in doubt. Jargon you were adept at—"Party policy, political direction, spirit, deviation, adherence, report, criticism"—were at least not so obtrusively used there and then. You were fascinated at first with words such as "mister, missus, party, seminar, credit card, bill, boss and long weekend." It was in such a state that every day I penned passages about Xinjiang and its grasslands, an old horse and thunderstorms. Was it romantic or pathetic? Was I trying to strike a balance, assert my own worth, reorient or hold onto my identity? Was there in this story of an old horse, a story in which nothing much happens, merely anxiety and yearnings for a place where I could feel secure and at ease?

I came to know the Japanese novelist Minako Oba while in Iowa. She later won an Akutagawa Prize,[4] one of Japan's most coveted literary awards. She invited me over to her place and cooked lunch. We talked in English and by writing down Chinese characters that were also used in Japanese. She wrote down Chinese characters for "sleepless" to describe her flight to the U.S. and "beat" and "beauty lies in melancholy" to describe her writings. Later I hosted her in Beijing and visited her home in Tokyo twice. Translator and poet Peter Jay from Britain was a raffish fellow with a charming manner and a disarming smile. He had translated into English classical Korean poems originally written in Chinese. As he had no knowledge of Chinese, he worked with someone who understood Chinese but was not well versed in classical poems. This was also how "Songs of Chu" by Qu Yuan[5] was translated into Russian: first by sinologist Nikolai T. Fedorenko and then edited and completed by the Russian poet Anna Akhmatova, who was in disfavor with the state for decades in the Soviet era.

I was barely a beginner in English but chatted merrily with other writers, with boldness making up for linguistic deficiency. I eagerly attended literary gatherings even though I could not understand much of what was being said. I became acquainted with the Russian-American novelist Grace Paley, who liked the English translation of my short

4. Oba Minako won her Akutagawa Prize in 1968 for *Sanbiki no kani* (Three Crabs) and the Tanizaki Prize in 1982 for her novel *Katachi mo naku.*

5. An anthology of classical Chinese verse dated to the third century BCE.

story "The Eyes of the Night," and Columbia University professor and biographer Frank McShane, whom I would meet a few more times in the years to come.

IWP hosted a Chinese Weekend and invited many writers writing in Chinese from across the United States. There I met Liu Nienling, writing under her penname Mu Ling Qi, and the versatile and gregarious Ou-fan Lee. We have since become good friends. I tried to present a balanced assessment of contemporary Chinese literature. I pointed out for example that we should not regard literary writings of new China before the "literature of the wounded" as totally worthless. I did not identify with the notion that exposé should be the sole function of literature. I advocated critical depth and intellectual insight, so that "compassion and healing would be possible after examination and dissection." I emphasized a personal commitment to, and responsibility for, making things better in new China, for I had played an eager part in its making. Merely venting anger was counterproductive. I had made similar remarks back in China. For example, I had questioned—given that the communal "big rice pot" system was rife with problems under the Gang of Four—whether we should mend or discard it. Would we all perish if the "big rice pot" were simply smashed? I wore my newly made Chinese tunic, the so-called Sun Yat-sen suit, when we debated such serious questions. My outfit contrasted with the three-piece suit worn by Shi-Kuo Chang, a professor of computer science from Chicago and author of the novel *Anger of Yesterday*. The mismatch brought giggles from the audience. Chang's novel was related to the "Defend the Diaoyu Islands Movement" in Taiwan. Professor Chang was a mathematician and had a reputation for his quick, computer-like mind. He might have written a novel about gambling from a mathematician's perspective.

Nieh Hualing invited me to dinner at Iowa River Power Restaurant on several occasions. This well-known restaurant is in an old building that was once a power station, with old wirings, pipes, and equipment retained for decor. Such use of industrial remains was rarely seen in China and helped me later to appreciate the architectural style of Centre Pompidou in Paris. The prevalent aesthetic aspirations in China then were till typical of an agrarian society in ascent.

I often ordered Alaskan king crab with baked potatoes and cheese.

A second serving would be packed as takeaway for my next meal. I reciprocated by hosting dinners there too, and Paul Engle once exclaimed after seeing me paying the hefty bill, "Hualing, you should stop this or Wang Meng will go broke . . ."

We traveled extensively during the last two months of the program and met more interesting people. They included Hsia Chih-tsing, Te-Kong Tong and Ming-shui Hung, all university professors in New York, and Ching-Jang Yao, a painter of the Photorealism School. Through his paintings of stunning detail and precision, I learned that modern art of the "capitalist" West was not all about cubism and abstraction. I also met Kwang Lum, a painter, calligrapher, and art collector: and the entrepreneur, mathematician, and author Wang Hao and his then wife Chen Youshi, known for her acerbic and blunt comments. I also met Afro-American novelist Toni Morrison who later won a Nobel Prize for Literature. I called on Professor John Fairbank at Harvard and told him that I had read his *The United States and China* while I was at a "May Seventh Cadre School" during the Cultural Revolution. Despite being a China hand, he seemed not to have understood how his book became widely known in China: it was circulated for criticism and denunciation, like other Western writings made available during the Cultural Revolution. I would not have known his name otherwise. He was a humble man almost in a Chinese way, saying that he had merely managed to learn a few Chinese characters. He pointed to the old armchair by the door of his modest living room and said it was there that Lao She had sat when he came to bid farewell before returning to China in 1949. He urged Lao She to wait and decide later. But he would wait no more.

The trip opened a window on America for me. I began to understand some of the American catch phrases and etiquette. My boldness and humor perhaps helped me. When I was interviewed by *The New Yorker* together with Ai Qing and Feng Yidai (staying at Columbia University as a visiting scholar then), I described my first U.S. visit as "very busy." When asked what I had kept myself "busy" with, I replied "meeting and dining." My gastric fixation, no less than my literary interest, brought a round of laughter. When asked about my impressions of America, I said, "All the girls are beautiful and all the dishes are delicious." The interviewer was enthralled. Paul Engle modestly interjected that he thought the girls were merely homely. At least I had shown interest, opened my eyes and pricked my ears to understand and absorb new information. I had seen other Chinese visitors timidly huddle in a corner at social gatherings and talking with compatriots about things of interest to them only. What a waste of the opportunity to get to know the world and to bring the world closer to us!

We also met the daughter of the deceased novelist Zhang Henshui. In the brief period of "let a hundred flowers bloom" in 1957, a new edition of Zhang's novel *Fate in Tears and Laughter* was published. However, once the "anti-*Rightist*" persecution started at the end of that year, his books were banned again. We had not heard of him until his quiet rehabilitation later when the "reform and opening-up" started. Such were the unpredictable turns of a writer's fate over the past decades.

In Los Angeles, Professor Perry Link took us to Hollywood and Disneyland. He reminded us that not all American families could afford to take their kids to Disneyland. Many were impoverished, living in hardship, and their quality of life poor. He spoke fluent Chinese and could even impersonate Chinese standup comedian Hou Baolin. It was regrettable that he was later deeply entangled in political strife about China. On the UCLA campus, I saw many sculptures and was struck by one of Henry Moore's. Moore was known for his semi-abstract sculptures containing hollow spaces. I was quick to point out that it looked like the "artificial boulders at Taihu Lake." People in China had long appreciated the grotesque, undulating forms of the famed lake boulders riddled with holes. Why should there be such an uproar and aversion to abstract art? People had protested that they could not understand this or that piece of art. But what should the yardstick of understanding be? If you believe you see the form of a dog or panda in a sculpture, would this qualify you as being in the know?

My most memorable encounter on this trip was with Professor Allyn Rickett in Philadelphia. Rickett had lived in Beijing in the late 1940s as a student at Tsinghua University and stayed on after Liberation. While studying there, he was given assignments by U.S. Naval Intelligence and provided some reports. When the Korean War broke out, Rickett and his wife Adele were arrested and put behind bars for espionage. Following mediation by UN Secretary General Dag Hammarskjöld they were eventually released and deported after spending a number of years in a Chinese prison,

Given such experience, which was unusual to say the least, they did not harbor any grudge against New China. Quite the contrary, they became staunch supporters of the People's Republic, having witnessed the country's transformation brought about by the revolution. The Ricketts praised the PRC in *Prisoners of Liberation,* a book of some renown they co-authored after returning to the United States. They even saw a ray of hope for humanity in New China. One particular incident precipitated this mindset. On the morning after his first night in prison, Mr. Rickett was distressed at not finding his toothbrush. When the prison guard saw this, he took out his own, rinsed it under the tap and gave it to Rickett. He hesitated, fearing it was not clean. Rickett came to realize that the guard did not mind *him using it,* while he himself, a convicted spy, had been bothered by the hygiene of the gracious gesture. This reminded me of lines from a poem by the Soviet poet Mayakovsky: "O Commune / all I have / is yours / except my toothbrush!" When even the toothbrush was offered for sharing, it was little wonder that Rickett was moved.

Mr. Rickett was also impressed by the practice of self-criticism widely encouraged in New China. Everyone competed to confess their own mistakes and shortcomings. To him, this was almost saintly. It was surely a path to perfection.

His glorification of the People's Republic caused him trouble. He was summoned by the House Committee on Un-American Activities. His refusal to change his views and retract his statements led to his being banned from teaching and left him in limbo for two decades. So being banished and put in an academic deep freeze, as it were, can also happen in the United States. He lived through immense hardships for a lengthy period. But by the time I visited Philadelphia in December 1980, he had already become a professor[6] at The University of Pennsylvania.

I was invited to his home for homemade *jiaozi* [Chinese dumplings]. His wife Adele had a Chinese name, Li You-An. She said the name was taken from *Li Yi-An,* a female Song dynasty poet whom she admired. She

6. W. Allyn Rickett, professor of Asian language and literature at The University of Pennsylvania.

visited China shortly after the normalization of Sino-U.S. diplomatic relations. Upon her arrival, she told Chinese officials about the prison sentence she served in China in the 1950s. The officials said that they knew all about it and it was a thing of the past and now she was a guest and friend. She said she felt a sense of great relief after hearing these remarks.

To me, Adele Rickett was one of those people who embodied great beauty, elegance, humility and kindness, the very image of perfection. Her smiles were not merely courteous, but were the most genuine and disarming, full of kindness to the world. Out of affection for China, she and her husband adopted two orphan girls from Hong Kong (adoption from China was not possible then). Their daughters grew up in the United States and spoke only English. When the family visited China later, people were amazed that their children who looked Chinese spoke English only, while they who were clearly American spoke impeccable Chinese. Adele Rickett died of illness a few years ago. Her friendship and kindness toward China will be remembered always. May her soul rest in peace!

Allyn Rickett invited us to a Mexican restaurant that had a rustic Mexican feel. Its interior walls were plastered with adobe and there was a fireplace in one corner though no fire was burning. Allyn commented at dinner that Americans had a transcendental attachment to China: if China could not be a friend, it would be a foe inspiring both hatred and love. They could never be indifferent. As if to bear this out, a gentleman at another table asked the waitress to bring a bottle of wine to us on him. Seeing that Ai Qing and I were visitors from a far away land, this was his way of wishing us a happy journey.

Allyn stressed to me that he hoped China would keep the tradition of revolution and Chinese writers would continue to be concerned with the laboring masses. He did not want to see them emulating Western writers in their indulgence in man's debasement and ugliness. His admonition was earnest, and in retrospect, prophetic.

At the University of Iowa, IWP writers were invited to interviews with the local media. One reporter asked me about the similarities and differences between then and the time when I wrote "Young Newcomer at the Organization Department." My answer was that it was the same author at different ages: I was twenty-two then and forty-six now. Still others asked about the extent of liberalization in the literary field in China and if there were constraints on literary expression. I cited my own experience in my response. In the 1950s, my writings caused me trouble, and now I was writing and publishing in a much more relaxed environment. I had freedom in my creative work, and my writings were acceptable to the socialist system of China. I felt good about that.

We only found out our transit visas for Hong Kong had expired when checking in at the San Francisco airport for our flight back to China. The visas had been issued by the British Embassy in Beijing and were valid for only three months. We had to retrieve our checked bags and fly to Los Angeles to get new visas from the British Consulate there. Such mishaps enriched my travel experience. Four months in the United States was not at all a short sojourn. A crop of corn or sweet potatoes would have ripened in the duration. I was already homesick. My daughter Yihuan's letters were getting alarmingly short: "Dad, sorry for not writing to you all this time. Talk to you. Bye."

Chapter 39

"Unrequited Love"

Following my return to Beijing in early 1981, I was reminded to heed the recent remarks by CCP leaders on ideological issues, as I was about to give a talk on my visit to America. Then in late summer or early fall of that year (or perhaps it was toward year's end), a series of study sessions were held for leaders from the literature and arts circles, including a few notable writers and artists. These sessions concerning political tendencies in literature and arts, organized by the CCP Propaganda Department and presided over by Zhou Yang, dragged on and on, but didn't seem to go anywhere. Various issues were debated, but questions remained unanswered. The inconclusive sessions were eventually called off when a controversy over *Unrequited Love* broke out. Then, a formal meeting on ideology was called by the CCP Central Committee. Domestic and international media coverage of the ensuing criticism of Bai Hua's *Unrequited Love* abounded, to which I could add little. However, works similar to his were not uncommon at the time. Why was *his* singled out and causing such a big stir?

The only explanation is that certain incidental factors converged in the case of *Unrequited Love*. Bai Hua, who wrote the screenplay, was one of the most visible writers at the time. He had a robust, outgoing personality, a quick wit, and a flamboyant style. He was more energetic and prolific than most of his peers. He was also brazen, thrived on controversy, and relished the limelight. He never shied away from playing cat and mouse with the powers that be. His prodigious output spanned poetry, fiction, drama, and screenplays. However, much of his creative output was marred by keeping to predetermined notions and lacking depth and enduring quality, even though he could be utterly imaginative. His most quoted dialogue in *Unrequited Love* was: *Why is the Buddha statue in the temple so darkened with soot? It is because of excessive incense burning by pious worshipers.* This is typical of Bai Hua's narrative style, about which he must have felt smug. Even in the most difficult years of the Cultural Revolution, he had the leisure as well as the resources to petition for a controversial film—*Chuang Ye* [Oil Industry Pioneers], which was rather daring of him to say the least. He was eager to show off and shine at the Fourth National Conference of Arts and Literature Circles. However, he didn't have much of a chance. A commentator from Shanghai described him as first and foremost an orator, a social and political activist, and only then a creative writer. He was officially on the payroll of the PLA and inevitably incurred the ire of certain top brass.

The *Unrequited Love* incident, however, was indicative of senior leaders' dissatisfaction with the state of literature in general, rather than annoyance over a single work or writer. They had found the leadership of the arts and literature circles, and of ideological work on the whole, seriously lacking. Some tightening up was in order. Like many others, I had hoped to give Bai Hua and Peng Ning, the film's director, some protection, not merely for their own sakes, but for the sake of the hard earned, relatively relaxed environment for literary expression. However, this proved to be wishful thinking.

I felt a personal aversion to criticizing *Unrequited Love*. In fact by the 1980s no literary figure of any standing was willing to criticize works of literature and art. With all the politically motivated and orchestrated criticism not far behind us, it was almost impossible to engage in literary criticism and not be seen as repeating a past atrocity. A critic deemed to have suspicious motivations or to give unpopular commentaries could easily ruin his or her own reputation. Things were such that senior leaders had to come forth personally to comment on certain literary issues. It was as if a general had to engage in street combat while the soldiers stood by. Such aversion resulted from the excessive political and literary criticism in the past, with Chairman Mao leading the way and orchestrating campaigns starting from his Yan'an days. After the founding of New China, there were again successive campaigns to condemn works of art and literature, among which was *The Life of Wu Xun*, a Chinese film about a beggar/educator. These culminated in the Cultural Revolution. Through such campaigns, Yao Wenyuan[1] shot up to his haughty perch on the CCP Politburo Standing Committee. Indeed for a time, toeing the political line in literary criticism became a path to political stardom.

In those years, when the political agenda mandated it, literature and writers often got the short end of the stick. Literature was fodder for the class struggle waged by the Party. A major political battle was often signaled by the condemnation of a novel or film, which was politically expedient and fed the public appetite for intrigue and conspiracy at the same time. Writers were often self-centered solitary creatures who could easily be incited to fight among themselves. Furthermore, it was always easier to go on the attack than to create a work of literature. Denouncing a writer is far easier than cultivating one, with quicker returns in political gain. Even the public, eager to have a piece of the action, was always ready to pounce on anything they saw as dubious in a work of literature.

By then, there had again been complaints by the reading public (parents with adolescent children in particular) and by government officials, as it was in the past, about the state of the arts and literature. Literary works were deemed too dark, dispiriting, and even amoral. They demanded rectification, or at least corrective measures. It was against such a background that the storm over Bai Hua's *Unrequited Love* brewed.

I tried to play down its political significance and mitigate the impact by pointing out that literature—with humor, compassion, feebleness, impracticality, and symbolism—always led to compromise and forbearance, rather than animosity and confrontation. The revolutionary fervor after the May Fourth Movement [ostensibly literary and cultural] in the early twentieth century had more to do with the rise of the CCP and various political forces than with literature itself. Without these forces at play, literary authors would have only been able to brew a tempest in a teapot.

My comments about not taking too seriously the impact of literature

1. Yao Wenyuan, 1931–2005, a member of the "Gang of Four," former Politburo member, was given a 20-year prison sentence after the end of the Cultural Revolution for counterrevolutionary crimes.

was rebuked from left and right. Those on the left accused me of trying to evade political control over the direction of literary causes, while those on the right thought of me as a defeatist, negating and trivializing their serious struggle.

What transpired in the *Unrequited Love* incident was a tug of war by various forces, which resulted in a stalemate and then re-alignment. Bai Hua eventually got a slap on the wrist. He engaged in self-criticism and retained some dignity. The *Reports of the Era* journal, with Huang Gang[2] as its editor-in-chief, which had been among the first to criticize Bai Hua, had to let go its editorial staff. Party leaders promptly and repeatedly reassured us (to what I felt was an embarrassing degree) that no one would be persecuted for their literary writings. Then all the noise dissipated as if nothing untoward had happened.

2. Huang Gang, 1917–? Journalist and editor.

Chapter 40

Unpredictable Political Fortunes

I came to know Hu Qiaomu[1] in the early 1980s. In the late summer of 1981, I received a letter from him commenting on my recent writings. (I was trying to fend off criticism of my borrowing of foreign literary devices such as "stream of consciousness.") He concurred that the free flowing, unrestrained narrative could also be found in classical Chinese literature, from *Chu Ci* [Verses of Chu] by Qu Yuan to the poems of the Tang dynasty greats. He even jotted down a poem of his own urging me to explore broader literary horizons. When he saw me later, he offered a customary note of modesty, saying that for want of a better metaphor he was not happy with the poem's ending. Obviously, a poem of instruction was hard to fashion.

He was essentially a man of learning. An avid reader, he delighted in talking about books. He was an articulate speaker, and his measured orations at forums could readily be transcribed into polished essays. He had an affable air, though I had heard he could be temperamental and severe in dressing down subordinates. I asked him for his view on Picasso. His reply was, "it would be difficult for a country like ours to accept Picasso." I noted a hint of objectivity, as if his view was not absolute and could be just one among many in currency. Was he hinting at diversity?

1. Hu Qiaomu (1912–1992), author of "Thirty Years of the Chinese Communist Party," the first officially endorsed text (published in 1951) on its history, had been Mao's secretary and then rose through the ranks to become a member of the Politburo and head of the Chinese Academy of Social Sciences.

Could judgment other than our own also be valid? He said there seemed to be no systematic deliberation on arts and literature by Marx and Engels and added with mockery that such a remark could be interpreted by others as heretical. So, even a senior leader with authority on ideology was not free from hesitation. I learned later that a debate was already raging in the press concerning Marxist literary theory. The contrarian view about the lack of such a theory, given only the occasional, though incisive, remarks by Marx and Engels on the arts and literature, was being criticized at that time.

I also noted that senior leaders were insulated to the extent of limitation. Security details and personal assistants hampered their interaction with ordinary people. Hu's residence was spacious, but somewhat spartan without any artwork on the walls. The newspapers and journals placed in his study were fewer than what I receive through complimentary subscriptions.

Hu apparently knew the craft of writing. After reading an essay of mine, he remarked that my experience in Xinjiang and Beijing had been the material of my fiction and my narrative had been informed by Chinese classical poetry. However, he warned against being trapped in the same style lest I should repeat myself. He was right.

He mentioned Wen Tingyun,[2] a Song dynasty poet, and Edgar Ellen Poe and said that they both possessed unique styles but failed to become true literary masters. This was his way of instructing me not to go too far down the path of "stream-of-consciousness," with which I could not agree more. I had long thought that stylistic idiosyncrasy might not be a good thing. It exposes an author's limitations and may lead to the closing of an inquisitive mind. I was glad to later learn of a similar view by Wang Anyi—one about not betting one's success on stylistic peculiarity. A unique style could be easily emulated and soon loose its uniqueness.

In the spring of 1982, I attended a symposium on contemporary Chinese literature at the invitation of Professor Jeffrey Kinkley of St. John's University in New York. I was approached by Yan Yuanshu from Taiwan and asked to support his appeal on behalf of Chen Ying-zhen,

2. Wen Tingyun, 812–870 CE, Chinese poet of the late Tang dynasty regarded as the first truly distinctive writer of *ci*, the song-verse style of poetry that dominated Chinese poetry during much of the late Tang dynasty and the Song dynasty.

who had been banned from traveling to New York. Chen was pro-Taiwan independence then. As an aside, both Chen and Yan have since become strong advocates of unification with the mainland, anti-independence, and even anti-American. Times have changed.

On the last day of the symposium, a Chinese student from Hunan read an accusatory paper attacking China's lack of freedom and appealed for action by Chinese writers. He turned out to be Liang Heng[3] who had got into trouble in China for his involvement in the student movement and had immigrated to the States after marrying Judith Shapiro, an American student studying in China then. He shouted: "Where are the Chinese writers of conscience?!" There was palpable suspense in the room. Someone in the audience heckled: "Let's hear from Wang Meng!" They anticipated drama. Do you support or oppose democracy? That was the question left hanging. If you were to oppose democracy on American soil, you would be seen as speaking for the Commies. If you voiced your support, you would be repudiating your own government. They couldn't wait.

I said with a grin, "Chinese writers are in China; I will soon be in Beijing and my fellow writer Huang Qiuyun in Guangzhou. We know what we should and can do for China's progress, prosperity, and democracy. Now I would like to ask you, sir, 'where are you?' So you are in New York, launching your roaring accusations. You want to tell us what we should do and accuse us of not doing it. If you want to help or save China, for starters, wouldn't it be more effective to do it in China, in Beijing, or even in Changsha for that matter?" There were chuckles from the audience. The tension subsided.

On another occasion during the symposium, I was confronted by Kee Fuk-wah, an author from Hong Kong. I had spoken about the tremendous hardships Chinese writers experienced, because of which they were respected by the reading public. I told my audience about a reader who tried to raise money by selling his blood so he could take a trip to visit his favorite author in Beijing. Liu Xinwu received thousands of fan letters, a selection of which he had compiled into a book. I

3. Liang Heng, 1954–, author of *Son of the Revolution,* his account of growing up in China during the turmoil of the Cultural Revolution.

declared my pride of being a writer of China. Kee sprang to his feet, shouting that Mister Wang had become a mouthpiece of the Chinese government. He was so fired up that his voice cracked. This prompted Mr. Li Yi, chief editor of *Seventies Magazine* (later renamed the *Nineties Magazine*, published in Hong Kong), to say, "He is out of his mind." After Kee was done with his shouting and agitating, I offered a cordial "Thank you!" as was customary in symposiums, which almost brought the house down. Kee has since mellowed and become rather mild when visiting the Chinese mainland as a member of Hong Kong writers' delegation on later occasions.

At Vineyard Haven in Martha's Vineyard, we met John Hersey, who was born in Tianjin. He had just returned from a trip to his birthplace. He managed to locate and visit the old house where he was delivered. It was then shared by several families. When he told them that it was his birthplace, the current occupants welcomed him and said they could even move out if he were to return. We also saw leftwing playwright Lillian Hellman, who was then in her nineties. Hellman had been a frequent visitor to Moscow during WW II and had met Vyacheslav Molotov. She asked me why I wanted to write. "Building bridges linking hearts and souls of the people," I replied. "Bullshit!" she said, to which I could only grimace.

In early summer 1982, a friend tipped me off about my possible nomination to the Central Committee of the CCP at its upcoming Twelfth National Congress. I felt perturbed, feeling not so much honor as anxiety. I had long thought of the Central Committee as being manned by career revolutionaries, true Bolsheviks with steely mind and piercing gaze, devoid of sentimentality and hardnosed about class struggle. I, on the other hand, was but a writer inclined to be free and unrestrained. I derived pleasure in words taking wing, in impassioned and nuanced expressions, in weaving intricate plots, in heartwarming laughter, in flights of fancy, irony, and satire. All this would hardly qualify me for membership in the esteemed Committee dedicated to serious political strife.

My wife and I took a trip to the seaside resort Beidaihe. We went by public bus and stayed at a guesthouse owned by a government agency. I agonized nightly over the prospect of a Central Committee perch for which I felt ill equipped. I marveled at this bizarre, unpredictable turn of fate: being plunged into political troubles and the abyss one moment and then crowned with unimaginable laureates the next. It would require strenuous efforts for me to live up to all the expectations that came with the grand political title. With so many years behind me but not as many published titles to my name, I desired to write more and realize my ambitious literary goals more than anything else.

I wrote the short story "Listening to the Roaring Sea" upon returning from our trip. I could not explain why I wrote such a story about a blind old man with a little girl and their conversations by the sea. I wrote about the murmuring of the calm sea, the roaring waves, the ocean's depth and infinite expanse. I wrote about forgiveness and moving on, a newborn bundled up in a quilt. I wrote about their chatting and falling into silence, understanding and incomprehension, the end and beginning of life, and calm and raging Nature. I asked which was more powerful: the surging waves or the craggy bluff that they crashed onto. I yearned for the solace of the vast ocean. I was reminded of the great philosopher recluse Zhuang Zi and the Tang dynasty poet Li Shangyin who wrote "*At the journey's end a gray-haired man / Yearning to be adrift in a skiff again.*"

I was nominated to be a delegate to the Twelfth National Congress of the CCP but was voted down. In an effort to instill a degree of democracy, a contested election was held to elect delegates to the Congress. One middle-ranking leader was said to oppose my nomination, citing my liberal tendencies. As a result, I did not muster enough votes. Only three people from Beijing literature and arts circles were elected. They were stage actor Yu Shizhi[4] and two traditional folk opera singers. This was my first brush with democracy. I was amazed that while overseas media reported that I lost credibility for speaking on behalf of the government, I was deemed to have liberal tendencies at home. The fact is, neither was true. Such contradictory perceptions only proved that I was an independent thinker and always held my own ground.

Now that I had lost the vote, I was invited to attend the Congress as a nonvoting delegate. In the group of nonvoting delegates from Beijing

4. Yu Shizhi, 1927–2013, stage actor and former deputy director of Beijing People's Theater.

were essayist Liao Mosha[5] and Ye Zilong, vice mayor of Beijing and former bodyguard of Chairman Mao. Ye recalled Mao telling him after the conclusion of the Eighth National Congress of the CCP in 1956 that he planned to retire and devote his time to writing. Ye's account is probably credible; Mao had likely *thought* about retirement then. However, this remained a mere idea due to a host of personal and political factors. Powerful as Mao was, in the end, he was not able to determine his own destiny. I noticed that there were oxygen tanks in the meeting room of this geriatric group of delegates. Elder Liao indeed became sick and convulsive while making his remarks, and needed to inhale a dose of air. Such was the First National Congress of the CCP after the Cultural Revolution: all venerable cadres were overly exhilarated.

We nonvoting delegates were brought back into the cavernous auditorium of the Great Hall of the People after votes for the Central Committee were cast. Sitting at the balcony level, I noted the name of Wang Meng in the list of elected alternate members of the Committee. I thought this could be my namesake. There was an announcement requiring all newly elected members and alternate members of the Committee to attend an afternoon session. I asked Chen Ye, a staffer from the personnel department of my Federation, to double check if I was actually the person. She came back with the confirmation, "Well, you made it big!"

I attended the first Plenum of the Central Committee of the Twelfth National Congress of the CCP with much unease and trepidation. It was a solemn occasion with a serious agenda for confirming the new politburo; chairman, vice chairmen, and the secretariat of the Central Committee as well as members of the Party's Central Military Committee. Everyone sitting through these proceedings looked cautious and discreet.

It was said that my nomination to the Central Committee was made at the suggestion of Hu Qiaomu and Wang Renzhong,[6] with support

---

5. Liao Mosha, 1907–1990, essayist and official in the Beijing municipal government, was among the first to be persecuted for their writings when the Cultural Revolution started.
6. Wang Renzhong, 1917–1992, former head of the Propaganda Department of the CCP and vice premier of the State Council.

from Deng Liqun.[7] My novel *A Bolshevik Salute* had probably caught Hu Qiaomu's attention. Wang Renzhong, who had recently returned to Beijing to become head of the Propaganda Department of the CCP Central Committee, had been urged by his daughter, Wang Xiaoli, an editor at the magazine *Modern Literature,* to develop good relations with leading writers. I was thus invited by Wang Renzhong to join him on a trip to Nanning, the provincial capital of Guangxi. I spoke with him about issues in public administration and grassroots discontent. He paid attention and had Wei Chunshu, party secretary of the city, come over for my debriefing. Deng Liqun presented a literary award to me at an event sponsored by the *Guangming Daily.* Of course, beside the patronage of these powerful individuals, a more important factor was the emphasis placed on bringing younger and professional members into the Central Committee.

In truth, this had not come out of the blue. My experience, prime-of-life age, and the success and popularity of my writings had in fact made me think at one time, in 1982, "Why Not Me?" But I immediately dispelled such a thought and decided that political eminence was not for me. I knew myself to be, after all, a writer, too emotional and sensitive to be much of a political leader. When the nomination became real, my wife Ruifang and I were both angst-ridden. She was more inclined to lead a carefree life, enjoy literature, and take things as they came. She was averse to politics and in particular to political strife and intrigue that this turn in her husband's career might entail. This had been true of her all her life.

Some novelists are fond of saying "fate and character are the same thing," meaning fate is determined by character. But character can change and fate is uncertain. In my youth, I had been unyielding and had literary aspirations and neurotic traits, and I unwittingly tried to outdo others. All this had contributed to my becoming a political outcast in the late 1950s and through the end of the 1970s. In spite of all this, I remained a patriot with compassion for the people. I had been trained by the CCP since youth, and had never wavered in my dedication to the revolutionary cause. Further, I was well versed in Party doctrines and principles. All the

7. Deng Liqun, 1915– ?, former head of the Propaganda Department of the CCP and member of the Secretariat of the CCP Central Committee.

inspiring notions about reform and opening-up in the 1980s agreed with me. Given all this, you really cannot say there wasn't some inevitability in my being nominated for the Party's Central Committee. Indeed, *if not me, then who?*

Chapter 41

A Fine Kettle of Fish

After being elected an alternate member of the Party's Central Committee at its Twelfth National Congress, I soon found myself embroiled in the debate on "Modernism."

It started with the publication of a book titled *A Preliminary Examination of Modern Fictional Techniques* by Gao Xingjian, then an interpreter at the International Liaison Office of the Chinese Writers' Union. This was an introductory booklet about modern novels in the West, touching on topics such as time and sequential arrangement, narrative voices, psychological descriptions and stream-of-consciousness. It stood out as unconventional, as most discussions on fiction writing then centered on archetypal characters, realism . . .

This booklet and other writings in a similar vein quickly became an issue. They were somehow construed as a wholesale attack on China in the name of Modernism. Hu Qiaomu singled out a literary journal, *Modern Trends in Art and Literature*. Its editor-in-chief was Xie Changyu,[1] who was politically well connected. However, one essay the journal published, "A Violent Tribe of Bards"[2] by Xu Jingya,[3] a poet from northeastern China, was thought to be subversive. After yet another essay titled "The Death

1. Xie Changyu, 1936–, literary editor, former vice chairman of Gansu Provincial Federation of Literature and Arts Circles.
2. The essay was first published in China in 1982 with a later English translation by Ng Mau-sang.
3. Xu Jingya, 1949–, Chinese poet and poetry critic.

of Orthodoxy" was pubished, its chief editor was named by Hu as an outright "gravedigger of revolutionary literature." Hu was so disgusted that he crossed out the customary prefix "Comrade" to Xu's name in a Party document.

The editorial board of the *Art and Literature Gazette* took an accusatory stance against Modernism. The gauntlet was thrown down to me, too. Tang Yin,[4] the executive deputy editor of the *Art and Literature Gazette,* mentioned my name on a number of occasions. Tang Dacheng,[5] a newly appointed deputy chief of the journal, also condemned modernism in my presence.

In retrospect, none of the proponents and detractors of Modernism, except perhaps Hu Qiaomu, truly knew what Modernism was. All were eager to wage battle without even rudimentary knowledge. It was truly absurd.

I had merely wanted to include changing narrative voices, multiple images and feelings, and poetic prose in my storytelling. I liked ingenious plots and clever turns of phrasing, and pushing the envelope. Feng Jicai and Liu Xinwu, who were also suspected of advocating Modernism, in fact remained writers in the tradition of realism. I was alerted by a sympathetic Ye Junjian,[6] a leading author who was then a member of the Secretariat at the Writers' Union with a portfolio for international liaison (the only senior officer at the Union who was not a CCP member). He asked someone to pass on a message that all the fuss about Modernism was directed at me personally.

I found the notion of conspiracy far-fetched. I was merely a man of letters and had no interest in ideological battles. Nor did I have any desire to challenge the literary establishment. Li Jikai,[7] a senior editor at the *Art and Literature Gazette,* urged me to be discreet. He was said to be eager to toe the correct political line and critical of writers supporting

---

4. Tang Yin, 1925–1997, critic and former president of Lu Xun Academy of Literature.
5. Tang Dacheng, 1928–1999, critic and former Party secretary of the Chinese Writers' Union.
6. Ye Junjian, 1914–1999, writer and translator, best known for his translation of Hans Christian Andersen's stories.
7. Li Jikai, 1933–, literary critic.

Modernism. At an internal meeting for leaders of the literary and arts circles, a senior leader laid out "guidelines" for criticizing Modernism, as if declaring yet another political campaign.

It turned out that Hu Qiaomu had decided to give me protection plus a stern warning. He affirmed, "You haven't gone too far." Hu also gave me a copy of John Galsworthy's essay repudiating Modernism. I remember a quote by Galsworthy to the effect that a shallow stream makes the loudest noise. Hu also suggested that I should get advice from the renowned scholar Qian Zhongshu and offered to make an introduction. He mentioned that Qian was in favor of Realism, Humanism, and Rationalism, and opposed to Modernism. However, Humanism later also got into trouble. He pointed out that my short story "A Dappled Horse" was not entirely proper. He also asked his college alumnus and friend Wei Junyi to pass on a further warning, "Don't indulge in Modernism." I thought, however, if I really wanted advice from Qian, I did not need to bother Hu for an introduction. What would Qian think? Besides, I had enough experience and sense to not blindly follow and embrace Modernism. I did not take up the offer.

Shortly afterward, Hu invited me to his home during the Chinese Spring Festival of 1983 and we had a delightful conversation. He even picked up the phone and instructed the duty officer of the Zhongnanhai [the central government compound] car pool to send a car so my wife could join us as well. After word got around, those who were attacking Modernism were so impressed with Hu's gesture that they backed off.

When I told Zhou Yang about Hu's advice and warning, Zhou was unimpressed. He was for more experimentation and less interference in creative work. He later went around advocating "getting rid of political clichés and archaism," and "a multitude of innovative paths for a common goal." He even singled me out at an award ceremony, saying that Wang Meng was an innovative writer and his literary experiments should be encouraged. He added that we did not want to end up having yet another Party propaganda cadre in place of a poet. He thus ran afoul of zealots at the *Art and Literature Gazette,* who forwarded him letters from readers critical of his views. This was something they did not have the guts to do in the past. Zhou by that time was no longer a deputy director of the Propaganda Department of the CCP Central Committee with the literature and art portfolio, but a mere member of the Central Advisory Committee. He was over the hill even though he still got himself extensively involved in cultural matters and remained outspoken. He did not step down when it was time, which was perhaps not terribly wise. But this only goes to show his unflinching dedication, devoid of calculation.

The *Art and Literature Gazette* in the end was not "rewarded" for its zealous attack. Party Secretary Zhang Guangnian of the Writers' Union, after consulting with other leaders, decided to change the biweekly journal into a weekly paper, reducing its size. Feng Mu was removed as its editor-in-chief and transferred to *Chinese Writers* magazine. Tang Yin, the deputy editor-in-chief, was transferred to the Creative Writing Training Center (later renamed Lu Xun Academy of Literature). Liu Xicheng, head of the editorial department, was transferred to the Research Institute of Folk Literature. Li Jikai went to the United States to visit family and never returned. My guess was that the affront to Zhou Yang led to this reshuffle. I met Li Jikai some years later in the United States, and by then he had no leftwing sentiments left in him. Anyway, after the reshuffle, the combative *Art and Literature Gazette* was no more, with its editorial team being disbanded and core members scattered.

There have been numerous accounts of the Modernism debate. In retrospect, four things stood out.

First, there was an apparent lack of understanding. Most, including myself, had only patchy knowledge based on Andrei Zhdanov's critique of Modernism found in dated Soviet era literature. We had little access to original texts of Modernist theory and literature. Gao Xingjian's booklet provided a scanty overview, but was far from thorough. It merely touched on techniques with little original commentary. However, with the Soviet-era precedent, nobody could afford disinterest and indifference. One particular theoretician, Chen Yong,[8] even declared that the debate was an inevitable struggle for China, which was menacing. Yet the reaction of the Party's central leadership was in fact rather muted. At one high-level CCP leadership meeting, when Hu Qiaomu harped on the modernist issue, someone more senior cut him short, "What modernist? I am a

8. Chen Yong, 1919–? critic and fomer editor-in-chief of the *Literarture and Art Gazette*.

modernist!" Apparently, he was not familiar with Zhdanov's critique, but his abrupt remark left Hu dangling and speechless.

Second, there was a tendency to generalize on the part of the leadership of literary circles. They would lump unrelated issues together and declare a trend, concluding that Modernism would topple the Party's exacting scheme of "Four Modernizations." According to their logic, Modernism equaled modernization of literature and meant an attempt to alter the scheme of four, making it an obnoxious five. Heaven knows what they were talking about.

Third, there was personal rivalry at play. The debate had been emotionally charged, and often verged on personal confrontation. This was in stark contrast to the criticism of *Unrequited Love* when even those with official responsibility for literary criticism were lethargic and evasive.

Fourth, boiling under the surface was a host of entangled issues, grievances that defied clarification. Writers and artists are sensitive creatures prone to disagreement. Leaders from the outside often missed the point, while those from within harbored prejudices. They would secretly promote their own agenda at the expense of anything outside their own literary specialization.

Another notable character in the Modernism saga was Comrade He Jingzhi[9], the newly appointed deputy head of the Propaganda Department, with a portfolio for literature and arts. He asked to see me after the conclusion of the Twelfth Party Congress. He told me that I should be prepared for criticisms, among other things, now that I was part of the Party leadership. I thought that I was still a writer and that writing had been and would be my career and my life. I could try my best to be a bridge between the Party and writers. I concluded that a few more critics would not change the condition of my existence. I had first met He Jingzhi in the 1950s. He'd sport a fashionable trench coat, typical of young men with a literary bent. He referred to my new novel *Young Newcomer at the Organization Department* as phenomenal. At the post-conference meeting, he said that since the literary community had just gone through a round of rectification (the *Unrequited Love* episode),

9. He Jingzhi, 1924–, poet and former deputy head of the CCP Propaganda Department and acting Minister of Culture.

it would take at least a while for it to degenerate again. It was evident he held an unsavory view of the literary community. He never raised the question of Modernism with me, though he hinted that someone's "underbelly" was being exposed.

At a seminar on issues of literature and art, Hu Qiaomu pointed out that the work to uphold the banner of socialist literature was far from done. Zhou Yang, however, talked about protecting writers and their creative efforts. By this time, he looked frail and his voice was raspy. He was evidently on the defensive, with age blunting his edge. This made me sad.

As I look back at this and the other storms I weathered, I feel more gratitude than resentment. I was able to transcend sorrow. Long gone are my youthful days when I relished melancholy for its aesthetic appeal. I have since grown into an old hack, with strength, insight, and indestructible optimism. That was how I felt at the end of the Modernism storm. I like the title of one of Liu Xihong's[10] novels: *You Cannot Change Me.* If I were to make a similar statement, I would instead say: *You Cannot Destroy Me!*

10. Liu Xihong, 1961–, Chinese writer.

Chapter 42

Taking the Helm at People's Literature

In 1985, at the recommendation of Zhang Guangnian, party secretary of the Writers' Union, I was appointed editor-in-chief of its *People's Literature* magazine. Prior to this, Zhang and I visited Zhou Yang, deputy head of the CCP Propaganda Department. Zhou, in Tianjin with the assistance of two scholars (Wang Yuanhua[1] and Gu Xiang[2]), was brooding over a paper on Humanism, which was to later land him in trouble.

When Zhou saw me, he indicated his satisfaction at having a younger chief editor take charge of the prestigious magazine. He then suggested adding a section for literary review in each issue. He was more interested in theoretical discourses than creative writing. He believed such a section could be a vehicle to convey Party leaders' intensions and guide literary output in the right direction. By his logic, revolutionary literature would be impossible without revolutionary theories. However, my experience taught me otherwise: theoretical interpretation could not come before works of literature. Guiding principles, no matter how appropriate, were never as effective for literary creation as for other endeavors.

In 1979, Zhou was in the limelight for his paper proposing three waves of "ideological emancipation," which was written in commemoration of the sixtieth anniversary of the *May Fourth Movement*. The first wave

1. Wang Yuanhua, 1920–2008, critic and former director of the Propaganda Department of the CCP Shanghai Municipal Committee; purged during the campaign against the Hu Feng Counterrevolutionary Clique in 1955.
2. Gu Xiang, 1930–, literary critic.

was the May Fourth Movement itself, the second the Rectification Movement in Yan'an, and the third the post-Cultural Revolution "Mind Emancipation." A few cadres at the Writers' Union were full of admiration for his sweeping synthesis, citing his essay as the only one worthy of the historical occasion. Accolades like that, however, backfired. In fact, using sweeping ideological notions to mobilize support and inspire commitment had become outdated. A change of mindset and a new approach became necessary as the nature of public administration in China began to change.

Back in the 1950s, *People's Literature* commanded great esteem. Only the most venerable writers had been appointed to its helm. Literary works published by the magazine became runaway successes, and their authors went on to garner national fame. It was generous to writers, too. I was paid twice as much by *People's Literature* for a short story. Only a few were qualified to lead this publication, while many more could take the top perch at the Writers' Union. You could be widely published elsewhere but still not be recognized as a writer of national repute if you had not made it into *People's Literature,* a platform reserved for the truly accomplished. The mere mention of any of its contributors—Ba Jin, Ding Ling, Ai Qing, Zhao Shuli, Cao Yu, Lao She, Liu Shaotang, Zong Pu—would make admiring readers tingle with excitement.

For the inaugural issue after my appointment (Issue No. 8, 1983), I wrote an essay "Not Merely for the Sake of Literature," declaring my editorial focus on social concern and progress. We also reprinted a short story, "Dressing Table Mirror" by the Anhui novelist Geng Hongxiang, as a reminder of the tradition of this people's magazine, i.e., compassion for the common people.

I tried to make the magazine more inclusive in its editorial selection. I was able to get notable authors of the time to contribute lead pieces for each issue, which included "May 19 Through a Telescopic Lens" by Li You; "A Kaleidoscopic View of Wang Fujing" and "Unlevel Playing Field" by Liu Xinwu; "Façade of the Capital" by Liu Shaotang; "Whirling World" by the factory worker-turned-writer Chen Jiguang; a selection of poems by Ke Yan in memory of poet Guo Xiaochuan; "You Have No Choice" by Liu Suola; and "Variations without a Theme" by Xu Xing. I also tried to promote short shorts and started a new section for literary reviews. Overruling an editor's objection, I decided to publish Liu Suola's novella, which became a literary milestone. I rescued from an editor's wastebasket the manuscript of "Kekexili," a short story by Anhui author Xu Hui.[3] However, my decision to print the short story "Three Deaths in One Night" by Hunan author He Liwei as the lead piece led to a small tempest. The story was written with a certain flair, an ambivalent theme, and in a somewhat eccentric style. Printing such a story caused a stir among leaders of the Writers' Union, and even raised the ire of Zhang Guangnian, who had long been my supporter. In the uproar, one venerable writer weighed in with his snide comment that nobody should put themselves above the Party.

This became rather interesting. I doubted this remark was meant as a stab in my back. He might even have said it with no ill intent. Eager to please by going the extra mile was his style. As the Uighur saying goes, ask him to snatch a hat, he will break someone's neck for effect.

I was out of town when the controversy boiled over, threatening a repeat of the Modernism debate. However, by the time I returned to Beijing, and after seeing the agitators eye to eye, the controversy quickly subsided. Was it a unique Chinese thing that those attacking others from behind would step back when being confronted face to face? I recall in Xinjiang when everybody in my work unit was instructed to move to a work camp, two of my colleagues dragged their feet and did not show up until months later. Their absence caused condemnation befitting heinous crimes. However, when the tardy pair eventually arrived after an interminable absence, everybody was cordial—as if nothing had happened.

I had grown frustrated with the singular approach in literary criticism, trumpeting the orthodox style and snubbing the experimental. I decided that change should start with me in both editorial and creative work. Though there was a limit to how much I could do, I tried to expand the scope of subject matter and styles that the magazine and I myself embraced. I wrote "Black Dragon Pond," which adopted an orthodox theme about changes in the new era and was promptly commended

3. Xu Hui, 1957–, Chinese writer and vice chairman of Anhui Provincial Writers' Union.

by venerable writer Sun Li. I followed that with a realistic account, "A Difficult Reunion," touching upon the issue of post-Cultural Revolution disillusionment and mind emancipation, which was applauded as a breakthrough by a fellow writer. My short story "The Deep Lake" had a new wave touch and depicted life of the younger generation and their anxiety. "Purple Silk Jacket at the Bottom of a Wooden Trunk" used the persona of an embroidered jacket as its narrative voice. I also began an autobiographical series entitled *Life in Ili*. The first short story "Ah, Mohammad Ahmed!" moved my wife to tears when she read the first draft. Tie Ning was also impressed by this story, and liked this ballad in particular.

Where will you bury me after I die?
Not by the roadside, I ask you.
Traffic and noise will never end.
Nor in the Gobi will I ever lie,
The sky is empty and the land bleak
And the desolation has no mend.

This was lifted from a Uighur ballad with a few tweaks when I translated it into Chinese. Some of its rustic and masculine appeal might have been lost in translation, with the tone becoming a bit too soft.

The protagonist is far from an ideal character. He even goes by a profane nickname. I wrote with much compassion about his good nature, wit, frustration, and suffering in the Cultural Revolution. I wrote about hardships and trials, losses and gains in the lives of other humble characters, and their passion, aspirations, and missed opportunities. The dialogue in the story was conceived in Uighur and rendered into Chinese. The countless days I spent toiling in the fields by the Ili River in the foothills of the Tianshan Range were not in vain. The baked flatbread and spicy mutton stew had nourished my body and soul. When I wrote those lines, I felt as if I were back among my Uighur brothers, though I was a world away in Beijing.

Nineteen eighty-three was also the year my father died. His health declined in the mid-1970s when he was at a "Cadre School" in Xianyang. He had been suffering from cataracts and glaucoma and was operated on by an ill-trained "barefoot doctor," to show his support for "socialist new things." He almost lost his eyesight as a result. Later he broke an ankle after a bad fall. People from my home village, including me, all seemed to have weak ankles. Slow healing caused muscle dystrophy in his legs. By the time my wife and I moved back to Beijing, he was both blind and lame. Overwhelmed by life back in the city, I was impatient and acted unkindly to him on two occasions. Once, he came to see me at my cramped apartment accompanied by my cousin. I had by then acquired some fame and endless visitors and admirers showed up at my door. I put up a note declaring "No Visitors Except on Tuesday Afternoons"; but it was no deterrent. Nobody thought it necessary to have an appointment to visit someone at home. I was at the end of my tether dealing with all the unscheduled callers that day and was irritated by my father's visit. On the second occasion, I became mad and scolded him after he'd written an article for a local evening paper about my childhood, which annoyed me. That was when I had just been elected an alternate member of the Central Committee.

During the Spring Festival of 1983, I became concerned about Father's health and was reminded of his fondness for Western delicacies. I bought some creamy and cheesy pastries that he liked and had them sent to his home. By early March, I learned that he had been hospitalized and his condition had deteriorated rapidly. He had abdominal bleeding and then lung and cardiovascular problems. To all who came to see him, he feebly repeated "thank you." He told everyone his fear of never being able to leave the hospital. He recalled memories of his mother, my grandmother. His last words were "it is tough even to die . . ." He fell into a coma and lingered a few more days before departing.

He had a passion for life and had known a few of its pleasures. He enjoyed eating out, swimming, horseback-riding, and dancing. But he also got more than a fair share of life's brutal absurdities and pains. His two marriages ended up complete failures. Toward the end of his life, he was not even able to see my younger brother and sister. In tears, he pleaded for my help, but I could do nothing useful, for those two siblings of mine held him in nothing but disgust. My sister had been on good terms with Father, before one incident changed that. When she was studying at Tsinghua University, he went to see her. Not finding her in her dorm, he told her roommates about her habits that fell short of his expectations.

His expectations were based on some assumed European etiquette. My sister found this unforgivable.

He had yearned for an ideal state of things and had his moments of bliss. But mostly he was a drifter. He cared for good health, but surrendered to unhealthy habits. He was gluttonous, but in old age he was not able to eat what he liked. He cared for his posterity but ruined any possibility of reunion. He was unsparing and mean in his criticism of others, and did it mostly behind their backs. He knew the beauty of many things but could approximate few. A man's life can be so wasted, and such a brutal folly, with everything ending up exactly the opposite of what he had hoped for. For a decade and more after his death, he returned again and again in my dreams, always a lonely man stumbling and limping away in a dark alley, as if half-drunk.

Wang Jindi, my father's name, was mentioned in writings about Zhang Dainian[4] and by historian Zhao Lisheng,[5] who thought him stubborn and eccentric. Zhao said that my father lived with me in his last years, which was not true. Both Zhang and Zhao mentioned the unfair political treatment my father endured. They both felt that whatever historical problems there had been with my father had long been resolved and should not be made an issue again. Such petitioning on my father's behalf caused Mr. Zhang some trouble in the 1950s. His being labeled a *rightist* had something to do with his words in my father's defense. I was touched by this.

A few other things during my tenure at *People's Literature* are worth mentioning. I regret even today that we didn't succeed in getting popular women writers—including Zhang Jie, Tie Ning, Wang Anyi, and Zhang Kangkang—to write for us. In fact, I had urged editors to seek their contribution and sent staffers to call on them in person. Regrettably, one senior editor of some repute rejected Zhang Jie's manuscripts for "Children from the Forest." In later years, I had heard him talking about his accomplishments, but he never had enough courage to recount his rejection of Zhang Jie's story. I also received much support from Xu

4. Zhang Dainian, 1909–2004, philosopher and chairman of the Chinese Society of History of Philosophy.
5. Zhao Lisheng, 1917–2007, historian known for his writings on history of landownership and peasant uprisings and translator of Soviet literature.

Weicheng[6] of the Beijing municipal Party Committee, who was responsible for cultural affairs and education. He recommended Chen Jiguang's writings and wrote a good review of my short story "The Wind on the Plateau," which was published in our magazine. We welcomed new writers, including Wang Zaojun,[7] Li Hangyu,[8] and Can Xue.[9] As I was an alternate member of the Central Committee, staffers heard my firsthand accounts after its annual plenums. But I also received admonition from a young person with high-level family connections. He urged me not to be involved in running a magazine—for I could easily get into trouble for publishing the wrong story, a risk to my political standing.

Some would say that an editorial appointment would not make a huge difference to a magazine. The difference I made was perhaps adding that snippet of extra advantage. I was comfortable with the mainstream and had access to the Party leadership, with a toehold in the Central Committee. I never thought there was anything incongruous in such a situation. But this did not mean my understanding of the creative process was any less. Unlike writers and artists who were not as well connected, I was able to consult and work with such CCP cadres as Xu Weicheng, who were thought by some as being on the far left. I was also bolder by an "extra inch" in pushing for "letting one hundred flowers bloom and one hundred schools of thought contend." What a difference that little extra could make to the magazine! Just to mention all the unconventional authors and unorthodox literary styles we were able to accommodate under my editorial hand!

I was, however, criticized by people from both the left and the right. Those on the left thought I had moved too far to the right. Those on the right deemed me an outright leftist. Those in the rear thought I was too avant-garde, and those riding on the cusp of change thought I lagged way behind. I was thought to be so many things, not fitting any pigeonhole. Hu Qiaomu and Zhou Yang both commended me. I had

6. Xu Weicheng, 1930–, former executive deputy head of the CCP Propaganda Department.
7. Wang Zaojun, 1947–, Chinese writer.
8. Li Hangyu, 1957–, writer notable for his stories based on environmental themes and rural roots.
9. Can Xue, 1953–, Chinese woman writer of short stories, novellas, and novels.

admired their scholarly attainment, generosity, experience, wisdom, and insight into matters of political significance. But even when compared with them, I still had that extra bit of advantage, in having artistic sense, tolerance, pragmatism and flexibility common to people with grassroots experience. This little extra, by "a mere inch" so to speak, had made all the difference. It also became a cause of envy for some. However, envy was unwarranted. This extra advantage was equaled by extra misery. I had in fact also been attacked from all sides, at times with no supporters.

In the early 1980s, literature gained an elevated status in the aftermath of the Cultural Revolution. In those heady years, one or two successfully published pieces could seal one's fame. In later years, novice writers found it hard to achieve the same and felt frustrated. At the height of literature's popularity, I wrote an essay urging "Let's Not All Crowd into the Straight and Narrow Path of Creative Writing."

I pointed out the limited role of literature and society's need for talented people in all fields of endeavor. Literature cannot feed on itself; it can only come from real life experience. From this perspective, literary writers should be amateurs practicing word craft after their day jobs are done. The number of salaried writers should be kept to a minimum. These remarks, decrying my own profession, were duly criticized by my mentor and friend Wei Junyi at one formal meeting of the Writers' Union.

Looking back at the literary scene of the 1980s, I was struck by how often truly refreshing and unconventional novels came forth. Ah Cheng's "King of Chess Games," published in *Shanghai Literature,* became a literary sensation. Then there were Cao Guanlong's "Strange Animals," Tie Ning's "Ah! Fragrant Snow," which established her literary reputation and was published by *October* magazine, and Tan Puren's "On the Plateau."

The era was not short on controversies either. Liu Zaifu's[10] exposition on the subjectivity of literature and dual composition of the literary character was criticized by writer Yao Xueying[11] in the weighty *Red Flag*

---

10. Liu Zaifu, 1941–, Chinese writer and literary critic. He left China and has lived overseas since 1989.
11. Yao Xueying, 1910–1999, Chinese writer of historical fiction; labeled a *rightist* in 1957.

magazine.[12] Yu Luojin's "A Spring Fairy Tale" was published in *Flower City Magazine* and some of her cynical and disturbing remarks, plus her unconventional conduct, caused a backlash. There were also mixed reviews of Can Xue's style and Gao Xingjian's experimental plays. Such controversies and nonconformity were nothing unusual. A new paradigm was emerging. Literature was exploring new frontiers; the intellectual life of the nation became robust and diverse. Hope and anxiety, conflicts and opportunities, trials and errors were attendant to progress.

Such pluralism was not limited to literature. Music stars and itinerant entertainers, Canton pop and oldies from prerevolutionary China, experimental art and sculpture . . . all gained currency. English lettering on product packaging, breathy and throaty voices in singing, discothèque, swag dance moves, and movies from the West that were screened in closed sessions, expanded our cultural horizons. Films that focused on China's poverty and backwardness, rock songs such as "Northwest Wind" and "Nothing to My Name," and the films *Old Well, Yellow Earth, Horse Thief,* and *Starry Night* caused great public excitement and animated debates. With freshly fashioned works of art and literature galore, there was jubilation and despair, affirmation and outrage, hope and admonition. But no one could be indifferent; no one wanted to miss the bandwagon, the once-in-a-lifetime opportunity, for a great ride or a lusty kill.

Beyond literature and popular culture, there were heated debates on adherence to communist principles, special economic zones, the legitimate number of employees for any private business (no more than seven, according to a Marxist tenet, for the economy to remain socialist), snubbing capitalist tendencies, paradigm shift, and adequate pay for intellectuals. The last arose from complaints about atomic bomb engineers earning less than street hawkers selling boiled eggs, and earth scientists less than barbers, though they all worked with similarly roundish objects. Reform of pricing control, breakthrough economic policies, managerial leadership (sidelining Party bosses), free expression, and access to information (e.g., allowing Guangdong residents access to Hong Kong TV signals) were all boldly proposed and hotly debated. I

12. A journal of political commentary published by the propaganda department of the Chinese Communist Party.

remember seeing a notice put out by the staff at a hotel in Guangdong, advising guests that as of the following day Hong Kong TV programs would be unavailable for three days, as an important government leader would be checking in. It happened that this leader was someone I knew well. Would he catch them out and censure their sneaky workaround? What could he do with all the expediency in the country at large in those heady days of reform?

Chapter 43

Member of the CCP Central Committee

Having served as an alternate member of the Central Committee since the Twelfth National Congress in 1982, I was elected a full member in 1985. I remained on the Central Committee through 1992, ten years altogether. At the committee's annual plenums usually held in the fall in West Beijing Hotel, I was party to the proceedings in which important decisions for the nation were adopted. They included policies on urban economic reform, party rectification, and the campaign against "spiritual pollution," all milestones in China's reform and ascendance.

The annual plenum was a gathering of the upper crust of the Party and government, the powers-that-be. Over the decade, I had seen Deng Xiaoping, Chen Yun, Li Xiannian, Hu Yaobang, party chiefs of all the provinces and government ministries, the top military brass, as well as renowned scientists, medical doctors, academics, artists, and exemplary factory workers and farmers who had been picked for their accomplishments. Even characters with storied pasts such as Hua Guofeng[1] and Wang Dongxing[2] showed up. I felt humbled in the presence

1. Hua Guofeng, 1921–2008, ex-chairman of the CCP (1976–1981) and Mao's chosen successor. He was edged out of Party leadership in the early 1980s after Deng Xiaoping took over de-facto leadership of the Party but retained central committee membership.
2. Wang Dongxing, 1916–, ex-politburo member and Mao's chief of staff and head of security forces protecting the central leadership; edged out of central leadership by the early 1980s but retained central committee membership.

of the political glitterati. The wisecracking, temperamental, and often untamed side of me would be quite out of place in the solemn proceedings that were overwhelming to say the least. At the same time, I marveled at the prowess of audacious CCP leaders in bringing together such a motley collection of seasoned and powerful personalities encompassing all societal sectors and professions, as well as ethnic nationalities. Through their respective nexuses, they helped the party achieve a level of cohesion within its ranks of tens of millions. Such a behemoth functioned with remarkable effectiveness and purposefulness, with policies swiftly adopted and regularly realigned. Much was accomplished while serious blunders were also made along the way. However, it had been able to get its feet under it, so to speak, and start over after each stumble. Its past failings had brought down scorn, repudiation and humiliation on itself. The ambitious, the speculative, and the scheming had also gravitated toward it. But in the end its power, nobleness, and patriarchic vigor overall were nonetheless undiminished. Its cause was surely a manly enterprise.

Those of us who did not hold senior Party or government positions had shared rooms at these conferences. In the first few years, I always shared a room with Chen Hanfu from Beijing. Gentle, humble and cautious, he was a former steam engine engineer (his locomotive was named after the late Chairman Mao) and then vice chairman of the Beijing Municipal Federation of Trade Unions. I also came to know a delegate from the military. His name was Wang Meng, too (though written differently in Chinese), and his hometown was next to mine. He had served as political commissar of the Thirty-eight Army Group, chairman of the National Sports Commission, and then Political Commissar of the Guangzhou Military District Command. As our surnames were the same, we were seated together following an order based on the number of strokes in the Chinese character for one's family name. I told him because of his wide renown in his hometown, I had been mistakenly greeted as Wang the Commissar when visiting a heritage temple there. He said he was often asked what he had written lately, being ennobled by his namesake but having nothing to show for it. He told me that during the Cultural Revolution, Central Committee meetings were shrouded in great secrecy. He would be gone, without telling his family, until after the sessions were over. By the time I became a member, all was much less uptight. I had often seen delegates, including once controversial characters, gather in front of the little kiosk casually chatting. There were also nightly film screenings and music and dance performances to keep delegates collectively amused.

Simple but nicely prepared meals were served for all, who were seated four to a table. Diners were discreet; there were no strident greetings or loud conversations. You could ask for a yogurt for desert, but would have to pay for drinks. I once bought a beer for a fellow alternate member who later became a senior leader in the national government. For such a small act of hospitality, I was teased for being the one who had become rich ahead of the pack. I can't recall how tea was served at the conference. But in the years when Hu Yaobang was the CCP General Secretary, only hot water was provided at meetings of the Secretariat of the Central Committee, which I attended in a non-voting capacity. You would have to pay 50 cents for a teabag to make your own brew. On one occasion, Ai Zhisheng, then Minister of Radio and Television, paid for my teabag as I didn't have any money on me.

There have been so-called insiders' tales of Chinese politics published in Hong Kong. Merely judging by their details about the Central Committee and Secretariat meetings, you can tell they were fabrications.

Reports read or circulated at such conferences were inevitably filled with jargon and clichés. You were supposed to be always "encouraged and inspired" by top leaders' speeches. All party decisions had to be "extremely important and timely." But breakout sessions touched on real political, economic, and social issues of the country. I learned much about China as we discussed issues such as human trafficking, managerial independence, heritage protection, family planning, employment, and grain production. I learned that China's problems had to be tackled with a pragmatic approach. A Party elder who had served as party secretary in a number of provinces and cities told me that the fundamental problem for China had been a lack of education and training for its people. This had been true with not only farmers and factory workers, but also cadres. Even so-called intellectuals lacked proper understanding. Therefore, the CCP's policy initiatives and ambitious goals could be hampered in execution. His words left me pondering.

The senior leaders were terse and to the point when they wrapped up each plenum session. Once, after the adoption of a policy on urban economic reform, Deng Xiaoping looked in good spirits and said offhandedly that this represented an addition to the Marxist political economy. He also said at the conclusion of a Central Advisory Committee meeting that without reform and opening-up, China would be trapped in a state of poverty, backwardness, ignorance, and savagery. Such poignant understanding lay at the bottom of his great political resolve. Zhang Guangnian's eyes brimmed with tears when recounting Deng's remarks to me (he had by then become a member of the Advisory Committee). The country had just come out of turmoil a decade long. There was great sense of uncertainty, poised as we were at the threshold of reform, about to "cross the river by feeling out the stones" as Deng famously said.

It was at one of the Central Committee sessions (the second plenum of the Central Committee of the Twelfth National Congress) when Deng Xiaoping talked about "spiritual pollution."[3] I had known the opposing views of Zhou Yang and Hu Qiaomu concerning an article on Humanism by the former. At a conference on March 13, 1983, commemorating the 100th anniversary of Marx' death, Zhou gave a keynote speech "On a Number of Theoretical Issues Relating to Marxism." He talked about Alienation and Humanism when trying to explain why the Cultural Revolution had happened and how fiascos like that could be prevented in future. He discussed the two archaic notions mentioned by Marx and said they had contemporary relevance. Hu Qiaomu, however, thought differently, declaring that such notions could be used to challenge communism and socialism and destabilize the Party's ideological footing. Deng's talk was a rebuttal to Zhou Yang and an affirmation of Hu's view.

This weighed heavily on me. I was meek-minded when it came to ideological strife, hoping for amity, not another round of struggle and then rectification. I did not want to see a philosophical discussion being silenced by political might. Zhou Yang was down on his luck, though given his seniority and status within the Party, he could have avoided such a fate. He was not a deputy head of propaganda any more, but acted

3. A political campaign from October to December 1983 launched by certain advocates in the CCP leadership to curb Western-inspired liberal ideas among its membership and the Chinese populace at large.

as if matters of literature and art were still his turf and his great concern. I had no experience with his domineering past. However, in the post-Cultural Revolution era, he seemed an old man babbling out parting words of wisdom. He acted as if he were the guardian saint of writers while in fact he was not universally liked. Older writers in particular viewed him with a twinge of pique. Then, he believed that theoretical development could determine the future of literature and overestimated the importance of his mission.

I have long thought championing grand theories is something an opposition party or revolutionaries would do. They can use inspiring theories to win popular support for the lack of a track record in power. However, once you are in power, your concern should be real action and change.

I tried to convince myself that the campaign against "spiritual pollution" might after all be necessary. We had had a phase of uninterrupted freedom over the past several years. *The Gulag Archipelago, Testimony: The Memoirs of Shostakovich, 1984,* and *We,* a novel by Yevgeny Zamyatin, all became readily available in China. Revelations of brutal persecutions of Yu Luoke[4] and Zhang Zhixin[5] and the publication of Yu Luojin's *A Spring Fairy Tale* had contributed to the collective condemnation of the Cultural Revolution and the extreme Left. Some cooling off, rethinking, and debate might not be entirely a bad thing.

I was convinced that Zhou Yang's sincerity and serious intentions would be acknowledged and his conclusions accorded due respect. We should be accommodating on matters of theoretical debate in the search for truth. Intuitively I would have sided with Zhou Yang. But I also knew that my personal choice did not matter in the larger scheme of things, and I needed to be calm and rational when political decisions were being made and handed down.

I wrote about my feelings at the time in an essay titled "Fall Musings." I wrote about the crisp air and vast skies of fall, when the harvest was brought in and the soil allowed to rest. Impending cold winds were yet to

4. Yu Luoke, 1942–1970, a young man imprisoned and executed for writing an article opposing the feudal "family bloodline theory."
5. Zhang Zhixin 1931–1975, a lecturer at People's University in Beijing who openly opposed the Culural Revolution and was executed after many years in prison.

thin out the bright foliage.

I welcomed the thinning of the autumn foliage. I took comfort in the knowledge that not all "thinning" was harmful. The intelligentsia could sometimes be overly agitated, unrealistic, and hugely impatient. Some feigned literary pretensions but were after all vicious and mean. Original thinking, true scholarship, and great literature of compelling moral power would only stand out after "thinning." Such is the virtue of autumn, of its clarifying force.

Such was my thinking after the start of the "anti-spiritual pollution" campaign. I learned to sing "The Way We Were" by playing a tape recording over and over. It is the theme song of a film about a student activist of the 1950s. The young woman is full of idealism and youthful innocence. She is uncompromising in her political pursuits, eventually parting ways with her husband. I recalled the film's final scene, in which she and her ex-husband see each other on opposite sides of a New York street, the latter with his new girl friend while she, flyers in hand, is still canvassing for her political cause. People and traffic slide by until they could see each other no more. Then the song rises, bringing tears to my eyes.

I saw in the heroine a kindred spirit. We were both destined to be the way we were. Because of larger political forces at play, it was impossible for me to lead a private and cozy life. Nor could I emulate the reclusive scholar Qian Zhongshu, or dedicated novelists such as Feng Zongpu of great sincerity and simplicity, Wang Zengqi and Jia Pingwa of great elegance and ease, Tie Ning of such sweet temperament, Wang Anyi[6] of intense focus and razor-sharp wit, the free and uninhibited Mo Yan, or the distraught and indignant Zhang Chengzhi. I was destined to lead a life of tribulations, to fend off attacks and accusations left and right, and, to be patient with forced composure, and to be able to laugh when seething with wrath.

My two-term tenure on the Central Committee allowed me to see the inner workings of the Party leadership and gave me political exposure and access. All this was also material for literature. I became less fallible,

---

6. Wang Anyi, 1954–, writer, chairwoman of the Writers' Association of Shanghai; notable writings include *The Song of Everlasting Sorrow*, trans. Michael Berry and Susan Chan Egan. Columbia University Press, 2008.

less prone to prejudice, and more politically savvy and less inclined to exaggeration and sentimentalism.

I must admit I was not entirely up to snuff as a Central Committee member. I was too caught up in my writing. I cared too much about literature with its evocative power through words and imageries, with its forms and styles; about individuality, creativity, a sense of fun, tears and laughter, kindness, innocence, and compassion; about the feelings of the common people and the richness of life experiences. I lacked fierce ambition, resolve, and the fighting instinct. I did not have the vigor and tenacity to overwhelm opponents. You would have to be manipulative and hungry for power, relishing it all the while, if you were to dedicate your life to revolution, or to a career in politics. I inevitably shied away from all this with an inclination or pretension to nonchalance, detachment, civility, and simplicity. I was even timid, guilt-ridden, and fearful when put in a position of political power. Being a writer had somehow prevented me from being too concerned about power or scheming for more of it. After all, I felt far more comfortable spending my time writing novels than being put on the pedestal of leadership. I disappointed senior leaders, my mentors, and my fellow writers, for my life's passion was not the pursuit of political power. This was the way I was. Had I tried to be anything else, I would have delighted none and disappointed even more.

Chapter 44

A Sense of Clarity and Serenity

My prose poem "Fall Musings," written in response to "anti-spiritual pollution," was motivated by a desire for a state of self-knowledge, clarity, and simplicity. I could not pretend to be the conscience of the nation, or the beholder of truth, as some would gladly do. We were all caught up in our own fleeting fancies inspired by our existential experiences and what we could comprehend. I would not think that our personal judgment and conclusions could be a panacea for all the world's ills and that anyone who did not agree with us should be held in scorn.

Clarity and serenity often eluded us. In reflecting upon what had happened during the campaign against "spiritual pollution" in 1983, only now do I realize that (a) there was no way you could turn the CCP leaders back when they decided to launch the campaign; (b) they had no intention of seeing a repeat of the persecution that had transpired in the Cultural Revolution repeated; (c) reform had to proceed under the condition of stability; (d) a man of letters could engage in a host of things that were more suited to him, and would both delight him and benefit the nation; and (e) time would solve everything. In time, clarity will replace confusion; justice will triumph over brutal force, and rationality over folly.

Not until 2006, however, did I reach that level of understanding. I remembered Spinoza, the Dutch philosopher, who was often quoted by my father as saying "Do not weep. Do not wax indignant. Understand."

Spinoza made his living as a lens grinder. Yet, around us we had too much weeping and waxing, animosity and ferocious attack, but not understanding. The so-called "anti-spiritual pollution campaign" that started as a precautionary "do not . . ." somehow turned into a public "cleansing." Over-eager zealots even assailed people's hairstyles, their wearing of pantyhose, and their reading undesirable books. Even Modernism became a target again. Gao Xingjian, who by now had achieved some repute for his experimental plays, was depressed. He had been a heavy smoker and thought he had lung cancer. He began to prepare for the eventuality of death, and on his bucket list was a long overland trip. His trek in western China resulted in his novel *Soul Mountain,* which won him a Nobel Prize.

At a high-level meeting, I heard someone of significant stature, a "somebody," citing anonymous "people's complaints" that "those advocating capitalism are being given a free rein and their opponents are being censured." Another person of similar standing echoed, "The question is what should be defined as socialist and what as capitalist." Such questioning and strenuous debate went on and on until they prompted a rebuttal from Deng Xiaoping.

A couple of months later, there was a hint from above that there should be no more mention of spiritual pollution. Writers felt relieved, and even rejoiced. Zhou Yang, who had been regarded as a source of "pollution," however, did not experience a respite. He was shown in media reports being ushered to various officially sanctioned events and conferences. He then had a bad fall in the bathroom when staying at a Guangzhou hotel and his speech became impaired.

I went to see him and he became alarmed when I mentioned a forthcoming meeting called by the Central Committee. "What meeting?" he asked with sudden focus. I calmed him, "Please don't worry, it will be taken care of." His friend Mei Shaowu[1] and his wife Professor Tu Zhen were also there. Zhou Yang then slipped back into his resigned state with a meek smile and the countenance of a sickly man. I was unsettled by his reaction. As someone once said, not necessarily with banal intent,

---

1. Mei Shaowu, 1928–2005, eldest son of the noted Beijing opera singer Mei Lanfang, and scholar of American literature.

that Zhou Yang had led (dominated) China's art and literary circles for decades and grown accustomed to his role of directing, and alternately defending and rectifying, Chinese literature and arts. I had great sympathy for him when he came forth with his reflections and apologies after the Cultural Revolution and his final determined attempt to put all his lessons and ponderings into one unified scheme. I had been willing to follow his leadership. It took me some time to realize that practical solutions for real problems are perhaps more important than mere concepts and grand theorizing.

I shall remain eternally indebted to Zhou Yang for his tremendous confidence in me and his kindness and generosity. I think of him often and still feel an affinity for him. His painstaking efforts in the 1980s could have turned out differently. After retiring to become a member of the Central Advisory Committee, he should have backed off. He shouldn't have been so naïvely confident, with that cocksure stance of "If not I, then who?" But he persisted. Such were Zhou Yang and other revolutionary stalwarts. They dedicated themselves to the pursuit of truth to the extent of putting their own lives in peril. When he joined the revolution, he was a true rebel against the establishment and a believer in Mao's cause, free from self-interest and calculation. His devotion also led him to rethink with tremendous pain after the Cultural Revolution the nation's approach to progress. He once described the two main lessons from the recent turmoil: China should not have attempted leapfrogging the stages of social evolution; its progress could not be achieved in isolation from the world. Regrettably, he did not elaborate on such worthwhile observations. He turned his attention to "alienation" and Humanism, which were somewhat removed from China's reality. Nonetheless, they were important notions that could have been acknowledged and accorded due reflection had he not hastily had the *People's Daily* print page after page of his weighty treatise. I still hope that someday we will have a more relaxed environment that would be tolerant of Zhou's notions and discussions to encourage unconventional thinking and innovation, and to approximate the truth.

With a decade of persecution plus a decade of Cultural Revolution behind me, leaving me with nothing but "lessons," I was no longer a young man. I no longer believed that theoretical notions should govern everything. I knew that life is much larger than theories. Life is about having common sense and dealing with reality, about avoiding harm and seeking improvement. Once you have been through enough setbacks and failures, you acquire the wisdom to make changes when necessary and to keep up with the times. None of the noble political notions that you presently hold close to your heart will matter as much, ten, fifty years down the road. Yet the river of life flows on forever.

However, before the campaign against "spiritual pollution" finally tapered off, its proponents did get their hands dirty in "cleansing" and rectification. They were intent on getting rid of "bad elements" and rectifying the ills in literature and arts. They contemplated launching a nationwide campaign, subjecting people of interest to scrutiny and investigation so as to criticize and help them and stop them from sliding farther down the hill. They wanted to see people cave in and repent with tears, as in the rectification campaigns of the past. A forum was organized at the request of a propaganda department leader, which was meant to be an occasion to hand down instructions from above, review unwanted tendencies, and bring everyone into line.

Luckily, not too long after the menacing start when the propaganda leader spoke stern words, and as the forum unfolded, its theme changed to unity and joint efforts for the greater flourishing of literature and arts. What had happened? How did a forum intended for condemnation turn apologetic? Apparently, there was resistance among the participants and perhaps an injunction from the top. This was a huge embarrassment for the one who convened the forum. Ba Jin was quoted as saying in his emphatic Sichuan accent, "no more criticism . . ." Ba Jin, of course, could say something like that as he was not a party member and was an elder in his eighties. Wang Meng did not voice his objections. Weighed down by my obligations and responsibilities, I failed to do what I should have done. At the time, all I wanted was to see all the problems with literary and arts circles abate and even disappear. I wanted more tolerance. I had hoped leaders would not be unduly perturbed by writers' impassioned utterances and hyperbole. For our part, writers would refrain from whimsical outbursts and histrionics. But who would listen? Reform in China had brought about not only great economic and social progress, but also controversies and growing pains. Uncertainty caused excitement and anxiety. Not only writers and artists, but also those in leading political roles, became tentative and at a loss about how to proceed.

Against this background, an essay by Zhang Xianliang in the *Art and Literature Gazette* caused a further stir. He claimed that in order to succeed in building socialism with Chinese characteristics, it would be necessary to build capitalism with Chinese characteristics first. He was condemned for blatantly advocating capitalism. The editorial team of the *Gazette* and leadership of the Writers' Union were also implicated because of their tacit consent for the essay's publication.

Zhang Xianliang is from the northwestern province of Ningxia. He was labeled a *rightist* when he was not yet twenty and was sent down to a camp to be reformed through labor in the late 1950s. He was restless by nature. When he was granted home leave at the start of the Cultural Revolution, he chanced upon a "rebel" group consisting of itinerant laborers in Xian. He joined them on the spot and never went home. He told me that he had planned to study economics after the Cultural Revolution. However, after failing to find a publisher for his academic writings, he switched to writing novels. His *Old Man Xing and His Dog* was an instant hit. Literary fame followed after a series of short stories with sad and poignant endings, peppered with references to *Das Capital*. In addition to writing stories, he was also known for his sensational remarks, such as intellectuals being subversive by nature, which was commended by that propaganda leader bent on getting rid of "spiritual pollution." In the 1980s, amid the general rant about the arrival of an information age, he declared to the nation he was about to launch an informational newspaper catering to Chinese writers. However, nothing followed. He also proposed on several occasions that there needed to be career writers dedicating themselves to the service of the state, like the ancient court poet. A great state such as China could afford a few such writers under government patronage, so he argued. He confessed that people like him who had been persecuted as *rightists* in the past were now beneficiaries of the reform, and hence its staunchest supporters.

Despite his controversial remarks, hollow upon examination, he was by no means a dissident with anti-socialist views. At most, he was given to pompous statements and relished public attention. His comment on capitalism first, with whatever characteristics, in his essay published by the *Art and Literature Gazette,* was just plain absurd and playful with no vicious political design. It should not be deemed as a manifesto against socialism. On the other hand, neither could it go unchallenged. The *Gazette* and the Writers' Union were put on the spot, and they had to do something about it.

I thought about Hu Sheng,[2] with whom I became acquainted in Central Committee meetings. I had read his booklet on dialectical materialism circulating as an underground publication before Liberation. I admired him a great deal. He mentioned to me his previous interest in Zhang Xianliang's writings. I told him about the problem that the *Gazette* and the Writers' Union now faced because of Zhang's controversial essay. I proposed an interview with Hu by a senior correspondent from the *Gazette.* He would speak in his capacity as president of the Chinese Academy of Social Sciences on the inevitability of China taking the socialist path, from both theoretical and historical perspectives. The interview was published in the *Gazette.* It brought the matter to a largely satisfactory end. There had been similar incidents where I tried to smooth things over, without the person embroiled in the storm even knowing it. The savvy Zhang Xianliang did not know that my hand had more than once got him off the hook.

The literary and art circles muddled along prompting frequent mentions and admonitions in the Party's internal circulars. It could be one writer denouncing politicians lacking conscience, and another criticizing so-called democratic dictatorship. Some writers cast doubts on the Party's tradition of strife and martyrdom. Yet others indulged in literary gatherings at scenic resorts. Nothing unbecoming ever happened at those gatherings, except for an odd pair or two who fell under each other's spell and were perhaps found in an unsightly embrace. Sha Yexin's play *The Impostor,* Li Ping's novel *When the Fiery Evening Clouds Disappear,* Ye Wenfu's poem "General, You Cannot Do This," and Liu Binyan's reportage each was mentioned for being problematic. Apparently there were people who snooped around and reported on suspicious speeches and activities of writers and artists. Once some writers at the Beijing

2. Hu Sheng, 1918–2000, revolutionary theoretician, head of the research office for Chinese Communist Party Chronicles and president of Chinese Academy of Social Sciences (1985–1992).

Municipal Federation of Literature and Art failed to turn up were censured for failing to turn up at a mandatory political study session and they were censured shortly after the session was over. Most writers and artists felt there was not enough freedom and openness and loathed any mention of criticism and rectification.

To the Party leadership, it all boiled down to one nagging question: whether the writers and artists were supporting socialism or secretly harboring something dubious. It was rather absurd that more than three decades after the founding of the People's Republic, writers and artists were still being viewed with doubt. Stage actresses could be deemed as too scantily clad on stage and writers too grudgingly, or not stridently, Marxist. Even montages used in films and singing in the Western operatic style could be problematic. If someone argued that matters of political significance concerning art and literature had all been resolved, the statement itself attested to an erroneous judgment. Thus after decades of ceaseless campaigns, criticism, self-criticism, political labeling, and reform through labor, the question of political orientation of writers and artists remained.

However, such a mindset was to become outdated toward the end of the 1980s. A new approach was emerging. It was not completely laissez-faire, but would aim to replace rectification for political purity with effective administration. Such an approach aimed to prevent acrimonious debates and sensationalism, nip in the bud "harmful ideas" before they got spread around, deal with specific issues without generalization, give greater freedom to creative writers—particularly leading ones—while subjecting publishing houses and their editors and managers to discipline and regulation. All this would come about later, but a trend was emerging.

Chapter 45

Memorable 1984

Going into 1984, I reflected on the unfathomable political tides that alternately swept me into the trough and heaved me up to the cusp. I came to the realization that personal efforts and destiny were at the mercy of greater forces. It was like being out in a skiff at sea—harmony with the calm ocean until the storm rises; you become utterly powerless in the grip of raging Nature. I had learned to refrain from political agitation, showmanship, and righteousness. I detested being judgmental, vengeful, and opportunistic. I should always guard against jealousy, grandstanding, and toadying to the powerful. Never would I stab people in the back.

The year 1984 was one of trials. In the aftermath of the "anti-spiritual pollution" campaign, clearheadedness, modesty, and discretion were called for. Moreover, my younger son Wang Shi's mental illness caused me a great deal of anguish. He had graduated from an Air Force missile technology college the previous year and landed a job at the No. 5 Research Institute of the Air Force. However, this was soon followed by a bout of depression. The illness was painful for both him and the family. The fear and darkness he felt must have been unbearable. There are no better descriptions for the sorrows of aging, illness and death than the Buddhist terms *bei, cibei* and *dabei,* their closest equivalents being pathos, immense pathos, or utmost pathos. Wang Shi told me every time he fell ill, the world around him turned opaque, and a murky gray. I was shaken. We all have our weaknesses. However, when you are struck by a mental illness, you are tormented by your lonely soul, unhinged and beyond your control. It was again like being in a tiny boat in the vast ocean, but this time you do not even have a compass. The ocean rages and thunder strikes. You feel like you are being plunged into utter darkness, a bottomless abyss, impenetrable and immense. You feel the overwhelming immensity of a towering iceberg. You feel lame and powerless, and you cannot hear or see. Of all creatures great and small, you as a human are the only kind that has self-knowledge and can ponder on the poignancy of life. You have needs and aspirations that cannot be fulfilled. Your anxieties weigh heavily as if for eternity. With all the good things in life, you fear their imminent loss; with all the adversaries, you fear their staying power. There are haunting illusions that you cannot dispel. You are never happy with yourself. You see endless pain inflicted on humankind: measles, hunger, sweltering heat and freezing cold, ferocious mosquitoes and sickening flies, poverty, and lack of status in society, disgrace and injustice.

I had to take him to the hospital again and again, waiting in line to register, trying to understand diagnoses and treatment options. I was scared, fearful of the unexpected. I tormented myself for not taking good enough care of him in his childhood and wanted to find out what traumatic experience over the last two decades had caused his present grief and what I could do to alleviate his pain.

Thankfully, his condition gradually improved. In 1984, I took a trip to Wuhan and took him along. We stayed at the prestigious East Lake Hotel thanks to arrangements made by Wang Renzhong, then director of the Party's Propaganda Department. I took long walks every day on a trail skirting the pretty lake and began to form thoughts for *The Transformer*, an autobiographical novel based on my childhood experiences. From Wuhan we took a cruise on the Yangtze going upstream to Chongqing. Then one day, my son declared he was healed. He told me that while taking a shower next to the ship's engine room, he felt something click in his head and came out the shower a healed man. It was unbelievable, but he did begin to smile, which he had not done for a long while. However, after we disembarked at Chongqing and were about to return home, he fell ill again. So it went, with much of 1984 being taken up by caring for my mentally ill son while working on *The Transformer* manuscript.

In June 1984, I took a brief trip to the Soviet Union. I headed a delegation of Chinese filmmakers to the Tashkent Film Festival. Afterward, we visited Samarqand, Tbilisi, and Moscow. Huang Shuqin, a film director from Shanghai, and an interpreter were in our group. I wrote about my impressions in a collection of essays which won popular acclaim and accolades from fellow writers. Li Yimang, former Chinese ambassador to Burma and director of external relations of the Central Committee, perceived political maturity and sophistication in these essays. They were later included in a 2006 anthology, *Eulogies for the Soviet Union.*

Life sometimes seems merely a string of missed opportunities and unfulfilled yearnings. You often do not get what you desire most. Ninety-nine point nine percent of youthful longings are not fulfilled in interminable youth. After you have put some years behind you, you only feel an unspecific sense of loss, more than gratification, when you have managed to realize some of your goals. My 1950s' dream of traveling to the Soviet Union was realized three decades later. By then nothing was the same any more. The Soviet Union was no longer the great nation that inspired my youthful aspirations. The camaraderie between China and the USSR was long gone. I yearned for the fame of a writer of renown. A quarter century later, had I achieved just that? I felt more self-doubt than confidence. When your adolescent dreams finally came true twenty or thirty years later, do you feel jubilation or mere sadness? When in your fifties you run into a heartthrob of yore, will you smile or struggle to hold back your tears? All the dreams of your youth will cease to matter. Your face lined with age, you are sober in the cool air of another dawn. All this is material for literature. You may stir and put pen to paper, but once the momentary urge is over, you have to watch out and swallow a glyceryl trinitrate as a precaution for your waning heart.

We met an official from the Soviet Ministry of Foreign Affairs who lectured me on the futility of seeking help from capitalist countries. Times had changed indeed. Now it was the Soviet Union that criticized us for bowing to capitalists. I also heard a Soviet radio broadcast denouncing China's right-leaning opportunism. These two countries always went opposite ways. At least this did no harm to and had in fact served China well.

In Samarqand, an ancient town I came to know through Uighur stories read in Xinjiang and had long hoped to visit, we were invited to a big lunch party at a Leninist commune. It started with a long speech, and everyone grew restless. I asked Anatoli, our Soviet minder and interpreter, a charming and energetic young man, who the big shot was. He shrugged and said, "Who knows? Chernenko, maybe?" We howled with laughter. But afterward, Comrade Anatoli began to avoid me. His invoking the name of the general secretary of the Soviet Communist Party in an irreverent manner could have caused him trouble. He must have thought that I was from China and feared what would happen if I were to report to the state security.

At Tashkent, we had an English interpreter, a warmhearted and cheerful young woman. We were invited to her home. She told us that her long-deceased father was a Chinese who married her mother when they were both in Mongolia. We met her mother too, who became angry when her daughter said she wanted to marry an American. The mother said she would kill her if she were to move to that faraway land.

We flew close to the arctic on our way home. The summer sun dipped low over the horizon to the north and rose untiringly a short while later and a new day began. I imagined that in the dark winter, the sun would barely rise above the horizon to the south before descending into darkness again. Such was the great North, in all its majesty and splendor.

I came to learn that the best way to deal with absurdity is to match it with an even more outlandish absurdity. A member of the Chinese embassy in Moscow was extremely arrogant and gave us stone-faced instructions on how we should conduct ourselves in what would be a very tricky situation, as if we were a bunch of sophomores. I proposed that since the situation was going to be so dire, we might just as well pack up and go home. This stopped him then and there. So, it goes to show that you can treat the paranoid with a greater dose of paranoia.

One day, we were scheduled to meet with the chairman of the Soviet Film Commission. The delegations from different countries all stood in a line waiting for their turns for an audience with him. Ten minutes past our scheduled slot, I decided to go back to my room. They could always come and fetch me when the Chairman was ready.

After returning from the Soviet visit, I took a trip to Shanghai. It was for an award ceremony organized by *Shanghai Literature*. I made it a point to go there to show my support for Li Ziyun, the embattled executive deputy chief editor of the magazine. After the award ceremony, we were put on an overnight ferry to Ningbo to visit a naval base at the invitation of the East China Sea Fleet. I did not get a wink of sleep as the engine thrummed and waves crashed against the ship's hull. In Ningbo, we were put up for the night in the guest quarters of a heritage building, an ancient library of a private collector in fact, and I tossed and turned in its century-old wood frame bed with an imposing canopy and curtains, exhausted but wide awake. On the third day of this grueling trip, I was woken up at three in the morning for a six-hour ride back to Shanghai to a seminar organized by the *Shanghai Art and Literature Gazette.* At the time, there was still animosity among writers in Shanghai in the aftermath of the "anti-spiritual pollution" campaign. I did not know the people at the *Gazette* very well. I did not want them to feel slighted. I was averse to factional strife, favors, and secrecy. I was also dog-tired; my mind went blank and my eyes glazed over as I was ushered into the seminar room. I managed to remember the need for caution. It was getting close to the end of 1984. I was growing in stature yet being always watched over by some. I could not drop my guard, give them ammunition, and inadvertently loose my perch and let those on the extreme right or left take advantage. Thus, the speech I pulled off was thought by many to be hazy and clueless. I quickly earned notoriety for this. Fellow writer Chen Chun described the speech as a hallmark of Wang Meng's ambivalence and his skittishly beating about the bush. This infamy was entirely of my own making, and there was no excuse for it.

Later in the year, I was invited by Li Zi, editor-in-chief of a literary magazine in Cangzhou, the prefecture where my home county is located, to give a lecture on "The Tradition of Social Commitment in Chinese Literature." The topic was chosen apparently in consideration of my position and obligations. This was my first visit to my hometown in forty-five years. At the sight of those vaguely familiar street signs, memories of childhood flashed back. I went to Nanpi, the county seat, and my home village of Longtang. The local cadres were warm and eager, but their clothes were tattered and patchy. The salinized soils yielded poorly and life was harsh. I felt saddened. They remembered people of my parents' and grandparents' generations when I mentioned the names.

But our old house had been torn down. I found my father's name in the local gazetteer, which listed all its proud sons who had gone to college. The trip greatly helped my writing of *The Transformer*. It was also a stark reminder of the harsh reality, and my being a native son, of this rural area in north China.

October 1, 1984, marked the thirty-fifth anniversary of the founding of the People's Republic. For the first time in my life I stood atop the Tiananmen Gate Tower to watch the military parade that Deng Xiaoping had called for. I had the chance to listen to his commemorative speech up close, and watched an impressive display of fireworks in the evening. In the moments before the parade started, the vast central boulevard was eerily quiet. Standing high on Tiananmen, I could see it stretch into the distant horizons, east and west. Then it began. Lavishly decorated floats rumbled down the square, and soldiers and civilians marched in giant formations, with flowers, soaring balloons, and pigeons for effect. It was all glory and grandeur befitting a nation with vast territories that was in ascendance after decades of extreme hardships. Then suddenly a group of students flashed a banner saying "Hello, Xiaoping!" which apparently was unscripted in the parade plan. Such spontaneity was touching. It had been long lost in all the organized hoopla of past years.

While watching the fireworks I bumped into Wang Feng, the former deputy director of the United Front Department of the CCP and Party secretary of Xinjiang, His daughter was on the editorial staff of *People's Literature*, so we felt close. He had left Xinjiang a few years earlier but still took an interest in what was happening there. He knew that I spoke Uighur and said he once recommended me to Deng Xiaoping for a position in the regional government. I was flummoxed. He then said with his heavily accented Shaanxi drawl, "But he fo*rrr*got." This of course was no result of amnesia. But it did reflect an element of chance and casualness in Chinese politics and personnel appointments, despite all the regimented seriousness of larger political schemes.

The celebratory mood continued into the following Spring Festival, which climaxed with mass jubilation. The skies turned pink with endless fireworks exploding all over the city. I had never seen such a collective celebration before in all my fifty years of life, and it was all spontaneous. I wrote a story, "The Legend of Renowned Doctor Liang," about two brothers with opposite temperaments and fates. After three decades of tumultuous changes, they were faced with the tantalizing, albeit uncertain, prospect of prosperity. They watched riotous fireworks exploding all over the city, eyes brimming with tears, with bitterness and resignation, gratitude and hope welling up in their hearts.

The most memorable event of 1984, however, was the Fourth National Writer's Conference. Voices from the four corners of the country competed for attention. Literary circles were again shown to be restless and contentious, to be anything but serene. Yang Xianyi[1] described the bickering at the conference as busybodies having nothing better to do so they did *it* to keep themselves busy. Another writer, Zhou Yiliang,[2] prophesied the futility of the self-righteous strife of the intelligentsia. But all this will come in the next chapter.

1. Yang Xianyi, 1915–2009, Chinese translator, known for his English translations of Chinese classics, including *Dream of the Red Chamber.*
2. Zhou Yiliang, 1913–2001, Chinese historian noted for his writings on Asian and Japanese history.

Chapter 46

Freedom of Literary Expression—A False Start?

The Fourth National Writers' Conference[1] opened at the end of 1984 and ran through early January of 1985. Zhang Guangnian, who assumed the Writers' Union's interim chairmanship in 1980 when former chairman, poet Li Ji, died on the job, was to step down at the conference. A new leadership team for the union was to be elected. Zhang gave a lengthy review of the literary cause in his parting speech. He commended the achievement of the writers in their thirties and forties. He also talked about freedom of literary expression and his take on the Party's policies concerning literature. For the first time, diverging views and opinions were voiced at a national conference like this. Delegates showed their support for Zhou Yang, while Hu Qiaomu was ignored. A sense of greater freedom was in the air.

That the conference could be conducted in such a manner at all was a marvel. Some were bothered by its unruliness, while others applauded its democratic spirit. The main event was an unprecedented election for the new leadership of the Writers' Union.

Zhang Guangnian also wore the hat of secretary of the CCP Leading Group of the Writers' Union. He had served as editor-in-chief of *People's*

1. Held in December 1984 through January 1985, it was an emotional gathering of writers after the Cultural Revolution, during which many were persecuted or banished into limbo and the Writers' Union itself was disbanded. The conference elected new leadership for the Writers' Union. Venerable writer Ba Jin was elected chairman and Wang Meng executive vice chairman, along with ten vice chairmen.

Literature before I took over. He was born in 1913 and was twenty-one years my senior. I came to know his work when singing the chorus for the "Yellow River Cantata" in my high school years. He wrote the lyrics for that monumental work under the penname of Guang Weiran. He continued to publish poems and literary reviews after Liberation, and kept his passion for poetry alive after he became a CCP cadre. He was pro-reform and thought it crucial for the nation's future, when dogmatic conservatives fiercely challenged reformers. Though he was not against necessary compromises, he opted to take a firm stance on matters of principle and was not afraid of antagonizing his opponents. He said that a life without daring to antagonize someone is too pathetic!

Zhang Guangnian's seniority, literary achievement, personal integrity, and clear-cut views won him respect and authority in the Writers' Union. He also had great respect for Zhou Yang, but was never too eager to pander to others trying to exert influence over the union.

I tried not to get too involved in the union's work, even though I became the editor-in-chief of *People's Literature,* the official publication of the union. I declined invitations to attend meetings of its Party Core. However, I dropped by Zhang's office often and enjoyed many a long conversations with him. But I warned myself not to get entangled. Those were my most productive years, and I maintained a rate of several thousand words per day. I knew only too well that my true worth lay in my writing.

By this time, Zhang was already seventy-one. He and leaders of the Party's propaganda and personnel departments had all approached me with the suggestion that I succeed him at the union. I resisted by saying that as I was in the most productive phase of my literary career and was yet to settle into my job at *People's Literature,* it would be best for me to assist the new leadership rather than taking full charge. I recommended Tang Dacheng as a candidate for the party secretary position. When asked by Zhang Guangnian, I also suggested that Feng Mu should be asked to stay on. Other candidates I voiced support for included the writers Bao Chang of Tianjin and Cong Weixi of Beijing. However, this incensed those who felt they were being overlooked. You cannot please everyone.

The election of the Union leadership ended in a surprise. Some hardliners were left out, and some ex-*rightists* were in. Ding Ling, Liu Baiyu, He Jingzhi and Cao Yu, who were all candidates for the vice presidency on the official ballot and would otherwise have been duly elected, were voted down. As Cao Yu was already president of the Chinese Theater Association, his not being elected was deemed understandable. The loss of other candidates, however, had a great deal to do with delegates' negative perception of them. At a meeting of the union's council to elect the conference presidium, Zhang Guangnian and I took turns to urge council members to vote for those who had been designated as official candidates, all in the interest of maintaining unity and balance. Both Guangnian and I were aware that we must be inclusive. I so exerted myself in canvasing that my voice became hoarse and I was literally in tears. But all this was to no avail. Delegates wanted to see drama and surprise. They had long felt that they were being controlled and neglected. Now that they had the opportunity to show their displeasure and anger, they were not about to give it up easily.

The bitterness of those being shot down was not hard to imagine. I sent people to call on them and mend soured relationships. I also made personal calls and invited them to participate in the union's work, e.g., as jurors for the Mao Dun Literature Prize. However, my efforts were snubbed. I could no longer remain impartial and detached. I could not shake off the cobwebs of dark animosity.

One senior CCP leader commented that such animosity was a legacy. It went back to the League of the Left-Wing Writers in Shanghai in the early 1930s and then the Yan'an era. It continued through the war and did not stop until the start of the Cultural Revolution when almost all writers were persecuted. However, it was rekindled when the Cultural Revolution was over and these persecuted old souls were brought back. Then they began passing away one after another. In their obituaries, their epic differences were all ironed out and they were invariably deemed as fighters for the literary cause having made outstanding contributions and their passing was a huge loss . . . Such accolades were meted out equally, and none outshined others in the final tributes they received.

Ding Ling, also a candidate for the presidium who was voted down, had been one of the writers I admired most in my youth. After her political rehabilitation, she said, "All the past bickering amounted to nothing and is water under the bridge. I am now immersed in the classical canon and philosophical musing, and my time is running out . . ." She said this with poignancy and resignation. However, I knew she could not let go entirely. In her last years, she devoted much of her precious time to launching and running the literary magazine *China,* after failing to register its original name "Chinese Literature," whose use was barred by existing English- and French-language journals of the same name. However, by then there were simply too many literary periodicals and the latecomer was fatefully disadvantaged. It did not have much of a chance, even though Ding Ling still had lingering clout and commanded a large following. It was just another literary publication that fell short of expectations, failing to deliver its promise of carrying forward the revolutionary literary tradition. She was also weighed down by discord in her editorial team. I did contribute an essay on literary styles that was published in two installments and generated some interest.

During the conference, I went with a senior CCP leader to see Zhou Yang in the hospital. By then, he was already in a vegetative state and was being fed through a nasal tube. When his assistant shouted into his ear that so and so and Wang Meng were there to see him, Zhou's eyelids twitched slightly. I was told by writer and former medical doctor Bi Shumin that eyelid movement is the last motor motion that a dying person has. It was saddening. We also visited Bin Xin, who was in good spirits. She even joked about her accomplishing what Chairman Mao once advocated: "Fear not being demoted, put in prison, stripped of Party membership, divorced, or threatened with death." Now, with Zhou Yang being incognizant and Ding Ling in a losing battle for the survival of her magazine, other literary giants were still at loggerheads with each other, their differing views on literature and arts threatening more clashes.

Back at the conference, in the first direct election of the Writers' Union leadership, Ba Jin received the most votes and the runners up were Zhang Guangnian and Liu Binyan. Behind them was either Lu Wenfu, or me, though I cannot recall the exact order. The results were published in the *People's Daily,* which made the whole thing even more dramatic. Liu and Lu were not even on the ballot. During discussions prior to the voting, some delegates petitioned for their inclusion in recognition of their popular appeal. I remember a few venerable writers of the Yan'an era passionately canvasing for Liu Binyan, claiming that he had a strong sense of moral duty and the death-defying courage to speak up. Thus, two more vice presidents were added. I became the executive vice president at the recommendation of the conference presidium. Some later complained about how badly the conference was run, citing Liu Binyan as the man in charge of the union. That simply was not true.

Getting or loosing an official position at the union really should not have caused so much agony. Writers are supposed to prove their worth through their own writing. Peking orders and hierarchies should be of no concern to them. In fact, there are writers, Sun Li, for example,who carry no grand titles but command enormous esteem. Ba Jin once complained that on his calling cards that the Writers' Union printed for him when he took overseas trips, official titles, such as vice chairman of the CPPCC,[2] chairman of the Writers' Union, and titles for various Shanghai local organizations, preceded "writer." He said being a writer was most the important thing for him, without which he would have nothing much to speak of. But that was left at the bottom.

But some people did care: now that they had lost their official titles at the union, their annoyance was beyond compare. Zhang Guangnian was unperturbed by angry reactions to the election outcome. However, election results aside, the liberal tendencies manifested at the conference were to soon cause serious concern to the senior CCP leadership.

2. CPPCC, Chinese People's Political Consultative Conference, the loose equivalent of the upper house of Congress.

Chapter 47

Who Am I?

Following the national writers' conference, Hu Qiaomu handed me an essay he had written and instructed me to publish it in the *Art and Literature Gazette.* It claimed that freedom of literary expression could never be absolute. This was apparently an attempt to address some of the tendencies shown at the writers' conference. In truth, although the Chinese Constitution provides for freedom of speech with its attendant obligations, no writer seriously expected an official endorsement of freedom for literary expression. No great works by literary masters, such as Qu Yuan, Li Bai, Du Fu, Cao Xueqin, Tolstoy, Balzac, or Cervantes for that matter, were created because they were guaranteed freedom of literary expression. Great works in world literature were often created under conditions less than ideal. Advocating literary freedom as a precondition was more like political posturing than literary concern.

I showed Hu's essay to Zhang Guangnian and Tang Dacheng, deputy chief editor of the *Gazette* and, after reviewing it with them, did some tweaking and wordsmithing myself. The essay was published in the *Gazette* as an editorial. Hu said he "admired" the nice job of polishing his draft and instructed it be reprinted by other papers.

A short while later, a few films were criticized for advocating Humanism and downplaying class struggle; these included *Dove Tree,* with a screenplay written by Ye Nan.[1] The CCP central leadership then decided

---

1. Ye Nan, 1930–2003, playwright.

to take away responsibility for the film industry from the Ministry of Culture and put it under the Ministry of Radio and Television, renaming the latter the Ministry of Radio, Television and Film. Such a move was perhaps to remove the influence of venerable cultural personalities thought responsible for the irksome films.

At a council meeting of the Writers' Union in early 1985, I made a comment that literature that was getting ahead of reality and prone to controversy would likely cause public concern. We should never underestimate this and must be prepared to take proper action. Freedom of expression has limits, subject to constitutional provisions and the "Four Basic Principles." However, when my remarks came out in the press, critics, my literary acquaintances in Hong Kong in particular, raised an outcry. Some claimed that my remarks simply wiped out the freedom won at the writers' conference.

With the benefit of hindsight (the realignment of film administration), some younger critics later realized that had I not come out with such a statement, the Writers' Union would have been seen as inept in putting its house in order. They recognized that Wang Meng might have in fact protected the Union. But of course Wang Meng could hardly be such a guardian of the union, given the mess it had got itself in. More serious problems would surface later.

For much of 1985 I had to deal with the legacies of the Fourth Writers' Conference, to "wipe its behind," so to speak; a rustic expression, a tad vulgar even, but entirely fitting. Some had vented their grudge so zestfully that they ended up having a hard time cleaning up. What consumed most of my energy in 1985, however, was *The Transformer,* my second novel after a gap of thirty-two years.

The novel was inspired by childhood memories. In preparing for the novel, I found them inevitably to be limited and incomplete. For a story that begins in China under the Japanese occupation, you would have to include the resistance movement, hardships under foreign occupation, and the clashes of various forces in times of war. Then there was also the theme of memory itself—the emotional entanglements and pain. One recurring image from my childhood was that of empty rooms; the rooms I had lived in, the bed unmade, warmth lingering. I left in such a hurry a long time ago, without a proper farewell. My soul would not be at ease without tying up all the loose ends with these rooms of yore.

I have come a long way, taking on immense responsibilities and committing to undertakings of significance to the Party and the nation. But for a lengthy period earlier on, matters of importance had nothing to do with me. In truth, nobody was destined to be a CCP member and to have great things in store for them. I wanted to revisit my past, put it in order, or at least bid it a proper farewell. If such a work proved less than epic, or not even a proper novel, so be it.

The urge to write was powerful, in spite of my positions at the Central Committee and *People's Literature.* I started my research at the Beijing Library, poring over faded newspapers and microfiches. I found publications from the Japanese occupation era and the postwar years prior to Liberation in 1949—*Xiao shi bao* (Little Facts Daily), *369 Pictorial, Ping Ming Daily* and the *World Daily.* I read about people in long queues outside a porridge kitchen in bitter winter cold, Japanese collaborators rallying in support of the bombing of Pearl Harbor, the start of the Pacific War, and the execution of Yoshiko Kawashima, a Manchu princess who became a Japanese spy. I found reports, which I used in my novel, about the "fourth campaign to enhance law and order" launched by the occupation regime, with one of its slogans calling for the "Elimination of Communist Outlaws and Rectifying Thought." Such totalitarian intent had portended its eventual collapse.

I holed up for more than a week in a deserted temple (Xifeng Monastery) in the Western Hills of Beijing in early spring 1985. With the help of Liu Yinnan of the propaganda department of the district government, I set up in a small corner room. My meals were brought in by a stranger. It was bitterly cold and I had only a small coal stove to keep me from freezing. My host gave me coal bricks and wood shavings to coax a fire with. I had learned how to keep a fire going when I was a child.

I wrote with abandon from dawn to dark. I had calluses on my knuckles and my back ached due to nonstop writing. I would write as many as fifteen thousand words a day. This was faster than copying text, for, when copying, you are slowed down by looking back and forth. Words poured forth, as I lost myself in immense sorrow and anger. No matter how fast I wrote, I could not keep up with my thoughts and the flashbacks of memories, the soaring and plunging of emotions. I was more like an actor on th stage: murmuring lines of impassioned dialogue, words flying like fury. I had never written in such an excruciating manner.

While snow was still in the shaded corners, tender weeds were peeking out of crevices in temple walls. During the day, there were a couple of construction workers working on temple restoration. There were also occasional visitors who stayed overnight in two others rooms. I would really have enjoyed a chat with them. Not speaking to anyone for a whole week was tough. I surprised, if not scared, myself. I had not thought it possible to work in that derelict room in self-imposed isolation for so long. I had thought that I would go mad in prolonged confinement. It is a weakness in the Chinese character, at least one of mine: an aversion to solitude; a compulsive urge to seek companionship, finding meaning and gratification only in communal life. In the West, however, single-person dwellings are everywhere.

I felt increasingly comfortable with the novel. All that was needed was some revision, expounding, and tweaking to finish the book. I took a two-week break over the summer, staying in an army sanitarium in Dalian, to polish the final draft. It was an old building in disrepair, with many rooms and a basement. Some of the windows and doors worn by age were left ajar. Wind came through; the creaking of doorjambs and birds chirping broke the erie silence now and then. The silence was broken by birds' chirping. There was the ever-present smell of disinfectant (this being a sanitarium) and of some strange incense burning. We had a few blackouts at night when thunderstorms hit. However, the haunted old building was a godsend. In the phantom echoes of the past, in urgent winds and pelting rains, I found myself back in an era of nearly half a century ago. There I was, with youthful optimism, intense concern for the motherland, and a yearning for a better tomorrow.

The other characters in the novel—people of my parents' generation—did not have the faith, confidence, and hope that I had. Their fleeting lives were filled with hardship and sorrow, loss and despair, suspicion and jealousy, hatred and pain. There was no forgiveness, no consolation.

I came to understand that solitude, sorrow, and sense of loss are conducive to a necessary state of mind for writing. People relishing companionship and with dogged faith and overconfidence are not ready for literature. They can be easily distracted by life's many temptations, and cannot possibly endure the arduous journey of writing, cannot abandon themselves to a world of imagination and words, of sparks of association and flights of fancy.

I sent out my manuscript upon returning from Dalian. I had thought about using the title *Deserted House*. The images of empty rooms in my childhood had been etched in my memory, always evoking a sense of loss and pain. Still, this did not fully capture the essence of the novel. I thought about using *Punishment* (which was the title for its Japanese edition published by Hakuteisha of Japan). Again it did not seem to fit. I eventually chose *The Transformer*, which I remembered was the name for a Japanese toy in my childhood, *karakuri ningy* in Japanese.

The ending of the novel was not satisfactory. I found it impossible to wrap it up. I passed judgment in the novel on my fellow countrymen, people of my father's generation, my home village, my family, and myself. I wrote about apathy and misunderstanding, envy and hatred, the animosity and meanness of perfectly decent folks. I told everyone: People, how ugly, sinful, witless, and pathetic you all are. In the end, however, I forgave everyone and cried my heart out for them.

Such were the days of the spring and summer of 1985 when I worked on my second novel. I had a feeling then that such a pure literary existence would be no more.

At a seminar organized by the publisher, Liu Xinwu coined the Chinese phrase "father-judging complex" when commenting on my novel. This was picked up by venerable writer Liu Baiyu when condemning the errors of the Fourth Writers' Conference. He said with scorn that there were people in literary circles who wanted to condemn their fathers. By extension, this meant condemnation of the revolutionary forefathers, which was quite menacing. In fact, the father character in the novel was not a revolutionary. Nor did he even want to be.

The Transformer was one of my most influential works, with its Italian, Russian, Japanese, English, Korean, and German translations being published. It was included in the *Modern China Library* series. When it came out in the Soviet Union, the first print run was 100,000 copies, which were quickly sold out. In early 1989, when Eduard Shevardnadze, the Soviet Foreign Minister and later Georgian statesman, visited China,

I was at the dinner hosted by his Chinese counterpart. Shevardnadze mentioned my novel and I joked that I was considering if I should switch to writing exclusively for Russian readers, as the first printing of its Chinese edition was only 29,000 copies in paperback plus a small quantity in hardback. Of course, after several rounds of reprinting in China, this was no longer the case.

A Western reporter (I cannot recall if he was with the Associated Press or some other media organization) asked for my thoughts when he compared me to Shostakovich. I told him China was different from the Soviet Union. (I remember Hu Qiaomu once commented that China had been ideologically better prepared for revolution than Russia was. I believed he meant Chinese intellectuals were more motivated for revolution.) I told him flatly I could not be compared with Maestro Shostakovich. I then raised my doubts about the authenticity of Shostakovich's memoirs being published by a Western publishing house. It has a passage describing the Kremlin's special facilities for people to wash their butts and change, as those summoned could be so scared of Stalin that they shit in their pants. Such exaggeration diminishes the credibility of the memoirs.

I commented with a sigh that a writer who joined the revolution would be praised as a martyr if he ended up being executed. If he survived and became someone of a certain standing, he would then have to endure all sorts of opinions and judgment. The literary world disdains the blessed and successful. There were those in China, and perhaps more outside China, who were bent on proving that the good guys had all perished in China, and that those "in official favor" (a phrase used by the reporter which, or at least in its Chinese translation, I detested) had to be the bad ones. They believed this to be true not only historically but also in the present. "In or out of favor" became a yardstick. Why such an appetite for hatred?

Such discussions were never pleasant. But Wang Meng was himself, and simply could not be likened to a Russian or an American. He could not be the kind of intellectual or martyr they expected him to be. But in fact he had been through trials and sacrifices. He had a track record; what did those critical of Wang Meng have? Wang Meng could have only taken the path of his choice rather than theirs. He joined the revolution when he was barely out of short pants. He was an idealist when it came to revolution. He had stumbled along but never renounced his convictions. He could only side with China, his vast, barren but endearing motherland, and its people. He would side with Chinese intellectuals and cadres, all pillars of society, who were committed to a good cause, and with friends who understood and wished China well.

These reporters came with a set of criteria which were not mine and by which they judged me inadequate. With their pitiful intellect and limitations, they could only accept an intellectual who was a nonconforming rebel. But Wang Meng had been a rebel a long time ago. He was even a member of an underground organization, intending to be a career revolutionary. But you cannot not be a rebel forever just for the heck of it. Reconstruction, reform, opening-up, and improving people's livelihood were far more challenging than bellowing out battle cries. Of course, the right to criticize is sacred, and criticism can be full of wisdom and conducive to progress. However, criticism was nothing new to me, and I had endured more than my fair share. Whenever people mention criticism, I cannot help thinking of Uighur farmers in the Cultural Revolution. They had to borrow the Mandarin phrase as there was no such expression in their own language. They also had difficulty in pronouncing certain consonants. Thus, the way they said "criticism" made it sound like "to be stuffed," "to be spanked," or even expletives if they were not careful when saying it. After this deconstructing in Uighur, I could hardly be solemn-faced when people talk about criticism.

What could I do but write? Fiction, *xiaoshuo* in Chinese, literally meaning "minor talk," can include anything unspeakable in solemn-faced "major speech." I wrote a short story called "Fireworks," which was based on my wife's initial ideas and sketches. It was about nightmares, ravens, and her experience of a younger brother's fatal illness that paralleled my own suffering in successive political campaigns. This was followed by two short stories "The Silence of Trees" and "Wind on the Plateau."

Some people are like towering trees: contributors, steady, tacit, and at ease with themselves. Some are like winds that constantly lash at trees to prove their worth. They may even succeed in uprooting trees, but more often than not their attempts fail. Then there are those dependent on trees: birds and butterflies; bugs and mites; lovers and loggers. Trees are noble with unspoken qualities and natural virtues, which I am determined to emulate. In contrast, we are often surrounded by too much pretention and hubris; resentment and jealousy; pettiness and indecision.

Two decades later, one young artist did a series of paintings based on "The Silence of Trees." He already had an exhibition of these paintings and will have a book published later.

"Wind on the Plateau" is about an intellectual's soul-searching and regrets. I admire people's courage and capacity for self-criticism. A publishing house in New York liked this story for its Soviet era feel, and its English translation was included in a collection of my short stories it published in 1993.[2] Such is the magic of literature in bridging cultures.

I became a personality defying categorization. All these descriptions could be true and fitting: I was dedicated to literature. I sat on the CCP Central Committee, genuinely commited, for a whole decade. I continued to write prolifically. I worked with a strong sense of duty and diligence in my assigned official capacities. I tried to play a positive and conciliatory role.

Who am I? I am no Solzhenitsyn, Milan Kundera, Alexander Fadeyev,[3] Konstantin Simonov,[4] Pyotr Pavlenko (the informer),[5] or Vsevolod Kochetov[6] (who had fond memories of Stalin), or for that matter, any other noble or notable Chinese writer. I can only be what I am; I can only be Wang Meng.

---

2. See *The Stubborn Porridge and Other Stories* by Wang Meng, trans. with an introduction by Zhu Hong, New York: George Braziller, 1994.
3. Alexander Fadeyev, 1901–1956, Soviet writer, one of the co-founders of the Union of Soviet Writers and its chairman from 1946 to 1954.
4. Konstantin Simonov, 1915–1979, Russian / Soviet author, known especially as a war poet
5. Pyotr Pavlenko, 1899–1951, Soviet writer, screenwriter for the film "The Vow," and war correspondent.
6. Vsevolod Kochetov, 1912–1973, Soviet / Russian writer and cultural functionary.

Chapter 48

Mexico City and West Berlin

At the end of my second U.S. visit in 1982, I traveled on to Mexico City and spent a week at the College of Mexico at the invitation of Flora Botton Beja of its Center for Asian and African Studies. Mexico was a thriving developing country. In the capital, downtown streets were congested and people thronged the sidewalks. Construction was going on everywhere. I felt oddly at home. I heard the infamous quote upon my arrival: "Poor Mexico, so far from God and so close to the United States!" It was in fact a world apart from the developed countries such as its neighbor to the north.

I visited the National Museum of Anthropology and was overwhelmed by the display of relics of ancient Mayan rituals, the instruments for disgorging human hearts for the worship of the sun. What dark impulses does such a bloody rite reflect? At the time, Chinese scholars were fixated on the inherent good of human nature. I thought that we must also recognize its darker side. How did this ancient people conclude that the sun's flame would wane, without a ready supply of human hearts in homage?

I attended a roundtable with writers from Mexico, Argentina, and Chile. It was to be the main event of my trip and was scheduled for June 17. However, it had to be postponed to June 21, as police closed down the college after receiving a tip about a time bomb ticking away somewhere in the building. As a result, an Argentine writer did not make it.

The theme of the roundtable was "Realism and Reality." The organizer explained that as this was a very broad topic, participants could talk about anything that interested them within its loosely defined scope. Flora Botton Beja was the moderator. She was feisty, gregarious, dashing here and there, wearing several hats: director of the China program at the Center, chief editor of a women's magazine, and radio host of a weekly program on topics about women and China. Thanks to her passion and enthusiasm, a collection of six short stories of mine was translated into Spanish within two months by Sinologists and Chinese students at the College. She distributed copies at the roundtable and the collection was later published in Mexico.

As it turned out, the roundtable was focused on my writing. There were five panel speakers, and it was open to everyone who was interested. There were about fifty attendants, including a former Mexican ambassador to China.

The discussion centered on two topics.

The first was my claim that I wrote for the people and for their benefit. Some in the audience questioned if Shakespeare thought about writing for the people when he contemplated his plots. They asked how I would define the abstract notion of the people. I replied that all good literary writers have great compassion for the people and sympathy for their misfortunes and sufferings. They rejoice in their joys and give expression to their aspirations. Of course, not all writers recognize this to the same degree, and some have insisted that writing is personal and refuse to admit their creative work has anything to do with the people. However, the intertwined relations between literature and the people, literature and society are a fact, not lessened by any writer's protestation. Chinese writers are perhaps more aware of this and readily admit they write for the benefit of the people. There is also nothing abstract about the notion of the people. The toilers in farm fields and on factory floors— everyone, including us, are the people. However, a girl in the audience disagreed. She said that Mexico, unlike China, had never had a revolution in the real sense. None of them in the audience was "the people"; they were merely members of the petty bourgeoisie.

The second topic was raised by a Mexican writer who found my novels somewhat depressing. This was echoed by a woman writer who said it was only natural because sorrow outweighed happiness in life. The Chilean writer Valdivieso disagreed and said Wang Meng's novels were full of faith in revolution and socialism, and his conviction that Chinese people were capable of solving their own problems.

I pointed out that the human condition is multifaceted and so are our emotional responses. I said happiness and sorrow, despair and struggle, success and setbacks are often intertwined. On balance, I am an optimist and full of conviction. Meanwhile, I am also a realist and recognize the challenges and problems we face in reality. Life's sorrows do not always come in battalions. I felt warm contentment and elation, not a hint of sorrow, as I was in the company of my appreciative Mexican friends. I also urged people not to make too much of the pessimistic, cynical, despairing feelings conveyed by writers in their writings. Indeed, those who imparted profound sadness leaving their readers in despair were not themselves prepared to take fatal amounts of sleeping pills any time soon. In fact, they might even be quite smug about the condition of their own life. The audience broke into laughter. Later I would often use Goethe's *The Sorrows of Young Werther* as an example when being asked such questions. The novel reportedly led to many an attempt of copycat suicide, but Goethe himself of course did nothing of the kind. He lived a long and passion-filled life, and even contemplated, at the age of eighty, the prospect of marrying a young woman. He was a rarity among writers, living a full and copious life into ripe old age.

The discussion touched upon the impulse of revolution, which excited me. When that girl in the audience claimed she felt unqualified to be a member of the people, had she been longing for a real revolution such as the one that China had gone through? It seemed indeed that revolutionary impulses and the inevitable disillusionment, which some Chinese scholars advocated in their "farewell-to-revolution" musings, were universal. I said at the session that revolution was the noblest and most sacred of human impulses. I did not elaborate then, as I would if I had thought more on the topic, that such noble aspirations could lead to rationality and eventual triumph, but could also result in irrational outbursts and hasty actions. More importantly, when victory is won, wisdom and rationality; harmony and moderation should prevail.

Many came up to shake hands and asked for my autograph at the end of the session. A local radio station asked for permission to read my stories on one of its programs. Such a warm reception was something I did not encounter in trips to America and Germany. I reminded myself that I was now in a third world country, the same as China. There was an affinity, and I was probably preaching to the choir. But it was nonetheless a delightful and gratifying trip overall.

My second visit to Germany was to the Horizon Arts Festival held in West Berlin. It was dedicated to showcasing arts and culture from the Third World countries. West Berlin at the time was an enclave within socialist East Germany. Khrushchev once referred to it as a cancer. In the early years after China established diplomatic relations with the Federal Republic of Germany, Chinese visitors avoided going to West Berlin, which was not recognized as part of West Germany by the socialist bloc.

In 1984, prior to our visit, the organizers sent a representative to China to discuss our participation. They especially wanted to have me there. However, the Writers' Association desisted, at first saying I had already visited Germany and other writers would be grumpy if I should go again. At the time, overseas travel was deemed a privilege and a perk. A compromise was made eventually: more than half of the invitees on the German list, including me, would be allowed to go, if the organizers also invited and paid for delegates recommended by the Union. I was to head the delegation, while writer Bao Chang would serve as deputy leader. The group included poet Fang Bin,[1] literary editor Liu Jianqing,[2] writer Xi Rong,[3] and Huang Zongying.[4] There were also younger writers such as Zhang Jie, Zhang Kangkang,[5] Shu Ting, Fu Tianlin,[6] Bei Dao, Kong Jiesheng[7] and Zhang Guofeng.[8] Huang Zongying, being a celebrity, was recognized by the cabin crew shortly after takeoff and upgraded to first class.

1. Fang Bin, 1914–1997, Chinese poet.
2. Liu Jianqing, 1927–1991, poet and literary journal editor.
3. Xi Rong, 1922–2001, writer of short stories and novels.
4. Huang Zongying, 1925–, film actress, documentary filmmaker and essay writer.
5. Zhang Kangkang, 1950–, Chinese writer.
6. Fu Tianlin, 1946–, Chinese poet.
7. Kong Jiesheng, 1952–, Chinese writer.
8. Zhang Guofeng, research fellow in German literature with the Institute of Foreign Literature at the Chinese Academy of Social Sciences.

It was in the early days of China's reform and opening-up and there was a prevailing sense of celebration. Everyone in the group was in a boisterous mood. The world also welcomed China's reform. West Germany seemed to have published more contemporary works of Chinese literature than any other European or North American country. Michael Kahn-Ackermann, the German translator of Zhang Jie's novel *Leaden Wings,* won a translation award at the festival. Professor Wolfgang Kubin of Bonn University organized several half-day panel sessions on my writing. Professor Martin Woesler talked about my short story "The Strain of Meeting" and Professor Rudolf Wagner discussed my short story "The Vagrant Son." Wolfgang Kubin commented on my "The Eyes of the Night," and the Chinese editor Liu Jianqing provided an analytical review. However, Kubin was criticized in the local paper, which derided his lack of literary sensitivity to translation. This caused him some consternation. Academics in Europe also have their woes.

Professor Kubin invited us to his home for Austrian porridge. It was cooked with different grains and nuts which made it somewhat like *la ba zhou,* a traditional Chinese porridge served on the eighth day of the month before the Spring Festival. We also visited Günter Grass at his home in West Berlin. This was the second time I saw him. He had a well-stocked cellar and seemed to have substituted water with wine altogether. He had a knack for drawing and there were several framed ink drawings of his, mostly sketches of animals, on the hallway wall. One was a snake with its reared head drawn in his image. He was a member of the German Social Democratic Party and we talked about our respective political involvement. He first visited China in early 1980. He wrote about being overwhelmed by the human multitudes at evening rush hour in Shanghai.

We met Pai Hsien-yung, a Chinese-American writer. Pai's father was Bai Chongxi, a former defense minister of the Nationalist Government in the 1940s. I had known his father's name when I was still a student in the pre-liberation years poring over newspaper stories of the war. Pai was pleased to see us. Zhang Jie noted his brightly colored shirt and joked about having one like it. Pai did not seem to mind and said he would swap his with Zhang Jie's.

We visited Lübeck, Bochum, and Bonn after the festival. German author Theodor Storm, known for his novella *Bee's Lake,* was said to have grown up in Lübeck. I did not know much about the novella but I liked the nice sounding rendition of its title in Chinese. It was a poignant story of two people sharing a childhood dream of a life together but eventually drifting apart.

I wrote "Organ Music in a Church in Lübeck":

Pulling the door closed,
I shut out the grief of—
Rock 'n Roll.
With the organ in the shadow,
A choir's angelic song
Soaring like rising stars.
Honest man
With polemic thoughts,
Hides a devilish farce.
I raised my glass,
Asked for lemon, please.
Will God play tricks?
I, who have forgiven,
Seek no forgiveness in return.

Chapter 49

Dialogue with Western Writers

The forty-eighth PEN International Congress was held in January 1986 in New York. Lu Wenfu and I received invitations to attend as special guests.

The organizers requested participants to prepare presentations on two topics. One was "The Writer's Imagination and the Imagination of the State" and the other, Cross-Cultural Dialogue. The first topic was mandatory. As Lu Wenfu chose the second topic, I had no choice but to tackle the first. Even today, I am still somewhat perplexed as to its exact meaning, having consulted many experts on the English language. I put together a draft commenting that the incongruity that if the government's imagination were imcompatible with reality there could be disastrous results, while the opposite would be by welcomed by all, including writers. A case in point was China's reform and opening-up. Wenfu talked with me about his paper and included some of my suggestions.

The organizers sent us complimentary return tickets and we flew on PanAm. Wenfu was particular about what he drank. He brought his green tea and declined all beverages served on board. When the meal was served, he fished out a mini bottle of Chinese liquor, to the amusement of cabin attendants.

We took a taxi from the airport to the St. Monica Hotel following the instructions of the organizers. I did not quite expect the yellow cab to be so dirty and the ride so bumpy.

We were given a stash of invitations and an elaborate program and asked to sign a copyright waiver upon our arrival. The last was for our talks and presentations at the conference. We were also given breakfast vouchers and cash to cover out-of-pocket expenses ($2,000?). The organization was efficient and the support staff kept to a minimum. We were left very much on our own. We could opt to attend conference sessions or chose to be absent. The same went for dinner parties and book readings. I thought then if such a conference were to be held in China, there would be a large secretariat, not to mention all the support staff for interpreting, transportation, catering, liaison, and newsletters.

Due to Secretary of State George Shultz's appearance at the opening ceremony, we waited outside in the cold to go through security checks for his keynote address in the auditorium of the New York Public Library. As soon as Secretary Shultz got started, some American writers began to heckle. I saw the Russian-American writer Grace Paley, whom I had known in Iowa in 1980, take off one of her shoes and start pounding on the table. When reading about Nikita Khrushchev's pounding the podium with his shoe during his infamous tirade at the U.N., I had wondered why, of all sartorial tidbits, he chose to use a shoe. Now it seemed this was a tradition.

I had no clue what the fury was about. I was later told that the Columbian writer and Nobel laureate Gabriel García Márquez had been denied a U.S. visa because of his association with Fidel Castro and his anti-American stance. Norman Mailer, president of PEN American Center and moderator of the session then spoke about his disgust at the conduct of his American colleagues. This of course caused yet more uproar.

I met my old friend Gunter Grass again, as well as Claude Simon, who had just won a Nobel Prize in Literature, and the hugely popular South African writer Nadine Gordimer. She began her talk by declaring, "Governments have no imagination." Her supreme confidence and moral superiority brought a round of applause.

I noted one speaker, Vasiliy Aksyonov,[1] whose novel *Ticket to the Stars*

---

1. Vasiliy Aksyonov, 1932–2009, Soviet and Russian novelist. His *Burn* and *Generations of Winter* were published in the West.

depicting the life of confused youths in the Soviet era I had read as a negative example of Soviet literature back in Beijing in the "Western Hills Reading Sessions." He talked about his disillusionment as an exile living in the United States. As soon as he finished, Gunter Grass rose to rebuff him, saying that the gentleman wanted us to be back into the Cold War. Aksyonov's humiliation was palpable.

My talk at the conference was ridiculed in *The New York Times*. It reported that all writers at the conference criticized and slighted their own governments, except Wang Meng, who was smug about his relationship with the government.

Judith Shapiro challenged Lu Wenfu, hinting that his script had been reviewed by Wang Meng beforehand and that his conduct in the United States was subject to Wang Meng's scrutiny. She had studied in China and was married to Liang Heng, an activist from Hunan who had been involved in the student movement of 1980. Her logic and presumption were at once naïve and fallacious. She was apparently indignant as if she had a scoop, some dirty secret. Lu Wenfu explained that as Wang Meng was a fellow writer and friend, it was only natural for us to share thoughts and compare notes, which was entirely different from what she had presumed. Professor Donald Stone, who had taught in China, also spoke about Wang Meng's contribution to Chinese literature and liberalization. He criticized Judith Shapiro for her provocation.

What could I say? American writers flaunted their pride in being free from, indifferent to, and morally superior over, government officials. This was indeed something Chinese writers were not very accustomed to. One woman writer with a Taiwanese background pointed out in her writing that the extent of freedom American writers enjoyed was unnerving to writers from China.

How should I respond? The best perhaps would be to say we were just different. One German writer once asked me how we could have survived all the hardships and turmoil. He said if he were to go through the same, he would have either killed himself or gone mad. His comments reminded me of empathy and putting myself in another's shoes. If I were an American writer, I would have felt extremely lonely and unfulfilled. In China, writers indeed lived eventful lives, be they good or bad, so much more than their Western counterparts. They even received letters from amorous fans, though I hasten to add that I had been somewhat of an exception. Some of my women colleagues concluded that the acid tone and political sentiments of my writings might have scared off many a potential overture.

Talk about a rebel heart and fighting for freedom, I had not only been a critic of the government, the Nationalist Government that is, but had risked my life in the struggle for its downfall. In new China, I had paid a personal price for my writings that were deemed critical of the government. What right had those gum-chewing writers of the free world to dismiss Wang Meng's applause for the highly imaginative policies of reform and opening-up adopted by the CCP leadership? What had they done and what price had they paid?

I wrote "To A.W. and in Reply to the New York Times," which was printed in the *Wenhui Daily* in Shanghai.

Chewing sweetened gum,
You heckled Secretary Shultz.
But "shush!"
You have more divorces
Than marriages,
You flash your banner of freedom
As if it were your new Chevrolet
or sleek stereo.
Now I know you are smug,
Yet you do not know my trials.
My underground activism,
All strife with no sugary gum.
But the court of special prosecution (of the Nationalist government to persecute student activists);
A gibbet was no imagination.
Victory turned sour;
A historic mistake
For one decade and
Yet another
Weighs heavy like the un-melting snow on the Tianshan Mountains.
Then today,
I embrace the blissful today,
And look forward to tomorrow.

I do not smoke pot and do
Cherish my wife.
Shaped differently by our experiences,
We need
Understanding,
In addition to a freely dispensed
"Thank you!"

Lu Wenfu was invited to dinner by a Chinese playwright who wrote the screenplay for the famous 1950s' film *Five Golden Flowers.* She stayed behind in the United States, after an officially approved visit and never returned. After the dinner, she asked Wenfu to sign the receipt, so she could get reimbursement from a political refugee organization. Wenfu was outraged and paid for the dinner instead. When he recounted this, I laughed at his little misadventure. Wenfu was always nice to everyone, which sometimes put him in an awkward corner.

I was asked by the *Nation* magazine to write an essay for its commemorative issue for the 210th anniversary of American Independence. I wrote "Things I Like About America": the Golden Gate Bridge, the cathedral in Boston, fiery maple foliage in the fall, and the song "The Way We Were." I wrote about the peculiar American accent and the highway grid. I wrote about its people's generosity, free spirit and intense interest in the new and untried. I concluded that if Americans could have a better sense of both their accomplishments and their limitations ,they would be even more endearing. I showed a copy of this essay to Anna Chennault;[2] she was full of praise.

I had also been asked if great literature was possible in China given its current political and social environment. I told my audiences it was my hope that China's political and social environment would continue to improve, and writers would have more and more freedom to write and earn more. I hoped more good things would befall Chinese writers. However, this did not mean there would necessarily be great literature. How did great writers like Cao Xueqin come about? Was it because

2. Anna Chennault, 1925–, widow of Lieutenant General Claire Lee Chennault, who directed the "Flying Tigers" to airlift military supplies into China to aid Chinese efforts during WW II , and an Asian-American politician of the Republican Party.

the Qing dynasty and Cao's living conditions then was so conducive to literature? What did Cao Xueqin mean by "my family lived on nothing but porridge and my wine was often bought on credit"? Could the Russian literary achievement at the end of the nineteenth century be attributed to Tsar Nicholas II's magnanimity and support of literature? Persecuting writers and sending them off to Siberia were more his thing. But of course, when things degenerated into such a horrible state as during the Cultural Revolution, when the very safety and lives of writers were in peril, literary creativity became unthinkable.

In so saying, I was trying to defend new China. I did not think it appropriate to politicize literature and a writer's worth and hold government accountable for the nation's literary achievement or the lack of it. But I had not imagined even such comments of mine could be attacked by the left in China. They accused me of downplaying the Party's leadership and attributing a writer's accomplishments only to their own creative impulses and the little acts of writing. They might just as well praise the Party for the literary success of Cao Xueqin, or the great eighteenth century writer Wu Jingzi, or even Tolstoy and Ivan Turgenev for that matter.

We had seen too much insanity, self-inflicted isolation, and paranoia. When I tried to communicate with people who knew little about China, trying to win their empathy, respect, friendship and valuable advice for the country, what I feared most were not foreigners' challenges and prejudices. With our cultural heritage, wisdom and historical knowledge, I could handle any outside challenges with ease, be they from politicians, celebrities, anti-communist diehards, or other adversaries. No, what I feared most were those ill-meaning compatriots and attackers from the rear. They would take your remarks out of context and compile incriminating reports based on untrue or incomplete coverage by the foreign media. They would submit these to leaders higher up the ladder in an attempt to destroy you and make it impossible for you to engage in cultural dialogue or maintain friendship with foreigners. Yet, those who harbored dark thoughts were incapable of cross-cultural dialogue. They would fail miserably at the moment of truth.

Before leaving the United States after the PEN conference, I bought a window mounted air-conditioner, a Westinghouse product. It was midnight when I landed in Beijing. The customs officer first requested duty payment for the air-conditioner. He then asked if I was the writer Wang Meng. I nodded and he simply waved me through. This too was China: writers were so respected that rules were sometimes bent. This window unit made a lot of noise but not much cool air. It thrummed like a locomotive whenever it was turned on. It did provide some relief from the sweltering summer heat for my apartment for a number of years. Then, I took it down and installed it in the farmhouse I bought at the Eagle Nest Village of Huang Song Yu Township in Pinggu District, outside Beijing. It lasted a few more years before its useful life ended, unlike most home appliances nowadays that are disposed of too soon for technology upgrades.

The young man who sold me the air-conditioner was filmmaker Xie Jin's son. He had moved to the States a little earlier and ran a small appliances store. I couldn't forget what he told me: Do you know what I miss most about China, Uncle Wang Meng? It's the political study sessions. We always had a roomful of people sitting around, smoking, dozing off, flipping through the papers, grumbling about corruption in the country at large. You could sneak off half an hour before your shift ended but still got your full day pay. What a deal!

Chapter 50

Becoming Minister of Culture

In early 1986, I was abruptly asked at a social function by an American journalist, "Are you going to become the next Minster of Culture?" I replied, "That would be terrible!" I did not know if it was my poor use of English that caused her to look befuddled. Humor was intended.

Word had gone out about a search for a new cultural minister, and various names came up. In May 1985, shortly after I returned to Beijing from the Berlin Horizon Arts Festival, I was asked to go to a meeting at a senior CCP leader's office on a Sunday. Others at the meeting included Tang Dacheng, Xu Weicheng, and Yu Shizhi, a stage actor and head of Beijing People's Theater. The leader got down to brass tacks right away and asked for recommendations. We tossed up some names which included Gao Zhanxiang,[1] Xu Weicheng, He Jinzhi (deputy director of the Propaganda Department of CCP Central Committee), Ai Zhisheng (newly appointed Minister of Radio, Film and Television) and Li Yan (either a secretary-general or a deputy director of the Propaganda Department). The senior leader was unmoved and made comments as to their unsuitability. Then all of a sudden he said, "What about any of you?"

Upon this everyone acted as if stunned. Modesty and pretension kicked in. Yu Shizhi in particular shook his head as if to dodge an invisible slap and whined, "Nah, nah . . ." It sounded like either "cannot" or "no good" in his mumbling. We all chaffed.

---

1. Gao Zhanxiang, 1935–, poet and former Vice Minister of Culture.

Then came a day in the early spring of 1986 when I was watching a screening of *The Gourmand,* a film based on a novella by my dear old friend Lu Wenfu, in the old ill-equipped auditorium in the sprawling compound shared by the Ministry of Culture, the Party's *Red Flag* magazine, the Federation of Literature and Arts Circles, and the Writers' Union. I was totally engrossed and smiled when the gourmand snubbed his matchmaker when she pitched how pretty the girl was, "A pretty face won't make a delicious dish!" Just at that moment, a staffer found me in the dark and whispered that I was wanted by the CCP Central Committee Organization Department.

So my candidacy became formal. I was alarmed. Although I had been invited to many high-level meetings and seminars and had collected a few impressive titles since my return to Beijing, I had never dreamed of being in charge of a government ministry. All I had hoped for was a role in enhancing the dialogue between the Party and writers, making useful recommendations, advocating rationalism, and mitigating the impact of ideological struggle. I had never imagined the role of being in charge, handing down decisions, taking on bureaucratic responsibilities, and always having the final word. I had declined the role of Party secretary of the Writers' Union—how could I even consider leading a government ministry? I went around asking for support. I told them I was still in my prime as a writer. Being a senior official in the government would be too painful for me. I had been deprived of the opportunity to write and publish in the past two decades. What a tragedy it would be if in the next two I would be kept from doing what I wanted most to do.

What I could not say out loud was: Why would I care about being a minister at all? To be on the receiving end of all the complaints and accusations? To be trapped in the "cultural circle" known for its bickering, vicious strife, and character assassination? I remember a conversation in the controversial memoirs of Shostakovich. It was between him and the party secretary of the Soviet Musicians' Union. The latter was quoted as saying "You think things at our Union are bad? Then look at the Writers': they could eat each other alive!"

Such internal strife could befall you in spite of yourself. When you are provoked and an arrow is aimed at your throat, can you stay aloof and pretend you don't care? Perhaps just for once you may want to find out who was behind the attack. Yet, once you get started, there is no easy exit. You assemble your allies and cronies while your attacker gathers his. Thus factions are formed, and you become an unwitting ringleader. You seethe with rage and your weak spots are exposed. This then wreaks havoc in your gut and affects your well-being. I shun those who are deft at internal feuding and inept at open dialogue. I recoil at the prospect of such strife, not out of ineptness, but because it is demeaning.

I called on Hu Qiaomu and Hu Qili[2] and asked Zhang Guangnian to petition Qiao Shi[3] on my behalf. Such a petition to dodge rather than seek a promotion was rare. I know that Zhong Renfa, chief editor of *Writers* magazine, had managed to extricate himself from a pending promotion. Another example is Huang Youyi of the China Foreign Language Publishing Administration. He declined a promotion to be its director-general. He stressed that he was after all an officer with functional expertise. I admired them both.

I was then asked by a senior leader at a meeting of the Secretariat of the CCP Central Committee in 1986. I explained that the good impressions the Party seniors had of me were due to the positive and reconciliatory role I had played as a writer. But if I were to be appointed the head of a government ministry and therefore had to deal with routine government matters, all my inadequacies and limitations would become apparent. I would end up loosing my credibility. What good would that serve?

Hu Qiaomu voiced his appreciation. He said he was personally acquainted with Wang Meng, who was speaking the truth. Hu's endorsement only solidified other leaders' opinion about my appointment. Xi Zhongxun, secretary of Central Committee Secretariat with responsibility for personnel and organization matters, summoned me for a talk. He was firm and urged me to oblige. He indicated that if I were still not prepared to accept the appointment, then a member of

2. Hu Qili, 1929–, member of the Politburo Standing Committee and Secretariat of the CCP Central Committee, stepped down in the reshuffle of the centeral leadership in the summer of 1989 and later was appointed to a lower post in the government as Minister of the Electronic Industry.
3. Qiao Shi, vice premier (1986–1988), member of the Politburo Standing Committee. Chairman of the National People's Congress (1993–1998).

the Politburo standing committee or even the secretary general of the Party might be the next to talk to me. He said I could continue to write and need not be too hands-on in administrative matters. I could always delegate those to my deputies. At the same time, being a minister could also be advantageous to writing, he added. He did not say if this meant a team of assistants and ghostwriters. Maybe I did not hear him correctly; he probably was not talking about writing novels. At the time, Party leaders and senior officials did not regard literary writing as a personal pursuit but rather an undertaking in the service of the Party and the people.

My wife did not like the prospect. She much preferred a simple life without my involvement in officialdom. She supported my resolve to write more. My daughter thought I did not look like a government minister at all. She was in senior high school then and had her own view of what a senior official should be like. She even had a codename for minister which is 1-3, like "Do Mi" in musical notation, by which she meant growing no taller than 1.3 meters in height, "not growing" [*bu zhang* in Chinese] being a homonym for minister. My son, on the other hand, thought that I should consider accepting, as this was a big deal and meant glory for the family.

The outcome of my conversation with Xi Zhongxun was that I should be prepared to serve as cultural minister for three years, which would allow the central leadership time to identify a suitable successor. I was somewhat dismayed. When I bumped into the writer Ye Nan, he said, "You are on the altar . . ." I knew this was his way of offering congratulations, or at least his words were not to be taken literally.

It was time for the annual session of the National People's Congress; Zhang Xianliang, Feng Jicai, He Shiguang and Ye Zhongmin, a well-known journalist with the *Ta Kung Pao* in Hong Kong, visited me at home. They insisted on knowing if rumors about my appointment were true. I tried to dodge their questions. Yet, Zhang Xianliang put words in my mouth, "a CCP member will always obey the Party's decisions." All this later came out in the Hong Kong paper. Feng Jicai told me that whenever he was asked by his overseas readers for his opinion, he would say Wang Meng was first and foremost a writer, a true writer at that. I appreciated that.

From a junior officer of the Youth League, to a budding young writer, a condemned *rightist,* a salaried writer, then a member of the CCP Central Committee, and now a member of the cabinet as Minister of Culture, I had come a long way. I could not say I was free from conceit, being tempted to feel smug about my "meteoric rise." What gave me satisfaction, however, was not the appointment to a certain government position, but rather the way it was bestowed on me, in spite of my protests. I knew so many who would expend great efforts in seeking certain appointments or opposing the same for others. Some would even proclaim they had been considered for this or that, a claim that nobody could verify. They would whine and even trot off to faraway lands when their efforts came to no avail. Feng Jicai's wife once talked about the three writers she knew well: Wang Meng was like the wise man Nasreddin Afandi in Xinjiang folklore—mirthful, regaling us with his tales while having everything going his way. In contrast, the second writer madly pursued official appointments and was inevitably disappointed. Zhang Xianliang was like a raffish outlaw—on the lam with his loot and woman.

Two years earlier, when I became editor-in-chief of *People's Literature,* there was an invitation from the French president François Mitterrand to Ding Ling and me to visit France. The Writers' Union did not inform me until some time later. They reasoned that given the appointment at the magazine, I should not turn around and hop off to France. They decided to send Liu Binyan instead. I had visited the United States in 1980 as a substitute for Liu Binyan. So our scores were settled over this "substitution" business. But I heard then that the French side was none too happy and thought me disrespectful.

In 1986, I received an invitation to give a series of lectures on Chinese literature at a university in Los Angeles. With the looming ministerial appointment, the visit would again be out of the question. I had to make adjustments to my life and my travels. Why couldn't this appointment happen five years later? At least till after I had a better grasp of English? Apparently I did not have everything going my way as I wanted. Had it ever?

In April 1986, I was named secretary of the Party Core at the Ministry. In June, at a session of the Standing Committee of the National People's Congress, my appointment as Minister of Culture was officially confirmed.

Right before I moved over to the ministry, my colleagues at the Writers' Union organized a farewell. I remember what Zhang Qie, then a member of the Secretariat of the Union, said to me. He declared that some words of encouragement were in order: One needs the power of high office to accomplish anything of significance in China; fret no more and just get on with it! I cannot recall his exact words but that was the gist. It certainly sounded like something from the popular song titled "Sis, Brace Yourself and Hit the Road" He was surely speaking from his heart.

I lived close to Tao Ran Ting Park where my wife and I often took long walks. At the time, the National Ballet and the Academy of Folk Operas were both nearby. I knew that once I took office, I would have a responsibility for these organizations, too. I had been living in their vicinity for three years but never thought that one day my work would be linked with them. I thought about the artists that I had been privileged to know and felt a special sense of affinity. I knew the beauty of the ballet, the theater, and music. Would I do them a service or would I end up only being their inadequate advocate? I remember an old army veteran sayng to me, upon hearing of my appointment, that a cultural minister would be judged favorably if his decisions did not end up causing harm to culture. Was he being sarcastic?

It is interesting to note that writers had been appointed Minister of Culture before. However, the ministry was in fact concerned first and foremost with the performing arts. Next down the list were the visual arts. Accomplished performing artists became stars; a few of them were even granted political privileges and a seat at the Chinese People's Political Consultative Conference. There was unending rivalry and bickering among artists, too. Most at that time they were unhappily living in cramped apartments and earning a paltry allowance of thirty cents for each performance in addition to their fixed salaries. Things have of course improved beyond imagination since. But at the time, they had to resort to ingenious means and appeal to senior officials for help to get more spacious lodging. Some had, out of despair, simply opted to leave the country. It was a time of great change. Artists began to regain respect and popularity. All of a sudden, I became related to these interesting characters, each with an impressive and strong personality. It was an odd union— a writer and a motley collection of renowned artists, but I felt I had known them for eons.

On my first day at the Ministry, my chauffeur, Zhang Shouzhong, came to pick me up. I stopped by at the Writers' Union, which was in the same compound, to collect a document. When I came out, the car was still waiting to take me to the ministry's offices, which were no more than a hundred yards away. The two organizations were disbanded during the Cultural Revolution, their offices taken over by other organizations. Now they were both squeezed into a compound formerly used by the Propaganda Department. The Writers' Union was housed in makeshift buildings constructed out of metal sheets after the massive Tangshan earthquake and did not move out of them until the 1990s.

I gave much thought to my first all-hands meeting with departmental heads. I invited former ministerial leaders, including former vice ministers Zhou Weizhi,[4] Lin Mohan, and Chen Huangmei. They were influential personalities that had occupied leadership perches at the Ministry for decades, commanding respect not merely because of their titles but also for their accomplishments. I stressed the need for evolutionary change. I borrowed the economic notion of "steady long-term growth." This became my approach: using concepts of socio-economic development and political affairs when talking about culture and arts. I made it a point to approximate editorial statements of the *People's Daily* and refrain from using cultural and arts jargon. I proposed maintaining the momentum of reform and of opening-up, upholding all de facto policies and guidelines. Problems should be dealt with on a case-by-case basis as they crop up, without resorting to constant policy overhauls. My goal was to maintain the stability of policy framework and not to change the established direction.

I felt my inaugural talk was appropriate, down to earth, and focused on critical points. It was commended by some senior CCP leaders after they read a post-meeting report. My approach proved better than making reactive and frequent adjustments to policies and guidelines. Zhou Weizhi was very positive about my respect for retired ministerial leaders. Lin Mohan grabbed my hand and said, "This must have been overwhelming

4. Zhou Weizhi, 1916–, songwriter and former Vice Minister of Culture; Chairman of the Chinese Federation of Literature and Arts Circles (2001–2006).

for you!" I believe he meant well. There were also ludicrous criticisms denouncing my approach as maintaining status quo and protecting the privileged.

At an anniversary celebration for *Chinese Literature,* which was published by the Foreign Languages Press, I was greeted with loud applause. I told the audience I rather hoped that I could get some cheers for what I had done when I exited the stage of my ministerial career.

The writer Lu Tianmin[5] delivered a missive, which read like a letter of condolence. He lamented that the only writer he had high hopes for was no more. The most intriguing letter was from Zhang Yu, a writer from central Henan Province, asking me to write an introduction for a collection of his short stories. He had been warned by others that Wang Meng was now a big cheese and had no time for writing introductions. He wrote that he refused to believe such nonsense and that a mere minister's hat was no big deal and should not affect Maestro Wang's literary ambition in the least. He sure knew which buttons to push. Flattery and exaggeration was his way of persuasion. If I refused him, I would be admitting my failing as a literary man. I obliged with a hoot of laughter.

I was summoned to a meeting of newly appointed heads of the cultural, media, and propaganda departments. We were billed as leaders for the transition into the new century. I felt the weight of obligation and a prolonged journey. So we had to remain at our jobs all the way into the next century.

A friend sent me a magazine published in Hong Kong which carried an article by Professor Ma Sen, a playwright from Taiwan, with his good wishes for the new cultural minister. Ma Sen was an alumnus of my high school. Back in early 1949, he had applied to join the southern expeditionary force of the People's Liberation Army before he was forced to join his family fleeing the mainland. We parted ways.

In May, I was invited to attend a forum on children's literature in Yantai organized by the Writers' Union. I had my first taste of pampering reserved for government ministers. I traveled on to Jinan and Qufu afterward. While in Qufu, I bumped into the Chinese-American scholar

5. Lu Tianmin, 1943–, Chinese playwright.

Tung Ting-shan,[6] who later wrote that local folks at Confucius birthplace saluted the newly appointed Minister of Culture with firecrackers. This was, however, untrue. The firecrackers were for a businessman's dinner party that evening. I regarded Mr. Tung as a friend. It was regrettable that even such a friend would report untruthfully on my first days of being a minister.

While in Yantai, I stayed at a guesthouse by the sea. Summer was yet to arrive, and the beach was deserted and quiet. I was touched by the serenity of the calm, empty sea. Before, I had always been at the seaside in the busy summer holiday season. I penned the following poem:

Thoughts adrift to the vast ocean
of yesteryears;
I swam in your wrath and sorrow.
A thin tidal line
Dividing continent and ocean
Along unexpected convergence.
I longed to be close,
So I can gaze on you,
Be embraced and sing your praise,
But never touch your depth.
Your murmurs and silence,
Your being, fluid and magnanimous,
Constant, too, as nothing diminishes you.
Sunrise strikes gold,
Moonlight stirs compassion.
Wind enrages you,
But always
In the great depth an untouched calm.
Like a child's dream without start and end.
You are unfazed
By the glories to your name.
Towering waves and plunging troughs,
Your immensity,
In endless ebb and flow,

6. Tung Ting-shan, 1922–2015, Chinese-American author, translator and literary critic.

Like furrows of an old man's face,
Sorrow in a young man's heart,
And muted sighs after one more praise . . .

The poem reflects Wang Meng's sentiments in 1986 when he was swamped in accolades and glory, and feeling smug about it, too. But there were also "dividing," "unexpected," "untouched calm," "wrath and sorrow," "silence," "fluid," and "praise, sighs." This is the "haughtiest" poem that I ever wrote, and I am still touched reading it today.

Chapter 51

Imperatives Galore

I soon settled into the routine of a minister's work. Every morning I would find documents stacked high on my desk requiring review, approval, or otherwise. Most concerned plans and budgets, construction projects, and ministerial events. Fewer than half related directly to culture and arts. Decisions on personnel issues, budgeting, and assets often put to the test one's knowledge and experience. I was big on delegation, with clearly defined roles and responsibilities for everyone, empowering them to solve their own problems. You could always criticize, penalize, or demote those who were not doing a good job. But you'd better not give direct instructions as to how their job should be done. Such an approach had many benefits: (a) not having to keep my nose at the ministerial grindstone; (b) junior cadres and established processes being given due respect; (c) no undue initiatives that a new minister is often tempted to launch; (d) building consensus and avoiding conflicts and confrontation.

I adopted a consultative approach in the ministry's Party Core, too, rather than deciding everything by vote. I would bide my time if any vice minister had reservations. It was customary for all in the leadership team to respect the opinions of the minister. Unless you were outright unreasonable, you usually could get your way. Things you opposed could at least be put on hold. The key is candor and devotion, rather than playing tricks or hiding things up your sleeve.

I also realized that various departments within the ministry had been functioning with established procedures for decades. You were limited in what you could accomplish even though you were the head honcho. Before long, I was faced with some knotty problems. One was a controversy over the film *Remote Mountains* in which two men, simply put, swapped wives. The film, which was nominated for best film of the year, was based on a novel by Jia Pingwa about conflicts both between and within two farming families against the background of rural reform. In one family, the husband was entrepreneurial and pro-reform while his wife was conservative. The other family was the exact opposite. Their rivalry and conflicts saw no end until the two men swapped wives. Such realignment brought harmony and prosperity to both families.

One senior leader was apparently unhappy about the film. I was asked by him to watch and comment on the film, although by that time the film industry was no longer in my portfolio. The film had been nominated for an award, but plans for an award ceremony were put on hold. I managed to see the film in a private screening, and then what? I decided to sleep on it. This was also one of Chairman Mao's tactics: let hot potatoes cool off. I then drafted a report to the effect that the film first of all had a positive theme in praise of rural reform. The novel itself, written by an accomplished author, had won critical acclaim. In the film, however, wife swapping became the focus, which had caused mixed reviews and reactions. I went on to say that being nominated for best film did not imply the film was perfect. Awards given by the jury were no substitute for public opinion. Award-winning films could still be criticized to encourage debate and future improvement. My last point was in fact inspired by similar comments made by Zhou Yang. I asked Vice Minister Gao Zhanxiang to put his signature on the report as well before submitting it to the senior leader. I did not want the spotlight on me only. The report was reviewed by the senior leader, and the case was thus closed.

There were also repeated efforts to arrange a concert tour by the Taiwanese pop singer Teresa Deng, who enjoyed a large following on the mainland. One newspaper even reported a telephone conversation with her, fueling further speculation. However, senior leaders differed on whether such a tour should be allowed. One was opposed to it, while another was all for it. Yet another said this should be left to the ministry to decide. None of these opinions could be ignored. One municipal cultural leader also threw himself into the fray, saying if the ministry could not decide, it could turn the matter over to his city.

My response was to seek clarification first. I wanted to know how it had all started, before landing in the lap of the ministry. I asked for all the files and found it was all a result of media speculation. There had never been direct contact between the singer and any mainland performing arts agencies or government departments responsible for Hong Kong, Macao, and Taiwan affairs. No one had met with her to talk about a tour. The singer herself had never formally indicated an intention to perform on the mainland. No proposal had ever been submitted to the ministry. Therefore the debate was pointless. The ministry had no intention or need to invite the singer, let alone to decline or ban her tour. There was no need to do anything until (a) the singer indicated an intention to tour; (b) a mainland performing arts agency was willing to sponsor such a tour. It would then be required to submit an application before which the ministry had no need even to consider such a matter.

The seeming problem that had bugged everyone did not even exist! I wrote a memo stating this fact and proposed a suspension of any further discussion and media reports. The memo was circulated among senior leaders who all felt happy about it. That put an end to the saga.

However, I could also tackle a problem head on. A couple of months before I reported to work at the ministry, a ban on commercially operated dance halls and discothèques was jointly issued by departments of propaganda, culture, industry and commerce, and public security. One young writer once told me that guards would patrol dance venues to nip in the bud any hint of canoodling among dancing couples. This sounded medieval. At one meeting, I heard Vice Premier Wan Li commenting on the necessity of dance halls and other entertainment venues to cater to people's needs. I decided to reverse the ban after I took office. I ordered an investigation and was told the reason for the ban was a concern about hooliganism and promiscuity. I pointed out that these would be easy to deal with: law enforcement agencies could conduct inspections, even dispatch uniformed guards to keep order or send undercover agents for sting operations. I added that having dance halls might even help track down the hooligans if they indeed tended to congregate there.

Such sarcasm helped me push through the policy reversal. Dance halls were hence legalized nationwide, with one provincial exception. The people's congress of that prosperous province in south China, otherwise quite open, adopted a decision in early 1987, after the reform-minded Party Secretary General Hu Yaobang stepped down, not to implement the policy legalizing commercial dance venues. That decision has not been officially revoked to this day. But it has long been rendered irrelevant. In fact, now there are just as many commercial dance venues there as anywhere else. But it did show the difficulty in accomplishing anything in China. The seemingly tame matter of dance venues had been subjected to changing policies and local resistance spanning decades. Many years later, the writer and critic Huang Miaozi wrote in a Hong Kong newspaper that as Minister of Culture Wang Meng had been decent to people, but he was short on any notable accomplishments. I protested when I saw him. When he asked what I had actually done, I gave him the example of reversing the ban on commercial dance venues.

I courted failure on another matter. There were quite a few retired scholars and senior ex-officials on the ministry's payroll who were regarded as authorities in their respective fields. I had a high regard for them and decided to hold regular sessions to hear their views. However, these sessions inevitably turned into collective condemnation of contemporary culture. In fact they were so outraged at the current state of arts and culture that they insisted that something be done lest revolutionary culture be doomed. Their bombastic voices roared in the ministry's conference room, as some of them had been trained for the stage. As it went, I had to say something. Otherwise, I would be seen hosting sessions to condemn contemporary arts and culture. Yet my comments only spurred further condemnation. The sessions led nowhere.

My successors have done the smart thing by doing away with these sessions. They would invite the retired scholars and senior ex-officials to an occasional dinner but were never foolish enough to encourage them to air their views. The motley bunch of bombastic old souls in the ministry's conference room became a thing of the past. Had I been too by the book? These people who had long since retired from positions of power liked to think their opinions still mattered. They were inclined to grumble self-righteously as if they were members of a shadow leadership team—they were incapable of harm, though.

My appointment also aroused the interest of the young and aspiring, some of whom requested an audience with the new minister. I tried to accommodate such requests, allocating no more than three quarters of an hour for each visitor, the duration of a school class. Visits by several women artists who were offspring of notable cultural personalities left a deep impression. An artist who was also a social activist asked me bluntly, "Do you genuinely want to be a good minister?" I said I would try my best to do a good job. Not missing a beat, she said, "If you are for real, then you must . . ." do this, take that approach, and create a new language. From the imperative of being a good minister to a new language, it was such a leap of imagination. I could only marvel at her unusual logic and reasoning.

A descendant of a notable artist proposed an all-encompassing new organization covering talent management, creative work, show production, ticket sales, promotion, and marketing. She seemed to have done a bit of research for her proposal, but I suspected her proposed enterprise would look much like a parallel ministry of culture, a department of arts, or a duplicate Federation of Literature and Arts Circles. How would it reconcile with the current structure? Reform was supposed to be improvement proceeding from present conditions, not creating everything from scratch.

There were also direct appeals to me for solving problems of all sorts. Once, an award-winning artist came to me. He had received an invitation to a music event somewhere in Latin America but could not find a sponsor to cover his international airfare. I could not help him either. The ministry, like any other government department, operated with an itemized budget. I could not change it on a whim and siphon off money for anyone who requested it. I simply could not put away a few grand for the sake of desperate artists who might need it.

Then there was also the problem of the housing shortage for ministry employees. I would get letters or instructions from very senior leaders regarding housing allocation for certain notable artists. I asked around and found that the ministry did not have spare housing units earmarked for those with special background or patronage. I could only respond by saying that I would try my best.

A senior leader whom I admired a great deal instructed me through an intermediary that I should focus on solving the housing shortage problem. If I made this my top priority, everything else would fall into place. I could only favor the messenger with a polite nod. Another former leader pointed out that guards at the ministry's front gate were too stern, as if guarding a garrison command. He suggested I should see to having the situation changed. Apparently, he was the people-friendly type. Again I could only acknowledge his suggestion but could not think of any alternative to the existing security arrangement.

My approach was to focus on what I should do while recognizing what I could not accomplish or change. You only know the limitations to your power when you are in possession of it. When you look afield from your perch, you see everyone else is either more senior or more experienced than you are. They have better connections or more powerful patronage. You run up against hallowed precedents and practices. Many things are already spoken of or subject to long established procedures. Inevitably you come to the realization that amid the billion-plus populace, scores of millions of card-carrying CCP members, and thousands of ministerial ranking officials in China, how infinitesimally insignificant you can be.

Chapter 52

Yes and No, Minister

Once, when he happened to be in the ministry, Liu Binyan asked me, "How does it feel?"

To begin with, you command respect and your words matter. Unlike at the Writers' Union, my instructions and comments were recorded, delivered to the intended recipients, and put into action. For years, I disliked the word "deploying" for getting arts groups to Beijing to perform. They were not cargo or troops that you could deploy. In the past, I had voiced my dislike but nothing happened. Now, I said it again and "deploying" was soon changed into "being invited by the Ministry of Culture" to perform in Beijing.

Another problem was that many graduates from arts colleges opted to leave the country upon graduation. This was a matter of public education costs (college tuition was paid for by the government at the time). Arts training cost the country much more than liberal arts and science studies did. I instructed that a procedure be developed requiring all who received state-sponsored arts education to fulfill a contractual obligation of service. My idea became administrative policy and stopped the exodus of arts graduates, some of whom were from influential families. I even censured a vice minister who granted favor in this context at the expense of the public interest.

In 1988, Gao Xingjian received an invitation from the German Academic Exchange Service (DAAD) to spend six months or longer in Germany as a painter-in-residence. He had visited Germany as a writer at the invitation of DAAD, whose sponsorship rules allowed only one visit per recipient. So DAAD bent its own rules and Gao now had a different designation as a painter. The officers at the Bureau of External Relations of the Ministry who were reviewing his application were befuddled. They agonized over how he had become a painter and were unable to come to a decision, stalling approval. When this was brought to my attention, I told them since the Germans recognized him as a painter and would cover all his travel expenses, why should we rack our brains over it? Everyone should be allowed to travel overseas as long as they were not involved in any criminal or civil litigation, serving a prison sentence, or in possession of important state secrets. The Bureau's mandate was planning exchange programs, not evaluating professional credentials. The English word "painter" did not imply any level of attainment as in its Chinese equivalent. It could even mean a painter of walls. Gao was soon given permission to visit Germany. But he never returned. Did I do right or wrong?

I have heard that Gao Xingjian's ink and wash paintings sold well, particularly after he won the Nobel Prize in Literature. Regrettably, to this day I have never seen any of his paintings.

Dilber Yunus, who later became an internationally renowned lyric soprano, was at the time a graduate student at the Central Conservatory of Music in Beijing. I took an interest in her as she was a Uighur from Xinjiang. I first met her in 1986 at the inauguration of the China International Exchange Association officiated by Ambassador Li Yimang.[1] I talked with her in Uighur, which surprised her. She was quite miserable because of her folks' opposition to her proposed marriage, as her fiancé was thought to be non-Uighur. I talked with Isma'il Ehmed, Minister of the Commission on Ethnic Affairs, also a Uighur, and we both signed a letter attesting to her fiancé's ethnicity. I then asked Saifuddin Azizi, former chairman of the Xinjiang Uighur Autonomous Region, to proclaim their union. I happened to be on a trip in Britain at the time of her wedding. I asked Vice Minister Gao Zhanxiang to offer congratulations on my behalf. I still feel good about doing all this for Dilber.

---

1. Li Yimang, 1903–1990, former Chinese ambassador to Burma and Deputy Head of International Liaison of the Central Committee of the CCP.

In August 1986, I visited Tibet for the first time to attend the Shoton Festival. It was a land of majestic mountains and an enchanting culture. The skies were so clear that they took on a jade-like quality. Towering monasteries clung to precipices and prayer flags fluttered in the highland winds. Everywhere there were people chanting and praying. I wrote a long poem "Tibetan Thoughts," which was published in the *People's Daily*. It was translated into Italian and won the Mondello Special Prize of International Literature.

In Lhasa, I got to know the soprano Tseten Dolma, who became famous for her deeply moving rendition of Tibetan ballads such as "Sing a Song for the Party" and "On the Golden Mountain of Beijing." I cared very much about this serf-turned-singer. When I learned that she lived in a cramped apartment, I talked with Wu Jinghua, Party secretary of the Tibetan Autonomous Region and filled him in on how the late premier Zhou Enlai had commended her. Tseten Dolma soon saw her living conditions improve, being appointed vice chairman of the regional People's Political Consultative Conference, a vice-minister-rank position that entailed better housing allocation, when the incumbent's term was up. A similar arrangement was later made at my urging for Paxia Yixian, a well-known ethnic singer from Xinjiang.

There were also occasions when my opinion was simply ignored. At a gala performance in honor of a visiting head of state in a small auditorium of the Great Hall of the People, I found the sound deafening. I had just read an article by the folk opera singer Xin Fengxia, who criticized the extensive use of sound amplification, saying it would destroy the folk-singing tradition. I commented on the problem several times and even wrote essays about it, but to no effect. I remember another occasion when two singers were about to sing an opera duet, a senior person barked, "Add a mike!" Technology brings convenience as well as destruction. This has been proven true in arts.

The Chinese National Academy of Arts, an entity under the Ministry, employs a large number of scholars and researchers on Chinese operas, music, and the arts. It also has institutes dedicated to the study of the arts from around the world, the Chinese classical novel *Dream of the Red Chamber,* Marxist art theories, and Chinese culture. I followed a recommendation by Su Yiping, Party secretary of the academy, to invite

Li Xifan from the *People's Daily* and Feng Qiyong, a professor of Chinese literature at Remin University, to head the academy. Even though Li Xifan had openly criticized me in the 1950s, I did not let personal vengeance got in the way. I detested unforgiving infighting and cronyism. Li proved an honest and conscionable man, though some of his views were conservative. He was surely beyond pettiness and opportunism. He was later urged to join those condemning me, but he stood his ground.

Luciano Pavarotti toured China in 1986, though the arrangements were made well before my tenure at the ministry. I took great interest in the tour, nevertheless. I said at the welcoming dinner I hosted at the Great Hall of the People that true art was without borders and Pavarotti belonged to Naples, to Italy, to all humanity, and by extension to China. Such a novel comment later became a refrain in remarks by my lieutenants on similar occasions.

General Secretary Hu Yaobang, who had just returned from a visit to Italy, invited Pavarotti to a luncheon at his residence in Zhongnanhai. Chinese singers Liu Weiwei and Peng Liyuan were also invited. A visit to Lijiang was added at Hu's suggestion after an exchange of superlatives about Guilin and Italian scenic sites between Hu and the Italian ambassador. Hu Qili, then the Politburo member responsible for culture and the arts among other things, also instructed the ministry to move Pavarotti's last concert in Beijing to the Great Hall of the People. The concert was a gathering of dignitaries and luminaries in the capital and became a highlight of the tour.

Pavarotti was excited, too. He went to the Great Hall of the People for acoustic testing and tried his hand at a set of ancient bronze chimes, unearthed from a site dating back twenty-two hundred years and now in the collection of the Palace Museum, i.e., the Forbidden City. He played the notes of "O Sole Mio" on the ancient instrument. He came on stage and exited, waving a white handkerchief, which added an air of elegance to his broad-chested frame. His soaring singing filled the cavernous hall. Listening to him, you felt you were being lifted by glorious music of great compassion, like an ocean swell. Everyone, faces glistening, was in blissful exultation. "O Sole Mio" was followed by an encore of the more romantic "Return to Sorrento." I was touched. In Pavarotti's singing, you sensed the wonder of life, the immensity of the universe, and a compassion for creatures great and small. You sensed the youthful vigor of Europe. As Minister of Culture and moreover as a member of the audience, I was immensely satisfied. It was one of those once-in-a-lifetime events.

Pavarotti was followed by Plácido Domingo. I was personally involved from the start and had a spirited discussion with the Spanish ambassador in Beijing about Domingo's tour. Given financial constraints then, we could not pay the usual performance fees and full international fares for touring artists. What we offered as the local sponsor was to cover all expenses once they were in the country. However, the Spanish ambassador requested the Chinese side to cover the international airfares for Domingo, his accompanist, and an agent as a gesture of Chinese hospitality and sincerity. I immediately concurred and offered to fly all three first class. We would also prepare special souvenirs to show our respect and friendship. I proposed that the ministry and the embassy hold a joint press conference to announce the tour. The ambassador was utterly pleased and agreed on all points. A little over a decade later, a concert by the three tenors in Beijing would command performance fees in the hundreds of thousands of dollars, which was a reflection on how far China had come.

A dozen years later, Domingo met the Spanish Ambassador again in Shanghai during another tour. This was the ambassador's second tour of duty in China (after his first in the 1980s). The reunion brought back fond memories, and Domingo added a paragraph thanking me in his message for the program.

In the 1980s, the Chinese People's Friendship Association with Foreign Countries proposed a concert by the Spanish-American singer Julio Iglesias in the Great Hall of the People. Given that he was a pop singer, I was uncertain if it would be appropriate and hence disapproved the proposal. Nowadays, such a consideration is no longer warranted. But I believe careful thought should be given to what type of performances are appropriate in what venue. In retrospect, I am not sure if my decision against the Iglesias concert was appropriate. I had bought Julio Iglesias' tapes when I was in the United States and liked his passionate singing. His song "To All the Girls I've Loved Before" evoked romantic feelings by its mere title.

In contrast to the tours of the two tenors, the visit by the renowned Italian author Alberto Moravia did not go quite so well. Moravia was born in 1907. He refused to collaborate with Mussolini during the war and was expelled from Italy. He published seventeen novels, twelve short stories, ten plays, and ten collections of reviews and travel writings. He was in the vanguard of new realism in Italian literature, and his *Racconti Romani* (Roman Tales) depicted hardship and alienation in the lives of the common people. He had also served as the president of PEN International. At the time of his visit, he was already in his eighties but showed a keen interest in China's reforms. He had hoped to meet China's senior leaders and write a book about China. However, his wish was not granted. Some speculated that it was his admiration for the classical Chinese novel *Carnal Prayer Mat,* professed in his meeting with me, that blew his chance. They believed that because of his favorable view of a novel deemed pornographic and banned in China, China's leaders refused to meet with him.

The truth is the State Council had a policy at the time regarding senior leaders' meetings with international visitors. Eligibility was limited to visiting officials above a certain rank and top honchos of multinational businesses, but not cultural personalities. The ministry tried unsuccessfully to get a meeting for the British violinist Yehudi Menuhin. After I was appointed minister, Menuhin would send me a card every New Year with a recent photo of him and his wife. I drafted a report to the State Council proposing adding accomplished cultural personalities to the eligibility list. This was later affirmed in principle.

I heard that Moravia was dismayed after his China visit. I made it a point to have the cultural office of the Chinese embassy in Rome send greetings and a bouquet of flowers to Moravia on my behalf every time I passed through or stayed over in Rome. I never heard from him.

I served in the cultural ministry for exactly three years and five months: from April 1986 through September 1989. To this day, the ministry has been taking care of me in many good ways. The leaders both current and past and staffers have treated me kindly. I feel indebted.

A short poem I wrote then was included two decades later in the commemorative issue for the fiftieth anniversary of the *Poetry* monthly. The poem was titled "A Traveler's Inn":

All you need is a key
Which one?
A random pick or by destiny?
With the code in steel
You enjoy a bottle of champaign or a feast
No questions asked.
Softer than love,
With soothing colors and tone,
The silent street below and foaming sea afar
Many mirrors and a lonesome you.
Can you endure the pampering,
Outdoing the comfort of home
Fussing like a cat's claws?
The solemn face of an elevator door
Swallows you and your haul,
And spits you out, bags and all.
No farewells and doors close,
So goes every traveler.
A hastily told story,
A strange but cordial world.
It belongs to you
Till time is up and out you go.

I wrote this poem in 1988 while still on the job as minister and doing reasonably well. I wrote about fatalism, random chance, manipulation, being pampered, many mirrors, one individual, solemn-faced elevator, no farewell—"doors close," "strange," "hastily" and time being up . . . feelings of a transient traveler; life of a minister.

Chapter 53

Swept Up in a Storm

In November 1986, about six months into my minister job, I attended a conference organized by the Writers' Union. Participants were mostly international scholars on Chinese literature, including Professor Göran Malmqvist from Sweden, Professor N. Fedorenko from the Soviet Union, as well as those from Britain, France, Italy, Japan, and Australia. The conference had been in the works for a long time, pending official approval by the Ministry of Culture. After I took office, the approval was soon granted.

The conference venue was in the Baoshan District of Shanghai. I insisted on attending as a writer and staying in the same hotel with all the participants. I asked Vice-minister Liu Deyou, whose portfolio covered international affairs, to host a reception at its closing. All logistics and planning, including the guest list, were handled by the international liaison office of the Writers' Union. One problem was a funding shortfall. Deng Youmei, head of international liaison at the Union told me that their budget was barely enough to cover accommodation and meals for formal delegates. Many journalists came, however, either having been invited or inviting themselves. Some writers brought along their own media friends. The Writers' Union was hard put to accommodate all, particularly at official dinners and receptions when per-head costs were high. So it was proposed that journalists be served meals at a separate venue, albeit at a lower cost. I did not raise objections to this arrangement, which proved disastrous. Journalists in China had to be treated well for their dedicated reporting.

Thus, following the welcome dinner from which journalists were barred, a storm was brewing. Some reporters came knocking, demanding an answer. My assistant failed to turn them back, and I had to come out of my room. I told them I was tired and what they came to discuss could be left to the following day. I became agitated after they refused to budge and quickly lost my temper and almost yelled at them. It was a fiasco.

There was also irony here. Government officials were urged to be close to the people. I had thought that, being one of them, I should stay at the same hotel with everyone, but almost ended up in a scuffle with reporters who'd been rubbed the wrong way. Had I behaved like a big shot, things would have turned out quite differently. I would have uttered nothing but words lifted from editorials of the *People's Daily.* I wouldn't even be seen except for a short appearance with a few remarks at the opening ceremony. Nor would I have opened my door to whomever came knocking and bothered myself with matters such as costs and guest lists for dinner—I could have passed the buck to the Writers' Union.

I realized you could not afford to antagonize anyone. Not journalists, nor anyone else: CCP leaders could determine your career future; shop assistants, the quality of your service and purchases; postman, the timely arrival of your mail; drivers, the safety of your transport; and journalists, your very public image. I was reminded of the saying I first heard in Xinjiang: a grain of sand can blind you; a small rock can cripple you. I must submit to Chinese conditions. I was a senior cadre now. As a French proverb goes, there are two titles, once acquired, you carry for life: minister or prostitute.

I must admit I had been unduly influenced by Western ways, having been to a few conferences overseas. Everything was so straightforward in pulling off a successful symposium: a professor with a bit of funding would be all it needed. He could be helped by his wife or partner. Costs would be kept to a minimum. Participants were advised in a written note as to what organizers would cover and what they would have to take care of by themselves. Journalists would make their own arrangements. But in China, there would have to be teams of people dedicated to liaison, security, transportation, logistics, publicity, etc., who may number as many as half of the delegates. The fiasco in Shanghai was caused by the lack of a capable media relations team. In China, you have to do it the

Chinese way. The minimalist Western approach was destined to fail.

In the winter of 1986, there was student unrest in several cities. Such unrest had occurred every time someone began talking about "democracy" in internationally defined terms. These stirrings would invariably end with someone in the leadership who started the talking being forced to step down. (I had no intention of opposing democracy. On the contrary, I wished there could be more and better democracy. However, I must also tell the truth: I did not want to see unintended damage.)

In January 1987, Hu Yaobang resigned as General Secretary of the Party.[1] Everyone in the Party and government departments relating to culture and ideology was shocked. I couldn't fathom why ideological strife could still be so intense after China had come a considerable way in its "reform and opening-up." You were never too far from the danger of being deemed extreme left or right, or being accused of supporting feudalism, capitalism, democracy or other ideologies. New ideas abounded: a socialist market economy, privatization, homogenization, and psychological complexes. Some were imported from Europe; all were relevant to and had a bearing on mankind and the fate of China. Then there were also the notions of literature being a playful pursuit, a "mad dog innovation" (in the words of writer Zhang Xinxin, the urge to innovate haunting us like a mad dog), a global village and even a breathy style of singing. They could all brew controversies and trouble. The 1980s was indeed an era of ideological strife and controversies.

In early 1987, there was a rumor that I might be replaced at the ministry. Oddly, by then I felt I wasn't ready to let go. I had been in my job not yet a full year; there was still much to be said and done. I did not intend to be a short-lived minister. I wanted to test China's possibilities in cultural development. I was encouraged by one incident. I was told someone had submitted two of my recent essays to the country's paramount leader (Deng Xiaoping), one of which was on Marxism and

1. When widespread student protests occurred across China in 1987 demanding more liberalization and democracy, Hu was criticized for his "laxness" and tolerance of "bourgeois liberalization," which was thought to have either led to, or worsened, the protests. Hu was forced to resign as Party general secretary, but was allowed to retain a seat in the Politburo.

published in *Dushu*. The other, a discussion of "let one hundred flowers bloom and one hundred schools of thought contend," was printed in *Red Flag* magazine. Those that submitted the essays could well have harbored some ill intention. Yet, Deng commented "well written" after reading them. Admittedly, the statements I made in those two essays were debatable. There was nothing extraordinary or profound about them. The fact that they did not bring me ill fortune in those eventful days of early 1987 showed that the country had indeed come a long way.

By the summer of 1987, things had settled down. I reflected on what had transpired and by now was ready to leave my ministerial position, preferably right then. Rather than causing others to toil over collecting evidence against me, I could vacate my perch voluntarily. I went to see Wang Renzhong and asked him to make my intention known to the Party's leadership. I told him it would be best for me to go back to writing. Wang only said it was "good thinking," but nothing followed.

While serving as the minister, I initiated China's first ever National Arts Festival. When the idea was first proposed, it was met with objections left and right. At a session of the Chinese People's Political Consultative Conference, one revolutionary elder criticized the notion as creating false festivity. This was quite vicious; as such an accusation had been used in the past to denounce dishonesty and frivolousness and to imply sinister intent.

I asked Xu Shiping, secretary to the Party Core of the ministry, to draft a commentary on the arts festival, which was published in the *People's Daily* in the early summer of 1987. It pointed out that proper policy direction was necessary for the flourishing of arts, but it needed to be supported by vigorous programs, or else it would be empty talk. We also sought help from Deng Lin, an artist-in-residence at the Institute of Chinese Painting and daughter of Deng Xiaoping, to obtain a handwritten inscription of "China Art Festival" by her father. With the endorsement of Deng, the lurking threat vanished.

There was a short description of this historic event in *A Day in History*, created by the National Library of China:

> On the evening of September 5, 1987, the first ever China Arts Festival was inaugurated in the Beijing Capital Gymnasium.

> The opening ceremony was officiated by Wang Meng, chairman of its organizing committee and Minister of Culture. Wan Li, honorary chairman of the China Arts Festival, member of the Politburo and vice premier, spoke at the ceremony. Over three thousand artists from different parts of the country gave stunning performances on opening night.
>
> The first arts festival was dedicated to Chinese traditional and folk music. Over fifty music groups from around the country gave close to 180 concerts in Beijing to 200,000 festivalgoers over the three-week period from September 5 through 24. There were also regional sites for the festival across the country including Shanghai, Wuhan, Lanzhou, Urumqi, etc. UNESCO Director-General Amadou-Mahtar M'Bow applauded the festival, saying "The organization of the first ever arts festival in China, with its ancient history of several thousand years, fully demonstrates the extent of China's reform and opening-up. It will not only have a significant international impact but also greatly contribute to the cultural progress of mankind."

I traveled to Urumqi to attend the opening ceremony for the regional site and was deeply moved by the traditional "Twelve Makams" performed by the Xinjiang Song and Dance Ensemble. Seeing this powerful performance was a rare experience for me. Saifuddin Azizi, the former governor, suggested on several occasions before he passed away that someone should compose a symphony based on "Twelve Makams." I had urged responsible comrades in Xinjiang to follow up. There were some discussions, but no real progress was ever made. I now take some comfort in knowing that "Twelve Makams" has been designated by UNESCO as an Intangible Heritage of Humanity.

That fall, the Thirteenth National Congress of the Chinese Communist Party was held in Beijing. At the time, the situation in Tibet had caught the nation's attention. I invited a Tibetan art troupe to perform in Beijing for the Congress delegates. Many leaders attended. When one leader who was originally from Xinjiang spoke impromptu in Uighur to welcome the artists, I was his interpreter. My years of hardship in Xinjiang benefited me in many ways, one of which was allowing me a good grasp of the Uighur language. The Party secretary of Tibet was impressed and said, "Next time Wang Meng is in trouble, please send him to Tibet." Just as Karl Marx wrote, history repeats itself, "the first time as tragedy, then as farce." Time changes everything. In the words of Confucius when standing by a great river, "It passes on like this, not ceasing day or night!" Never will there be perpetual wailing and whining, or unending festivity or jubilation. Only empathy, compassion, and a knowing smile endure.

Chapter 54

Seeing the World

During the three and half years I was Minister of Culture, from the spring of 1986 to the fall of 1989, I visited many countries as head of the Chinese government's cultural delegations. I took these trips keenly aware of the honor and my obligations, and the experience was also a great eyeopener for me.[1] I also visited every province and all the major cities of Mainland China, as well as Hong Kong, Macao, and Taiwan. I was fortunate to have had such opportunities to see the world and to rid myself of self-conceit, prejudice, ignorance, and gullibility. I felt blessed living in an era of reform and opening-up. I am grateful to all the friends and organizations (mostly Chinese embassies and foreign educational institutions) for their facilitation and hospitality.

My first official visit as cultural minister was to North Korea in October 1986 at the invitation of Jang Cheol, Minister of Culture and Arts. Pyongyang looked squeaky clean, and pine trees lined almost every street. However, there were only occasional vehicles in the street, which would jolt the pretty policewoman into a frenzy of waving her baton.

---

1. Countries and cities visited: North Korea, Thailand, Japan, India, Nepal, Bhutan, Singapore, Malaysia, Indonesia, the Philippines, Vietnam, Turkey, Jordan, Georgia, Uzbek, Kazakhstan, Russia, Britain, the Netherlands, Belgium, Romania, Bulgaria, Poland, Hungary, Switzerland, Greece, Germany, France, Spain, Italy, Austria, Sweden, Norway, the United States, Mexico, Canada, Australia, New Zealand, Egypt, Algeria, Morocco, Tunisia, Mauritius, Cameron, South Africa, Ukraine, Estonia, Lithonia and Iran, plus stopovers in Monaco, the Vatican, Denmark, and Luxemburg.

Local residents were required to walk if distances were within three bus stops, so as to save scarce fuel and engage in exercise at the same time. We stayed in the Korea Hotel, a multistory building with hardly any guests. Chinese-made goods were everywhere. Our hosts' eagerness was heartening. As I stepped off the train, the local leader at Hamhung gave me a bear hug that knocked my glasses off. I also got to know our North Korean interpreter. We called him Little Kim, and his Chinese was impeccable. He told us Korean proverbs and folk stories. One was "*Kimchi* in the kitchen jar next door somehow tastes better." The other was about a skinflint scraping soybean paste off the legs of a fly that had landed on his pickles.

The city of Pyongyang was literally a shrine for the eternal glory of Kim Il Sung, with a North Korean style Arch of Triumph and ubiquitous monuments dedicated to him, and universities and cultural palaces bearing his name. Regrettably, we did not get an audience with the supreme leader. In the following May, however, I had the opportunity of accompanying the visiting Kim at a private gala in the small auditorium of the Great Hall of the People. He gave me a porcelain knickknack with two exquisitely made globes one inside the other. In fact, I had been given the same during my earlier visit to Pyongyang. I also bought a few pairs of chopsticks made of stainless steel which I have not seen anywhere else. Steel chopsticks from South Korea are hollow and light, while the North Koran ones are solid, angular, and heavy.

I visited Thailand in February the following year. My impression of Thailand was a nation with people of disarming kindness and honesty. An official at the Ministry of Education told me he had studied in Britain, married a British girl, and worked for a number of years in America. He now felt like a stranger in his own country. He reminded me of other third world intellectuals I had met and their struggle with cultural dislocation. I strongly believe that overseas education was useful and necessary. However, I had also seen many Chinese émigrés overseas, including those who were successful—becoming tenured professors, owning businesses, making loads of money, and owning expensive properties—feeling like foster children in an adopted home. There was always a sense of being out-of-place. Could this be merely a reflection of my parochialism?

My meeting with Princess Maha Chakri Sirindhorn in Chiang Mai was most memorable. I was advised that the princess usually met foreign visitors for no more than fifteen minutes. I rose to bid farewell when the time was up, but the Princess bid me to stay. I rose again after thirty minutes, but the princess said we had yet to talk about literature. She had a penchant for writing and had published children's stories and travelogs. We talked for nearly fifty minutes before I took leave, not wanting to take up any more of her time. I heard later that she planned to translate my novella *Butterfly* into Thai. Her translation was completed in the 1990s and published by a Bangkok publisher. We met again on each of the Princess' subsequent visits to China. In 2001, she came to study at Peking University for a month and visited me at home. She was an avid learner, and impressed people with her friendly and charming simplicity. We have maintained our friendship, exchanging greeting cards every New Year.

I visited Japan in April 1987 at the invitation of the Japanese Foreign Ministry and the Japan-China Cultural Exchange Association. The invitation was also extended to my wife, who until then had never traveled abroad. I was overjoyed. However, approval for her travel was not granted, though my predecessor had taken his wife on a visit to Japan. Well, circumstances may have changed. The Japanese foreign minister, Tadashi Kuranari, had just been appointed. He was very cordial. At his welcome dinner, he showed me a few rope tricks, and was quite a professional! I realized that there were many ways of building goodwill and enhancing friendship.

The Japan-China Cultural Exchange Association had a leadership team of luminaries. Its chairman, Yasushi Inoue, was stern and self-composed, the artist Higashiyama Kaii was solemn and ceremonial, the playwright Koreya Senda was square and smooth, the musician Ikuma Dan had an air of elegance, and the novelist Tsutomu Minakami was sharp-witted. Another writer, Ryotaro Shiba, later became associated with Lee Teng-hui and his pro-indepenence activities, joined forces with the separatists, and left the Association. He passed away, as have all the others some time later. I feel sadness for their passing.

At a reception during our visit, an elderly Japanese woman approached me with tears in her eyes and said in fluent Beijing dialect, "I lived in north China during the war . . ." Upon hearing her words, my childhood memories flashed back. The alley of my childhood home had Japanese families of men in the occupation troops. Their kids sang a rhythmic song as they played a hand clapping game. At the eastern end of the alley, Japanese music wafted out the low windows. Why did this old lady have tears in her eyes? Did she also suffer during the war? Was there some past that she remembered with pain? How did she feel when China was mentioned now?

In the fall of 1987, I had an opportunity to visit Italy. I traveled to Sicily for the Premio Letterario Internationale Mondello award. We took the southern route via Sharjah and after a refueling stop continued on to Rome. We then flew from from Rome to Palermo, the Sicilian capital. The venerable poet Feng Zhi and younger poets Shu Ting, Zhou Tao, and Ye Yanbin were also invited to the award ceremony. They had to make an additional stop in Frankfurt, as their tickets were purchased by the host organization, which made their journey even more grueling. We all arrived in the early evening, which was well past midnight in Beijing. We were taken straight to a welcome dinner, which seemed to go on forever. There was an almost forty-minute pause between each course so that guests could have time for conversation. However, all the Chinese guests were flat tired, and Feng Zhi groaned in despair, "When is it going to end?" Such was our first taste of Mediterranean hospitality and formal dining. Shu Ting was clever and found an excuse to leave early, saying she needed to take elder Feng Zhi back to the hotel. She grinned cheekily when departing, delighting in my misery. After a while, other Chinese guests also left, leaving only me behind for the sake of Sino-Italian friendship. I sat and dove into the formal courses, finishing up the deserts, cheeses, drinking up the after-dinner spirits, and then black tea and coffee. By the time I rose to make my way to my room, I could hardly move my legs.

The award ceremony at Mondello, a seaside community of Palermo, was presided over by a former chief justice. The Italian cultural minister was there because of my attendance. A representative of the Italian national government appointed to Sicily also attended. I made the following acceptance speech:

> When humanity is bogged down by daily trials, when lust is supported by technology, when strife sharpens human intellect and intellect furthers strife, leading humanity to the brink of self-destruction; when life has become such a hassle that the essence of life is forgotten; when art is overwhelmed by kitschy thrills and exotic colors, will poetry help? Will it save the soul of the modern man?
>
> Poetry is ancient. Poetry clashes with poetry. Even computers can compose verses now. Pathetic poetry!
>
> Before the last of poetry disappears, shouldn't we take another look at poetry?"

I met Doris Lessing at the award ceremony. She won the prize for Best Literature in a Foreign Language, while mine was a special award. The best foreign literature prize had been proposed for me. However, as I couldn't decide if I could attend the award ceremony, it was decided that the prize should be given to Ms. Lessing.

Lessing had lived in South Africa for decades and wrote sympathetic stories of black people's lives. Many of her writings as well as her later work, *The Golden Notebook,* were translated and published in China. Her writings demonstrate a bright and fluid style and have been widely used in school textbooks around the world. Thus, her name is well known among students of English.

She and I were drawn to each other because of our love of swimming. I hit the sack early every night and rose early the following morning. As the hotel was right by the Tyrrhenian Sea, I walked to the beach and swam every morning. Out of security concerns, my Italian host sent a pair of bodyguards (one man and one woman), who were neat in appearance and sparing of words, to provide protection. People who had seen the movie *Godfather* might conjure up scary images of Sicily. However, Palermo was actually a quiet and sleepy town. Unless you were involved in dealings with the Mafia, nobody would bother you.

On my way to the beach every morning, I would see the slender and remarkably fit Doris Lessing on her way to the swimming pool. We bid each other good morning, chatted about the great feeling of swimming in the morning and felt altogether amicable.

I saw her again in 1988 when I visited Britain and invited her and

Margaret Drabble, well-known British novelist, to visit China. When their visit took place five years later, I had already stepped down as minister. They visited me at my humble home to talk about old times. I met with them again when I visited Britain in 1996. Margaret Drabble introduced me at my lecture, praising my "great sense of humor." She also joined Doris Lessing at a welcome dinner hosted by an Anglo-China cultural organization.

For the visit to Britain in January 1988, I was in London as a guest of honor at a publishers' conference. Other guests included Suzanne Mubarak, wife of the Egyptian president, Nigerian writer Wole Soyinka, and Indian Foreign Minister Singh. The conference was followed by a tour of Britain. I met the Prime Minister, Mrs. Thatcher, in the VIP lounge before an opera. She wore a woolen dress of striking blue. She mentioned the names of several Chinese leaders whom she said she knew well. She carried herself with a haughty air, even as she was being cordial. She did have style.

We visited Eton, the public school that had groomed generations of politicians and civil servants. The pupils wore frocks on formal occasions, followed high society etiquette, and had a stuffy manner of speech. On our way to Eton, we stopped to visit a modern art gallery. One particular piece was a screen showing an endless loop of speeches by Mrs. Thatcher, which I did not quite understand. I also met Mark Fisher, shadow minister for the arts, and I talked about reading socialist writings by members of the Fabian Society in my youth. Things that I did in my youth suddenly became relevant four decades later, as I sat with someone of real Fabian lineage in a country where it had all begun!

Ji Chaozhu, the Chinese ambassador to the U.K., hosted a reception in my honor. Former Prime Minister Edward Heath was invited but showed up about half an hour late. I was told that for such social occasions, he would time his arrival, being either punctual or late, and decide how late he should be, in the case of the latter, by the visitor's stature. It was an interesting example of the famed British etiquette.

I also made a few remarks in English when I met with Richard Luce, Minister of State for the Arts. He grunted to his associates, "You didn't tell me he could speak English!" which was amusing. Luce was a slender fellow, articulate and elegant. However, his rash comments on Hong

Kong later earned him criticism by the Chinese side, so I was told.

The most elegant of the group was Sir David Orr, chair of the British Council. His cheerful and disarming manner was most unforgettable. I learned from him what it took to be a gentleman. I had met him before when he visited Beijing with Sir Edward Heath. At the time, Heath was in China at the invitation of Deng Pufang[2] to guest conduct a symphony orchestra in Beijing to raise funds for the China Disabled Persons' Federation. He then went on to conduct a benefit concert in Shanghai, at which Jiang Zemin, then mayor, also conducted a short piece.

During my 1987 trip to Italy for the Mondello literature award, I also met Bertolucci. I had talked with him before over the phone when I stopped over in Rome on my way to Algeria. The call was arranged by Chen Cun, a Chinese actress in Bertolucci's film *The Last Emperor*. Bertolucci was a member of the Italian Communist Party. Both the Italian president and General Secretary of the Italian Communist Party wrote letters on his behalf to Chinese leader Hu Yaobang, asking for support for his film production. Therefore, upon learning I was in the country, Bertolucci, who had just finished postproduction of the film, postponed his trip to London and arranged a private screening for me. The British producer of the film ordered Maotai from a local Chinese restaurant to celebrate. Later, however, I had to answer questions from the National People's Congress for the privileges given to Bertolucci for on-site shooting in the Forbidden City, which was thought to have skirted heritage protection regulations.

Through my travels over the years, I had made many friends around the world and throughout the country, some of whom have since departed this world. People pass away and the world moves on. Just as Confucius had said standing by a great river, "It passes on like this, not ceasing day or night!"

---

2. Deng Pufang, 1944–, chairman of Chinese Federation of Disabled Persons and son of Deng Xiaoping; physically disabled after a serious injury caused by Red Guards during the Cultural Revolution.

Chapter 55

The Wonderful World—A Sequel

I visited Romania, Poland, and Hungary in November 1987. Romania had a certain quaint charm in the era of Nicolae Ceausescu. It was early winter. I saw Caucasian-looking men and women clad in old-fashioned overcoats at bus stops and low-rise apartment buildings everywhere in a city that seemed to have defied modernization. Everything reminded me of the world of Balzac's *The Human Comedy* or those of Cervantes, Dickens, Hugo and Guy de Maupassant, worlds that I had come to know through their novels. From an aesthetic point of view, being locked in the past could be more appealing than development, the old Europe preferable to the new. That is also how a writer's perspective could differ from and even contradict that of political leaders.

Bucharest had delightful lakes and woods. Being in a capital city, you still felt close to nature. In my early morning walks, I was touched by the sight of tall trees and their autumn foliage and flocks of birds alighting on a placid lake. I ambled in cobblestoned alleys with good-looking cats and dogs lurking in doorways, thin smoke rising from chimneys, and doors with ancient number plates on them slowly opened and shut. Eastern Europe, falling behind in economic development, looked endearing to me, a sightseer on a hurried journey.

There were often blackouts. Television programs were in black and white except when "Leader" Ceausescu and his wife Elena Ceausescu popped up; then the broadcast would switch to color. I recalled a saying of Laozi, rendered literally: "How can you bully the weak as if they are infants?" But that was how Ceausescu treated Romanians. I remember the protest of my Greek-American English teacher when I proposed a toast to Elena Ceausescu in Iowa. I was trying to make a point about Chinese-Romanian friendship in the presence of a Romanian friend, not realizing how the Ceausescus were viewed in the world. At that time, China was one of Romania's few remaining allies.

The chair of the Romanian Cultural Commission was a high-energy physics professor who still taught graduate classes. I was much impressed. I wondered if it was better to put a real intellectual in charge of culture. Would his intellectual attainment help him do a better job? Would he remain a scholar with independent thinking and hence unruly to the higher-ups? I racked my brains with such seemingly laughable questions.

The Polish cultural minister was a non-communist. He was short, with small eyes, and had a calm air about him. He lamented the lack of humanism in capitalist culture, with the prevalence of consumerism and commercial excess. A Chinese diplomat had once told me that sometimes non-communist thinkers could be more staunchly revolutionary than their communist counterparts. I later heard similar comments on capitalism from the cultural ministers of Hungary and Morocco, and I began to realize that the humanist tradition was still alive in Eastern Europe and beyond. My conversations with cultural personalities in Eastern Europe on Humanism influenced my views on the topic in later discussions back in China.

While in Poland, I visited a museum of horse carriages at a town called Łańcut. We marveled at those lavish vehicles that looked to me far more stylish than today's Lincolns, Chevrolets, Mercedes, or BMWs. I was touched by the poignant tales about their departed owners, many of whom had to flee the country during the war, leaving behind everything, including their prized buggies. Such endings made me ponder: wealth and glory are but transitory; museums and man's lamentations endure.

The visit to the Royal Castle in Warsaw gave me inspiration for better management of the Palace Museum in Beijing. The Royal Castle was reconstructed after it was burned down by the Nazi army during the war. The new Royal Castle restored its grandeur and has become a holy shrine. Reverent visitors are required to change into protective shoes before entering. I thought of the Palace Museum in Beijing (i.e.

the Forbidden City), which had become like an amusement park where merrymaking visitors ate and drank, and dallying young men tickled their girls. The exquisite imperial back gardens were trampled by hordes of careless tourists, causing damage to many precious ancient plants. Upon returning to Beijing, I immediately proposed restrictions on food and beverage vending inside the Palace Museum and raising the price of admission, hoping to limit the number of visitors and reverse its slide into a fairground. However, the proposal was rejected by the price control agency. Of course, nowadays its admission is much higher. So are those of other public parks and heritage sites in China. The uniqueness of the Palace Museum is yet to be fully appreciated.

I had long heard of the beauty of Budapest, a city with the Danube running through it. Regrettably, exhaust fumes from heavy traffic on the bridge connecting Buda and Pest were choking. Bulky Soviet era architecture and statues solemnly dominated the cityscape. The Hungarian cultural minister, a dashing college professor, held forth like a torrential river, his topics ranging freely from modern Western philosophy and ancient Greece and Babylon, to the Orient, Marxism and art theoreticians of Marxist lineage in Hungary, and then finally to Georg Lukács, who narrowly escaped execution in the aftermath of the 1956 Hungarian Incident. The minister also spoke good French and his love for France was all too evident. My colleagues thanked heaven for having Wang Meng with them; they would be hard put to respond to that volley of intellectual pronouncements. The minister demonstrated his verbal dexterity, while I was no slouch in the rhetorical back and forth, flaunting leftist ideas of the West and criticism of capitalism and its lack of humanism that I had picked up along the way. At the end of the animated exchange, I threw in an invitation for a lecture tour in China to be merrily conducted in French.

I was then invited to speak at a seminar organized by the Hungarian Writers' Union and PEN Center. I talked about Chinese writers and Chinese society, citing the recent several-fold increase in beer prices. This struck a chord with my Hungarian peers. They roared in unison, "We are socialist brothers!"

In March 1988, I took a trip that included Morocco, Turkey, and Bulgaria. The Moroccan cultural minister was a talkative scholar. He hosted a late night welcome dinner on my arrival. As I sipped a chilled drink at nine, waiting for appetizers which did not come until well past eleven, I was both delighted and dismayed, being rather particular about my sleep. I was in for a ride from which I could not disembark. The dinner was served in the style of French haute couture. The minister's residence had a large garden, quite a notch above our "apartment buildings for high-ranking cadres."

The minister talked about the significance of OPEC, which had changed the old world order. He gave me copies of his writing on the topic. He also criticized some Islamic nations that did not pay enough attention to protecting their own languages and cultural traditions. From there he went on to the demise of humanism in capitalist societies, a topic which Chinese intellectuals had only picked up in the early 1990s. In a lighter mood, the minister told me a political joke: both Soviet and American heads of state were invited to see a computer simulation of their respective countries' future in fifty years' time: the United States would have come under communist rule, while all Russians would have switched to speaking Chinese.

I also visited Casablanca, a city with a strong European feel not far from Rabat, the Moroccan capital. I remembered the film *Casablanca* and felt like traveling back in time to the era of WWII. Military campaigns in the North African theater to some degree paralleled the Siege of Stalingrad and the Battle of Pingxinguan[1], which I knew well. On our way to Casablanca, we passed a sports stadium that was built as a foreign aid project by China. I also remember the massive display of fresh flowers in the lobby of a hotel where we had lunch.

In Turkey, I was asked by our host about China's reform and economic development. I told him about the rapid growth and the problem of inflation. After learning the inflation rate of the previous year in China, he shook my hand and offered his congratulations—it was apparently no match for inflation in Turkey.

With help from staffers at the Chinese embassy, I offered my toast in Turkish to end my remarks at a welcome dinner. I was able to pull

1. A major battle fought between the Eighth Route Army of the Communist Party of China and the Japanese Army on September 25, 1937, at the beginning of China's Resistance War against Japanese Agression

this off thanks to my Uighur language skills.[2] The Turkish cultural and tourism minister was intrigued and promised to do the same in Chinese when he visited China.

Istanbul, a city of great magnificence, straddles the continental divide of Europe and Asia. The transcontinental bridge was built with European technology, while a new bridge under construction was all Japanese engineering. That weekend, a belly dance parading as an ancient court dance was performed for us in an old castle, all of which was rather amusing.

In Bulgaria, I met with Bulgaria's top leader, Todor Zhivkov, who talked about his hope for a quick end to the war in Afghanistan, which message I duly reported to the Chinese leadership via the embassy. He also mentioned preferential treatment for writers in Bulgaria—when the writers' union and the national security agency were both vying for a resort facility on the Black Sea, he ordered that it be given to the writers. Another example of such beneficence was his invitation to a writer who had been critical of him to spend time with him in the presidential quarters. The writer was said to have greatly modified his views after such an experience. Was his proximity with the leader a blessing or a burden? How, in retrospect, would he view and recount this experience years later?

By that time, Bulgaria had also started its own brand of reform and opening-up. When the twenty-first century dawned, most countries in the former socialist bloc had done the same, following a trend that first started in China. However, the Soviet Union and the Eastern Bloc collapsed soon after their reform got underway, while China has become stronger the further it pushed its reform. There is a world of difference in outcome.

In March 1989, I visited Australia and New Zealand for the first time. I attended a literature festival in Australia and saw Margret Drabble again. When touring the seashell-shaped Sydney Opera House in near darkness, I almost fell into the orchestra pit if not for my quick reflexs, grasping the railing. I saved myself from a bad fall but suffered a rupture in the webbing between my left thumb and index finger, yanked by the

2. Uighur is a Turkic language with 8 to 11 million speakers, spoken primarily by the Uighur people in the Xinjiang Uighur Autonomous Region of Western China.

weight of my 150-pound body. I attended a piano recital by a Greek pianist in the Concert Hall and also saw a play, *Being with the Queen,* in the Playhouse. The play was about an Australian who traveled to England in the hope of getting help from the Queen. He ended up returning without having a chance to see anyone from Buckingham Palace. Without the aid of scenes and props, the actor used quite a bit of pantomime to mimic a flight attendant. Such miming had been a technique used in Chinese theater for centuries.

The culture minister of New Zealand was friendly and rather laid back. He took me to the Parliament House for lunch and introduced me to the prime minister and some of his cabinet peers. He asked me if the appointment of former vice premier Gu Mu, whom he had met during his visit to China, to be vice chairman of the Chinese People's Political Consultative Conference, was a promotion or otherwise. After hearing my explanation, he remarked that such an arrangement was wonderful. In New Zealand, he said, once you lost an election you would have to pack up and vacate the office the following day. "It is harsh," he said.

In Auckland, I met sinologist John Minford, who gave me a copy of *The Story of the Stone,* his translation of the Chinese classic *Dream of the Red Chamber.* I also visited a Maori community and was surprised to find Chinese modernist poet Gu Cheng (who later killed his wife and then himself) in the welcoming party. He was dressed in a Maori outfit and wearing a white hat in the style of a Chinese muslin prayer cap. We were flown in a small charter plane arranged by our New Zealand host after we missed our scheduled flight. I was seated next to the pilot, which was quite an experience.

Seeing Gu Cheng, I pondered the fate of Chinese poets living abroad. They might have been discontented with their lot in China, which was understandable. But coming all the way to settle in New Zealand had not made things any easier. Wearing a small white cap made him look outlandish. He would have been considered an eccentric back in his own country. But was he more of an outcast in New Zealand? His tragic end must have had a lot to do with his frustration and disillusionment.

My last overseas visit in my capacity as cultural minister was to France, Egypt, and Jordan in May 1989.

The French Minister of Culture at the time was Jack Lang, who was a famed liberal politician. He hosted a luncheon in my honor and invited the novelist and 1985 Nobel Laureate Claude Simon, who arrived looking rather subdued. Simon wrote strangely constructed prose. He had traveled in the Soviet Union, the Middle East, and India. He divided his time between working in his vineyard and writing novels, and was disdainful of all decadent tendencies in society at large. Such a mode of living was what the Chinese writer Zhang Wei had fancied and described in his stories. Simon and I had met before in New York, and his appearance and air of humility reminded me of the venerable Chinese writer Ba Jin.

At the lunch were also Pierre Cardin, a fashion entrepreneur eager to do business in China, and the French pop singer Mireille Mathieu, who had performed in China. She had learned to sing the Chinese song "Jasmine Flowers." When I hosted a dinner for her at the French restaurant Maxim's in Beijing during her tour, she had insisted on my singing the song together with her. At the minister's lunch, a Sinologist served as interpreter. He was not allowed to eat at the table and could only munch on two chocolate bars that he had brought with him. He grumbled jokingly to me in Chinese, "What human rights are there if I am not even allowed to eat . . . !"

At a reception hosted by the French Foreign Ministry, I saw Gao Xingjian and Li Hanhua, who both had worked in the liaison department of the Chinese Writers' Union and spoke French. Gao was later awarded a Nobel Prize in Literature, and Li won a Goncourt prize for his novel *Red Sorghum* (not to be confused with Mo Yan's novel of the same title).

In Jordan, I met the younger brother of King Hussein and some local writers. I was invited to be an honorary member of the Jordanian Writers' Union and was presented with an official certificate. I visited the ancient site of Petra and walked its *Siq*, a narrow path through towering cliffs on either side. The kilometer-long path opened onto the impressive rose-red monument of Khazneh. In Jordan I swam in the Dead Sea. Its high salinity made swimming akin to floating and it was difficult to get back on your feet once you lay flat in the water. We also visited King Hussein Bridge on the Jordan River at a Jordanian-Israeli border crossing, with a heavy military presence on both sides.

Toward the end of May as I wound down my trip, I made a stopover in Thailand and met with my Thai counterpart. The Thai minister asked, "Why don't you stay here for a few more days. We can play Mahjong and you can return when the situation in China settles down . . ." He of course said this in a joking manner. It seems that all the agonizing and pressing matters in the world could seem irrelevant and insignificant when you assume a different perspective. However, I could linger no more. By this time, I had no stomach for jokes. I felt heavy-hearted and prayed that China would not sink back into chaos after so brief a lull.

As cultural minister, I also hosted many visitors from around the world. They included Brazilian writer Jorge Amado, who in the 1950s had achieved fame akin to that of the Chilean poet Pablo Neruda. I also met the Japanese writer and former Japanese Communist Party member Hiroshi Noma, Director of the U.S. Information Agency Charles Wick, and Soviet Cultural Minister Vasily Zakharov. I met with government cultural delegations from San Marino, Mauritius, Benin, North Korea, and Pakistan, and writers' delegations from the United States, the Soviet Union, Malaysia, and Germany. There was also a women's delegation from Iran. The women officials from San Marino wore traditional costumes and looked as if they had stepped down from a Renaissance painting. The Iranian women delegates were interested in how China dealt with imperialist cultural infiltration after the founding of the People's Republic. Benin delegates plunged right into their scheduled activities after an exhaustingly long flight. I admire their ardent spirit.

The head of the Soviet writers' delegation, Sergey Mikhalkov, chairman of the Russian Federation of Writers, wrote the lyrics to the country's national anthem. He was a great conversationalist. He regaled us with a tale about how a cat coaxed a mouse out of hiding. Ready for an ambush, the cat mimicked a dog barking. The mouse assuming that the cat was gone, stepped out into the cat's waiting claws. The cat later bragged, "It always helps if you can speak a foreign tongue." I retold his tale to many a charmed audience. Mikhalkov also said that heading a delegation of writers was like taking a traveling zoo on tour. By the end of his visit, Mikhalkov became fascinated with the aphrodisiac aspect of traditional Chinese medicine. In short, he was, forthright, rowdy and humorous—all typical Russian traits.

Vasily Zakharov was appointed Minister of Culture in the Gorbachev era. He appeared earnest and humble. He quoted Gorbachev saying that the Soviet Union needed more democracy and socialism. He told a joke about an actor being nominated to be Minister of Culture during the Stalin era. When asked if he would be up to the task, he replied, "Not a problem. I have played Peter the Great!" Zakharov visited Shenzhen and bought a telescopic fishing rod that pleased him immeasurably. I pictured him as a merry angler, casting far into a tranquil river.

Chapter 56

Not Giving Up on Writing

I continued to write fiction while serving as culture minister.

"Shadow of a Centipede" was a short story that starts with an engineer who hears rumors about his hair, which somehow looks better than his peers'. People suspected that it was fake just as another rumor about his promotion to director general began to circulate. He was so bothered that he became slack in his work and went for a test to prove that his hair was genuine. But people refused to believe it despite the medical evidence. A mere "I don't believe it" cast a vanishing spell over all facts. His rivals spread more rumors about him, all of which were duly reported to him by his friends to show camaraderie, while all he wanted was to banish them from his mind.

Then he was snared; he became obsessed with the prospect of being a director general in spite of himself, hoping that it would nullify all rumors. If only he could become a director general, all the accusations about his hair, even the style of his hat, coat, pants, shoes and the embarrassing blemish of a corn on the underside of his foot would be blown away. When a man who had never thought about becoming a director general became obsessed with the idea, he was willing to charge ahead: he could indeed have fake hair. In the end, he even believed a centipede dwelled in his belly.

> Five days later, when he woke up in the morning suddenly filled with hope, a spirit he seemed to recognize blew a puff of cold air as he was tying his shoes.

> The spirit hissed through its teeth and cold air blew into his shirt collar and hovered over his navel. Then he felt an abdominal pain. "Ugh," he groaned, "Get out, you nasty worm that I cannot see! Don't you know I have medical reports from the hospital . . . ?'
>
> Then a small voice came from inside his belly.
>
> "Your hair! You have stolen others' hair; you have dyed and played tricks with your hair! Doctors can only prove you are temporarily free from inflammation, cancer, clots in your veins or stones in your gall bladder, but they cannot prove you haven't played tricks with your hair. What's more, it is all very well that you believed in the Friendship Hospital, but why should we, too? We will continue to attack your fake hair, and we will win if we persist! We have already sent a sample of twenty of your hairs to the lab at the Council of the Sick and Dead Hairs for testing, just so you know . . ."
>
> His belly voice was booming, indignant, and unstoppable. How could his belly become like this? He passed out with a groan.

I thought this piece was written with true feelings and had a unique narrative. However, people took little note.

In 1987, I wrote a short story, "A String of Choices," about a man with toothache but unable to decide on treatment options. He made multiple appointments with dentists, only to be confounded by their divergent opinions, paralyzing him with indecision while his toothy woes persisted. A TV drama based on the story was made, but never aired.

> President Shi's eloquence flowed on; he was conversant with all the famous examples of toothache as well as all pertinent theories and schools of thought, from ancient to modern, native and foreign. From the fifth left upper molar of Napoleon to the auction of the dentures of Hitler's mistress, Eva; from the front teeth of the newly excavated female mummy of the Eastern Han dynasty to the qualities of the Buddha's tooth and its efficacy on various occasions—he was conversant with them all. Then he went on to the great controversy between the conservative and the radical schools in treating toothache,

which has been raging for centuries. Just as he was at the height of his eloquence, I screamed, 'It's killing me!' and fainted dead away.

President Shi was most apologetic. He was also modest. He declared that he was only the president of the Toothology Society and was not a practicing doctor at a dental clinic. He explained that the society was an academic organization and then proceeded to inform me that all dentists at the county level were supervised by the Handicrafts Management Office of the county government and that their licenses were issued by Agricultural Market Control officers. He kindly pointed out to me that my toothache was too down-to-earth, too mundane to arouse his interest. He offered me the use of his collection, including *The Toothache Encyclopedia, The Complete Guide to Toothache, Suggestions for Tooth Protection,* and other reference books.

Reading those books plunged me into the depths of confusion. I painfully realized that teeth are mortal but knowledge boundless. In the act of pulling, the teeth are there, but after the act teeth are nonexistent. Lost in boundless despair in a toothless, boundless world, I woke up and found myself a modern man.

My wife's elder brother, who had just returned from research and study abroad, scolded me roundly for my ignorance and condemned President Shi for wallowing in useless words . . . He pointed out with great perspicacity that there was no such branch of science as toothology . . . I geared myself up for another extraction . . . My colleagues at the department admonished me to make sure that I got hold of a male doctor for the operation . . . Friends and colleagues poured out their own experiences, lessons to be drawn, warnings for the future, tricks for an easy way out, rules to stick by, and so on, all relating to the art of dealing with the aching tooth. As the sayings go, The scholar offers words, the rascal offers gifts . . . Alas for my scholarly tooth.

I stood in line for three days running, waiting my turn, but my turn never came. It was said that all the registry slips had slipped out through the back door. The masses at the front gate, tormented by bad teeth, were seething with anger . . . I

> went home and told my wife everything. My wife said, "We have our own back door!". . . set out with two bottles of Maotai wine (don't blame me if they were fake; I can't tell the difference) to call on my wife's cousin many times removed, a certain Mr. Liu who was department head at one of the offices at the Ministry of Health. Mr. Liu told me first that he was supervisor for hospitals of Chinese medicine, that he had nothing to do with Western medicine . . . and second that he disapproved of Western medicine on principle. Mr. Liu informed me that famous physicians of the West had personally told Chinese medical students studying abroad that the future of medicine is embedded in China and will flourish in China, that it is preposterous for them to go west to study, that in fact it was scholars from the West who should make the pilgrimage to China to pluck the fruits of wisdom. He added that Picasso had owned up to Chang Ta-ch'ien that art is found only in China (I saw this in a recollection by Wang Zengqi but need to take it with a pinch of salt) . . . I was so overjoyed that for the moment I even forgot my toothache . . . I have finally learned that science without philosophy or science plus philosophy but without being armed with backdoor connections would get me nowhere, cannot even save my teeth.[1]

This story reflects my musings on the Chinese condition. We had long debated over the right approach to national revival, but had been bogged down by indecision and a lack of practical solutions to immediate problems. In fact, different approaches may all be valid to a degree, like dental treatment options. However, in the heat of argument, people had all but forgotten the sorry tooth of the sickly man.

I wrote two more short stories in a similar vein, one of which was "Fur Elise."

> I woke up the folks in the middle of the night. I asked them if the bluish Sun in the sky was actually our wall clock crowned with a Nobel laureate? My wife said nonsense and the sun wasn't up yet. Why don't I go and have two fried balloons

1. Translated by Zhu Hong and included in *Chairman Mao Would Not Be Amused,* edited by Howard Goldblatt, Grove Press, New York, pp. 73-76.

sunny side up? That'd stop my loose bowel movement and pump more air into me. My son pushed me aside and flipped back to slumber after announcing he would marry that elder woman who plays Chinese violin if he did not succeed next year in getting a visa to go overseas. My dad remembered there used to be nine suns in the sky but all of them grew big, took on wings, and were not seen again. My daughter vowed to become a Toyota salesgirl but needed a grand to get a degree by correspondence learning. But that could all be reimbursed later by her employer. My wife said if I did not eat all the apples, the apples would rot and their prices might rise again.

I got up and went straight to the bus stop with a shovel on my shoulder, intending to plant a tree. I pictured the canopy of my tree becoming a helipad before a mushroom cloud would rise. I started digging a hole in the ground but found a toad, a talking, flattering and novel-writing one at that. Not only could it croak, it was also capable of half a dozen exotic tongues including barking, neighing, bellowing, and cooing. I wondered from which country it had returned armed with all these learned tricks. I asked why it was not wearing large-rimmed sunglasses. It said it cared about its image and did not want to give people ideas. Then I realized why I was hopeless in getting further promotion and fame. The bus arrived with all its wheels gone. Passengers chipped in with ping-pong balls, mothballs, black plums, jingle bells, and flatbreads as substitutes for the wheels. I was chosen by a democratic vote to go and push the bus, as the bus driver and the conductor sat idle. I was so vehement in bus pushing that I was spotted by a talent scout for the National Sports Commission and named head coach for middle distance runners and sprinters. But I quit after a month, grumpy about commission leaders not providing me with a blazer, a table lamp, a sofa, mosquito repellent, a diary book, a leather jacket, and the like. I became a novel writer instead and joined a writers' club and was put up in a hotel. But the hotel manager took to me and invited me to take a puff of liquefied natural gas. She asked me if I could betroth myself to Beauty Enhancement Porridge Inc. as its honorary chairman, claiming the company had registered its patent with

> a trans-Atlantic multinational company and was entitled to a fifteen-day waiver of the corporate income tax. The porridge contained Vitamins U, V, W , X, Y and Z and a total of over twenty four hundred organic matters and inorganic salts. It had passed all the tests of government agencies and received certification for quality and efficacy for turning slanted eyes into stunning deep set ones and for boosting physical growth, with a positive side effect of extending one's leg length by four centimeters.

Was all this hallucinatory nonsense? It was a reflection of the collective excitement, restlessness and euphoria of the 1980s, when nothing seemed impossible, restrictions were lifted, imported goods and music became popular, and foreign jargon gained wide currency. The tone and style of the stories were not incidental, nor were they an indication of madness or linguistic jumble. They reflected the spirit of an era of wild imagining; an era when everything seemed to be up for grabs. People were secretly saying, "Let's all try and make some quick dough before the Communist Party wakes up!" They figured that the CCP would sooner or later go after the rich.

These were the heady years of the 1980s. It is now fashionable to feel nostalgic about the 1980s. I take great comfort in that I have left behind some inimitable writings about that era; I had not lived through it in vain.

In retrospect, taking every opportunity to write novels while serving as minister was hardly a recipe for success. It smacked of contrivance, recklessness, and compromise. Even though I had dutifully reported to work, convened requisite meetings, passed down and implemented all official policies and solved problems when necessary, doing all these diligently and by the book, the question begs asking: Was I a good minister? In fact, I had thought that by not giving up writing I could perhaps better serve as a bridge between the Party and writers. I received a greeting card at the end of the year wishing me good health and good health for Chinese arts and the intellectual community in the coming two decades. There was an element of flattery surely, but I appreciated the sentiments it conveyed.

I could switch quickly to the writing mode. I was always ready to write, often finding it hard to put down my pen and hold back the urge. I could be on a two-hour flight and once I'd landed and checked into the hotel, I would, settle in with a hot pot of tea, and write right up to the time for the dinner engagement. I told people I seemed to function with two minds—one for work: official meetings and speeches; the other for composing stories. I could filter out all noise and interference when I wrote. My folks felt troubled when they heard my talk of having two minds. Back in my Xinjiang days, being of two minds meant intending to collaborate with foreign agents, which was perilous to put it mildly. My writing of course had nothing to do with that agent business.

My life as a minister was also material for literature. In my work, I had seen much haste and blundering, maneuvers and intrigues, arrogance and corruption. But on balance, I had seen more dedication to national revival, passion for change, patriotism, and altruistic dedication. I had seen effectiveness and coherence, decisiveness and moral courage, devotion to the welfare of the people and mankind. We cannot expect all writers to be concerned about national destiny and the future of mankind. It is only natural that some writers would prefer to write about their cultivated taste, the good old days, or even their dalliances and misadventures. They might be adept at composing sardonic, grumpy, and even outrageous passages. But concern for politics, philosophy, and affairs of the world at least should not be deemed a weakness in an author.

I had often wondered during the 1950s when reading confidential documents of the Party why they could not all be made available to the public then or later. In them, we could actually sense the concern, tolerance, understanding, and arduous exploration by the Party. Seeing officialdom as completely corrupt or senior leaders as immortals were equally erroneous and far from the truth.

In addition to writing short stories, I also wrote many poems, essays, and literary reviews. Poetry writing was often viewed as sophomoric and petty bourgeois. Poetry seems mostly associated with romantic souls, rolling meadows, and solitary, self-indulgent musings. However, when we have all become hardened in our rush through life, a poem or two to revive sensitivity and mellowness can be very worthwhile. Writing literary reviews, on the other hand gave me an opportunity to guide, to be a bridge, and to promote harmony. It was also served as an exercise in discipline and honing a sensitivity to nuance. My essays "When Literature Ceases to Have Sensational Effect" and "Freedom and Weightlessness" were first published under the pen name Shan Shi [Mountain Rock] by the *Art and Literature Gazette* and reprinted in *The People's Daily*. The Chinese expression for sensational effect was first coined by me borrowing a favorite word of my wife's. She was a high school physics teacher and was in the habit of using such terms as "cause and effect." The expression soon gained currency in China, which was a collective contribution by my wife and me to the literary glossary.

The pen name Shan Shi was merely a combination of the given names of my two sons. However, one overseas China-hand imagined a link between this penname and those that had been assumed by groups writing during the Cultural Revolution. He was clueless.

People often find it hard to resist a spoiler, being eager to know the ending first. If the ending was not what they liked, they would rather not bother with the journey of reading and exploring. We have all grown accustomed to such a way of thinking—as long as we are happy with the ending, it doesn't matter if there is anything wrong with the process; if the tally is what we expected, the sloppy calculation doesn't matter.

My fellow writers and readers, I love you all. Yet sometimes I cringe and want to cry, seeing your intellectual reach. I despair over the abundance of writers and shortage of discerning readers. But what's really in excess and what's amiss?

Chapter 57

"Leaving Home at Eighteen"

In early 1987, Ruifang mentioned to me "Leaving Home at Eighteen," a short story by Yu Hua in *Beijing Literature.* This was one of his best short stories. Its plot has some clever twists but its descriptions of the psyche of a new generation are most ingenious—a generation that was irreverent, wide-eyed with wonder, dare-devilish, and infinitely hopeful. It also has a great title—a young man at eighteen embarking on a long journey, a metaphor for adventure and coming of age. It is powerfully evocative. I wrote an enthusiastic review titled "Youthful Musings."

In 1983, during a trip to Guizhou, I came across a short story by Shi Ding, "A Road at the Foot of a Mountain," which was published in the journal *Mountain Flowers.* I admired its rustic touch and precise and nuanced phrasing. I recommended it to *Fiction Monthly.* It also won a prize for best short story of the year. Shi Ding later became chairman of the Zunyi Municipal Federation of Literature and Arts Circles. His political career also took off. He was appointed vice mayor of his city and elected a member of the standing committee of the Eighth and Ninth Chinese People's Political Consultative Conferences.

I also liked "You Cannot Change Me" and "Black Forest," two short stories by Liu Xihong. In the 1980s, Guangdong and Shenzhen, where Liu lived, were heralding economic reform. Hu Qiaomu cited a short story about a reform-minded man having to move to Shenzhen after setbacks in his hometown. Hu complained that it was an imitation of stories written prior to Liberation when aspiring young men and women flocked to the liberated areas to join the revolution. I chuckled and thought about the cheerful ending of the Broadway musical "Fiddlers on the Roof" in which the impoverished left their home village for America.

I was also moved by Can Xue's *Dialogues in Paradise,* which has a touch of melancholy, bitterness, and exotic beauty. I wrote a review delighting in the discovery of a new talent even though her unconventional writings were somewhat esoteric and had been criticized by older writers. I pointed out that tolerance of writings like Can Xue's would be a positive sign of greater spiritual dimensions of our nation. As some had complained that her stories were difficult to comprehend, I tried to offer my interpretation as well as commentary in my review. Readers were too used to stories with an obvious theme and a straightforward moral, complete with a good start and ending. It would take strenuous efforts to get them to accept literary experimentation and innovation. Can Xue later said that my favorable review protected her from attacks planned by certain leaders.

I had long thought myself an elder friend who gave her support and protection when she was in need. In the 1990s, she often complained to me how difficult it was to get stories published. She faced a dilemma: if she continued with her unique approach, she could repeat herself; if she abandoned it, she would lose her identity. I helped to introduce her to literary journals such as *Flower City*. However, a few years earlier I received a letter from her which sounded almost like a denunciation. She had found my writings outdated and not readable anymore. How would I carry on when a woman writer of a certain unique style thought I was getting on?

We had all hoped China could be at least tolerant of unconventional literary styles. However, sometimes writers of such uniqueness would rather resist inclusion and shun others who were not like them. You thought you were a champion of advocating inclusiveness as the ocean accepts all rivers that flow into it, no matter how remote and incongruous their origins might be. Then one small stream renounces the ocean. Such was the state of the literary community.

A word about writer Zhang Xinxin is also in order. She demonstrated her extraordinary literary talent through her novel *On the Same Horizon*. Some CCP leaders, however, were unhappy about her writing, which was deemed modernistic and emblematic of blatant individualism. At about the same time, *Chinese Youth* magazine reported a debate on the meaning of life following a reader's letter, which turned out to have been planted by the magazine itself. Both Zhang's novel and the debate were thought to illustrate ideological confusion in the nation. A literary critic of some repute then published an essay criticizing Zhang, which caused much alarm. I had admired Zhang's talent and decided to lend her support. I made it a point to seek her contribution to *People's Literature* as soon as the heat was off her and published her essay "Married Daughter Returning Home." However, she was said to be repulsed by a later essay of mine, in which I commented on the general bearing of Chinese writers, citing Ba Jin and Zhang Chengzhi as writers who wrote in great agony and Zhang Xinxin as delighting in the act of writing. She declared that Wang Meng was bent on detracting her.

Perhaps I was too conceited. I believed in genuine criticism, which is important to literature. I was forthcoming with my opinions and comments. Had I done wrong? Was I the one who was persecuting or antagonizing writers?

Zhang Xinxin also organized a rare literary festival, gathering a group of writers in front of an audience in the Capital Stadium, with a program of singing, book reading, and dance performances. Zhang had studied theater directing and proved a capable organizer. This was plausible only in China; parading a motley collection of writers on stage would be quite impossible in another country. Solitary writers are seldom known for their gregariousness or stage appeal. Readers interested in their books may not necessarily be impressed by their looks. Li Zhun once said, "Better not to meet a writer in person for more often than not you'd be disappointed." A poet who started a relationship through correspondence with a fan agreed to meet in person with her only after their wedding date was fixed. His fiancée almost passed out when she saw him for the first time. This is a true story.

At this literary festival in 1987, I was supposed to read from my early work *Long Live Youth* in the spotlight on stage. As the festival approached, however, there was student unrest around the country, and then the resignation of General Secretary Hu Yaobang. People became edgy and worried about what might happen at the festival. Unusual precautions were taken, including a ban on picture-taking by the audience. In the end, the whole thing, which was meant to be a celebration, was tense and subdued, though it concluded without incident.

In 1988, the National Museum of Art sponsored an exhibition of nude paintings which caused a sensation. A former female colleague from my days at the district Youth League committee asked me what aesthetic value there was in all those naked buttocks. I did not know what to say. I had learned during my travels abroad one essential difference between Chinese and Western sartorial approaches—the former to clothe and conceal; the latter to emphasize the beauty of the body.

This was followed by an avant-garde exhibition at the same venue. I did not go to see the exhibition at first, fearing it might cause a fuss. The show was considered rather vulgar and came under much criticism. Some exhibits were said to appeal to foreign tastes by design. For sensational effect, gunshots were fired by one exhibitor standing in front of his installation—a red box resembling an old English telephone booth. There was feetwashing in public view (behavior art?) and helium-filled condoms floating like balloons. Angry viewers wrote in the visitor book condemnations of Wang Meng for not banning such a show. There was an anonymous letter claiming a bomb had been planted at the exhibition venue. People can have such violent reactions to art works they hate. This is something worth mulling over. I got a call from a Beijing municipal leader suggesting the show be shut down.

I did not wish to see the show, and its closing becoming an ideological issue, much less a political one. I recalled discussing art appreciation with my Australian counterpart when visiting a modern art gallery in Sydney. My Australian friends told me that they were often uncertain about how to judge modern artworks, which could be truly artistic and innovative or simply rubbish. Some creators of modern art could be geniuses while others charlatans. However, it would be best to leave them to the test of time and the judgment of the academic community and public at large, rather than having the arbitrary decisions of government officials. It would be better to err on the side of tolerance than restrictions that would stifle creativity. Whatever was destined for the garbage dump would find its way there sooner or later. I found this approach by and large more plausible. Thus, I proposed at a meeting of the ministry's Party Core that the National Museum of Art should only showcase art works judged by consensus to have reached a certain high standard. New and experimental works should be excluded from shows at the museum for the time being. On the one hand, they should be treated with caution but, on the other, nor should they be hastily labeled decadent or reactionary. We could say that they had estranged themselves from the art-viewing public, would likely cause discomfort, and could be better shown in venues of less impact and assessed there.

We also decided, given the bomb threat, to temporarily close it for three days to conduct security sweeps. The original closing date remained unchanged, now that the show was cut short anyway after the closing for security reasons. I proposed not starting an ideological debate about it, thus avoiding potential friction between the government and artists, much less between the government and the viewing public, which would do more harm than good. Many years later, this avant-garde exhibition became the subject of a thesis by a graduate student in Chinese studies in the United States.

I only had a quick tour before the show was shut down for the bomb sweep. I did not see anything worthy of my support or protection, or deserving overreaction. Overall, I did not have a high opinion of the exhibits. Thenceforth, similar predicaments have been resolved by adopting the spirit of my decisions made at the Ministry's Party Core on this controversial exhibition.

Chapter 58

An Old House in a Beijing Alley

I moved into an old courtyard house at No. 46 Bei Xiao Jie Alley in 1987. It had been the residence of the CCP elder and former vice minister of culture Xia Yan.

Earlier still, a certain relative of Li Zongren, former president of the overthrown Nationalist Government, had lived there. During the Cultural Revolution, Premier Zhou Enlai moved the renowned linguist Li Jinxi to this house so that he could be protected [from marauding Red Guards]. Li was the inventor of a phonetic notation system for the Chinese language and had once been Chairman Mao's teacher. I had known Li's daughter Zhong Hong from his wife's earlier marriage when she worked in the literature and arts division of the propaganda department of the Beijing municipal Party Committee. Li Jinxi died in the house.

Xia Yan had lived in a courtyard house near the Beijing Railway Station before. He was evicted from the house during the Cultural Revolution. With his political rehabilitation when the Cultural Revolution was over, he moved into this house in Bei Xia Jie alley. I had visited him when he lived there. His bedroom faced south and was sunny, though quite small, barely six square meters. It was next to a larger living room of twenty square meters, with another bedroom of about ten square meters next to it. There were two more rooms on the east side of the courtyard and three on the west, each roughly ten square meters. The kitchen and dinning room were on the south side. The house had no patio, and rooms were not set deep into the back. When Xi Zhongxun, the senior CCP leader visited Xia, he found the place too cramped and arranged to move Xia's family into a more spacious house at Rong Xian Alley near Xidan. After I moved into this house, Li Ziyun, Xia's former secretary, said I had literally stepped into Xia's footsteps.

Kitty-corner from my house was a large courtyard where two successive vice chairmen of the National People Congress had lived. Guards were stationed at its gate. People of the older generation in Beijing preferred courtyard houses. Living in contact with the earth is good for you, so they would say. In the summer, sitting in the courtyard as the sun set, I relished having a slice of water melon, chilled green bean soup, or noodles cooked in the old Beijing fashion. On a windy day, however, it could be dusty, which made eating in the courtyard impossible. In the winter when it snowed, we would make a snowman. However, over the years, we had less and less snow. Often, it would be just a light dusting that never got anyone very excited.

Outside the courtyard door to the right, there would often be a food cart selling deep-fried flatbread in the morning. I was an early riser and would often stand in line in my flip-flops to buy my breakfast. Someone in the neighborhood saw this and told a playwright. This for a while became an example of my easy manners much talked about among my literary friends. I had always tried to avoid loosing touch with the ordinary people. I never completely gave up riding my bicycle and the bus—I still do it at least once or twice a year just to be in touch.

There was an old plum tree in the courtyard. For lack of proper pruning it did not yield well. A Chinese mahogany tree planted by Xia Yan's daughter grew vigorously and its bulging roots made the ground of the courtyard uneven. The new leaves in the spring were a delicacy. However, I was mostly away when they were in season and rarely had an opportunity to try this prized vegetable. There were also a persimmon tree and a pomegranate tree that were planted after we moved in. The little pumpkin shaped persimmons were sweet and juicy. However, lacking proper harvesting tools, we only picked low hanging ones that we could reach from the flat roof. Turning a lovely orange-red in the fall, they were a stunning sight to behold. Then later in the fall, they fell one after another, each with a slight thump, stirring sadness and regret.

In blossom, the pomegranate would remind me of a verse by the

Tang dynasty poet Li Shangyin, "Laugh not at pomegranate flowers missing the spring/Sadder were those that flower and wither earlier still." The pomegranate does not flower until well into June, later than most other fruit trees. I had been critical of the melancholy in Li Shangyin's poetry—"flower and wither earlier still." I had come to learn that poets were more inclined to feel dejection and a sense of loss, which was the true constant of life. Mere mortals simply could not be exuberant and bursting with vigor all the time, like soldiers ever ready for battle.

I lived in the courtyard house for twelve years; longer than I had lived anywhere else. I moved out on Labor Day in May 1999. Its former occupant Xia Yan and his daughter Shen Ning came to visit once. People visit their old homes and friends of yore, as if to open and reseal a treasure trove of a long cherished past.

Living in a courtyard house, you are in touch with earth and the elements. When it rains, you see raindrops splashing in the puddles. You hear wind howling and forcing its way through the crevices. You see shadows of spiky boughs crawl across curtained windows as the bright moon traverses high in the night sky. You feel the shift of seasons, the summer dews and winter frost, and the break of dawn, more keenly than you would in an apartment tower, where you might not even notice a passing storm.

The nocturnal chorus of crickets in late fall makes your mind wander. Then there are bugs both in and outside the house; scurrying centipedes, flies, mosquitoes and the stink beetles. But oddly I had never spotted any cockroaches, which perhaps only thrived in communal apartment buildings.

More awe-inspiring were the resident rodents. Their nightly athletic meet in the attic helped me understand how people in Beijing *hutong* houses lived in the old days. There was no effective way of getting rid of them. We decided to keep a cat, as cats in those days were still keen on catching an occasional rat for dinner, unlike the ones fed with pet food nowadays that have lost all interest in wild game.

In this courtyard house, I entertained friends from the Japan-China Cultural Exchange Association, including Yasushi Inoue, Ikuma Dan, Junko Sata, Ikeda Ryoichi, and Ken Yokokawa. We sipped tea and soda while sitting in a circle in the courtyard and spent many a happy hour.

Novelist Chiung Yao from Taiwan and her husband Ping Xin Tao, founder of Crown Publishing also came to visit. I saw a very disarming Chiung Yao who was modest, energetic, and honest. She had read some of my novels, including in foreign language translations, and said with admiration, "Yours is true literature!"

I invited my elementary school teacher, Mrs. Hua Xialing, to my home. She moved to Taiwan after the war. Finding her was a saga in the first place. I had asked a Singaporean businessman, Poh Choon Ann, for his help. Mr. Poh's wife was Bao Lala, a well-known Taiwanese pop singer, who made frequent concert appearances on the mainland in the 1980s and knew the Performing Arts Agency under the ministry well. Mr. Poh sought help from his contacts in the education community in Taiwan and was soon able to locate Mrs. Hua. However, when he called her by telephone, he mispronounced her name, which caused alarm. When he mentioned my name and told her I had been a minister, she said she knew no such person. He only managed to win her trust after mentioning his wife's name.

The thaw in relations between both sides of the Taiwan Strait began just around that time. In the following months, things moved fast. Many Taiwan veterans returned to the mainland to visit families they had left behind. I finally had a chance to see Mrs. Hua. She had become a specialist in preschool education. Separation and reunion are emotional moments. What is lost may be miraculously regained. The stories of our lives lived through tumultuous decades, no matter how they may end, have inspiring and redeeming power.

In this unpretentious house, I also received many other visitors from far and wide, including Doris Lessing, Margret Drabble, Graham Carleton Greene—Chair of the British Council and Graham Greene's nephew, Soviet sinologist Nikolai Fedorenko, Soviet writer Vladimir Sorokin, Richard Trappl, director of Confucius Institute at the University of Vienna, Japanese scholar Shigetada Kawanishi, German sinologist Wolfgang Kubin, and Michael Kahn-Ackermann, director of Goethe Institute in Beijing. The house was also steps away from the People's Literature Publishing House and SDX Joint Publishing Company. I could easily walk over to their offices. Fellow Chinese writers, editors, and journalists who walked through my door were simply too numerous to mention.

I also had some unlikely visitors there. One of them was a young man from my home village in Nanpi, Hebei Province. He came for my help to help him find a job. He also asked if I could help his brother who was in prison for stealing a bullock. I of course could do neither and was hard put to make him understand. Then from Xinjiang, my adopted home province, came two men with their food cart selling barbecued mutton on skewers right outside my house. Smoke from their brisk business hung over us in daily, but I could do nothing. Then a garbage collection station was set up near the house, adding noise and stench to the incessant smoke. By then I was ready to move out.

It was in this house, on October 1, 1988, that I wrote the letter to the CCP Central relinquishing my official position, at what many thought was the height of my ministerial fling. I referred to the early promise that I would be in the job for only three years. Now that I was two and half years into my term, I proposed that my successor be named as soon as possible so that I could go back to writing.

This was followed by a talk with a senior CCP leader who was sympathetic and agreed to start the process of selecting a successor. I recommended a few candidates, including He Jinzhi and Gao Di,[1] but was urged to be patient. The CCP leader hinted that no quick decision should be expected. Besides, I had been doing my job reasonably well.

I had an inkling that had I continued in the minister's job for three or more years, I would have been beyond redemption. I could have become accustomed to and even relished the trappings of power. After all, discerning hidden messages and achieving precision; allowing a minimum margin of error and steeling myself at the moment of truth; taking up challenges and being blessed with political patronage could all be too tempting. Wasn't it said that politics was a calling for real men; men who were undaunted by political strife and never duck in the face of a formidable challenge?

By the fall of 1988, I had made up my mind. Of course, such a decision would seem to others as defying reason. I decided to quit in

1. Gao Di, 1927–, former secretary of Jilin provincial CCP Committee who was then deputy director at the CCP Central Party School.

order to continue writing, with a determination akin to that when I quit smoking years ago. In early chapters I mentioned that I started smoking with the thought of eventually giving it up. I kept testing myself to make sure smoking was a choice—I could quit when I so determined. The same held true with my being the cultural minister. I had contemplated the time and manner of departure, on the day I took the job. I must apologize if such a thought was irresponsible and a letdown to those who had high hopes for me. But in truth I had never been able to banish the thought. Whenever I was in a meeting that dragged on forever, and whenever I was being attacked, I thought it was high time that I step down.

The old courtyard house has long since been torn down. A road cuts through where it used to stand. From dawn to midnight, traffic speeds past where I once lived. No. 46 Bei Xiao Jie Alley was gone for good. When the roadwork was underway, my grandson went by the site one day and brought back a rusty spout. He thought we might want to keep it as a memento. We did not show much interest, and it was not seen again.

At times I felt a tinge of regret, not at the old house's disappearance and the fading of its memories, but at what I had and could have accomplished in the twelve years I lived there. I had been too busy with all manner of things. In that house, I wrote the *Seasons* quartet, *Assassination—3322*, a number of novellas and short stories, and my essays on *Dream of the Red Chamber*, the Tang dynasty poet Li Shangyin, and Humanism. I also translated from English into Chinese short stories by American and New Zealand writers. It was unlike any other place where I had lived, where I felt completely at home and with an untroubled conscience, living a simple and uneventful existence. Memories of my past often flash back, as I recall my days at No. 46 Bei Xiao Jie Alley, with a smile and a feeling of indistinct melancholy, of ephemeral moments that are no more. All things come to pass. As the Russian poet Alexander Pushkin once said, what we are left with is only the past and its remembrance.

Mr. Qu Weigang, manager of an artists' retreat near Yantai owned by the Chinese Federation of Literature and Arts Circles, came to visit and brought me a porcupine. We all liked it very much. However, it vanished after the first night, probably having escaped through a small sewage hole under the wall. In such a big city, what would be the fate of this tiny creature? That is one mystery associated with the old house that remains unsolved. In my days there, we rarely saw crows but often cheerful magpies. They bring good omens, as Chinese country folk like to believe. This perhaps was the reason why the place always meant hope for me. After all these years, I still have feelings for the magpies and the lone porcupine still at large; I wish them all well.

About the Translators

Zhu Hong, former member of the Chinese Academy of Social Sciences, was a visiting professor at Boston University from 1992 to 2005. Her translations from the Chinese include the following: *The Chinese Western: Stories of Contemporary China* (Ballantine Books, 1991), *The Serentity of Whiteness: Stories by and about Chinese Women* (Ballantine Books, 1992), *A Higher Kind of Loyalty: Autobiography of Liu Binyuan* (Pantheon, 1990), *The Stubborn Porridge and Other Stories* by Wang Meng (George Braziller, 1994), *Will the Boat Sink the Water? The Life of China's Peasants,* by Chen Guidi and Wu Chuntao (Public Affairs, 2005), and *China 1927: Memoir of a Debacle* (MerwinAsia, 2013).

Formerly a translator at the Chinese Ministry of Culture, **Liu Haiming** has published several works of translation. His translations from the Chinese include: *A Century of Chinese Fashion 1900–2000* (China Books, 2016) and *The Peace Hotel, A Non-fiction Novel* (Shanghai Press, 2015).